JAYAPRAKASH NARAYAN

SELECTED WORKS

Volume Three (1939-1946)

Jayaprakash Narayan

SELECTED WORKS

Volume Three (1939-1946)

Edited by
BIMAL PRASAD

Issued under the auspices of
Nehru Memorial Museum & Library

MANOHAR
2003

First published 2003

ISBN 81-7304-353-1 (Series)
ISBN 81-7304-465-1 (Vol. III)

Published by
Ajay Kumar Jain for
Manohar Publishers & Distributors
4753/23 Ansari Road, Daryaganj
New Delhi 110002

Typeset by
A J Software Publishing Co. Pvt. Ltd.
New Delhi 110005

Printed at
Lordson Publishers Pvt. Ltd.
Delhi 110007

CONTENTS

Appendices

ILLUSTRATIONS

FOREWORD

The Nehru Memorial Museum & Library takes pride in releasing the third volume of the *Selected Works of Jayaprakash Narayan* in the birth centenary year of the great leader. The period covered by this volume, September 1939 to April 1946, is a period of great historical significance from the Indian as well as the world point of view. This was the period which witnessed the Second World War and the launching of the Quit India Movement—generally considered to be the most powerful upsurge of the Indian people for independence since the great revolt of 1857. The documents included in the earlier part of this volume, covering the period 1939-43, show the pioneering role which J.P. played in preparing the ground for a mass upsurge right from the time of the outbreak of the World War. According to him, the struggle, in order to be successful, would have to be partly based on violence and conducted through an underground organization. Although this view remained controversial, there is no doubt that his daring escape from the Hazaribagh Central Prison in November 1942 gave a fresh lease of life to the Quit India struggle.

This volume also shows the beginning and earlier development of J.P.'s aversion to the methods adopted by the Communists both in India and the Soviet Union as also his growing attraction for some of the Gandhian values which in later years propelled him to abjure violence and some of the basic tenets of Marxism itself. In fact, this marked the first stage of his journey to Democratic Socialism and then to Sarvodaya. Particularly interesting in this volume from this angle are his letters to M.R. Masani from prison in 1945-6.

I hope this volume will be found useful by those who not only wish to study the evolution of J.P.'s political thought but also an important period of Indian history and especially our freedom struggle.

O.P. KEJARIWAL

ACKNOWLEDGEMENTS

It is a pleasant duty to thank all those who have helped in preparing this volume. As in the past, Dr. O.P. Kejariwal, Director, Nehru Memorial Museum & Library, always took keen interest in its early completion and willingly extended all help whenever required. I am deeply grateful to him for this. I must also thank Dr. N. Balakrishnan, Head of the Research and Publications Division, who fully shared the Director's interest in the project and extended all necessary cooperation.

Among those who helped in collecting and arranging materials for this volume I would like to first mention the contribution made by Ms. Deepa Bhatnagar and her team of researchers, namely, Dr. Amrit Varsha Gandhi, Ms. Usha Syed Ali and Ms. Priyamvada Shome from the Research and Publications Division of the Nehru Memorial Museum & Library. By the time they were withdrawn from this project with a view to enabling them to concentrate on the projects in their own Division, the J.P. Project, thanks to the sustained efforts of Dr. Kejariwal, was able, for the first time, to recruit its own research staff in reasonably sufficient strength, consisting of Sri J.L. Gera, Dr. Maya Gupta and Ms. Sangita Mallik (Research Officers); and Sri S.A. Abidi, Dr. Kapileshwar Labh and Sri Vasudev Lakhanpal (Assistant Research Officers). They took over from where Ms. Bhatnagar and the members of her team had left and rendered all necessary assistance and cooperation both in completing the manuscript and in seeing it through the press. I am sincerely thankful to all of them.

My thanks are also due to the administrative staff of the NMML, particularly to Sri Deshraj, Administrative Officer, for their willing co-operation whenever required. Ms. Deepa Sharma ably attended to almost all the typing work in connection with this volume. Towards the end she was joined by Ms. Neha Bhardwaj. As in the past, I could also count on the cooperation of Sri Anand Bhushan Sharma as and when necessary.

BIMAL PRASAD

INTRODUCTION

Most of the items included in this volume throw light, among other things, on J.P.'s stand, articulated from inside prison as well as outside, on some of the critical issues relating to the strategy and tactics of the Indian struggle for freedom between 1939 and 1945, as also his attitude towards the stands of some other stalwarts of the freedom struggle like Mahatma Gandhi, Jawaharlal Nehru and Subhas Chandra Bose. Among these particular mention may be made of the items which show J.P.'s insistence from the commencement of the Second World War that the Congress must adopt a policy of total opposition to the use of Indian men and materials by Britain in its war effort; his suggestion sent from the special camp jail at Deoli (Rajasthan) in 1941 that some of his comrades of the Congress Socialist Party (he particularly mentioned one of his comrades in Bihar, Basawan Singh) should go underground and prepare for an armed struggle against the British; and his two letters to the Fighters for Freedom sent from the underground in 1943, during the brief respite from prison won by him through his escape from the Hazaribagh Central Prison (then in Bihar, now in Jharkhand). In these letters be emphasized that the suppression of the great mass upsurge in August-September 1942 did not mean the end of the struggle, which had to be carried on till final victory was achieved. He also debunked the notion that efforts being made then by leaders like C. Rajagopalachari for a settlement with the British Government might somehow succeed and suggested ways for continuing the struggle, violently or non-violently, depending on the circumstances and the inclinations of particular freedom fighters. J.P.'s jottings (including comments on a number of books) and letters while lodged first in the Lahore Fort (1943-5) and then in Agra Central Prison (1945-6) will be found useful in understanding his reactions to some of the major political developments in India during those years. They also illustrate his growing revulsion (which had already begun during 1939-40) for the tactics employed by the Communists both in India and abroad, particularly in the Soviet Union, and his growing fascination for certain Western democratic principles and practices as well as for Gandhian values. This was the precursor of his shift in later years first to Democratic Socialism and then to Gandhism or Sarvodaya.

I

The volume opens with J.P.'s statement issued shortly after the outbreak of the Second World War on 3 September 1939. Here he adopted a forthright stand that the Congress had no option but to oppose, with all the strength it had, the use of Indian human and material resources by Britain in its war which was clearly being fought in order to safeguard its imperialist possessions. This, he argued, was the only course which could be adopted if the Congress were to prove true to the stand taken repeatedly in its resolutions in the recent past on the war issue. Asserting that the British Government had actually committed aggression against India by ignoring the repeated declarations of the Congress in those resolutions to the effect that it would not tolerate India being dragged into the war by the fiat of the British Government, he observed:

> What answer can there be to this British aggression against India than the most determined resistance? If we have any self-respect and if we maintain our objective of complete independence, we cannot possibly do less. Resistance in such circumstances is not opportunism but a political and moral necessity.
>
> By all means let us dismiss from our minds all thought of bargaining. There should be no question of obtaining concessions or even freedom in exchange for support in Britain's war. For freedom bought at the price of participation in war dictated to us is no real freedom at all. We can conceive of no concessions which can justify India's participation in this war.[1]

As is well known, the Congress Working Committee did not accept this view. Through its long resolution adopted on 14 September 1939, even while registering its strong protest against the action of the Viceroy in committing full support to the British war effort on behalf of India and indeed making the country a party to that war, offered to support that effort if India's independence was assured. When that resolution came before a meeting of the All India Congress Committee at Wardha on 9 October 1939, J.P. moved an amendment to that resolution on behalf of the Congress Socialist Party. That amendment declared that the Congress would not only be unable to accept any piecemeal advance towards India's freedom, but would also refuse to entertain a settlement of the issue of freedom which pledged in advance the country's support to the British war effort and directed the Working Committee 'to give immediate effect to the national policy of resistance to Britain's War'. The amendment, of course, was lost by 181 votes to 64.[2]

Not deterred by this, J.P. went on propagating his view about the imperative need for non-cooperation with the British war effort wherever he had an opportunity of doing so. The British Government, however, soon

[1] For text see, item no. 1, pp. 1-3 of this volume.

[2] Ibid., pp. 3-4.

adopted measures to put a stop to such propaganda. For a speech delivered at Jamshedpur (then in Bihar, now in Jharkhand) J.P. was arrested on 7 March 1940. This was about two weeks before the commencement of the next annual Congress session at Ramgarh (in the same region), where the Congress, dissatisfied with the British response to its demand for a clarification of British aims in the war and the position of India in that context was expected to decide upon its future course of action beyond the resignation of Congress Ministries in the provinces (which had already taken place). The statement made by J.P. at his trial on 15 March 1940 will have an honoured place among the memorable documents of our struggle for freedom. Pleading guilty to the charge levelled by the prosecutor, he observed:

> Regarding the speech for which I am being prosecuted, I cannot say how fat it succeeded in achieving its ends. But nothing would please me more than to learn that it did have some success in impeding the effective prosecution of the War. I shall deem the heaviest punishment well earned if I am found to have succeeded in this.
>
> As for the charge of endangering the defence of British India I think the irony of it cannot be lost upon us. A slave has no obligation to defend his slavery. His only obligation is to destroy his bondage. I hope we shall know how to defend ourselves when we have achieved our freedom.[3]

The reactions of Gandhi and Nehru to J.P.'s arrest show the high position which he had by then acquired in the nationalist ranks. 'He is', observed Gandhi, 'no ordinary worker. He is an authority on socialism. It may be said that what he does not know of Western socialism nobody else in India does. He is a fine fighter. He has forsaken all for the sake of the deliverance of his country. His industry is tireless. His capacity for suffering is not to be excelled.'[4] Nehru commented that the news of J.P.'s arrest was of vital importance for he was 'one of the dearest and most valued of our comrades' and his arrest signified the 'determination of the Government to declare war on the Congress'.[5] J.P.'s imprisonment at a time when most of the Congress leaders were still untouched, further raised his stature and increased his popularity, particularly among the youth.

After this term of imprisonment was over, J.P. was immediately arrested again and kept, without trial, in the special camp jail at Deoli, in Rajputana (now Rajasthan). This again marked him out as one of the leaders who were the special targets of the Government's policy of repression. Two events which occurred in Deoli increased his prominence. The first was a sequel to his efforts to provide guidance to his colleagues and followers from prison. He was caught by the jail staff while trying to smuggle out

[3] See item no. 26, pp. 46-8.

[4] Jayaprakash Narayan, *Socialism, Sarvodaya and Democracy*, ed. Bimal Prasad (Bombay, 1964), Introduction, p. xv.

[5] *Selected Works of Jawaharlal Nehru*, ed. S. Gopal, Vol. X (New Delhi, 1977), p. 347.

letters to his comrades through his wife, Prabhavati, who had been allowed to see him. The purpose of these letters was to prepare for an armed struggle against the British.[6] The Government published these letters in the press throughout the country, hoping it would tarnish J.P.'s image as a person who, in spite of belonging to the Congress, was preaching recourse to violent methods. It perhaps also thought that this would drive a wedge between him and his colleagues and followers on the one hand, and the older leaders and workers of the Congress on the other. Actually, the impact was just the opposite, as J.P. rose higher in the estimation of the Indian people. Even those who did not approve of his methods forgot their differences for the time being, and applauded his courage and single-minded determination to see the country free as soon as possible. Their mood was reflected by Gandhi's statement which, while calling upon the Congress to retain its faith in non-violence, questioned the Government's right to condemn J.P.: 'Frankly, all nationalist forces, no matter by what name they are described, are at war with the Government. And, according to the accepted canons of war, the method adopted by Jayaprakash Narayan is perfectly legitimate.'[7] Shortly after this J.P. undertook a fast in support of certain demands of the prisoners at Deoli, including disbandment of the camp prison and repatriation of all the prisoners to their home provinces. The fast continued for thirty-one days and was broken only after the main demands were met. This again turned the attention of the Indian people towards J.P. It was widely felt that the Deoli prison camp was disbanded largely through his single-minded efforts even at the risk of his life.

II

Repatriated to Bihar, J.P. watched the onward march of the freedom struggle from his cell in the Hazaribagh Central Prison. While there was exhilarating news of the adoption of the Quit India Resolution by the All India Congress Committee in Bombay on 8 August 1942, and the popular uprisings which followed in various parts of the country after the arrest of the Congress leaders, that about widespread depression and demoralization in the wake of the suppression of those uprisings worried him. He found it more and more galling to sit idly in prison while such a momentous struggle was going on. At last, with the cooperation of some of his trusted comrades, he managed to scale the walls of the prison on Diwali night, 8 November 1942, together with five other fellow prisoners. This daring feat made J.P. a national hero in the eyes of the Indian people. Once out of prison he established contact with other underground leaders and infused a new life into their efforts. Among his most significant contributions at this time

[6] See item no. 32, pp. 80-99 for the text of the *Deoli Letters*.

[7] See Appendix 19 for the text of Gandhi's statement.

were his two letters to 'Fighters for Freedom', one issued in February and the other in September 1943. They show J.P. at his best, analysing the nature of the 1942 struggle and providing inspiration and guidance to those of its soldiers who had managed to elude arrest till then.

In his first letter, he exhorted the fighters for freedom not to be demoralized because of the apparent suppression of the 1942 rebellion and remarked: 'The history of all revolutions shows that a Revolution is not an event. It is a phase, a social process. And during the evolution of a Revolution, tides and ebbs are normal.' The Indian Revolution, he explained, was at a low ebb at that time not because of the superior force of the British, but for two other reasons. Firstly, there was the lack of an efficient organization that could provide effective leadership to the mighty forces that were released by the August uprising. Secondly, there was no programme which could be placed before the people after the first phase of the uprising was over. So the main task was to remove those shortcomings and prepare for the next phase. Boldly asserting that recourse to violence was unavoidable in performing these tasks, he observed: 'I have no hesitation in admitting that non-violence of the brave, if practised on a sufficiently large scale, would make violence unnecessary, but where such non-violence is absent, I should not allow cowardice, clothed in Shastric subtleties, to block the development of this revolution and lead to its failure.'[8]

In his second letter issued some months later, J.P. expressed his views on this subject in a slightly different way. While remaining as convinced as before that violent means were necessary to carry on the struggle for freedom effectively at that time, the main thrust of his argument now was that there was no justification for carrying on a controversy on the issue of violence vs. non-violence. 'Every fighter for freedom', he wrote, 'is free to choose his own method. Those who believe in similar methods should work together as a disciplined group. And the least that those who follow a different path should do is not to come in the way of one another and waste their energies in mutual recrimination.'

Another issue to which J.P. devoted considerable space in his second letter was the effort being made by certain leaders to end the political deadlock in India. He tried to show that such an effort would harm India's interests and described those who were engaged in it as 'saboteurs of the freedom movement'. According to him, a continuation of the political deadlock would be helpful to India by showing that India remained unbeaten and the spirit of resistance continued.

J.P. also took this opportunity to pay tribute to Subhas Chandra Bose, who had escaped to Germany and from there proceeded to South-East Asia to take command of the Indian National Army. In line with their changed policy of supporting the British war effort after the German invasion of the

[8] See item no. 41, pp. 110-15.

Soviet Union in 1941, the Communists were then denouncing him as a quisling. Obviously referring to them, J.P. remarked: 'It is easy to denounce Subhas as a Quisling. Those who are themselves Quislings of Britain find it easiest to denounce him. But nationalist India knows him as a fervent patriot and as one who has always been in the forefront of his country's fight for freedom.' J.P., however, took care to emphasize that India's freedom would not come as a gift from the Japanese people, but would depend primarily on the strength and resources of the Indian people themselves. According to him, it was impossible for the I.N.A., however large, to defeat the Allied armies in India; this could be done only by the Japanese army. But in that case, the latter would not hand over India to the Indians whatever the understanding between the Japanese Government and Subhas Bose. 'We must be ready', he said, 'in the event of an Axis-Allied clash in India to seize power ourselves. Only if we are ready to make this attempt can outside help, such as Subhas' National Army be of value to us and Tojo be prevented from annexing India.'

Behind such thinking lay a new vision of India's role in the world as the leader of all the peoples struggling against imperialism and fascism. At a time when one section of nationalist leadership (represented by Jawaharlal Nehru) was inclining towards the United Nations and the other (represented by Subhas Chandra Bose) towards the Axis Powers, J.P. asserted that if the Indian people continued vigorously with their struggle for freedom without being deflected by talks of ending the political deadlock, India would gain 'the leadership of the third camp of the common men of the world' for whom neither Allied nor Axis victory held any prospects of liberation and happiness. Affirming that the interests of the common man of both sides demanded the end of the war, J.P. pointed out that this could not be brought about by 'Churchills and Roosevelts, Hitlers and Tojos'. Nor did he bank upon the Soviet Union or the Labour movement in Western Europe. The future, according to him, lay with the common people of the world, and India must seek to rally them together for strengthening the forces of peace and freedom. As he put it, India alone represented 'the aspirations and promptings of the disinherited and dispossessed of the earth. . . . We work for the defeat both of imperialism and fascism by the common people of the world and by our struggle we show the way to the ending of war and the liberation of the black, white and yellow.'[9]

J.P. was not content with writing inspiring letters for distribution among freedom-fighters; he also tried to lay the foundations of a guerilla force which he called Azad Dasta. In order to evade arrest he had selected a spot in the terai region of Nepal, close to the borders of north Bihar, for this purpose. While he was engaged in training the officer cadre of this force,

[9] See item no. 42, pp. 116-34.

he, along with six other colleagues, including Rammanohar Lohia, was arrested by the Nepalese police, but all of them were rescued by the trainees and their sympathisers. It was with this organization in mind that J.P. had written at the end of his second letter to freedom-fighters that some progress had already been made in 'developing a guerilla movement'. He had high hopes from such a movement, but could not get sufficient time to expand it into a large force. The second letter was dated 1 September 1943. On 10 September, J.P. was arrested at the Amritsar railway station while travelling from Delhi to Rawalpindi, thus returning to prison exactly ten months and ten days after his escape from it.

Lodged in the Lahore Fort, J.P. had to go through a long period of interrogation and torture and had to pass several months in solitary confinement. He was allowed out, handcuffed, only in the mornings and evenings for an hour for exercise,[10] but all this failed to cow down his spirit in any way. He remained firm like a rock in his determination not to divulge any secrets regarding his activities since his escape from the Hazaribagh Central Prison or regarding those of his friends underground. He also conveyed to his tormentors that he remained as determined as ever to continue the struggle, where necessary with violent means, for India's freedom from British rule. Along with Lohia, who had also been brought to the Lahore Fort after his arrest in 1944, he was transferred to the Agra Central Prison in January 1945. Although all the top leaders of the Congress were released in June 1945 (Gandhi had already been released in 1944 on medical grounds), J.P. and Lohia were considered too dangerous to be included among them and were released only in the middle of April 1946.

III

Some time after the end of his interrogation and torture J.P., even though still kept in solitary confinement, was provided with newspapers as well as writing facilities like paper, pen and ink. Not being in a mood to write his autobiography or any other serious work, he utilized them to jot down his reactions to some of the political developments then taking place outside the prison as well as his reflections on certain long-term issues which appeared important to him. At the same time, within the limits permitted by Government rules, he exchanged letters with some of his friends and well-wishers. A perusal of his correspondence with M.R. Masani, his old friend and colleague in the C.S.P., will be found particularly rewarding. For they provide us with intimate glimpses of the subtle changes taking place in J.P.'s thinking during 1944-5 regarding some of the important

[10] For a detailed account of the nature of J.P.'s life in the Lahore Fort after his arrest in September 1943 see item no. 45, pp. 145-7.

ideological problems of Socialism. Both his reflections in the Lahore Fort and his correspondence with Masani show his growing aversion to Communist methods, and growing attraction for Gandhian values as well as Western democratic principles and practices, particularly their emphasis on the liberty of the individual and on free and fair elections.

All J.P.'s jottings (including comments on a number of books which J.P. had then been reading) and his letters during 1944-6 must be carefully perused in order to realize their full significance. All that can be done here is to highlight some of the important points emerging from them. The first point which strikes us is J.P.'s dislike for any move which seemed to him likely to dampen the spirit of rebellion ignited all over the country during the Quit India uprisings in August-September 1942. Because of this, the release from prison of some Congress leaders in 1944 did not enthuse him at all. For he was convinced that it would lead to no constructive result (on this point, recording his agreement will the Viceroy, Lord Wavell) and at the same time have a negative impact on the people's spirit of rebellion.[11] For the same reason, even while expressing his happiness at the release of Gandhi as it had taken place because of his ill health, he wondered what its political fall-out was going to be.[12] Later on, when Gandhi came out with some criticism of the underground activities of the revolutionaries[13] and some Congressmen, raking up the issue of non-violence, began to openly attack them, J.P. felt hurt and exclaimed: 'Violence, it seems, is a terrible sin, but only when used against British rule.' In this connection he referred to the efforts then being made by Gandhi to have an understanding with the British on the basis of which a national government might be established and engage itself in galvanizing the Indian people for the British war effort.[14] He felt even more hurt and indeed bitter at some of Gandhi's comments on the Quit India Movement, decrying it for its non-adherence to non-violence and stressing that it was not a Congress movement. Noting his jottings on those comments under the title: 'A revolution is disowned because it failed', he remarked: 'I feel bitter because I find we have been badly let down—not I personally, because I openly preached violence and was therefore prepared in the event of failure for severe censure and excommunication. But, thousands, rather lakhs, of Indian patriots have been let down.'[15] J.P. was also strongly opposed to C. Rajagopalachari's formula for the settlement of Congress-League differences based on the acceptance by the Congress of the Pakistan demand in principle and to the infructuous Gandhi-Jinnah talks held on that basis. He thought that the creation of Pakistan would not

[11] See item no. 46, pp. 149-52.
[12] Ibid., pp. 177-83, 186-8.
[13] See Appendix 27, pp. 341-2.
[14] See item no. 46, pp. 198-9.
[15] Ibid., pp. 202-5.

solve the communal problem and would be, besides, extremely harmful for India and all sections of the Indian people, including the Muslims, on whose behalf the demand for it was being put forward.[16]

IV

As mentioned earlier, among J.P.'s significant jottings and letters while in prison during 1944-6 are those which illustrate the shift of the central point of his political ideology from Marxism to Democratic Socialism, without totally renouncing Marxism. This, of course, did not begin in 1944, but much earlier and had a lot to do with his as well as his friends' experience of working with the Communists and the developments in the Soviet Union in the 1930s. J.P. and his friends did not like the political line being pursued by the Communists in India in the early 1930s, based on opposition to the Congress and the Civil Disobedience Movements launched by it and decided to set up their own separate organization, the Congress Socialist Party, wedded to Marxism but functioning within the framework of the Congress. However, some of them, particularly J.P., continued to hope that some day the Communist Party would see reason and decide to work in cooperation with the Congress Socialist Party, as both the parties drew inspiration from Marxism and the only dividing wall between them was their divergent attitude towards the Congress. When therefore the Communist International, at its Seventh Congress in 1935, modified its previous line and advised their affiliated parties to work in cooperation with leading nationalist organizations even though they might be led by the bourgeoisie, J.P. was immensely pleased, for the door was now open for the realization of socialist unity in India, one of his fondest dreams during those days.

The sequel is described in detail in his pamphlet entitled *Socialist Unity and the C.S.P.* prepared in 1940 and published in 1941. The doors of the Congress Socialist Party were thrown open to members of the Communist Party of India and the latter not only entered the C.S.P. but also utilized it to enter the Congress and secure important positions in both the organizations. Their main interest, however, was not in building up an united front with the C.S.P., but in utilizing the opportunity to either capture it or to expose it as a non-Marxist party, and project the Communist Party as the only party of Marxism in India. J.P. was so fascinated by the dream of socialist unity that even when there emerged clear evidence of such designs on the part of the Communist Party, he, as General Secretary, continued to pursue the programme of fraternizing with the Communists. Indeed he did not agree to give up this programme even when four of his leading colleagues—Rammanohar Lohia, M.R. Masani, Achyut Patwardhan and

[16] Ibid., pp. 153-8, 188-90, 215-19. For the text of the Rajagopalachari formula see Appendix 26.

Asoka Mehta—resigned from the National Executive of the C.S.P. in protest against it. The Communists were finally expelled from the Congress Socialist Party only in 1940, when it became clear that any further delay would only add to the loses of the Congress Socialist Party. It is characteristic of J.P. that he accepted all the responsibility for the disastrous consequences of his policy for the C.S.P. But what is more significant, from the point of view of the evolution of his political thought, is that this experience created in him a deep aversion to the Communists and their methods and a conviction that it would never be possible to achieve unity with a Communist Party, at any rate, as long as it remained affiliated to the Comintern.[17]

The doubts, first born in 1929-30, about the ability of the Comintern to understand the nature of the political situation in India were now further confirmed. And with all this there developed growing doubts about the nature of the Soviet experiment itself. The stories of numerous purges and trials being carried out under Stalin contributed further to those doubts. J.P. began to feel more and more that there must be something basically wrong in the Soviet experiment to lead to what seemed to him a negation of Socialism. He now ceased to look upon the Soviet Union as a model for Socialism and while continuing to proclaim his faith in Marxism, in reality he was increasingly drawn towards Gandhism and absorbed some of its important tenets like the need for decentralization in administration and commitment to certain ethical values in politics. At the same time he was also becoming conscious of the necessity of nurturing some of the Western values of democracy in order to avoid the pitfalls of Soviet Communism.

If the pamphlet describing his experiences of working with the Communists shows how J.P. was being repelled by the latter, the draft resolution prepared by him and submitted for consideration at the Ramgarh session of the Congress (March 1940) under the title '*An Outline Picture of Swaraj*' marks the beginning of his shift toward Democratic Socialism. Here we have the picture of a democratic socialist society in outline: the law of the land to be based on the will of the people freely expressed by them; guarantee of full individual and civil liberty and cultural and religious freedom; abolition of all distinctions of birth and privilege and guarantee of equal rights to all citizens; social justice and economic freedom to be the guiding principles of the political and economic organization of the State; all large-scale production to be under collective ownership and control. While the political and economic organization of the State, the draft asserted, would conduce to the satisfaction of the rational requirements of every member of society, material satisfaction would not be its sole objective. On

[17] See item no. 31, pp. 57-79. For a more detailed account of J.P.'s exertions for uniting all Marxists in India, see M.R. Masani, *Bliss was it in that Dawn . . .* (New Delhi, 1977), pp. 120-41.

the contrary, it would aim at creating conditions for healthy living and the moral and intellectual development of the individual. With this end in view, the State would endeavour to promote small-scale production carried on by individual or cooperative effort for the equal benefit of all concerned. The life of the village would be reorganized, with a view to making it self-governing and self-sufficient in as large a measure as possible.[18]

This draft while incorporating the essential ingredients of Socialism, indicates the emergence of a new trend in J.P.'s thinking, clearly distinguishable from the thrust of his first major treatise on Socialism published in 1936 under the title *Why Socialism?*[19] His jottings and letters during 1944-6 show a further development of this trend. Thus in his jottings on 27-8 February on the economic problem likely to be faced by India after the achievement of independence he firmly takes a socialist position and writes:

> By the economic problem I do not mean merely the problem of poverty or industrialisation or any such economic problem in the ordinary sense of the term. I use this term here in a much more fundamental sense, namely, the determination of the basic economic principles on which Indian economy shall rest in a Free India. . . . We believe that unless a deliberate, conscious attempt is made at the very outset to bring the nation's economic life under the guidance and control of the State, not only would that life be made to serve the end of Indian capitalism, but soon enough would the State itself be converted into the latters' subservient tool.[20]

In his jottings on 22 July 1944, however, J.P. added another significant dimension to his views on development (to which he stuck till the end of his life)—something quite rare in the universe of discourse of socialist thinkers. Writing under the caption, 'Bricks of Society', he admitted that in the conditions in which the majority of our people lived in those days, it was quite natural to think first of means for alleviating their suffering by securing their material well-being. Undoubtedly, he observed, 'first man must live and, therefore, those conditions have first to be created in which he can live happily, i.e. as far as happiness can be derived from the satisfaction of material needs'. But then he added that 'in laying the foundations of the Indian nation and the future free society of India, it is not sufficient to pay attention to the material aspects of life alone. The human aspect, though not urgently demanding our present attention, is perhaps even more important than that of material well-being.' He further added: 'A nation is made up of individuals, so it should also be our aim to

[18] See item no. 27, pp. 48-50.

[19] Text in *Jayaprakash Narayan: Selected Works*, Vol. II (New Delhi, 2001), pp. 1-89.

[20] For details of J.P.'s views on various other issues connected with economic policy see item no. 46, pp. 158-63. The lines quoted here occur on pp. 159-60.

so mould the character of every individual that we become eventually not only a nation of prosperous but also of good men.'[21]

V

Such writings show that, inspite of his differences with Gandhi on the issue of sticking to non-violence in the struggle for freedom, J.P. was coming close to Gandhi's thinking on some of the most fundamental issues of development. At the same time, however, he continued to draw inspiration from Marx. This is very well brought out by his comments on a large number of books sent regularly to him by Masani, as well as his correspondence with the latter. These must be perused by the readers themselves in order to have a full idea of the elements of change and continuity in J.P.'s thinking during 1944-6. Here it may suffice to highlight some of his comments as his ideas developed. Thus describing Eric Fromm's *The Fear of Freedom* (1942) as 'the most valuable book' he had read till the time of jotting his comments (2 October 1944), J.P. wrote:

> Fromm has great respect for Marx and is impatient of those who misrepresent or misunderst and him. Marxists have often overlooked the dynamism of the human organism and have emphasised only the role of society and social forces in moulding human psychology. We should be thankful to Fromm for his corrective, by which he has brought us nearer to Marx, for Marx was always conscious of the creative or active principle in human nature. He could not be the revolutionary he was, unless he recognised that not only history made man but also that man made history—a phrase common to both Fromm and Marx.[22]

At the same time J.P. was impressed by Fromm's concern with the evil effects produced by over-centralization and regimentation in the Soviet Union and his prescription of Democratic Socialism as the remedy. As J.P. puts it: 'Fromm is conscious that socialisation of production means bureaucracy and manipulation of the individual and points out that the solution of the problem is one of the major tasks of the present. A balanced system of centralisation and decentralisation must be evolved so as to reconcile large-scale social planning with freedom for the individual.'[23]

The more J.P. read about the details of the Soviet economic organization based on over-centralization and regimentation, the more he became convinced that the Soviet model of economic and political development could not be reconciled with a democratic system of government. Thus he wrote to Masani in January 1945: 'Burnham's *Managerial Revolution* has affected me rather strongly in the sense that it has made me realise that the problem is much harder than I had thought it to be: I mean the problem of democracy and economic planning.'[24] After going through Arthur Koestler's

[21] See ibid., pp. 195-8.

[22] Ibid., pp. 227-8.

[23] Ibid.

[24] J.P. to Masani, 20 January 1945, ibid., p. 259.

Darkness at Noon, full of criticisms of the Soviet economic and political organization, J.P. commented: 'A fine book. Shall keep it.' He further added: 'The section on Russia is superb. I agree 100%. . . . The suggestion at the end regarding the way out gives body to my own thoughts. Except for the language, there is page after page in this section of the book which I could have written myself.'[25]

In view of this trend in J.P.'s thinking it is not surprising that he was immensely pleased with Masani's pamphlet, *Socialism Reconsidered* (1944) where he openly expressed his disenchantment with the Soviet experiment and raised doubts about the validity of Marxism itself. After going through it J.P. wrote to Masani: 'I do not know if you will feel happy or begin to doubt your sanity if I tell you that I nearly agreed with you hundred per cent! Well, the world does change, doesn't it?'[26] Yet although quite disillusioned with the Soviet experiment J.P. had not yet given up his faith in Marxism. Writing to Masani about several anti-Marxist as well as anti-Soviet books sent by him, J.P. remarked in his letter in the first week of June 1945: 'Looking at the signs of the times, it seems to me Minoo, that I'll be the only benighted Marxist left in this country, as also the only unregenerate materialist.'[27] A few days later, he further clarified his position: 'By the way one of my letters to you has created a rather embarrassing situation. When I wrote from Lahore that I agreed nearly hundred per cent with your *Socialism Reconsidered* I was thinking largely of your treatment of Russia. I do not mean to suggest that I disagreed with the other parts, but my agreement with them was not nearly as complete.'[28]

Similarly, although J.P.'s reverence and admiration for Gandhi had gone on growing and he was attracted by several of Gandhi's ideas and techniques, he continued to differ strongly from him on the strategy to be followed in the struggle for freedom as also on the ideological issue, the natural concomitant of his continuing to cling on to Marxism. His letter to Gandhi dated 6 October 1945 is quite revealing in this respect. In a bid to correct Gandhi's estimate of J.P.'s ideological position, formed after hearing Prabhavati's report after her meeting J.P. in the Agra Central Prison, he wrote to Gandhi:

> It is true that in some areas of thought I have been drawn quite close to you. This has given me much happiness. However, I continue to regret that in the area of basic principles I still find myself as far away from you as I ever was. I feel that my field will not only get away from yours, but will also become totally separate. Because of the recent turn of events I find myself moving speedily in this direction.[29]

[25] Item no. 56, J.P. to Masani, 5 July 1945, p. 270.
[26] J.P. to Masani, 21 April 1944, item no. 46, p. 249.
[27] J.P. to Masani, 6 June 1945, item no. 55, p. 268.
[28] J.P. to Masani, 5 July 1945, item no. 56, p. 272.
[29] Item no. 59, p. 275.

J.P.'s letter to Gandhi cited above also reveals his total unconcern with the issue of his (J.P.'s) release from prison inspite of the fact that almost all the prominent leaders of the Congress had already been released four-five months earlier. Perhaps reacting to the concern expressed by Gandhi in his letter to J.P. under reply, the latter wrote:

> Although prison is not a place for human beings to live, still I assure you that I am neither counting the days of my release, nor thinking that I am engaged in any penance. In revolutions, it is inevitable that some die, some are ruined and some languish in jails. Where is the question of any kind of deliberation on this. Thousand are still languishing in jails—in future also thousands will continue to languish.
>
> The wilted flowers of the rainy season in our garden have now acquired wrinkles of old age. The seedlings of autumn flowers are peeping up from the veil of the earth to replace them. Now most of my time is spent in looking after their growth and in imagining which flowers will brighten which corners of this small world of mine and cover which garden-beds with their smile. The prevailing circumstances convince me that I shall be able to see the fulfilment of my imaginings.[30]

VI

The twenty-seven appendices given at the end of the book follow the pattern set in Volumes I and II. They contain either those documents where J.P. was one of the signatories or those to which he reacted at some length in his writings included in this volume.

During most of the period covered by this volume J.P. was either in prison or underground. We could not, therefore, find any photograph of his to be included here. We have tried to compensate for this, to some extent, by including the facsimiles of some of his handwritten letters and a jotting by him during this period.

1. Why Congress Must Resist War: A Political and Moral Necessity [after 3 September 1939][1]

In the war crisis that faces the Congress and the country we stand four square against war. We see no reason for any departure from the policy of resistance to India's participation in Britain's wars. The oft-repeated arguments in Congress resolutions for the past four years are as valid today as ever before and we hope that the Congress will put its repeated declarations into effect without further delay.

The Congress had sounded the warning that it would not tolerate India being dragged into war by the fiat of the British Government. The British Government has chosen with haughty disdain to ignore this warning. Not only has it proceeded with war preparations and the transfer of Indian troops overseas but it has presumed to declare war in the name of the Indian people.

Actually, the Government has declared war on the Indian people. In pursuance of that act, it has in defiance of a resolution of the A.I.C.C. rushed amendments to the Government of India Act through Parliament which destroy all remnants of that Provincial Autonomy on the basis of which the Congress formed Ministries in the provinces and has framed the Defence of India Ordinance which snatches away such few civil liberties as still existed and which is a fair replica of Hitlerism applied to Indian conditions.

What answer can there be to this British aggression against India than the most determined resistance? If we have any self-respect and if we maintain our objective of complete national independence, we cannot possibly do less. Resistance in such circumstances is not opportunism but a political and moral necessity.

By all means let us dismiss from our minds all thought of bargaining. There should be no question of obtaining concessions or even freedom in exchange for support in Britain's war, for freedom bought at the price of participation in war dictated to us is no real freedom at all. We can conceive of no concessions which can justify India's participation in this war.

The Indian National Congress has pledged itself to the use of 'peaceful and legitimate means'. It has expressed its abhorrence of wars and rejected the arbitrament of arms for the settlement of international problems.

How then can it possibly support a war which, despite the professed devotion to democracy, is nothing but another inter-Imperialist conflict?

The war of 1914-18 was also proclaimed by the British Government and its allies as a 'war to end war' and as a 'war to make the world safe for democracy'. That war despite its successful termination with India's support, brought neither democracy nor peace to the distracted world. Its net result

[1] *Yusuf Meherally Papers*, Nehru Memorial Museum & Library (hereinafter referred to as NMML).

was the Treaty of Versailles,[2]—that fabric of monstrous injustices that in time has produce Hitler[3] and the war of 1939.

Shall we then repeat the mistakes of the past?

Shall we not rather realize that neither side to this conflict is free of the guilt of war? Fascist Germany can expect no sympathy from us. But can there be any sympathy—much less support—for Imperialist Britain which, in attempting to maintain its rule over one-fourth of the surface of the globe, has consistently sabotaged all attempts at justice between nations and the achievement of world peace?

On Britain must fall the responsibility of wrecking within ten years of each other the two most noble of international endeavours of modern times—the Disarmament Conference and the application of economic sanction against Italy for its aggression against Ethiopia.

If Britain is at war today with Germany, it is not in defence of Polish democracy, which in any case never existed, but out of fear of German expansion which successive attempts at appeasement had not succeeded in stemming and which was threatening the security of its Empire. Where was Britain when the freedom of Manchuria, Ethiopia, Spain, Austria and Czechoslovakia was successively sacrificed and the League of Nations slowly strangled to death. War is a continuation of politics and the only change is one from a diplomatic to a military defence of the Empire. The British ruling class must therefore share the guilt of this war along with the German and other ruling classes.

There can be no hope that this war which in its origins is a war of imperialist rivalries will, as the war progresses, change automatically its imperialist character into one for democracy and world peace. No victory of either side followed by a dictated peace, as at Versailles, can encompass this. Such a transformation can only be effected if the peoples of the warring countries shake off the yoke of their masters. What better place for such an effort than India—dragged into war at the heels of its foreign rulers—and what fitter object of destruction than the British Empire, which is the biggest single obstacle to world peace?

It is urged by some that the Indian people have not the strength to perform

[2] The Treaty of Versailles signed in 1919 along with a series of associated agreements brought a formal end to the First World War. It redivided the territory of the defeated Central Powers, restricted the size of Germany's armed forces and established the League of Nations.

[3] Adolf Hitler (1889-1945); German dictator; founded National Socialist German Worker' Party, known as Nazi party, 1919-20; wrote *Mein Kamph* in prison, 1924; appointed Chancellor of Germany, 1933; violated the Treaty of Versailles and pursued certain policies which are generally considered responsible for the outbreak of the Second World War; committed suicide after Germany's defeat, 1945.

this historic task, that the country is not ready for a struggle. When one's self-respect is trodden on, there can be no question of waiting till one is strong enough to assert it. It is the will to resist that matters.

We are convinced, however, that given the call, the people of India, whose sense of national self-respect and desire for independence are violated by this war, that is thrust on them, would give a resounding answer. The real question is whether the Congress will lead the struggle that is inevitably bound to develop or whether it will stand by—nay, try to prop up a decaying order—and let history pass it by.

We stand today at the brink of a great decision. If the Congress would be true to its ideal of complete national freedom, its abhorrence of war and all violence, and its aspirations for a new world order based on democracy, justice and peace, its decision can be none other than one for immediate and unconditional resistance to this war.

2. Proposed Amendment to the Working Committee's Resolution on War Crisis, A.I.C.C., Wardha, 9 October 1939[1]

The A.I.C.C. endorses the statement of the Working Committee and declares that the present war which has arisen out of the desire of imperialist and fascist powers to maintain and extend their colonial territories and which is being waged with that end in view runs counter to the aim of the liquidation of imperialism and fascism foreshadowed in the statement. That aim necessarily involves full and unfettered freedom of every people in regard to internal as also external affairs. The Congress therefore will not only be unable to accept any piecemeal advance towards India's freedom, but will also refuse to entertain a settlement of the issue of freedom which pledges in advance the country's support in this War. Only after freedom is won and the foundations of an Indian State laid will it be possible to take decision on the question of War, which moreover, will be informed by the ideals and methods of work to which the Indian people have learnt to subscribe under the leadership of the Congress.

In view of this and of the continued utilisation of the country's manpower and resources in the war despite the declared policies of the Congress, the A.I.C.C. directs the Working Committee to give immediate effect to the national policy of resistance to Britain's War.

[1] *AICC Papers* (NMML). The proposed amendment sought deletion of a part of the resolution moved by Jawaharlal Nehru (see Appendix 3 for text of the resolution), beginning with the words "The All-India Congress Committee, however, does not wish to take etc. etc." and ending with "the rights of all minorities to which the Congress has always pledged itself", and in its place proposed the above amendment which was lost by 181 votes to 64.

3. Speech while moving the Amendment at A.I.C.C., Wardha, 9 October 1939[1]

We know imperialism can't fight for world salvation. The aim of the war is not to establish democracy. If new democratic forces arise in England, Germany and France, and the Governments of these countries really espouse the democratic cause then we may help them. In strengthening our own democratic forces we would be helping the world democratic forces. You would not be removing the root causes of Imperialism if you help the Governments of Chamberlain[2] and Daladier.[3] The argument that if Indian independence is declared we would to that extent weaken British Imperialism is not correct.

What we get in this manner, can also be taken away by the same agencies—witness for example the Government of India Amendment Act. There is only one way out: tell the British that they may shoot us down but we shall not help them.

We must steel our hearts for struggle. We shall go forward not by helping the British Government but by opposing them. This would be in accordance with Congress policy.

[1] *National Front*, 22 October 1939.

[2] Arthur Nevelle Chamberlain (1809-1940); British Conservative statesman; Prime Minister of British, 1937-40.

[3] Edouard Daladier (1884-1970); French statesman; served in First World War, 1914-18; member, Chamber of Deputies from 1919; identified with Radical Socialists; Premier of France, 1933, 1934 (for 11 days), 1938-40; arrested after collapse of French defence, 1940 and liberated, 1945.

4. Note on Gujarat Congress Socialist Party, 22 November 1939[1]

I find from reports received that Comrade Dinkar Mehta[2] and those who have formed a faction with him in the Gujarat C.S.P. have been conducting a very indecent public controversy regarding my decision to appoint Comrade Kamlashanker Pandya[3] to conduct and control the affairs of the Gujarat C.S.P. in the present circumstances of emergency. This controversy is an anti-party activity and is designed to undermine the organization and discipline of the C.S.P. I warn party members concerned that they are doing no service to themselves by such ill-advised action. It was open to such of them as

[1] *Brahmanand Papers* (NMML).

[2] For biographical note on Dinkar Mehta see *JPSW*, Vol. I, p. 122

[3] For biographical note on Kamalashanker Pandya see *JPSW*, Vol. I, p. 122.

cared to appeal to the National Executive against my decision. Till the judgement of the Executive they had no option but to submit to my decision. To indulge in a public controversy over such an internal party affair is the last thing they should have even thought of doing. As it is, the National Executive cannot help taking a serious view of their action.

I should like to utilise this opportunity to explain my decision which has caused a storm in the cup of a faction in the Gujarat C.S.P. The war council of the National Executive decided soon after the European war began that in the circumstances created it was not possible for the party's branches to function in a normal manner, and therefore, the constitution of the provincial parties should be suspended and their functioning placed on an emergency basis working through committees from above. The provincial parties were informed of this in due course. There was no thought in this arrangement of any manner of disciplinary action or any such thing, being involved, and no provincial party has taken it in this light.

In the case of such provincial parties, where there was internal conflict due to the presence of factions, prone to outside influences, it was decided that the provincial machinery should be set-up by the All India Centre. In the case of Gujarat and certain other provinces this was done. Comrade Dinkar Mehta is really angry because I did not choose him but chose Comrade Pandya. There would have been no storm had my choice fallen on Comrade Mehta. In that case I would have been hailed as an apostle of Socialist unity. It is a pity that personal pique should have been allowed to go so far and to do such injury of the Party. In the situation that has been created, I have no option but to explain why I did not select Comrade Mehta to guide the destinies of the Gujarat Party in spite of the fact that he is my Joint Secretary. I did not do so because I had no confidence in Comrade Mehta that he would loyally follow the policy laid down by the All India Party. I had complete confidence in this respect in Comrade Pandya. It may sound strange that a Joint secretary of All India Party should not enjoy this confidence. It is strange, but then it should be remembered that Comrade Mehta held the position of a Joint Secretary not because he has distinguished himself by his ability or his services to the Party, but because in our anxiety for Socialist unity we thought it desirable to give one of the secretaryships to that faction in the Party to which Comrade Mehta belongs.

I have noticed that Comrade Mehta has in this connection also dragged the name of Comrade Nabakrushna Chaudhury[4] of Orissa. It was quite unnecessary for him to do so. Some months back when I had gone to Orissa, it was the general desire of the Party members, there, including that of

[4] For biographical note on Nabakrushna Chaudhury see *JPSW*, Vol. I, p. 66.

Comrade Panigrahi,[5] the General Secretary, to hand over the entire charge of the Party to Comrade Chaudhury. But the latter was unwilling to take this responsibility then in the interest of the Party itself. I met Comrade Chaudhury again during my last southern tour after the war began and then he was ready and even eager to take up the responsibility. He has it now and I have no doubt that he is the best man in Orissa for it and he would discharge it brilliantly.

Regarding the abuses that Comrade Mehta has heaped on the head of Comrade Masani,[6] I need not say more than this that Comrade Masani had nothing whatever to do with my decision. His name has been brought in because of the obsession that he has become to those who hate him for resisting the attempt to destroy the C.S.P. in the name of Socialist unity. Comrade Masani's contribution to the building up of the C.S.P. is a part of national history now and his position in the Party or in the country is not going to be affected by the squeals of some people.

Before I conclude I should like to say how disagreeable it is to me to have said all this, but the manner in which Comrade Mehta and his friends have carried on this indecent controversy left me no other option. Any further controversy will only injure those who participate in it.

[5] Bhagabati Panigrahi (1906-43); one of the prominent leaders of the freedom struggle in Orissa; influenced by writings of Marx; organized relief operations in Orissa during drought of 1924 and floods of 1926-7; participated in the Non-Cooperation Movement and imprisoned; organized Communist Party in Orissa and 'Nabajug Sahitya Sansad' at Cuttack, 1935; participated in the political agitation in Dhenkanal and Ranpur States; convicted in Orissa Conspiracy Case, 1939.

[6] For biographical note on M.R. Masani see *JPSW*, Vol. I, p. 66.

5. Comment on M.A. Jinnah's Statement on 'Deliverance Day', 18 December 1939[1]

In his latest statement[2] on his so-called 'Deliverance Day'[3] Mr. Jinnah[4] has made a reference to a secret letter supposed to have been sent by the Bihar Provincial Congress Committee to me as President of the Gaya District Congress Committee. I have received no letter of the nature Mr. Jinnah alleges, nor has my office at Gaya done so.

Mr. Jinnah says in his statement that the letter has been published and remains yet uncontradicted. I do not know who has published it and where.

[1] *Tribune*, 20 December 1939.

[2] Refers to the statement of M.A. Jinnah issued at Bombay on 13 December 1939 published in the *Bombay Chronicle*, 14 December 1939.

[3] M.A. Jinnah issued an appeal to Muslims on 6 December 1939 at Bombay to celebrate 22 December 1939 as thanks-giving and 'Deliverance Day' after the resignation of the Congress Ministries.

[4] For biographical note on M.A. Jinnah see *JPSW*, Vol. II, p. 155.

It has not been contradicted simply because no one concerned has even seen it. The letter is pure invention.

I should like to add that I do not find anything objectionable in what, according to Mr. Jinnah, the imaginary letter says. To ask Congressmen to work for Hindu-Muslim unity is no crime. Nor can there be any objection to Mussalmans of India raising their voice against the attempts of the Muslim League to sabotage the independence of their country. The activities of the Muslim League have amply demonstrated how a few of its misguided leaders have made it an obstacle to the country's progress. Any Mussalman, who loves his country and loves freedom, must raise his voice against this.

6. To Provincial Secretaries and Members, Congress Socialist Party, 31 December 1939[1]

Sangharsh Office
Lucknow, U.P.
31 December 1939

War Circular No. 2

Comrades,

It appears that there is a lot of confusion in the minds of Party members as to the present policy and programme of the Party. This confusion has been made worse by members of the Communist Party and certain other leftists who, while they continue to talk of socialist and leftist unity have left nothing undone in the last few weeks to destroy even the existing measure of unity—for unity is a process and not an isolated incident. It has served the purpose of these people to propagate falsehoods about C.S.P. policy and create confusion and even rebellion in the ranks of the Party. I am, therefore, placing before you a short resume of the policies we have followed since the beginning of the war and our present programme. I shall prepare separate circulars on socialist and leftist unity and certain other subjects, which shall be sent to you in due course.

The first War Circular was sent to you in September.[2] In many cases it was personally delivered to Provincial Secretaries. Along with this circular were sent copies of the National Executive's first statement on the war adopted at its meeting of September 6, at Lucknow. Subsequently, a statement on Why Congress should resist war[3] was circulated and after that a war-issue of the *Congress Socialist*[4] appeared. In these documents the position of the Party was explained and in the circular certain instructions were given.

[1] *Brahmanand Papers* (NMML).

[2] Not available.

[3] See item no. 1.

[4] Not available.

The circular instructed Party Organizations to propagate the National Executive's statement on the war in meetings, through leaflets and the ordinary press. It is a matter of regret that several Provincial Parties were not able to do even this much. Then, leading members of the Party were asked to tour their Province, giving particular attention to student centres, to explain the Party's stand and to gain support for it. Party organizations were instructed to enrol volunteers for the coming work and to make arrangements for the printing and distribution of literature. They were also asked to develop independent party initiative. With regard to the statement of the Working Committee, Party members were asked not to attack it, while taking care to stress the Party's own position regarding the war.

The Executive's first statement and my subsequent statement which was also published in the *Congress Socialist* explained the Party's position, i.e. the position the Party desired the Congress to adopt. What was this position and wherein lay the difference between it and that of the Working Committee?

There were three positions before the country. The first was that of Mahatma Gandhi,[5] who stood for unconditional support to Britain, though his support was to be only moral. The second was that of our Party: unconditional opposition to the war and to the British Government in India which had dragged India into it. This meant immediate mass direct action. The third was the position of the Working Committee, which in effect was a compromise of the two (without any such conscious attempt at compromise of course). The Working Committee demanded of Britain a declaration of its war aims with particular relation to India and promised to associate itself with the war if these aims were the ending of imperialism and fascism in the Empire as elsewhere. This too implied struggle (for no such aims were actuating Britain in this war) but somewhat indefinitely.

As you will see, the Party's stand was of immediate struggle, without the formality of a declaration of war aims and without negotiations and without bargaining. The war is an imperialist war and Indians cannot fight for Britain in order that Britain might hold their country more firmly down. Not even a free India would have anything to do with an imperialist war except to use it to destroy imperialism elsewhere. This position the Working Committee did not accept. Later, when the A.I.C.C. met at Wardha,[6] we again put the Party's position in the Committee in the form of an amendment[7] to the resolution of Pandit Jawaharlal Nehru. The Committee rejected our position by an overwhelming vote.

The next question before us was, what were we to do? The policy of the Congress had been determined by the A.I.C.C. There was no further

[5] For biographical note on M.K. Gandhi see *JPSW*, Vol. I, p. 41.

[6] Refers to the A.I.C.C. meeting held at Wardha, 9-10 October 1939.

[7] See item no. 2.

possibility of changing that policy. The National Executive[8] which was meeting at Wardha decided that we must adjust ourselves to the verdict of the A.I.C.C. and utilise the resolutions of the Working Committee and the A.I.C.C. for anti-war propaganda and organisation for struggle. The following among others were the decisions of the National Executive at Wardha:

(1) To carry on vigorous anti-war propaganda, including demonstrations, political strike, etc.
(2) Activising Congress Committees for anti-war work.
(3) In the Punjab and Bengal, where application of the ordinances had made open anti-war work difficult or impossible, Party members to defy the law so as to keep up public morale (but taking care not to sacrifice too many of their cadres) and to raise a popular agitation against ordinance rule.
(4) In the Congress Provinces (the ministries were still in office there) if a specific ban was placed on Party members against any action which they were entitled to engage in (this was done in Kerala by the Madras Government), the ban to be defied.
(5) To push the enrolment of volunteers.
(6) To carry on other normal activities of the Party, particularly on the labour and peasant fronts.

We were to continue this programme till the end of October and the Executive or the War Council had to meet in November to review the situation. The question was discussed as to what should we do in case the Congress delayed action and the ministries continued in office. It was generally felt that if the Congress took too much time and there was unreasonable delay, something drastic would have to be done. No decision was, however, taken about it except that we should wait till the end of October. Pandit Jawaharlal had stated in the A.I.C.C. that the Working Committee expected an answer from the British Government in a few days and that in any case the Committee would not wait indefinitely. Before the end of October the Viceroy made his statement.[9] Immediately after, the Working Committee met[10] and adopted a strong resolution declaring that this was an imperialist war, that the Congress cannot give any cooperation to it and that the Congress Ministries must immediately resign, because they cannot associate themselves with a war which has been forcibly imposed upon the country and the aims of which

[8] Refers to the National Executive meeting of the C.S.P. at Wardha, 10 October 1939.

[9] Refers to the statement of the Viceroy on India's political future issued at New Delhi, 17 October 1939.

[10] Refers to the Congress Working Committee meeting at Wardha, 22-3 October 1939.

include the holding down of India by force as a subject country and the maintenance of imperialism. Further a call was given to prepare for all eventualities including civil disobedience chiefly through the constructive programme and propaganda for the Constituent Assembly. For the first time since the beginning of the war, the Working Committee took a bold and courageous step and it was made clear that it was only a first step towards bigger things. The resignation of the Ministries changed the atmosphere in the country and removed an inner obstacle—the opposition of the parliamentary group to struggle and its pull in the direction of compromise. If it did not completely remove it, it at least lessened its influence considerably.

The War Council met again to discuss the situation. Its statement has already appeared in the Press. The decision which the council reached was that the resignation of the ministries and the declaration of non-cooperation with the war were two forward steps towards struggle and therefore, there was no necessity of any independent action to force the issue. Our policy must be to continue the policy we had been following of intensive anti-war propaganda, organisational preparation for struggle, attention to utilizing the critical situation (rise in prices, etc.) to energise the peasant and labour movements, to popularise the Constituent Assembly, in short to endeavour to create such a mass ferment that a countrywide struggle may become its natural issue. We are still in this stage. Congress policy has again begun to stagnate and it is our task to see that pressure is constantly applied so that the next step may soon be taken. What is our programme now? Party members keep on asking us this question. You should understand that there cannot be a new programme every day. The following is our present programme. You will have done a good deal if you carry it out:

1. Anti-war propaganda through meetings, demonstrations, strikes, rallies, leaflets, pamphlets. The imperialistic nature of the war must be explained.
2. Propaganda about the position of the Congress, and Constituent Assembly. National unity expressed through the Congress should be emphasised and the attempt of reactionaries and communalists to check the progress of the country by becoming tools of imperialism must be exposed. The nature of the constituent Assembly must be explained and attempts to vulgarise it criticised and opposed. Its revolutionary import must be stressed.
3. Particular attention to propaganda among Muslim masses and the other minorities.
4. Propaganda particularly among Congressmen for launching mass civil disobedience, which must include non-payment of rents, revenues and other taxes.

5. Propaganda and organisational preparation for no-rent and no-tax campaigns.
6. Enrolment of volunteers for struggle and their training. Volunteers' pledge and training should be non-sectarian. Where possible Congress Committees should be persuaded to take up this work.
7. Activitisation of Congress Committees. Try to reach the four anna members and the primary committees.
8. Development of the labour and peasant movement. The rise in prices, the restrictions on organisation, the drive against militant trade unionists should be utilised for intensification of the partial struggles.
9. Work among students. They should be prepared to give up their studies en-*masse* to join the struggle when it starts.
10. As a matter of discipline, to participate in fulfilling the constructive programme.

Do carry out this programme and do not let the grass grow under your feet. Our resources are limited, but even with limited means we can achieve a lot. Do not lose sight of the fundamental objective of creating mass pressure for the launching of a struggle—a mass struggle which must draw millions of people. As I have said above, Congress policy has begun to stagnate again. Many of you are restive and want us 'to do something', meaning thereby to start civil disobedience. It would be unwise to do so now. The Congress itself is moving towards struggle, howsoever slowly. Drastic action may become necessary to force the pace. But the time has not come as yet. It may not come. For the Congress cannot escape struggle. Time is with us if we are active. We have a lot to do. Let us turn to the immediate tasks I have listed above. The struggle will issue from them.

Before closing the circular I should like to touch briefly upon the communist propaganda about our so-called adventurist plan of launching civil disobedience ourselves. Our friends have propagated a lot of lies about this matter as about many others. The first thing you should note is that the Party had never actually decided to launch upon an independent course of action. In the course of discussion among ourselves (as even in discussion with some of you) certain alternative policies that the Congress might adopt were discussed with the policy of the Party in each case. Two of these possibilities were unconditional support to the war and compromise after a period of pressure and bargaining. We had even informed the Congress Working Committee that the Party would not agree to cooperation with the war on any terms and if the Congress did, it would oppose that action of the Congress and oppose the war. You should understand that these were discussed merely as odd possibilities. The Executives did never think that the Working Committee or the Congress would go over to the side of imperialism as one document of the C.P. which viciously attacks us alleges. The Executive as a whole always believed, as it does today that the Congress would eventually fight and that our main task was to strengthen the conditions and elements of struggle inside the Congress and outside. Nevertheless, our course of action in case the other possibilities became realities or, if the Congress took too much time to make up its mind and the Congress ministries continued in office, had to be discussed and made clear. It has been the general feeling in the Executive, as also among party members, that in anyone of the above events the Party itself should have launched civil disobedience. I should like you, however, to remember that it was never thought by the Executive that the Party alone could fight and overthrow imperialism. Our action when taken would have only served to force the pace of the general political movement in the country. It was neither to earn cheap martyrdom nor to quench our 'Gandhian' thirst for jail-going, nor to 'rehabilitate' our Party that this course of action was conceived of. Our action would have been in the nature of an irresistible pressure on the Congress Organisation and the people generally towards struggle. The position that the C.S.P. occupies in the Congress Organisation would have given to our action a special force; at any rate cooperation with the war or neutrality towards it would have become impossible for the Congress. The ministries would have had to go. Remember all this discussion was with the Congress ministries in the background. However, any such drastic action became unnecessary in view of the further development of Congress policy in the direction we had thought it must take—the resignation of the ministries, the non-cooperation with the war and the preparation for civil disobedience. The Communists have called this policy adventurism, menshevism and the rest of the abuse-terms in their dictionary—and of course Gandhism. We are Marxists when it suits them and Gandhites when it does not. The biggest political joke in the country is that the Communists are shedding tears that the C.S.P. by its 'adventurism' is disrupting national unity.

I have said above that Congress policy has again begun to stagnate. Many of you are again eager for 'action'. I have already said that 'action' would be unwise now. You must concentrate on the programme given above. Remember we can never be too well prepared. There are seven lakh of villages in India. Ask yourself how many of them you have prepared for non-payment of taxes and rents. There are numerous factories. Thousands of Congress Committees and hundreds of thousands of students. How many more volunteers can you recruit and train? Have you reached the families of the soldiers and the police in the villages. There is work on all sides. Use your own initiative and work. And do send some reports to me.

A word about certain organisational steps that we have taken during this period. When the war began in Europe and the ordinances were promulgated, it was very uncertain how things would develop in the country. In any case it was desirable to put our organisation on an emergency basis. Accordingly, the Executive appointed a War Council to take all necessary steps in the emergency. The Council decided that the constitutions of the Provincial Parties should be *suspended*. This did not mean that the Parties were to be dissolved. Only that their working was not to be according to the ordinary rules and provisions of the Constitution, because in an emergency it is necessary for small committees to function and for quick decisions to be taken and for strict centralised control. Accordingly, the Provincial Parties were asked to set-up their own emergency machinery subject to the approval of War Council. Practically all the Provincial Parties have done this. In some Provinces such as Utkal and Gujarat where there was conflict within the Parties, the machinery was set-up by the All India War Council itself. The Communists have set-up a howl over it, because it has not suited them. They have advised rebellion in the Party ranks. I warn you all against yielding to such pressure. The Communist Party is going full-steam ahead with its attack on the C.S.P. and the usual campaign of lying and vilification and creating of internal confusion is on. We cannot allow this to go on. We cannot prevent them from attacking us. Nor are we worried about that. We did not worry in 1934-5 when we were much weaker. We are less now. But owing to our anxiety for unity we have admitted a number of Communists (when I use the term Communists I mean members of the C.P.I.) into our Party and these are openly acting today as the agents of the C.P.I. and doing their best to undermine the C.S.P. We do not want to attack the Communists in retaliation and we do not want to undermine the C.P., but we cannot allow them to break-up our Party like this. We must reorganise ourselves. I earnestly appeal to you to help us in this task. You worry about Socialist unity? Well, I have worried long enough about it and worked for it. We are not opposed to socialist unity. But what are we to do in the face of the Communist attack on us? If we reorganise our Party, that is surely not going to break-up unity, if it means real unity. Let there be two parties with honest differences criticising each other and honestly cooperating with each other in actual work. That might lead to unity sometime. But the present policy of the Communists negates the whole basis and even objective of unity. It is grounded on their exaggerated estimation of their ability to crush the C.S.P. Their leaders have openly boasted of crushing C.S.P. unity indeed. Let us build-up our Party as homogeneous Party without outside agents. Let us not grow inward and worry overmuch about little groups. Let us grow outward and reach the masses with confidence in ourselves and in our Party. As I have said in the beginning, I shall send you separate circulars about socialist and leftist unity and certain other problems.

This will do for the present. Please circulate this circular to as many Party members as you can. Translate it in you Provincial language and multiply it. And carry out the programme given above and send reports.

7. To Provincial Secretaries and Members, Congress Socialist Party, 1 January 1940[1]

Lucknow
1 January 1940

Comrades,

I am enclosing a statement on the new independence pledge.[2] You will see that we cannot take the new pledge[3] and that we should take the pledge of 1930.[4] You must get the old pledge printed in large numbers for this purpose.

The statement also gives a programme for that day. Please study it carefully and try to carry it out. See how many villages you can reach. If you can influence any Congress Committee, try to get them to adopt this programme. It is not in the least contrary to Congress policy. You can also arrange for the sale of small national flags on that day, just as popies are sold by the imperialists on armistice day. If students', and workers' one day strikes and Kişan rallies and marches (marching to district or taluk headquarters) can be brought about, it would be an impressive demonstration. You should also arrange for the distribution of simple leaflets on the war and the impending national struggle. I shall try to send you sample texts for these leaflets. There is no time to lose. Start your preparations as soon as you get these instructions.

With greetings,

[1] *Brahmanand Papers* (NMML).
[2] See next item no. 8.
[3] See Appendix 3.
[4] See Appendix 1.

8. Statement on the new Independence Pledge, 4 January 1940[1]

The new Independence Pledge as drafted by the Congress Working Committee has created unfortunate difficulties. It is substantially the pledge of 1930.[2] But sentiments have been introduced into it which make it difficult for Socialists or rather for all those Congressmen to whom the constructive programme is not an article of faith, to take it.

Whatever ambiguity the language of the pledge had in this regard has

[1] *National Herald*, 5 January 1940, Statement issued at Lucknow.
[2] See Appendix 1 for Congress Working Committee Resolution on Independence Day, 26 January 1930.

been removed by Mahatma Gandhi's recent article[3] in *Harijan*.[4] Indeed, it is this elucidation of the meaning of the pledge that has compelled me to make these observations. Mahatma Gandhi writes that those who do not believe in the constructive programme are bound not to take the new pledge and makes it clear what that belief constitutes.

It is unfortunate that a national pledge should have thus been made a matter of sect. I have no doubt that large numbers of Congressmen have worked for the constructive programme not out of faith, but because it was the Congress programme. Can they take the pledge? If not, only the faithful to fight for and win independence? What about the millions of Indian people?

Speaking here for the Congress Socialist Party, I must say that while we have never obstructed the constructive programme and have often cooperated with it, we never accepted it as the only or even as an adequately effective weapon in our struggle. We recognised its value as a channel of approach to the masses and as an instrument of social amelioration. But we always stressed its inadequacy and its unscientific social philosophy.

We advanced for our part a new programme, that of labour and peasant organisation, as the foundation of a revolutionary mass movement. Our views regarding these matters have remained unchanged. Rather they have been strengthened by the helplessness of the national leadership in the present crisis. Yet, we are prepared in the present circumstances to carry out the constructive programme because the nation's High Command desires it. But we cannot make an ideological recantation, nor can we give up our own programme of work.

We are prepared to spin, as some members of our party are doing, as a matter of discipline; but it would be dishonesty for us and renunciation of Socialism if we profess faith in Khadi which the new pledge requires. We believe in industrialisation and socialisation of production. Khadi has its place as all handicrafts must have in a balanced and planned economy, but we do not believe that Khadi will remove the grinding poverty of the seven lakhs of Indian villages as the pledge asks us to believe.

To my mind the pledge should have been so worded that every Indian who loves the freedom of his country and is prepared to work for it in a peaceful manner could have taken it. The number of such men in our peace-loving country is legion. The Working Committee should have been content with this and for the rest, it should have left it to zealous satyagrahis to inculcate by word and deed that faith is required in its new pledge. As it is we find ourselves in the painful position of not being able to take this pledge. Members

[3] Refers to Gandhi's article published in the *Harijan* dated 30 December 1939. See *Collected Works of Mahatma Gandhi*, Vol. LXXI, pp. 50-2.

[4] An English Weekly started from Poona in 1933 by the Harijan Sevak Sangh.

of the Congress Socialists Party shall, therefore, take the original pledge of 1930 and in doing so they shall do nothing that will give any semblance of hostility or rivalry to their action. They shall do their best to make the Congress programme for 'Independence Day' a glorious success. I should add that if the construction we have put upon the pledge is mistaken, we should be happy to take it in the company of the rest of our colleagues.

It is with great reluctance that we have raised this voice of dissent. Since the beginning of the present world crisis the Congress Socialist Party has scrupulously avoided conduct that would weaken the hands of the Working Committee and affect the prestige or strength of the Congress which in the midst of the age-old disintegration of the Indian nation is the only integrating factor and which is being assailed today on all sides by reactionary tools of imperialism. But we would have done harm to our cause if we had not placed our views before the people regarding this vital matter.

I hope that the spirit in which we have viewed this matter would be appreciated by the Working Committee and those of our colleagues with whom we have the misfortune to differ in the midst of such a crisis and on such a day as January 26.

We have no knowledge what programme the Working Committee has fixed for this day, apart from public or private taking of the pledge. But we on our part fervently desire to make of it a day for as great an anti-war demonstration as for self-preparation and national mobilisation.

Let there be meetings everywhere, let us try to see that every village takes the vow of independence, let every household hoist the national flag, let students come out of their schools and colleges on that day and let workers lay down their tools. Let there be rallies and marches of the peasantry, let millions of Indians take a vow on that day, along with the vow of independence, that they would have nothing to do with this imperialist war. Let us make this day a solemn and glorious day of oath-taking for the nation's deliverance from British imperialism and the horrors of a war with which the Indian people have now nothing to do and, yet, into which they are being dragged against their will.

9. Clarification of Statement on the new Independence Pledge, 6 January 1940[1]

Since the publication of my statement on the new Independence Pledge a number of friends enquired if it was not possible to take the new pledge itself, leaving those words which expressed belief in the constructive programme. They pointed out that the taking of the old pledge might involve the holding of separate meetings which would not be desirable.

[1] *Bombay Chronicle*, 8 January 1940. Statement issued at Lucknow.

I fully agree that it is not desirable to hold separate meetings and I have, therefore, no objection to party members taking the new pledge omitting the words.

I wonder if they cannot get Congress Committees to agree to allow them to read the old pledge in their meetings.

10. To Yusuf Meherally, 8 January 1940[1]

Lucknow
8 January 1940

Dear Yusuf,

You must have received my statement on the independence pledge.[2] I hope it has appeared in the daily press also on that side. Subsequently, I issued another statement[3]—just a small one—saying that there was no objection to taking the new pledge itself leaving out the words that express belief in the constructive programme. I am enclosing a copy of the statement.

I have prepared a circular[4] on our present policy which I am sending to you in a separate cover. Please see that it is properly circulated among Party members and sympathisers. A good summary may even be published in the daily press there. It should be translated in Gujarati and Marathi also. Let me also know what you, Minoo and Asoka[5] think of it. The thesis is not ready, yet, but I shall have it ready in a few days.

I am going on tour today for a fortnight. Please reply here. The letters will be redirected.

How are things on that side? What is the situation in Gujarat and Maharashtra? How are things in Bombay? Are you in a position to undertake a tour in the South. Before we call the Executive, we should have done two things: the thesis should be ready and all the Provinces should be visited and our members informed of everything we propose to do.

It is likely that I shall be going to Wardha about the 7th or 8th. I'll go from there to Bombay.

With greetings,

Yours affectionately,
Jayaprakash Narayan

[1] *Brahmanand Papers* (NMML).
[2] See item no. 8, 4 January 1940.
[3] See item no. 9, 6 January 1940.
[4] Refers perhaps to circular dated 31 December 1939. See item no. 6.
[5] For biographical note on Asoka Mehta see *JPSW*, Vol. I, p. 122.

11. To Swami Sahajanand Saraswati, 10 January 1940[1]

c/o Sangharsha
Lucknow
10 January 1940

Dear Swamiji,
Respectful Salutation,
I am very sorry that I haven't replied to your letter till now.[2] I thought that I would send the letter by hand after reaching Patna, but going there is being delayed. I had gone in between but could not write to you.

Before commenting on the issues on which you have given your opinion, I would like to write about something personal. I came to know from Basawanji[3] & Kishori Babu[4] that you said in Calcutta that I have insulted you five times. I was astonished and grieved at this remark. I am not among those who keep on pouring out their heart before everybody. I keep my feelings within my heart only. But since this issue has been raised, I assure you, whether you believe it or not, that I have always respected and still respect you from the core of my heart. My respect for you will always remain intact. I cannot think of insulting you even in my dreams. Due to some misunderstanding, I might have committed a mistake but, believe me, you are among those few people whom I respect very much. There can be political differences between us—which are apparent today—but my respect towards you will always remain the same.

Now a few words about the questions raised by you. The core of your thesis is that the Congress will not fight. I do not agree with this. Why I do not agree cannot be explained in brief. You have quoted many examples in favour of your view. The other side of the view can also be supported by quoting similar examples and by the same authors. But it is not necessary to prove this by examples. There are many forces in the Congress (and some of them are quite powerful) but this does not mean that Congress will not fight. This fundamental difference between our views is the cause of other

[1] *Swami Sahajanand Saraswati Papers* (NMML). Original in Hindi.

[2] Not available.

[3] Basawan Sinha (1909-89); took part in the Non-Cooperation Movement, 1920; joined Hindustan Republican Army, 1925; participated in revolutionary activities and imprisoned several times; joined C.S.P., 1936; participated in the Quit India Movement 1942; arrested, 1943, released, 1946; associated with the All India Railwaymen's Federation, its Vice-President, 1946; member, Bihar Legislative Assembly, 1952-7, 1957-62, and 1971-9, and Bihar Legislative Council, 1962-8; Minister, Bihar Government, 1967, and 1979.

[4] For biographical note on Kishori Prasanna Singh see *JPSW*, Vol. I, p. 142.

differences arising between us. Therefore we need not go into that. However, I would say this much that I consider separation from the Congress quite wrong. I also consider it bad that people involved in active politics stay out of class organisations so long as the Congress does not start a struggle, the first half of the united programme prepared at Lucknow[5] should be followed. This is my view and this is what was also decided at Lucknow.

I will say two things about Left unity. The issue of united command was raised in Lucknow. I opposed it and laid stress on the united programme. A united programme was prepared but instead of following it unitedly our Communist friends started attacking us. A united command was formed in Lucknow minus the C.S.P. God knows what this united command did! There were no obstacles on our part. A united war council was formed in Bihar. It also met with the same fate. Who was to be blamed for that? I learned from Basawanji that you said in Calcutta that our united command was not formed in Lucknow. I was surprised at this and when Shankarlal[6] returned from Calcutta to Patna I enquired about this in presence of Farid.[7] He replied in the affirmative and said that a committee had been formed there. I don't know what the exact position is. The least I could understand at Lucknow was that such a committee was formed.

Well, whatsoever abuses I have to face now, I have always stressed and strived for working together in harmony. If you are aware of the present activities of those who shout in the name of Left unity, you can very well see what beautiful means have been adopted for unity—'either join the united command or your head would be smashed', this is the slogan for unity! If I am not forgetting, this disease of 'unity' is being spread in Bihar also and you will see that in the name of unity, such discord would be spread at places where the work was carried out so far with cooperation and where we could achieve something. This will spoil everything. As far as I am concerned, despite all the differences you will always find me ready for cooperation as before.

Rest on meeting,

Yours,
Jayaprakash

I am sending my circular[8] by next post, detailing the existing policy of C.S.P.

J.P.

[5] Refers to the agreement arrived at after the Lucknow Congress in April 1936 between the Communist Party and the C.S.P.

[6] For biographical note on Lala Shankarlal see *JPSW*, Vol. I, p. 157.

[7] For biographical note on Faridul Haq Ansari see *JPSW*, Vol. I, p. 156.

[8] Perhaps refers to Circular dated 31 December 1939. See item no. 6.

12. To V.B. Karnik, 10 January 1940[1]

10 January 1940

Dear Comrade Karnik,[2]
I received your letter of Jan. 5 this morning. It was redirected here from Gaya. I did not receive the first letter that you mention.

Regarding the independence pledge our attitude has been made clear by me in my statements: either to take the old pledge or the new one leaving out the words that express belief in the constructive programme. The latter alternative became necessary in view of the undesirability of holding separate meetings. More than this we do not want to do. A campaign against the pledge (I mean the part of it that is not acceptable to us) would be definitely harmful. At least that is how it appears to me. The tendency that you want to fight against can be combated in a more positive manner. By mixing up the fight with such a psychologically important thing as the independence pledge, you would be doing harm to your cause. Please do consider this point. If Comrade Roy[3] is there please convey my opinion to him and tell him that in spite of all that has happened I still have great personal regard for him.

I should further point out that your attack on the pledge goes farther than ours. You have been attacking the Congress creed (of peaceful means) itself. We on the other hand are in the given conditions in full accord with that creed. Thus a joint campaign between us becomes still more out of the question. Please do not however take this as signifying our refusal to work with you regarding other matters about which we might be in agreement.

With greetings,

Yours sincerely,
Jayaprakash

[1] *M.N. Roy Papers* (NMML).

[2] Vasant Bhagvant Karnik (1903-); one of the prominent leaders of Trade Union Movement; participated in the Non-Cooperation Movement, 1921; Managing Editor, *Independent India* which later changed its name to *Radical Humanist*; Editor, *Freedom First*; first General Secretary, Radical Democratic Party and Indian Federation of Labour; Publications include: *M.N. Roy: Political Biography*, *N.M. Joshi—Servant of India*, *Trade Unions in India—A Survey*, *Strikes in India*.

[3] For biographical note on M.N. Roy see *JPSW*, Vol. II, p. 124.

13. Statement on Externment of Seven Jamshedpur Labour Workers, 11 January 1940[1]

I wish to draw the attention of the public generally, and of the Congress Working Committee particularly, to a news item that has got lost in the columns of the daily press. Recently, seven labour workers, of whom four are members of the Congress Socialist Party, were bundled out of Jamshedpur for no cause that was given out.

Jamshedpur is the most vital industrial centre of our country. It is the heart of the heaviest Indian industry, steel and iron, and has the largest single industrial plant in the British empire. The industry is not only connected with the most vital natural resources of the country, but also supported by the taxpayer in the shape of a State bounty.

Thus if there is any industry in India that should be worked in accordance with the wishes of the taxpayer and wholly in the national interest, and the workers of which should enjoy special State protection and security, it is the Tata Steel and Iron Works. Yet, what is the situation there?

I wish to refer to the present position only. Since the beginning of the war, the Tata works have practically become a military industrial unit, ministering to the needs of the Imperialist Government. The city of Jamshedpur has become a military area and production brought entirely under the control of the foreign Government. The normal life of the citizens and the working class movement has been placed under numerous restrictions and freedom of speech and organisation has been severely curtailed. The latest example of the latter is the externment of the seven trade unionists.

This somewhat obscure piece of news thus brings to light three important facts: the utilisation of the nation's most vital resources for imperialist purposes, the suppression of civil liberties and the suppression of the workers movement in pursuance of an imperialist war.

The Working Committee has declared that it would resist the utilisation of Indian resources in this war. Can there be a more fitting case for resistance than the present one? The Working Committee must conserve the nation's natural resources, must defend its own policy and must stand by the 40,000 workers of a city that is under a near military rule.

The war crisis has made clear, what was always a truism, that the workers' struggle is coterminus with the larger national and social struggle. It is easy to see now that the exploitation and supression of workers means the suppression of civil liberties and militarisation of industrial production. It is the workers of Jamshedpur who are fighting against the utilisation of Indian resources for the war and for civil liberties.

[1] *National Herald*, 12 January 1940. Statement issued at Lucknow.

The two causes are one and the same. The super-capitalists, who own the Tata's profess nationalism when it suits them, but today they will pay no heed to the Working Committee's declaration of non-cooperation with the war. Only action on the part of the workers of Jamshedpur, a general strike, can check the imperialist offensive and secure the wages and other demands of the workers and restore to them freedom of speech and association.

The Working Committee while it prepares for a nationwide offensive, must turn its attention to this matter also so that it may transfer its policies from paper to action.

14. To M.R. Masani, 12 January 1940[1]

c/o Sangharsha
Lucknow
12 January 1990

Dear Minoo,[2]

I am sorry that I had not replied to your letter yet. Before your letter came a friend had informed me that the news of your renunciation[3] had appeared in the Amrita Bazar. I was not entirely unprepared for it, but I had certainly come to believe that you had changed your mind. The drift in the country apparently changed it again. Well, I cannot say that what you have done has been a desirable thing in any sense of the term; though I can imagine that you had no alternative. But if any alternative was open to you, it has been a great mistake. However, the thing is done and till something begins to happen in the country, there is nothing better to hope for, I suppose.

Do write what you are doing now and how you are. I cannot imagine how you can occupy your restless energy out of politics.

Have you had a chance of seeing a circular[4] that I have just sent out? I would like to have your opinion on it. The plans for the future are also being made. I hope we shall get them through without much difficulty.

There is just a chance that we might meet in the first half of February in Bombay. But do reply soon.

With love,

Yours,
Jayaprakash

[1] *M.R. Masani Papers*, National Archives of India (hereinafter referred to as NAI).
[2] For biographical sketch of M.R. Masani see *JPSW*, Vol. I, p. 66.
[3] Refers to renunciation of M.R. Masani's political activities.
[4] Refers to item no. 7.

15. Interview to Press regarding the activities of Subhas Chandra Bose and rift in the Socialist camp, 18 January 1940[1]

Question: Comment on Subhas Chandra Bose's recent pronouncements and activities?

Jayaprakash Narayan: Subhas Babu's[2] recent activities and statements[3] have caused me great distress and I should like to make it clear that he is not justified in associating all leftists with his views. This is not the time for mutual sniping, much less should a former President of the Congress indulge in it. The present position does not require a vendetta between the right and the left. Nor, today, when we are on the eve of a struggle, can the Congress be divided into such compartments. Many Congressmen, an overwhelming number I suspect, who do not fall into the conventional category of leftism, are eager for a struggle today. The anti-right vendetta would only drive them away from those who are leading the ill-conceived leftist offensive.

Subhas Babu would do much greater service to the struggle if, instead of rallying leftists for a holy war upon the rightists, he concentrated upon, for instance, raising a volunteer corps of fifty thousand young men in Bengal and upon fighting against that paralysing suppression of liberties, which is ordinance rule, in Bengal. These two actions would drive Subhas Babu's rightists much nearer to struggle than all his massed offensive against them, which will only bring demoralisation and confusion in the national ranks.

In this connection, I cannot help expressing my deep concern over the turn of events in the Bengal P.C.C. I hope there is sufficient sense in all the parties in Bengal and the Working Committee to save the Congress from going into utter bankruptcy in one of the foremost provinces of the country.

Q.: Comment on Press reports regarding rift in Socialist Camp?

J.P.: It has surprised me to read in some newspapers[4] about differences between Acharya Narendra Deva and myself on the new Independence Pledge. It is through these papers that I have learnt of these differences for the first time. I had issued my statement on the new pledge with complete approval of Acharya Narendra Deva and we hold identical views on charkha and the rest of the constructive programme. Acharyaji has already contradicted similar reports in an interview to the press.[5]

[1] *National Herald*, 19 January 1940.

[2] For biographical note on Subhas Chandra Bose see *JPSW*, Vol. I, p. 114.

[3] Refers to the statement of Subhas Chandra Bose regarding the rightists and the leftists issued at Madras on 12 January 1940 (see the *Amrita Bazar Patrika*, 13 January 1940), interview to press at Bombay on 13 January 1940 (see the *Amrita Bazar Patrika*, 14 January 1940), and speech at Bombay on 13 January 1940 (see the *Amrita Bazar Patrika*, 15 January 1940).

[4] For report of rift in the Socialist ranks on the issue of Independence Pledge see the *Bombay Chronicle*, 13 January 1940.

[5] For report of the interview of Acharya Narendra Deva at Lucknow on 12 January 1940 see the *National Herald*, 13 January 1940.

16. To Swami Sahajanand Saraswati, 19 January 1940[1]

c/o Sangharsha
Lucknow
19 January 1940

Dear Swamiji,
Respectful Salutation,
I hope you have received my earlier letter.[2] I am sorry for being unable to attend the Kisan Council.[3]

I learnt from a letter from Pandit Dhanraj Sharma[4] as also from some other letters that there is dejection among the comrades in Bihar because of differences between us. I fail to understand how such things get publicised. However, it is a fact that such things do not remain secret for long. Our differences are purely political. There is nothing personal about them. There is nothing particularly wrong in differences of opinion. I want that whatever work we have done in Bihar should not suffer and our workers should march ahead with enthusiasm and unity. Something should be done for it. If you approve, myself or both of us could issue a statement or write an article about it in the *Janata*,[5] as you wish. Or we can collect the workers and talk to them. In no way should the work in Bihar suffer nor should there be confusion among the workers.

I hope you will think over this matter. Reply to me here itself.

Yours,
Jayaprakash

[1] *Swami Sahajanand Saraswati Papers* (NMML). Original in Hindi.

[2] See item no. 11 (10 January 1940).

[3] Meeting of the Bihar Provincial Kisan Sabha Council was held on 12 January 1940 under the presidency of Sahajanand Saraswati.

[4] For biographical note on Dhanraj Sharma see *JPSW*, Vol. II, p. 222.

[5] A Hindi Weekly started from Patna in 1939. It was edited by Ramvriksh Benipuri.

17. Interview to Press regarding Dominion Status, 23 January 1940[1]

Question: Would Congress Socialists submit to Gandhiji's leadership if an honourable settlement is arrived at between Gandhiji and the Government on the basis of Dominion Status?

Jayaprakash Narayan: Congress Socialists will never accept a settlement

[1] *National Herald*, 24 January 1940. Interview at Lucknow.

on the basis of Dominion Status. The only honourable settlement which I can conceive of is fulfilment of the Congress demand for a Constituent Assembly and I know that this cannot come through a settlement with imperialism but by fighting and uprooting it.

18. Comment on Gandhi's article entitled 'The Dissentients', *Harijan*, 26 and 30 January 1940[1]

Mahatma Gandhi's article on us 'dissentients'[2] requires that we make our position clearer. When he wrote to me that our opposition was just and proper and that we could not have taken any other line,[3] I thought he had fully appreciated our point of view. It appears from his article, however, that I was hasty in thinking thus.

In his article Gandhiji has raised various issues and when two widely divergent ideologies like Gandhism and socialism meet they bristle against each other at a thousand points. I shall have to confine myself to the main points.

We have declared our inability to accept certain portions of the new pledge of independence. The reason for this is not that we are unable to 'tender discipline' as Gandhiji seems to think. I believe that we are capable of the severest discipline in the interest of the struggle for freedom.

Non-violence is the way of democracy and conviction cannot be forced down on unbelieving throats in the name of discipline. If our interpretation of the addendum to the pledge had been that we were to spin and carry out the constructive programme merely as a matter of discipline, we would have taken the whole pledge with pleasure. I said as much in my statement. These were the words, I used. "I should add that if the construction we have put upon the pledge is mistaken, we should be happy to take it in the company of the rest of our colleagues."

We could not have made our position clearer or simpler. But no one with the requisite authority cared to tell us that our interpretation was wrong, that there was no question of accepting the charkha as an article and faith, and that we were to vow to spin only as a matter of discipline. A word from Mahatma Gandhi or Babu Rajendra Prasad would have cleared the position as it can do even now. I know that Pandit Jawaharlal Nehru has interpreted the pledge differently, but all that Gandhiji has written about it confirms us in the belief that an ideological clean-up is in process and that interpretation is nearer the truth.

[1] *National Herald*, 26 January and 30 January 1940, and *Searchlight*, 30 January 1940. It was also published in the *Amrita Bazar Patrika*, 26 January 1940.

[2] See Appendix 6 for the text of Gandhi's article.

[3] Mahatma Gandhi to J.P., 19 January 1940; see Appendix 5 for the text.

Mahatmaji writes that if he were in my position and felt able to tender discipline he would have remained indoors and silent. I do not think so. If he had interpreted the pledge in my manner, he would have done exactly what I have done. As he wrote in his letter to me, he too could not have done anything else.

As for preaching open revolt and frustrating the designs of an ineffective leadership, I have not cause to indulge in any such heroics, as I do find myself capable of tendering discipline. We a handful of socialists, cannot fight alone and win Swaraj. The whole Congress must fight and the Congress can fight today only under the leadership of Gandhiji. And Gandhiji imposes conditions for his leadership. We accept these conditions unreservedly. These conditions, however, cannot be a change of faith and a recantation. We recognise the economic value of charkha in the present conditions. We also want to promote communal unity and to remove untouchability. We regard khadi as the symbol of India's freedom and unity. We shall spin, but we cannot say that the charkha can resuscitate the seven hundred thousand villages of India, nor that the ideal of Gandhiji's *Hind Swaraj* [1909] is acceptable to us.

Open revolt may be for men like Subhas Babu. For us it means disruption and disintegration with nothing positive and greater to replace what we destroy. We believe we can march forward by mutual adjustment and disciplining our differences to needs of united action. If, however, there is to be no action and a settlement is reached and freedom remains in the distance, the obligation for discipline vanishes and we are free to choose our own path of advance.

This is not the place to dwell upon our attitude towards spinning and the constructive programme. Some weeks after Tripuri we had prolonged talks with Gandhiji at Delhi[4] at which we discussed our respective programmes and the relations between the two ideological groups within the Congress—the Gandhite and socialist. At the end of our three days' talks we found ourselves much closer to each other and Gandhiji also remarked that he had drawn nearer to us.

He had apprehensions about our programme of labour and peasant organisation leading to violence. We explained to him our own anxiety to keep these movements strictly within peaceful limits and he felt reassured at least about our own attitude. He no doubt continued to believe that there were irresponsible people in these movements who were thoughtless and reckless enough to foster a spirit of violence, but he was able to see that our influence was exercised on the side of peaceful and ordered mass struggle.

In his article Gandhiji, quoting my words that we had emphasised labour and peasant organisation as the basis of a revolutionary mass movement,

[4] Refers to the meeting of the Socialists with Gandhi in Delhi from 28 to 30 March 1939.

adds that he dreads the language used. To a revolutionary like Gandhiji, who had played with fire and stirred up millions to action, the words need not cause any fear. I do not mean by them bloodshed and chaos. Revolution need not always be red in tooth and claw. We had explained to Gandhiji at Delhi and I had again explained it to him at Abbottabad that our aim was to lay the basis for a country-wide non-payment of rents, revenue and taxes and general strike by workers in industry and transport. We mean by these peaceful and regulated but mighty mass conflicts that would paralyse and end British rule.

We had explained it to him that in our view it was essential in order to bring the peasantry and the industrial workers to the requisite kind of consciousness and organisation to organise them into peasant and labour unions on the basis of their immediate and ultimate economic interests. We have always believed that the motive of economic emancipation must be applied to the masses to fire them to great deeds of suffering and achievement. This the charkha does not do or does very infinitesimally.

In advancing our own programme it should be remembered that we never opposed Gandhiji's programme though we often criticised it. If there was any opposition it was in the first few months of our life as a socialist party. Since then experience taught us that not only we may not oppose the constructive programmes, but we must incorporate parts of it in our own. In my report to the Lahore Conference[5] of our Party I had drawn the attention of those members of our Party who were working in the kisan movement to such constructive activities to supplement their work, as village sanitation, primary education and adult literacy, village industries and agricultural improvement, etc. I had pointed out that a kisan worker cannot always be engaged in an economic satyagraha and he must serve the kisan and make himself more indispensable to him [the latter] in this fashion.

Gandhiji seems to have attached more meaning than I had intended to the words 'the helplessness of the national leadership in the present crisis'. I did not mean that the leadership was ineffective, but I cannot help feeling that if the Congress had accepted our programme and worked it these five years, our leadership would have been in a position to deal much more firmly and with greater confidence with the present crisis than it is in a position today. The fear of the unknown, the fear of the movement of the seething masses, the fear of 'red ruin' would not have numbed action as they seem to do today. Nor would the communal dragon have appeared so awesome. I suggest to Gandhiji that the Congress did not accept our programme not out of fear of violence but of class prejudice. I think it was within the strength and competence of our vast organisation to have kept in check and control the waking leviathan—the dispossessed millions of this dispossessed land.

[5] Lahore conference of the Congress Socialist Party was held on 12-13 April 1938.

Lastly let me assure Gandhiji that what he calls 'red ruin' would come not because a few Socialists would beckon it forth, but when his great experiment with peaceful revolution fails. We shall give him our full cooperation in this experiment because a Marxist cannot be dogmatic about violence and non-violence. But he must not rush us too fast. He says he cannot lead an army which has doubting lieutenants. We do not aspire to be his lieutenants, we are content to be his privates. But if this is taken to be rhetoric, then let me point out that Gandhiji puts up with the imperfections of his followers; let him put up with our doubts as well. We are at least honest in marching with him. He draws his inspiration from God. Few men in history have claimed to do so, and they have been great men who have moved peoples and made history. We have no God. History is our only guide and its science our only inspiration. But Mahatma Gandhi is making history. He is a stupendous force of history. We must march with history.

19. To Yusuf Meherally, 5 February 1940[1]

Lucknow
5 February 1940

Dear Yusuf,
I never thought that you too were such a bad correspondent. On my side I have not done so badly lately. Don't you think that you should keep me in touch with what is happening on your side?

Most probably the Executive will meet on your side sometime in the third week of this month. I shall write more definitely later.

I am enclosing a copy of an article that I wrote in reply to Gandhiji's that was published in the *National Herald* and the *Amrita Bazar Patrika*.[2] Barelvi[3] did not consider it worthwhile to publish it. I did not know of it till I asked Gurudeva[4] to find out how many papers had published it. I am sending it to you to make what you can out of it. It was very much liked on this side.

I am leaving for Patna now. Reply c/o *The Janata*.

Yours affectionately,
Jayaprakash

[1] *Yusuf Meherally Papers* (NMML).

[2] See item no. 18 (26 and 30 January 1940).

[3] S.A. Barelvi (1891-1949); journalist; Joint Editor, 1920-4, and Editor, 1924-49, *Bombay Chronicle*; President, Journalists' Conference, Lahore, 1930, Gujarat States Peoples' Conference, Ahmedabad, 1934, and All India Newspaper Editors' Conference, 1945; member, Working Committee of the All India Muslim Majlis, 1944; and Indian Delegation to U.N. Conference on Freedom of Press, Geneva, 1948.

[4] Gurudeva Sharan; a prominent socialist leader in Bihar; closely associated with J.P.

20. "Where I Differ from Mahatma", 7 February 1940[1]

Since the outbreak of the war talks have begun of a settlement between the Congress and the British Government. At first these were confined to the drawing-rooms of the Congress ministerial parties and the dens of those leftists who are convinced that the Working Committee and Mahatma Gandhi are intent on selling the country as a safeguard against the upsurge of the masses. Lately, however, these talks have become common and spread to the remotest bazars where the news of Mahatma Gandhi's impending interview with the Viceroy has reached.

Methods

That Mahatma Gandhi should talk of a settlement is not surprising to those who know his methods of thinking and acting. It is futile to take every statement of his as an index of further demoralisation. He has never placed a fight in the forefront. He has always first negotiated and bargained, pleaded and cajoled and turned his hands to non-violence only when persuasion failed. He has often said that he does not fight for the sake of fighting.

When he advocated Congress acceptance of office, he wrote that he expected to make them an alternative to both a bloody and a bloodless revolution. India knows that, in spite of his pleadings on bended knees, the Mahatma has fought not once but many times when he failed to get what he wanted. The same Mahatma says in the present crisis that he would fight even if he were alone if he did not get what he and the Congress wanted. Yet, the bazars of India and its homes buzz with talk of a settlement.

Final Sanction

The Working Committee has pointed out that the final sanction behind its demands is civil disobedience and has asked Congressmen and Congress organisations to prepare for that eventuality.[2] The General Secretary[3] of the All-India Congress Committee has given repeated instructions to that effect. It is clearly not the duty of Congressmen to go on whispering about the futile word, settlement. The demands of the Congress have been clearly formulated. Well and good. As far as we humble soldiers of the Congress are concerned, we have to keep in mind only two things—our duty to prepare the country for a nationwide struggle and to keep ourselves in readiness for

[1] *National Herald*, 7 February 1940.

[2] Refers to the resolutions passed by the Congress Working Committee at Allahabad (19-23 November 1939) and Wardha (18-22 December 1939).

[3] For biographical note on J.B. Kripalani see *JPSW*, Vol. II, p. 210.

it, uninfluenced by talks of settlement and secondly not to allow any one, however great, to reduce the demands to which we are pledged. Let us remember that if dominion status is foisted upon India it will not be the fault of one individual but of the 3,000 delegates and more who represent the 40 lakhs of Congressmen and crores of others who want independence.

Dispossessed Millions

I am not among those leftists who believe that Mahatma Gandhi is afraid of the masses or is an agent of Indian capital and will sign a pact with British imperialism on behalf of Indian capitalism. I am convinced that Gandhiji wants the freedom of his country as much as any leftist does and he wants this freedom not for the vested interests but for the dispossessed millions.

Soon after the Rajkot fast Gandhiji had gone to Delhi in connection with the Chief Justice's arbitration.[4] While in Delhi he also met the Viceroy[5] I had gone to Delhi at that time to see Gandhiji and in the course of a talk I told him that many people thought that he was discussing with the Viceroy some manner of adjustment on the federation question. Gandhiji has immense self-control, but I noticed that the colour of his face heightened as he replied, with unwanted asperity "Jayaprakash tell these people that whatever Gandhi may do, he will never sell his country". I should, therefore, plead with all my fellow critics of Gandhiji and Gandhism that they should remove all question of motive from their criticism. We unnecessarily weaken our case by attributing motives to Mahatmaji and the Working Committee.

[4] In 1938 the people of Rajkot started satyagraha against the ruler of Rajkot, Thakore Dharmendra Singh, demanding people's rule. On 15 August 1938 a peaceful meeting of satyagrahis was lathi-charged and a large number of satyagrahis were put behind bars. Negotiations were carried on with the ruler in consultation with Vallabhbhai Patel and Mahatma Gandhi. On 26 December 1938 a settlement was arrived at about establishing responsible government in Rajkot. According to one of the terms of the settlement, a committee of ten persons was to be appointed to draft the constitution, seven of whom would be those suggested by Vallabhbhai Patel. But Singh did not honour the agreement. He rejected the seven names suggested by Vallabhbhai Patel, substituted four names and appointed the Committee accordingly. Therefore the struggle was restarted on 26 January 1939. Gandhi met the satyagrahi prisoners at Rajkot on 28 February-1 March 1939 and decided to go on fast in support of their cause from 3 March 1939. The Viceroy Lord Linlithgow suggested interpretation of the settlement by the Chief Justice of India, Sir Maurice Gwyer. Accepting his suggestion Gandhi ended his fast on 7 March and went to Delhi on 15 March 1939. On 3 April 1939 Gwyer gave his award that Singh was bound to appoint only those on the committee who were suggested by Vallabhbhai Patel.

[5] Gandhi met the Viceroy on 15-16 March 1939. For biographical note on Lord Linlithgow see *JPSW*, Vol. II, p. 240.

Nationalist Hold

Let me make it clear at the same time that in an organisation like the Congress which embraces almost all classes in the country, there are bound to be men and interests who would accept any settlement in order to avoid the unsettlement and insecurity that comes with civil disobedience. The Indian industrialist class would naturally be anxious to see the nationalist hold grow upon the Central Government in order that it may secure for itself the plums which the new industrial activity resulting from the war will bear. This class will undoubtedly damn independence and the Constituent Assembly both, if they mean economic unsettlement in India and loss of present profits. Individuals undoubtedly there are in the Congress who will give expression, consciously or unconsciously, to these interests.

Then there is the parliamentary mentality which according to Gandhiji has come to stay. A fair sample of this mentality is the recent speeches[6] of Mr. Rajagopalachari,[7] Mr. Bhulabhai Desai[8] and Mr. Munshi.[9] Further, it will not take much to satisfy the urban middle class which is always ready to welcome an increase in the scope of employment as Swaraj will provide. This class too will have its own influence on Congress decisions. The danger of a settlement short of our fundamental demands, is therefore, real and the necessity of vigilance against it urgent. But it would be a mistake to simplify this danger in terms of the motives of an individual, however powerful, or of a conspiracy against the Congress by its own national executive.

Need of Warning

Thus fully accepting the bonafides of our leaders, I yet feel the necessity of raising my voice against the policy that is being followed at present. My protest is based on two counts. First, my quarrel with Gandhiji is on the

[6] Refers to the speeches of C. Rajagopalachari at a public meeting at Madras on 2 February 1940 (see the *National Herald*, 3 February 1940), Bhulabhai Desai at a public meeting at Madras on 4 February 1940 (see the *National Herald*, 6 February 1940), and K.M. Munshi at a public meeting at Bombay on 1 February 1940 (see the *National Herald*, 3 February 1940).

[7] For biographical note on C. Rajagopalachari see *JPSW*, Vol. I, p. 174.

[8] For biographical note on Bhulabhai Desai see *JPSW*, Vol. II, p. 209.

[9] K.M. Munshi (1887-1971); prominent Congress leader; participated in the national movement and imprisoned several times; Home Minister, Bombay Government, 1937-9; founder and President, Bhartiya Vidya Bhawan 1938-71; member, Constituent Assembly, and its Drafting Committee 1946-9; Minister of Food and Agriculture, Government of India, 1950-2; Governor, U.P., 1952-7; one of the founders of Swatantra Party, 1959.

same count on which conceivably Dr. Rajendra Prasad may have a quarrel with him. Immediately after the Viceroy spoke at the Orient Club,[10] Rajendra Babu declared that Congress had nothing to do with Dominion Status and the Congress demand was for complete independence. Some days later when the Working Committee was meeting at Wardha[11] he again stated that there was nothing in the Viceroy's speech for the Working Committee to discuss. Yet a day or two later Gandhiji declared that he found germs of a settlement in that same speech. We, too, thought like Rajendra Babu that there was nothing in the Viceroy's speech which the Congress could even look at. So our surprise was great indeed when Gandhiji published his article.[12] The Viceroy spoke of nothing more than dominion status to be conferred upon India at an uncertain date. The Congress parted company with dominion status more than ten years ago and its is difficult to imagine that it can revert to it. When the Congress has rejected the whole concept of dominionhood, how can it find germs of a settlement in a vague promise of it?

Mental Elasticity

Soon after Gandhiji's declaration millions of Indians reiterated the oath of independence which included severance of the British connection. It is difficult to see how dominion status of any variety can be squared up with severance of this connection. Yet, in Gandhiji's elastic mind the two things are reconciled. It is not for the first time that Gandhiji has shown such mental elasticity.

In his famous letter[13] to Mr. Polak,[14] written sometime ago, he said that he would accept dominion status if the right of secession were inherent in it.

[10] Refers to the speech of the Viceroy Lord Linlithgow at the Orient Club, Bombay, on 10 January 1940 making a plea for ending the constitutional deadlock.

[11] Refers to the Congress Working Committee meeting at Wardha, 19-21 January 1940.

[12] Refers to Gandhi's article entitled 'The Dissentients'. See Appendix 6.

[13] Refers to Gandhi's letter to H.S.L. Polak dated 27 January 1937 in which he stated, 'Owing to the pilgrimage to Travancore, it has not been possible for me to write to you earlier. Your question is whether I retain the same opinion as I did at the R.T.C. of 1931. I said then and repeat now that so far as I am concerned, if Dominion Status were offered in terms of the Statute of Westminster, i.e. the right to secede at will, I would unhesitatingly accept it.' See *Collected Works of Mahatma Gandhi*, Vol. LXXI, p. 322.

[14] Harry Solomon Leon Polak (1883-1959); friend and co-worker of Gandhiji in South Africa; Assistant Editor, *The Transvaal Critic*, later joined *Indian Opinion* and became its Editor in 1906 during Gandhiji's absence in England and a full-fledged Attorney in 1908 after having served an apprenticeship with Gandhiji; visited India as a representative of the Transvaal British Indians in 1909; was arrested after the 'Great March' into the Transvaal in 1913.

The stand of the Congress is not merely to have this constitutional right but to have the secession in fact and to start with it.

Gandhiji told me once that he was not a *but-parast* (idol-worshipper). That is, he is not a worshipper of words, such as Lenin,[15] who used to liken those who flung quotations in his face to the chicken that could not get out of the circle drawn around it. Gandhiji is after the substance. That is why he coined the phrase "substance of independence".

Substance of Independence

I too, as a Marxist, am not a worshipper of form. Substance is what matters. But while the form does not determine the substance, the substance invariably determines the form. In other words, if we really get the substance of independence, we will have the form of independence too. If we do not, then we may be sure that we do not have the full substance and we have been fooled and cheated.

Now, I do not want to be cheated. I know that we can get only what we have the strength to get, but I should know what I am getting and should call it by its proper name. If, for instance, we are not able to sever the British connection, we do not do without a British Viceroy, we do not control our foreign policy and our armed forces, I would know that I do not have the substance of independence. We would have in that case a party of people having a limited rule over the country under the protection of British arms.

Marks of Sovereignty

By whatever name that may be described it cannot be called independence. The marks of sovereignty are not empty marks but are expressions of the capacity of a nation to stand up alone in the world by virtue of its own unaided strength. Can such a strength come through a settlement? We might conceivably arrive at a mid-way house. But are we aiming at mid-way houses today?

Has our generalissimo been empowered to lead us to that goal? Did we on January 26, avow solemnly to make that the destiny of our nation?

[15] Nikolai Lenin, originally Vladimir Ilyich Ulyanov (1870-1924); Russian communist leader; founded and edited revolutionary periodicals, *Iskara*, 1900-3, *Vperyod*, 1905-6, *Zvezda*, 1910-12, and *Pravda*, 1912-14; became leader of the militant wing of the Russian Social Democrats—the Bolsheviks, 1903; led the 1917 November Revolution and overthrew the Provisional Government; became President of the Soviet People's Commissars—the Sovnarkom, remained the active head of the Soviet Government from 1917 till his death in 1924; writings include: *The Development of Capitalism in Russia*, *What is to be Done?*, *Imperialism, The Highest Stage of Capitalism*, and *The State* and *Revolution*.

In this present world where the established order of empire and domination is crumbling, can we not set our goal further up and march to it steadfastly, assisted by forces of history and without resting at mid-way houses?

I do not know what germs Mahatmaji has discerned in the offer of dominion status, but if he insists on his old interpretation of independence, I should like to tell him frankly and unhesitatingly, and on behalf of all young India, that we cannot then accept his leadership. For, that is not our goal. What he calls the substance of independence is only the gilded form of empire. There is no basis for a dominionhood in India.

Basis of Fighting

This much is patent even to Englishmen, as is evident from the articles,[16] published in the *Cambridge Review*,[17] reproduced by Mahatmaji, in the *Harijan* of January 20. It may be well to say that it is foolish to fight for the sake of fighting. Nobody wants to fight for the fun of it. But how else can the sanctions be created which, and not British arms, would be the basis of Indian independence? The merit of a revolution is that while it destroys the established state it also creates a new one strong enough to take its place. Does Gandhiji fear that such a revolution is not possible in India today? If it is not, let us have the courage to admit that we are not ready for independence yet. It is time that every Congressman answered this question for himself. If we are ready for independence, it implies that if the British power were withdrawn today, we would be able to maintain internal order and to defend ourselves against aggression from without.

Internal Strength

It is necessary both for the withdrawal of the British power and the creation of internal strength that we fight and the masses fight. A revolution is the universal participation of the people in political and social change. This universal participation is what we mean by fighting. A settlement between the plenipotentiaries of the people and the foreign power can give the people no sudden powers and capacities of defence and maintenance of order; therefore, a settlement can give us neither independence nor its substance.

It is a different matter that we desire a settlement for its own sake. In that case, let us boldly confess that we are putting the ideal of independence in cold storage for the time being. It may, again, be a different matter that we

[16] See *Collected Works of Mahatma Gandhi*, Vol. LXXI, pp. 106-7.

[17] A journal of the Cambridge University published by the Cambridge Review Committee.

do not consider ourselves strong enough to achieve independence and therefore feel compelled to settle with the enemy. In that case, too, we should have the courage to say that we do not want independence today. In both these cases there will be a clarification in the Congress and those who want nothing less than independence may choose their path, however fool-hardy it may appear to some of the elder statesmen. This is my first quarrel with Gandhiji on the question of objectives and definitions.

Power-Politics

My second quarrel is on the ground that a settlement, even if it is an honourable settlement, would line us up with British imperial power-politics. A settlement presupposes both giving and taking. The British Government are obviously anxious for a settlement. The reasons are that they want, firstly, a peaceful India; secondly, India in the British orbit of world politics; thirdly, the support of such moral forces as the Congress, Mahatma Gandhi and Pandit Jawaharlal Nehru represent, and fourthly, an opportunity to utilise the industrial and agricultural resources of India for the Allied cause.

If the British Government concede us the right to a Constituent Assembly after the war they would want the above things now. The question is, should Mahatma Gandhi and the Congress allow themselves to be exploited for the designs of the British Government? The Congress believes in democracy and the end of imperialism. Chamberlain represents neither anti-imperialism nor democracy. He has played the role of a foster-father to Fascism in Europe and is the head of a great imperial system. To settle with him is to leave him a free hand in Europe and in the rest of the world. That would mean betrayal of freedom and democracy everywhere. Let us be clear that the present is not an ideological war. It is a war for world domination, for colonies, for empires. It would be a tragedy for the world if Indian resources, moral and material, were thrown on any side in such a war.

And why should India remain in the British orbit of world politics? The natural orbit of a free India is China, the Soviets and the Muslim States of the Near East. A free India must be the pivot of an alignment of the great democratic powers of Asia. Why should we, by settling with Britain, commit ourselves to British foreign policy in world affairs? India must have her own foreign policy and that is bound to come into conflict with British policy. The latter is and has been anti-Soviet. A free India must have the closest friendly relations with its powerful neighbour, the U.S.S.R., and trade and commerce must grow between them. India, China and Russia must be the nexus that will banish imperialism from the world and usher in an era of a cooperative world society. British policy cannot for a moment tolerate this.

Historical Parallel

It is to prevent India from moving towards this nexus that Chamberlain wants to appease us and to use us as his tools. Chamberlain wants to fool Gandhiji, as Lloyd George[18] fooled Wilson.[19] I know the analogy does not fit four square; but it is fundamentally the same thing. The last war was won by Lloyd George by fooling the British workers into believing that the war aims of the Allies were noble and disinterested and no secret treaties existed for a division of the world amongst the three great Allied Powers. Col. House[20] has shown how Wilson was dexterously used by Lloyd George to give just that moral glow to the war in the eyes of the British workers which was necessary to win their willing cooperation. Today the British workers unfortunately do not require much window dressing from Downing Street. But it is likely that as this senseless war progresses they will begin to see things for themselves. Nevertheless, Chamberlain requires a moral tone to persuade the American democracy again to pull the chestnuts out of the fire for him.

What better instruments can Mr. Chamberlain find than the goodwill of Mahatma Gandhi and the moral support of the Indian National Congress?

If the Allies have Mahatma Gandhi on their side they can fool the workers into believing that their cause is just. They can fool world opinion. Above all, they can fool America. And once again a historic deception may lead to the perpetuation of empire, of capitalism and of the ideal of world domination.

Happily, the U.S.S.R. stands as a great guarantee against such a disaster and it is unlikely that Europe will witness a repetition of the Versailles atrocity.

Pawns in the Game

We in India have, however, our own duties and responsibilities. Let us beware lest we should become pawns in the game of imperial power-politics.

Mahatma Gandhi, as the tallest among living men, carries a great burden

[18] David Lloyd George, 1st Earl of Dryfor (1863-1945), British statesman; President of Board of Trade, 1905-8; Liberal Chancellor of the Exchequer, 1908-15; Minister of Munitions, 1915-16; Secretary of State for War, 1916; Prime Minister, 1916-22. Author of *War Memoirs* (1933-6), and *The Truth about the Peace Treaty* (1938).

[19] Woodrow Wilson (1856-1924); Professor at Princeton University, 1890-1902, and its President, 1902-10; Governor of New Jersey, 1911-12; President of the United States of America, 1913-21; author of the famous *Fourteen Points*.

[20] Edward Mandeff House, known as Colonel House (1858-1938); American diplomat; the Friend and confident of President Wilson (from 1912); personal representative of the president to European nations (1914, 1915, 1916); chief presidential liaison with Allies during First World War; appointed to act for U.S. in negotiating armistice with Central Powers (1918); secured Allied acceptance of Fourteen Points, which he had helped to draft; member of American commission to negotiate peace (1918-19) and of commission to frame the covenant of the League of Nations.

on his shoulders. Not only the fate of 350 million Indians is in his hands, but also in a large measure the future of the world. History will judge him severely as it judges all those who have a critical role to play.

Col. House records that Wilson was at least distrustful of the Welsh Wizard. Mahatma Gandhi has faith in the Viceroy's sincerity. Let him, therefore, be doubly cautious. If he settles with Chamberlain, he will settle with a hangman of freedom and democracy, peace and justice. There are forces being born in the womb of this war which will end Chamberlain and the order he represents.

Why should we settle with a dying order and give it a new lease of life?

World Order

Let us pause to consider what we get in return. We give a lease of life to imperial power politics and get nothing more than paltry constitutional makeshifts in the present. For, all the bigger things will be in promises to be given in future. But will Chamberlain or the order he represents survive the war to give us anything?

Intelligent people everywhere agree that this is very unlikely. If so, should we by settling with the present British Government lend them our moral support, allow them to use us as a pawn in their power politics, permit them to exploit our country's resources, cooperate with them in carrying on the King's Government, in short, constitute ourselves into an ally of imperialism? The answer is a clear 'no', and a 'no' that must resound from every nook and corner of the country. Swaraj will come but let us not barter away for a shadow of it all that we have earned through the sufferings and sacrifices of two generations.

21. Statement in Support of Abul Kalam Azad's candidature in Congress Presidential Election, 12 February 1940[1]

The Congress presidential election is drawing near and rather unexpectedly there is to be a contest. For the guidance of the members of the Congress Socialist Party I should like to state the Party's position in this contest. It is perfectly consistent for Comrade M.N. Roy[2] to contest this election, because he believes in displacing the present leadership with another revolutionary one. We, on the other hand, consider this attempt to be destructive of Congress unity which, in the present crisis, has become even more impor-

[1] *Tribune*, 13 February 1940.

[2] For biographical note on M.N. Roy see *JPSW*, Vol. II, p. 124.

tant than heretofore. We believe that today when we are on the eve of a great national struggle if the Congress as a whole is to march forward, it can do so only under the leadership of Mahatma Gandhi. As long as the struggle exists, it would be suicidal to fight Gandhiji and to attempt to displace his leadership. To vote against Maulana Azad would be to repudiate the leadership of Gandhiji in the present crisis. We must, therefore vote for Maulana Abul Kalam Azad. I should like to add that in spite of our serious differences I have great regard for Comrade Roy and should have been happy to support his candidature had it been politically possible. When I met him recently at Patna, I explained our position to him and he fully appreciated it.

In the end I should like to say that apart from the political reason for our support to Maulana Azad, I consider Maulana Saheb to be also eminently suited for the presidentship. His great learning and breadth of vision, his noble record of patriotism and service, his freedom from partisan politics will fit him prominently for this highest office as gift to the nation.

22. Statement on Subhas Chandra Bose's Anti-Compromise Conference, 29 February 1940[1]

The Congress Socialist Party is against compromise but so is the Congress. The Ramgarh session of the Congress[2] will in itself be the biggest anti-compromise conference in the country. The recent statement of the Congress President[3] has also made this clear. This does not mean that strong influences for compromise are not at work. We must oppose these. But in opposing them we must not oppose the Congress itself. Mass demonstrations against forces of compromise are necessary. But these demonstrations should not be against the Congress, nor aspire to become its rivals. They must contribute in a positive manner towards national solidarity. I am afraid the proposed anti-compromise conference does not fulfill these requirements. Its basic assumption is that the Congress Working Committee is going to enter into an alliance with imperialism and has relinquished the task of winning independence. Any action based on this assumption would logically and

[1] *Searchlight*, 1 March 1940. The Anti-Compromise Conference was held at Ramgarh on 19 March 1940 under the presidentship of Subhas Chandra Bose.

[2] Refers to the annual session of the Congress was held on 19-20 March 1940 at Ramgarh in Bihar.

[3] In an interview to Press on 26 February 1940 Rajendra Prasad, then Congress President, clarified that no compromise between the Congress Working Committee and the British Government could be valid unless it had been ratified by the A.I.C.C. See the *National Herald*, 27 February 1940.

necessarily disrupt the Congress and destroy national solidarity. The entire background of the conference is disruptive. Among the elements that make up this background are the piqued revolt of Subhas Babu against the Working Committee, the breach in the National Front in Bengal and the threat to carry this breach forward beyond the frontiers of Bengal, the talk of a parallel Congress, the talk of a neo Swarajist Party, the encouragement given to communal organisations such as the Hindu Sabha and the Muslim League, etc. Added to all this is the recent statement[4] of Subhas Babu that the anti-compromise conference if successful would eclipse the Congress. I cannot conceive how any Congressman can desire to eclipse the very organisation to which he belongs. These considerations make it impossible for us to associate ourselves with the proposed conference.

[4] This refers to the speech of Subhas Chandra Bose at a public meeting at Shraddhanand Park, Calcutta on 17 February 1940. See the *Amrita Bazar Patrika*, 18 February 1940.

23. Gandhiji's Leadership and the Congress Socialist Party [before his arrest, 7 March 1940][1]

The policy that the Congress Socialist Party has followed in recent months with regard to the Congress has come in for a good deal of criticism. I believe, however, that a little dispassionate thinking would show the correctness of its policy. Unfortunately, the prevailing atmosphere is not too conducive to dispassionate thought. There is mutual distrust and ill-will, deliberate confusion of issues, empty heroics. In certain quarters it is the fashion to attribute motives to whoever disagrees with you. Thus, it has been suggested by some of my leftist friends that my recent policies have been dictated by my desire to be elevated to the Congress Working Committee. This way of political understanding throws some light on the depths to which a section of the left movement has descended. If my friends find such a motive behind my policies, it is little wonder that in every move of the Congress Working Committee they sense a deal with imperialism!

It is in public interest to refer—even at the risk of indecorum—to a personal matter. Since my membership of the Congress Working Committee is on the brain of some of my friends, I should like to tell them that the doors of the Working Committee have, since the time we were first appointed on it [1936], been always open to me and to some other leading members of the C.S.P. I resigned my membership in 1936 of my own accord, and since have refused

[1] Published as Congress Socialist Tract No. I by All India Congress Socialist Party, Bombay; also in *National Herald*, 4 April 1940.

a seat every time it has been offered to me. At the Haripura Congress,[2] Acharya Narendra Deva[3] and Achyut Patwardhan[4] refused their seats that were offered again by the then President, Babu Subhas Chandra Bose. At Calcutta,[5] Dr. Rajendra Prasad again invited us to serve on the Committee, which offer he repeated at Bombay,[6] but Acharya Narendra Deva again declined the offer on behalf of the Party.

I should add that our refusal of membership never implied any disrespect to the Congress Working Committee, to be a member of which is a great honour. Nor did it imply our deviation from the principle of composite leadership which we have always held as we hold it even today.

Surrender to Gandhism?

To turn now to the subject-matter. Our present policy has been attacked on the ground that it is a surrender to Gandhism. Socialism versus Gandhism is not the present issue, however. We are faced with the task of preparing for and launching a national struggle against imperialism. This is not a socialist but a nationalist task to be carried out by Socialists, Gandhians and others. Our only crime, therefore, is that we continue to insist on the unity of the Congress as the only guarantee of national unity and a national struggle. Our further crime is that we insist that unity of the Congress involves the unity of its leadership, because we cannot, particularly in such a crisis as the present, split the leadership and keep the Congress together. Our still further crime is that we are being guided not by what is good for the Congress Socialist Party or for that heterogeneous and vague thing called the Left, but by what is good for the whole, the left and right together. We believe that we have reached a dangerous point when certain sections of the left have begun to look upon themselves not as a wing of a body, but as a whole body itself, with interests distinct and separate from the body of which they are a part.

The Congress Socialist Party was formed not to develop into a rival to the Congress, but to work within the Congress, to strengthen it, to mould and shape its policies. In the five years that the Party has functioned, it has succeeded appreciably in influencing Congress policy. A number of Congress decisions bear clearly the impress of our propaganda. Due to the pioneering work of the Party, since the depressing days of 1934, when civil disobedience had to be called off, and all through the upsurge of parliamentarianism, a vigorous left wing developed in the Congress which even penetrated the

[2] Haripura session of the Congress was held on 19-21 February 1938.

[3] For biographical note on Acharya Narendra Deva see *JPSW*, Vol. I, p. 61.

[4] For biographical note on Achyut Patwardhan see *JPSW*, Vol. II, p. 162.

[5] Refers to the A.I.C.C. meeting at Calcutta, 29 April-1 May 1939.

[6] Refers to the A.I.C.C. meeting at Bombay, 24-7 June 1939.

ranks of the leadership. The programme of peasant organisation which we placed before the Congress, though unaccepted officially by it, yet won the approval of quite a number of provincial and other Committees and a large number of Congressmen. But inspite of all our efforts the official programme of the Congress is still Gandhiji's programme of 1920. Also, while a new leadership has arisen, the predominant leadership is still in the hands of the Old Guard. The old leaders have been at the helm for twenty years. During this period they have led three major struggles and numerous partial ones. They have brought new life, new strength, new consciousness to the masses. They represent a vital national force—still the most influential in the country.

The Mistake of Subhas Bose

In these circumstances, what are we to do, particularly when a world crisis demands immediate action? Conceivably, given another five years the balance of influence within the Congress and the country could have been changed and the old, as always, would have given place to the new. I should interpolate a remark here that even today the influence of the left leadership would have been much greater had Sjt. Subhas Bose followed the advice of our Party and had the communists and other leftists the guts to tender the same advice to him. We advised Subhas Babu, inspite of all that had happened, not to resign from the Presidentship of the Congress. Had he followed our advice we would not only have escaped all the sorry developments of the past months, but we would have also had a Working Committee with a large leftist voice. Subhas Babu himself would have been the President, Pandit Jawaharlal Nehru would have been the General Secretary, Sjt. Sarat Chandra Bose[7] and two leftists would have been among the members. It will be remembered that this was the minimum arrangement to which the Old Guard was agreeable. Unfortunately, for reasons best known to him, Subhas Babu thought it better to resign and organise his Forward Bloc. In what manner his resignation helped the country only he and his supporters can tell. I think there would be few impartial observers who would deny that his resignation and subsequent activities have delivered disastrous blows at leftism within the Congress.

Through Uncoloured Glasses

Let me revert to the question, in the present circumstances, what is our duty? To answer it, first let me ask whether we have any other instrument than the Congress for waging a national struggle and maintaining national unity? Throughout history we have had to contend with disintegrating factors

[7] For biographical note on Sarat Chandra Bose see *JPSW*, Vol. II, p. 242.

and sometimes they have even overwhelmed the forces of national unity. Even today, excepting the Congress there is no other consolidating factor in our social or political life. The Congress represented and still represents, and from all appearances, will continue to represent (much as the communists and the Forward Bloc may dislike the prospect) the widest, the strongest front against imperialism in India. If India goes to war with imperialism with any chance of success, that war has to be waged under the tricolour flag. People talk loosely of kisans, mazdoors, youths and students, as if they stand outside of the Congress. What are meant by these generic terms, however are the Kisan Sabha, the Trade Unions Congress, and the Students' Federation. These bodies have potentiality for the future, but at present, except in a few provinces, their organisation is elementary. Their role in our national struggle will be important, and it must be the task of Socialists as well as of other progressive elements to make that role even more important by strenuous organisational work. Their role is, however, clearly of an auxiliary character. The Congress must lead the struggle and the active cooperation and participation of these bodies will be an added factor of strength. But it is crystal-clear that today, neither the Kisan Sabha nor the Trade Union Congress in their present stage of development can hope to fight imperialism with, any degree of success. That task unquestionably belongs to the Congress.

This is the situation facing us when looked at through uncoloured glasses. The Congress alone is the country's salvation. And let us remember that Congress means the whole and not a part of it. A limb torn from a body does not have its proportionate strength and ability. It merely dies.

Gandhiji & National Struggle

I have said above that we are faced today with preparing for and launching a national struggle. I have shown that this struggle can be launched by the Congress alone. Now, let us examine another set of facts. The effective leadership of the Congress is in the hands of Gandhiji. It is obvious that if the congress starts a struggle today it would be in accordance with the programme that Gandhiji lays down. We can influence that programme but we cannot determine it. The technique of the struggle would therefore naturally be the old Gandhian technique, whether any one likes it or not.

An acceptance of these facts does not mean surrender to Gandhism. We have not ceased to propagate Socialism. We have not stopped working in the Kisan Sabhas and Trade Unions and developing the peasant and labour movements. The first strike for a War-bonus was led by the C.S.P. in the Gaya Cotton Textile Mill and the first War-bonus victory was won by the Dalmianagar workers under the C.S.P.'s leadership.[7] In Bihar, the U.P., Bombay, Bengal and elsewhere members of the Party have been as active as before in the struggles of the workers. The same is true of the peasant movement. Where work has suffered in these spheres, it has been due to the withdrawal of Party cadres into the new activities of preparation for the national struggle—such as intensive organisation of the Congress Committees and intensive propaganda, volunteer organisation, etc.

However, the situation in which we find ourselves is not such that we can expect to develop the national struggle out of our own plan of action. We carry on our own work and propagate our platform, but at the same time, we desire an immediate struggle. When we know that there is no prospect of a struggle being started under any other leadership but the present, is it not a mistake to attack the leadership, to seek to discredit it, to weaken it? Shall we thereby bring the struggle nearer or push it away?

United Front & National Struggle

All these years we have heard the theories of United Leadership and United Front propounded. Now, when the hour has arrived to put these theories into practice, to act up to them, gutless revolutionaries are scurrying away from their implications. United leadership, was held to be necessary in the interest of a united national struggle. This theory was mouthed incessantly by our communist friends, at a time when the Congress was engaged in parliamentary work and struggle seemed distant. Now when the parliamentary work has been given up and the Congress is on the eve of struggle, our communist theorists have thought it wise to fling their theory to the wind and concentrate on attacking the present leadership. In this manner they will only contribute to the sabotaging of the struggle. The other day, I heard a Communist comrade, who holds an office in a provincial Congress organisation declaim vehemently at a Kisan Conference against the Congress creed of peaceful means. It is fortunate that there are not many persons in the Congress foolish enough to repeat such folly. There is no surer way to sabotage struggle today than for Congressmen to go about decrying peaceful means.

I think it is necessary for us to realise the limitations in which we have to work. By disregarding them we only strengthen them. A fight against the leadership now is not only inadvisable, it is positively harmful. If a national struggle as opposed to sectional, factional or partial can be launched by Mahatma Gandhi alone, it is suicidal to fight him. It is necessary to lend him our fullest cooperation and loyalty in everything that is preparatory for struggle. If, then there is no struggle we may part company with him and then take the responsibility of the struggle ourselves if we have the strength. Revolt against the present leadership in the manner of Subhas Babu, or attack on it, in the manner of the communists, both are harmful and are proving to be so.

Communist Bungling

Some people believe that in these circumstances, the Congress Socialist Party becomes superfluous. I should like to remind friends that we are to be guided by what is good for the whole movement and not by the necessity of blowing our own trumpet at all times. If our policy is correct, the C.S.P. will draw strength from it and as in 1934 show again that of all the groups mouthing Marxism, it is the only one that understands how to apply Marxism to India. This is not the place to go into the matter here, but it would be interesting to show how at every critical stage in the last five years the Congress Socialist Party showed the way and others followed or proved their folly. In 1934, the wise Communists were out of the Congress and were out to destroy it. We were in it and to build and strengthen it. In 1936 they too filed in, to build or to destroy history alone will show. In 1936 the C.S.P. opposed the acceptance of Ministerial Offices by the Congress. The communists were first for accepting them with a radical programme. Later, when they found that the anti-ministry cry was becoming popular in the Congress left, they veered round to it so that they may not be isolated. During the General Elections, the C.S.P. supported the Congress wholeheartedly. The communists opposed the Congress in one constituency, to repent at leisure. At Tripuri[8] they spoke passionately of unity and united leadership but again the fear of isolation drove them to action which could lead only to contrary results. At Calcutta,[9] the C.S.P. boldly advised Sjt. Subhas Chandra Bose to withdraw his resignation from the Presidentship; the communists lost their guts and kept mum. Coming to recent events, the C.S.P. did not subscribe to the addendum to the Independence Pledge; the communists swallowed it. One hopes that they are faithfully carrying out their vow; otherwise there is danger that fraud may be discovered and Mahatma Gandhi may refuse to launch the struggle after all!! The C.S.P. supported Maulana Abul Kalam Azad, the communists were neutral. The Communists declared in a public statement that voting for Maulana Azad would mean supporting the policy of the Working Committee. Strange argument! When the communists voted for Roosevelt[10] in America, did it mean that they supported the whole of Roosevelt's policy? In such a thing as a presidential contest one votes for the

[8] Refers to the fifty-second session of the Indian National Congress held at Tripuri, 10-12 March 1939.

[9] Refers to the A.I.C.C. meeting at Calcutta 29 April-1 May 1939, where Subhas Chandra Bose tendered his resignation from the presidentship of the Congress.

[10] Franklin Delano Roosevelt (1882-1945); American statesman; Governor of New York, 1928-33; President of United States, 1933-45; countered Depression with 'New Deal' legislation; kept U.S. out of the Second World War until Japan attacked Pearl Harbour in December 1941.

candidate whose election would advance the nation's cause generally. If one must have a president with whose policies one must always be in agreement, one has only one course open, i.e. to set-up a candidate every time, from one's own Party or Group. There are thousand and one ways of expressing one's difference from the Working Committee and this both the C.S.P. and the communists have been doing. Voting for Maulana Azad could never have prevented Communists from pointing out their differences from the Working Committee. I agree that it would have prevented them from calling Maulana Azad an agent of imperialism! Then a last instance. The C.S.P. clearly dissociated itself from the Anti-Compromise Conference the communists were neutral to it. Their growing neutrality is an index to their growing political impotency.

I had not intended to devote so much space to this matter. The list can be enlarged, more so when we leave the realm of policies and enter into that of tactics.

To return to my point. Far from becoming superfluous, the Congress Socialist Party has to be in the forefront of the struggle and the preparations for it. It must remain, as it has been so far, the active element in the Congress Committees, guiding them in organisational and agitational work. It must, by carrying on its mass work continue to prepare that basis for struggle that is more important than anything else. It must influence Congress policy by criticism and propaganda as it has done so far. The time has come for the Congress Socialist Party to work out what it has preached so far, even more vigourously in the future.

24. Appeal to the Left Wing to maintain Unity in the Congress, 7 March 1940[1]

It is a matter of deep regret to me that in this hour of crisis when National and Congress unity is so essential, there are so many disruptive tendencies at work. The task of maintaining unity in the Congress rests on the shoulders of the Leftists much more than those of others. Unfortunately, Left Wing infantilism is dragging the Congress to ruin. It is the duty of Congress Socialists, above everything else, to fight this disruption unmindful of the calumny that a section of the Left may heap upon them. Since its birth, the Congress Socialist Party has stood for balanced and sane policies. The necessity of adhering to the principles of united front and composite leadership is greater today than ever before. Let these principles guide our actions.

[1] *Searchlight*, 9 March 1940. Appeal issued just before his arrest at the residence of Phulan Prasad Verma, Patna, 7 March 1940.

Acharya Narendra Deva and I have already commented upon the draft Congress resolution.[2] Mahatma Gandhi and Dr. Rajendra Prasad's later statements have only confirmed our interpretation of the resolution. Let petty bickerings cease and let us close up the ranks. The Congress is in dead earnest about civil disobedience. This will be the country's final struggle for freedom. I hope that every Congressman will rise to the occasion and will not rest till freedom is achieved.

[2] See Appendix 7.

25. Clarification on proposed Kisan rally, 7 March 1940[1]

Some confusion is being created between the Anti-Compromise Conference and the Kisan Rally that are to be held at Ramgarh at the time of the Congress. The two are separate things. The Kisan Rally is being organised by the Bihar Provincial Kisan Sabha with the full concurrence and cooperation of the Congress Socialist Party. The Kisan rallies have been held regularly during Congress sessions for the last few years. I appeal to all with whom I may carry any weight to make the rally a great success this year.

[1] *Searchlight*, 9 March 1940. J.P. issued the statement before his arrest at Patna.

26. Statement in the Court of the Deputy Commissioner, Chaibasa, 15 March 1940[1]

I have been charged with trying to impede the production of munitions and other supplies essential to the efficient prosecution of the war, and with trying to influence the conduct and attitude of the public in a manner prejudicial to the defence of British India and the efficient prosecution of the war. I plead guilty to these charges.

These charges, however, do not constitute a guilt for me but a duty which I must discharge regardless of the consequence. That they also constitute an offence under certain laws of the foreign Government established by force in this country does not concern me. The object of these laws is diametrically opposed to the object of nationalist India of which I am but a humble representative. That we should come in conflict is only natural.

My country is not a party to this war in any manner, for it regards both German Nazism and British imperialism as evils and enemies. It finds that both the sides in this war are driven by selfish ends of conquest and domi-

[1] *National Herald*, 19 March 1940.

nation, exploitation and oppression. Great Britain is fighting not to destroy Nazism, which it has nurtured, but to curb a rival whose might can no longer be allowed to grow unchallenged. It is fighting to maintain its dominant place in the world and to preserve its imperial power and glory. As far as India is concerned, Great Britain is fighting to perpetuate the Indian Empire.

Plainly India can have no truck with such a war. No Indian can permit the resources of his country to be utilised to buttress imperialism, and to be converted through the processes of the war into the chains of his country's slavery. The Congress, the only representative voice of nationalist India, has already pointed out this sacred duty to the people of this country. I as a humble servant of the Congress have only tried to fulfil this duty.

The British Government on the other hand in utter disregard for Indian opinion has declared India a belligerent power and is utilising Indian men, money and materials for a war to which we have pledged our uncompromising opposition. This is in the nature of an aggression against India, no less serious in the circumstances than German aggression against Poland. India cannot but resist this aggression. It therefore becomes the patriotic duty of every Indian to oppose the attempt of the British Government to use the country's resources for its imperialist ends.

Thus the charge framed against me of trying to impede the efficient prosecution of the war is only the fulfilment of a patriotic duty. That the British Government should consider what is a duty for a patriotic Indian to be an offence only proves further its imperialist character.

Regarding the speech[2] for which I am being prosecuted I cannot say how far it succeeded in achieving its ends. But nothing would please me more than to learn that it did have some success in impeding the effective prosecution of the war. I shall deem the heaviest punishment well-earned if I am found to have succeeded in this.

As for the charge of endangering the defence of British India, I think the irony of it cannot be lost upon us. A slave has no obligation to defend his slavery. His only obligation is to destroy his bondage. I hope we shall know how to defend ourselves when we have achieved our freedom.

I consider it fortunate that I have been prosecuted for Jamshedpur speech. This important industrial centre, which I consider the most important in the country, is peculiarly backward politically and from the point of view of the labour movement. I shall derive some satisfaction in prison, where I expect

[2] J.P. addressed a labour meeting at "G" Town Maidan, Jamshedpur on 19 February 1940 calling upon the workers to carry on the fight for War bonus, and to develop the struggle to the higher level of fighting British imperialism for the attainment of freedom of the country. He emphasised that the workers should resist the War by all means and also the compromising attitude of the Congress High Command towards British imperialism. For a report of the speech see *Searchlight*, 24 February 1940.

inevitably to find myself from the thought that my arrest and incarceration for a speech delivered there has attracted to that city the notice of the political and labour leaders of my country. It seems scandalous to me that the country's most vital resources should be so wasted in a war to which we are so firmly opposed. And it seems no less scandalous to me that while labour throughout the country should be reacting vigorously to the conditions created by the war, Jamshedpur labour should carry on as if nothing extraordinary has happened. May, at least, the demand for a war bonus gain some momentum from this prosecution.

Before concluding I should like to add that lest as an Englishman you should misunderstand me I should make it clear that in impeding the prosecution of the war, I have no desire to help Germany or to see Germany victorious. I desire the victory neither of imperialism nor of Nazism. Yet, as a Congressman and a socialist I have nothing but goodwill for the British and German peoples. If India's opposition to Britain's imperialist war ensures a Nazi victory, it is for the British people to decide whether they would have Nazi hegemony or victory with real democracy at home and in India.

If the people of Great Britain remove their present rulers and renounce imperialism with its capitalist parent, not only India but the freedom loving people of the whole world would exert themselves to see the defeat of Nazism and the victory of freedom and democracy. In the present circumstances, however, India has no alternative but to fight and end British imperialism. Only in that manner can it contribute to the peace and progress of the world.

I am conscious, Sir, that I have made your task easier by this statement. I do not regret it. In the end I thank you for your courtesy and consideration during this trial.

27. An Outline Picture of Swaraj: Draft Resolution for Ramgarh Congress, 15 March 1940[1]

The Congress and the country are on the eve of a great national upheaval. The final battle for freedom is soon to be faught. This will happen when the whole world is being shaken by mighty forces of change out of the catastrophe of the European war. Thoughtful minds everywhere are anxious to create a new world—a world based on the cooperative goodwill of nations and men.

[1] *AICC Papers* (NMML). Draft of a resolution sent to Gandhi for consideration by the Ramgarh session of the Indian National Congress, March 1940. Though not discussed there in view of the decision to adopt only one resolution, that dealing with the immediate political situation, it was liked by Gandhi, who published it in the *Harijan* of 20 April 1940 with his own comments. For the text see Appendix 8.

At such a time the Congress considers it necessary to state definitely the ideals of freedom for which it stands and for which it is soon to invite the Indian people to undergo the utmost sufferings.

The free Indian nation shall work for peace between nations and total rejection of armaments and for the method of peaceful settlement of national disputes through some international authority freely established. It will endeavour particularly to live on the friendliest terms with its neighbours, whether they be great powers or small nations, and shall covet no foreign territory.

The Law of the land will be based on the will of the people freely expressed by them. The ultimate basis of maintenance of order shall be the sanction and concurrence of the people.

The free Indian-State shall guarantee full individual and civil liberty and cultural and religious freedom, provided that there shall be no freedom to overthrow by violence the Constitution framed by the Indian people through a Constituent Assembly.

The State shall not discriminate in any manner between citizens of the nation. Every citizen shall be guaranteed equal rights. All distinctions of birth and privilege shall be abolished. There shall be no titles emanating either from inherited social states or the State.

The political and economic organisation of the State shall be based on the principle of social justice and economic freedom. While this organisation shall conduce to the satisfaction of the rational requirements of every member of the society, material satisfaction shall not be its sole objective. It shall aim at healthy living and the moral and the intellectual development of the individual. To this end and to secure social justice the State shall endeavour to promote small-scale production carried on by individual or cooperative effort for the equal benefit of all concerned. All large-scale collective production shall be eventually brought under collective ownership and control and in this behalf the State shall begin by nationalising heavy transport, shipping, mining and the heavy industries. The textile industry shall be progressively decentralised.

The life of the villages shall be reorganised and the village shall be made a self-governing unit, self-sufficient to as large a measure as possible. The land laws of the country shall be drastically reformed on the principle that land shall belong to the actual cultivator alone and that no cultivator shall have more land than is necessary to support his family on a fair standard of living. This will end the various systems of landlordism on the one hand and farm-bondage on the other.

The State shall protect the interests of all classes but when these impinge upon the interests of those, who have been poor and downtrodden, it shall defend the latter and thus restore the balance of social justice.

In all the State-owned and managed enterprises, the workers shall be represented in the management through the elected representatives and shall have an equal share in it with the representation of the government.

In the Indian States, there shall be complete democratic government established and in accordance with the principle of abolition of social distinction and equality between citizens. There shall not be any titular heads of the States in the person of rajas and nawabs.

This is the order which the Congress envisages and which it shall work to establish. The Congress firmly believes that this order shall bring happiness, prosperity and freedom to people of each and every religion in India who together shall build on these foundations of great and glorious nation.

28. To M.R. Masani, 14 June 1940[1]

Hazaribagh Central Jail
Hazaribagh
14 June 1940

Dear Minoo,
I cannot tell you how sorely grieved I felt the day you were not allowed to see me. That the government would still be so inconsiderate and wooden I could not have believed. However, it gives me some satisfaction to find that the bureaucracy is sometimes capable of seeing its mistakes. I understand you have its permission now to interview me.

It was very good of you to have come. The message that I had sent you was not a joke. There were, and are, certain things which I could have told you alone. I cannot write them, naturally. But I might just mention that one of the things I wished to tell (as I do now) to change your decision. There is nothing irrevocable in life. I respect your strength of will, but feel compelled to say that it were far better to turn it to a worthier cause. I have learnt a great many lessons in the past year, and if both of us could begin all over again—this is not impossible despite the verdict of romanticists—we could make things hum. Do think over the mattere and do not just throw it out of your mind's window. In about four months I expect to be at freedom again. I am nourishing the hope that when we meet then, we would not fail to come to a satisfactory agreement.

As for the other matter, considering the present situation, it might well wait till my release. It would be an unqualified pleasure to see you here, but I have not the courage to put you to all the trouble all over again. Moreover, I have stopped my interviews due to all manner of irksome interference which I had to put up with. In any case you can always write. Do write often

[1] *M.R. Masani Papers* (NAI).

and tell me all you can about yourself and other friends.

I have yet to thank you, Asoka,[2] Leelubhai and Dantwala[3] for the excellent books. Will you kindly thank them on my behalf? *The Grapes of Wrath* is an astounding thing. I have read nothing so forceful and realistic since *Yama the Pit*. Such vividness combined with such scientific probity. Wodehouse, of course, never fails to cheer up the gloomiest hours. I had a hearty laugh all through and read it all at a stretch. *Hoghen's Dangerous Thoughts* is still at my desk. I am at his mathematics these days.

Why is the Maulana[4] so silent? His voice ought to be resounding from one end of the country to the other. Do speak to him about it. He had promised to send me foreign periodicals. He has not kept his promise, even ceremonially. Will you remind him of it? And will you also select a few periodicals and send them? The censorship is quite stupid here, yet we must try. Please ask the Maulana to send me some recent books on China except *Red Star Over China*, *China Fights Back & the Kuomintang* and *The Chinese Revolution*. Also a book bearing some title like *Japan over China or Asia*.

I expect to hear from you within a fortnight.

With the best of wishes and lots of love.

Yours,
Jayaprakash Narayan

[2] For biographical sketch on Asoka Mehta see *JPSW*, Vol. I, p. 122.

[3] Mohanlal Lallubhai Dantwala (1909-91); educated at Bombay (M.A.); specialized in agricultural economics, served at College of Commerce, Ahmedabad, 1936-45 and Bombay University since 1945; President All India Agricultural Conference, 1960; Chairman Agricultural Economics Committee, Indian Council of Agricultural Research; Chairman Committee of Experts on Unemployment Estimates, etc.

[4] Maulana—refers to Moinuddin Harris, one of the prominent leaders of the Congress Socialist Party in Bombay and a devout Muslim.

29. To Jawaharlal Nehru, 20 July 1940[1]

20 July 1940

Dear Bhai,

You can imagine how recent events have grieved and hurt us. Rajaji has stabbed us in the back. It was a great relief to know that you and Khan Saheb[2] opposed the infamous thing. But is that enough? All of us here expect

[1] *Brahmanand Papers* (NMML).

[2] Khan Abdul Ghaffar Khan (1890-1988); also known as Badshah Khan and Frontier Gandhi; started *Pakhtun*, a Pashto monthly; took part in anti-Rowlatt agitation, Non-Cooperation, Civil Disobedience and Quit Indian Movements, and served long terms of

you and beseech you to lead the opposition in the A.I.C.C. and the country. You should resign your seat on the Committee. After a settlement, i.e., if it comes about, you must leave the Congress and form another political organisation to fulfil the remaining part of the political task and the main part of the social task of the Indian revolution. Will you do it? Perhaps you all appreciate that Rajaji's resolution[3] sounds the death-knell of the Congress. The fear of dividing the Congress becomes unreal now. Gandhiji has been magnificent in his own way, but his support will, if not positively at least negatively, incline towards the traitors. Vallabhbhai[4] and Rajaji have not hesitated to break with Gandhiji. Will you hesitate to fulfil you obvious historic task? I do not know how much you will achieve. But, in any case you will have blazoned out a glorious path for those who will come after you.

This has not been written in passion or anger, but coldly and deliberately.

With Love,

Yours,
Jayaprakash

P.S. I expect to be out by the middle of October.
Itd. J.P.

---

imprisonment; founded the Khudai Khidmatgars, 1929; appointed member of Congress Working Committees, 1940; strongly opposed partition of India; member, Pakistan Constituent Assembly, 1947; arrested 1948; joined Pakistan National Party, 1957; recipient of Nehru Award, 1967, and Bharat Ratna, 1987.

[3] See Appendix 9 for C. Rajagopalachari's resolution.

[4] For biographical note on Vallabhbhai Patel see *JPSW*, Vol. I, p. 68.

30. To Subhas Chandra Bose, Secret, 1940 (exact date and month not available)[1]

Dear Comrade,

I am writing this letter not without considerable anxiety. Anxiety, because I am not sure how you will receive it. I do not know if you will take me seriously when I say that at no time did I bear any personal ill-will against you. There were political differences, which I did not try to hide. But anything more than that there never was. On the other hand, I have always admired your courage and steadfastness. And now, when it has been driven home to me, I admire your prescience and foresight.

Here I have been turning in my mind. Recent events have led me to reorient my entire thinking. I admit that the Anti-Compromise Conference and the

---

[1] Sisir K. Bose (ed.), *Crossroads: The Works of Subhas Chandra Bose, 1938-40*, Calcutta, 1981.

stand that you and Swamiji[2] took have been completely vindicated. I shall say so publicly at the first opportunity I get.

I am writing to make an extremely important suggestion which I request you earnestly to consider. The suggestion concerns the whole course of our future action and the development of the revolutionary movement in India. I have discussed it here with Swamiji, who is favourably inclined. We have yet to discuss it in greater detail, the results of which I shall communicate in due time.

I have already sent the suggestion to C.S.P. friends outside. Possibly some of them will see you in this connection as also the Anushilan friends.

Before coming to the suggestion itself I should like to give briefly an idea of how I look at the present situation and the immediate future.

To my mind our basic task today is to chalk out a line of action that is fundamentally independent of the Congress. This task shall lose none of its importance or immediacy in the event of the Congress launching upon civil disobedience. There is not an iota of doubt left that civil disobedience if started would be for no greater purpose than that of forcing concessions out of imperialism. The Delhi resolution[3] is by no means dead and buried as Jawaharlal suggests. It will be resurrected immediately as the British Government shows any willingness to compromise. At all events, therefore, the certain prospect before us is that of a Congress reconciled with imperialism at a price—high or low, depending upon the exigencies on both sides.

Hitherto the basic assumption of our work in the present had been that the Congress was the chief instrument of political action—a multi-class front (with the workers and the national bourgeoisie constituting the extreme ends) against imperialism. Our work henceforth must proceed on the opposite assumption entirely: that the Congress is no longer the main basis for political action. I am not suggesting that the Congress has lost its hold over the masses (though the opposite is more true today than at any time in the last few years: the masses have lost what hold they had over the Congress), or that it has exhausted its role of offering opposition to imperialism. Indeed the present situation makes such an opposition appear most likely. But its object would be the achievement of something as demanded by the Delhi resolution. Nor is there any chance whatever of our influencing the Congress in the present circumstances.

Here it is necessary to note the change that has taken place in the Congress. It indeed remains a broad-based mass organisation, but its leadership is more then ever concentrated in the hands of a coterie that is anti-masses

[2] J.P. sent this undated letter from prison, through a special messenger, to Subhas Chandra Bose while the latter was preparing for his escape from India. The letter is preserved in the archives of Netaji Research Bureau, Calcutta and was identified by J.P. to be his own during one of his visit to Netaji Bhawan. See Bose, n. 1, p. 111.

[3] See Appendix 10 (Delhi Resolution, 7 July 1940).

(anti-labour, anti-peasant, even anti-democratic to an extent), and completely bourgeois in ideology and sympathy. The peasant, labour and left national influences have been isolated. In these circumstances it would be a great folly to look to the Congress for a mass revolutionary action. Also we cannot vaguely expect to give a 'revolutionary turn' to the Congress struggle if and when it starts. We must rule out every possibility of it.

There is a further consideration why we must endeavour in the present to lay down a basis for political mass action independent of the Congress. The task of the Congress was the achievement of national independence. This task could have normally been fulfilled in a revolutionary manner only; and the Congress was expected to tread the revolutionary path (with its vacillations) up to a considerable distance. In the present circumstances, however, there is every likelihood of this task being fulfilled to the extent desired by the Congress (as at present constituted) through a compromise with imperialism. Doubtless pressure is required for compromise and doubtless Congress would continue to exert this pressure (even going to the length of some form of direct action). The power however which Mr. Rajagopalachari hopes to 'capture' by offering the blood and sweat of millions of the Indian people cannot be complete independence. It would be just as much of independence as Mr. Rajagopalachari and his 'Congress' would dare to have consistent with their desire to retain British military and economic tutelage (in order to protect their 'independence' from aggression from without and 'disorder' within, and to safeguard and preserve the economic status quo). It is not too much to expect that this sort of arrangement would not be repugnant to the British ruling class under certain circumstances that may arise sooner rather than later.

This leads us to the conclusion that we have reached the end of a stage. The united offensive of the Indian people (national bourgeoisie, urban middle class, peasantry, workers) against imperialism is at an end. The national bourgeoisie and a section of the middle classes (the upper strata) are deserting the struggle (in the name of national defence, etc.) They will have seized a certain amount of power from imperialism, but they cannot be expected to fight on till every vestige of imperialism is destroyed. The task of destroying what would remain of imperialism and of carrying forward the democratic revolution devolves on the workers, peasants and the lower middle classes. Thus in the second stage in a country like India the role of the peasantry must be predominant and this stage is mainly the stage of the agrarian revolution. This means that the period of the bourgeois revolution (an agrarian revolution is also a part of it) is not over and the stage of the proletarian or socialist revolution has not yet arrived. But the first part of the bourgeois democratic revolution (the period of united front struggle against imperialism) is over, and the second and last part, that of the agrarian revolution, begins.

Here again I am not suggesting that the agrarian revolution has actually begun in the sense that the peasants have taken the initiative with themselves of seizing the lands of the Zamindars, of driving them out of the villages, of taking possession of large holdings and distributing them among themselves. This indeed has not begun as it did in China in 1927. But what I wish to point out is that the preceding stage of the Indian revolution has reached its end, and now we must positively and clearly prepare and work to usher in the next stage.

There is also some talk in certain quarters of establishing soviets immediately. This is 'leaping to defeat' in Stalin's[4] words—leaping over a whole stage. Unquestionably it is the Kisan Sabhas that exist and that will arise everywhere that will play the predominant part in the present and be the organic precursors of real peasant soviets. (We need not borrow the word soviet. Kisan Sabha is a good enough, easily understood name with a revolutionary tradition.)

The foregoing implies that we have to direct our chief attention from the Congress to the Kisan Sabhas. The fact that the Kisan Sabhas are not to be found in large numbers and their organisation is not as widespread as that of the Congress need not deter us. Given the proper approach the appropriate slogans, they can be made to rise up like mushrooms.

My emphasis on the Kisan Sabhas should not be taken to mean that we are to neglect our other activities and our work side by side for the proletarian revolution. The working class movement must continue to receive our utmost attention.

Some people get exercised over the question if we should leave or remain in the Congress. To me the question is of secondary importance. The main thing is that for us the Congress no longer remains an instrument for revolutionary action and that therefore we must prepare an independent basis for such action. We may continue in the Congress as long as it serves any useful purpose. But we cannot continue to ask the masses to look to the Congress for their economic and political emancipation. To keep the masses tied up to the Congress is to do them the greatest disservice and to sabotage the revolution. It is our clear duty to remove the dependence of the masses upon the Congress. For this we need not ask the masses to turn against the Congress. We must, however, do two things: one positive and the other negative. We must explain the character of the present Congress leadership in plain terms to the masses (negative). We must build-up their own instruments of struggle and teach them to depend solely upon those.

Such being our tasks as I conceive them, the first thing that has to be done is to build-up a revolutionary ideology, i.e. a revolutionary socialist party. As far as my own party, the C.S.P. is concerned its framework has become too inadequate for the task before us. The present is a golden opportunity to

[4] For biographical note on Joseph Stalin see *JPSW*, Vol. I, p. 101.

bring together all revolutionary elements into a revolutionary party. The fact that we shall start on a clean slate should make it possible to unite the several revolutionary strands in the country. And here is my suggestion. Let us form a new revolutionary party out of the C.S.P., the Anushilan, the Forward Block, the Kirti,[5] the Labour Party and other such groups or elements. A party based squarely on Marxism-Leninism, independent of all other political organisations and parties. I think this is eminently possible if you only wish it. The C.S.P. may or may not be kept going merely as a cover and platform for the new party and particularly to function within the Congress as long as we consider it feasible to do so.

I have not mentioned the C.P. among the elements from which the new party has to be built, because the C.P. by its very constitution and the constitution of the C.I. cannot merge its identity in another socialist party. Even if they profess to do so that would be merely to get an opportunity of entering the other party and capturing (i.e. disrupting) it. The new party thus should be distinct from the C.P. but there should be a working alliance between the two.

This does not mean that I conceive the new party as being anti-C.I. We should indeed have contacts with Moscow and seek the aid of the Soviet in our revolution. It must, however, be free to follow its own policies without dictation from Moscow.

I conceive the new party as an entirely underground party of whole-time revolutionaries. Its activities must include (I cannot complete the sentence. You will understand).

This is in short my proposal. I am in deadly earnest about it. And I request you to consider it in all seriousness. I expect to be out by the end of next month. I shall try to meet you during your trial. In the meanwhile kindly discuss the matter with friends there, particularly the Anushilan friends. You may send me your tentative advice through Sharmaji.[6] If we are able to carry out this plan we shall be able to do something on a big scale in India.

Apart from the party, we need mass organs of struggle and for seizure of power. I see these in the Kisan and Mazdoor sabhas chiefly. These will have to be united in a mighty union of peasants' and workers' unions (Congress of Peasants' and Workers' Soviets). The formation of this union should be one of our objectives in the immediate future.

I hope you are keeping good health and are having your well-deserved rest. We are quite well here.

With best wishes,

Your
Comrade

[5] Kirti Kisan Party.

[6] For biographical note on Dhanraj Sharma see *JPSW*, Vol. II, p. 222.

31. *Socialist Unity and Congress Socialist Party*, 1941[1]

The last half-a-dozen years, that is, the years since the end of the civil disobedience movement in 1934, saw a phenomenal rise of the socialist movement in this country. The history of this rise is largely the history of the Congress Socialist Party.

Before the Party was formed in 1934, soon after the cessation of civil disobedience, socialism could hardly be said to have been in the picture of Indian politics. It had received a certain amount of publicity at the time of the Meerut Conspiracy case;[2] but it secured no place for itself in the political life of the country, and appeared to the people rather as an article of foreign importation. In 1931, Shri M.N. Roy, when he returned to India secretly, formed a party of his own. But that party too remained practically unknown, and did not as much as create even a little ripple over the surface of Indian politics. The utterances of individual radical nationalist leaders like Pandit Jawaharlal Nehru and Shri Subhas Chandra Bose, had attracted to a degree the attention of a section of the middle class intelligentsia. But there was no organised movement worth the name. It would be no exaggeration, therefore, to say that it was the Congress Socialist Party that in 1934 put socialism on the political map, and in the six years of its life, continuously enlarged the orbit of its influence.

These last six years of the socialist movement have been as full of rich experience as they were full of difficulties. We shall deal here only with one of the many problems that faced it. No question was of more interest or greater importance to the socialist movement than what might be described as the question of 'socialist unity'. Today, nothing is of greater importance than to examine the experiences gained regarding this problem, and to draw lessons for future guidance. While the matter is of some interest to the general public also, it is of the utmost importance for members of the Congress Socialist Party. Not only has all the relevant material never been published before but there is also a persistent attempt by enemies of the Party to misrepresent the whole case. It is hoped, therefore, that this pamphlet would

[1] Jayaprakash Narayan, *Socialist Unity and Congress Socialist Party* published by Sind Congress Socialist Group.

[2] On 20 March 1929, thirty-one communists, including Philip Spratt, Benjamin F. Bradley, Muzaffar Ahmad, Shaukat Usmani and S.A. Dange were arrested in different parts of the country and charged with conspiracy to deprive the King Emperor of the sovereignty of British India. The accused were tried by the Court of Special Sessions at Meerut in January 1930 and received sentences varying from twelve to three years. An appeal against the convictions was filed in the High Court at Allahabad on 24 July 1933 and the verdict was announced on 3 August 1933 reducing the period of some of the sentences. By the end of 1933 all the accused except Muzaffar Ahmad, S.A. Dange, Philip Spratt and Shaukat Usmani were released.

be of considerable use to members of the Party and its friends, and serve not only to inform but also to guide them. At the same time it is our hope that it will be found to be of some service also to the public in general.

The phrase 'socialist unity' is at best a vague phrase. Does it mean the unity of all those who call themselves Socialists? And what is the meaning of unity? Co-operation, unity of aim and purpose, or unity of organisation? There are all manners of people who claim to be socialists. There are people among the Liberals who profess socialism. Gandhiji calls himself a socialist. There are others, like the Congress Socialist Party, who consider that the only true socialism is Marxism. The problem that we are considering here is the problem of the coming together in one party of all those groups and individuals who stand by Marxism.

Let us consider how this question presented itself concretely when the Party was formed. Then we shall consider the vicissitudes through which it had to pass and its present position.

At the time the Party was formed, there were two other socialist groups that professed Marxism, and aspired to have an all-India basis. These were the Communist Party and the Roy Group. There were also at that time or shortly afterwards certain local Marxist groups, such as the Punjab Socialist Party and the Labour Party (Bengal). From the very beginning the Party desired to bring together all these local and national groups in order to form one united socialist party. As would appear from the present position, the Party largely failed in this endeavour. It failed, however, not because it lacked initiative or spared effort, but because of the sectarianism and disruptiveness of the other parties, particularly of the Communist Party. We shall now turn to the history of this failure.

The Roy Group

We shall first deal with the Roy Group. The Group greeted the formation of the Party with enthusiasm. Some of its members were associated with the Party from its foundation, and the Group as a whole took up an attitude of good-will and cooperation. The Party in its turn invited members of the Group to join it. In a few months practically the whole Group was within the Congress Socialist Party, and the hope was aroused that at least two of the three parties were soon to become one. But this was not to be.

Here, we may draw attention to an interesting fact—a fact that would emerge clearly from this narrative as we go along. Our Party, because it grew out of the very heart of the national movement, occupied a very strategic position in it. This led every other party that came along to try to capture the Congress Socialist Party so as to take advantage of the position it occupied. When, this was not possible, it was sought to destroy the Congress Socialist

Party as an obstacle to the rise of others. This is what happened in the case of the Royists and the Communist Party.

At the time the Roy Group joined the Party, there was hardly any difference expressed with the basic politics of the Party. But within the next year, i.e. some time before the second conference of the Party at Meerut in January 1936, certain difference began to appear. The difference was set forth in a document that said in essence that the Party should not at all be developed as a socialist party but as the left wing of the Congress; it went further and said that the Congress Socialist Party as a socialist party should indeed be liquidated.

Here again we may draw attention to another interesting fact. The basic difficulty in the path of unity was the ridiculous idea held by every miserable little party that it alone was the real Marxist party, and that every other party had therefore to be exploited, captured or destroyed. The Roy Group was also a votary of this inflated creed. It was natural for it therefore to consider the development of another socialist party as unnecessary and harmful. It was much better to have a left platform which it could animate and dominate. All this was unfortunately not clear to us at the beginning, and we took seriously the profession of unity of these groups and parties. Indeed, the ideal of unity had so far got the better of our judgement and understanding that this did not become sufficiently clear to some of us till the parties concerned themselves tore off their masks.

When the said Royist document was placed before the National Executive at Meerut, the two Royist members of the Committee repudiated it completely, and supported instead the Thesis of the Party (known as the Meerut Thesis)[3] that stated clearly that the Party was and must remain a Marxist socialist party. When the matter was taken to the Conference, the Royists were divided. Some voted for the Executive's Thesis, a few produced an amendment which made a veiled attempt to revert to the repudiated document. They were completely routed. After that single instance in which a point of important difference was brought to light, the Group worked as if it would soon merge completely with the Party. Difficulties were indeed experienced with them here and there, as in the labour movement in Bombay, but these were not ideological differences.

This situation continued till some time after the release[4] of Shri M.N. Roy from prison towards the end of 1936. To begin with, he was friendly to the Party and even played with the idea of joining it. But soon enough he began in his public statements to make indirect attacks on the Party and its basic policies. Statements such as 'there should be no party within the Congress'; 'abolition of zamindari is a remote issue'; 'there should be no

[3] See *JPSW*, Vol. II, Appendix 1, for text of the Meerut Thesis.

[4] M.N. Roy was released on 20 November 1936.

organisation of the peasantry apart from the Congress committees' (the Party had taken a leading role in forming Kisan sabhas and raising the issue of abolition of landlordism) found frequent places in his public utterances. He, however, allowed his followers who had joined the Congress Socialist Party to continue to remain in it. But not for long. Suddenly, at the time of the Delhi Convention in March 1937, he decided secretly to withdraw his followers from the Congress Socialist Party. Why he did so was never publicly explained. Perhaps he left the anomaly of the position in which the leader and his followers found themselves in two different camps. He must have found out that the Congress Socialist Party could not become his tool, nor a convenient pedestal for the eminence he wished to attain. Whatever be the reasons, the fact is that the Royists soon after trooped out of the Congress Socialist Party. While staging their resignations they invariably attacked the Congress Socialist Party for weakening the Congress. After that the main political activity of Shri M.N. Roy and his *Independent India* was to discredit and denounce the Party. They failed to capture it; therefore, they must destroy it.

Thus after more than a year and a half of close cooperation, our Royist friends left us with a parting kick. The entire responsibility of disrupting the measure of unity that had been achieved must be laid at the doors of the Royists, and above all of Shri Roy. However, judging from the present activities of the Democratic People's Party, it does not appear as though the cause of socialism suffered so very frightfully after all from that parting of ways! Yet, what can be said of Shri Roy cannot perhaps be said of all his followers. Undoubtedly, some of that Group could have served socialism well, had they not been bogged in Royism.

II

The Labour Party (Bengal)
The Punjab Socialist Party
The Punjab Kirti Kisan Party

Before taking up the story of our relations with the Communist Party we shall dispose of the three other parties mentioned above.

The Bengal Labour Party started with an attitude of strong hostility towards the Party. The Party on the other hand endeavoured from the very beginning to wear down this hostility and persuade the Labour Party to enter into a united front pact. Very soon our efforts were successful, and a joint Board was set-up with an equal number of representatives of the Bengal Congress Socialist Party and the Labour Party to coordinate the activities of both the parties. Some time later the Labour Party merged with the Communist Party; thereafter our relations with it were the same as with the latter. After some time the Labour Party split away from the Communist Party and once again became an independent party, working in alliance with the Forward Bloc. Our relations with it now, as with the Forward Bloc, are friendly and based on mutual cooperation.

As for the Punjab Socialist Party, which was formed largely out of the old Naujawan Bharat Sabha,[5] the Party was able to achieve complete success with it. The Punjab Socialist Party was from the beginning well-disposed towards the Party, and willing to join it. There were for some time certain ideological obstacles in the way; for instance, the Punjab Party's strong antipathy for the Congress. However, in the course of time these obstacles were removed and the Punjab Socialist Party merged with the Congress Socialist Party.

We might also mention here the Punjab Kirti Kisan Group. Our relations with this group have always been friendly; and at one time a large number of Kirti comrades were members of the Punjab Congress Socialist Party.

III

The Communist Party of India

Let us now turn to our relations with the Communist Party of India. The story of these relations falls into four parts or periods: the first, beginning from the birth of the Party to the Meerut Conference in January 1936; the second, from January 1936 to August 1937; the third, from August 1937 to the beginning of the European War; the fourth, from the beginning of the War till the present.

The first period was marked by the bitterest hostility on the part of the Communist Party, and by ceaseless attempt at cooperation and unity on that of the Party. It might be added that the Party's attitude remain consistently unchanged throughout. Even today inspite of the renewed hostility and belligerency of the Communist Party our attitude of cooperation as between the two revolutionary parties continues. Only the perspective of unity no longer remains due to the experiences hereinafter described.

As soon as the Party was formed it was faced with malicious and bitter opposition from the Communist Party. It was described as a 'left manoeuvre of the bourgeoisie', and as 'social fascist'—hackneyed expressions of the international communist movement. Not only the Communist Party of India took up this attitude of belligerency; but even its mentors in Britain, such as

[5] Naujawan Bharat Sabha: Founded in 1928, it was a secret revolutionary organization to liberate the country and collect funds for the defence of imprisoned revolutionaries in connection with Lahore conspiracy case. Bhagat Singh was one of the founders of this organization.

Mr. Palme Dutt,[6] did likewise. The communist movement throughout the world was at that time following an extremely sectarian policy prescribed by the *Sixth Congress of the 3rd International*—a policy aimed at giving a clear-cut identity to the communist parties. This was done everywhere by attacking all other parties that worked in the name of socialism or organised labour. Indeed, the hostility shown to the socialist parties was often greater than that shown to the bourgeois parties. The fruits of this policy were strife and bitterness in the world socialist movement.

In India too, it must have been intolerable to the Communist Party to find an independent socialist party in existence. Immersed in its own narrowness and pettiness, it must have seen its monopoly of Marxism direly threatened: and it girded up its loins to give battle.

How did the Party react to this foolish opposition? It did not counter-attack; it did not return the vituperation; it did not seek to thwart or defeat the Communist Party. It recognised in the Communist Party a sister revolutionary party, although following at that time a foolish and disastrous policy. In contrast with the Communist Party's policy of hate and strife, it opened up the perspective of a united socialist party, to be evolved by a slow convergence of all socialist streams. To make a beginning it actually proposed to enter into a united front arrangement with the Community Party. The latter had at that time an open platform in the Red Trade Union Congress—one more of the products of the foolish policy they were following at that time. The Party negotiated with the Red Trade Union Congress and succeeded in persuading it to sign a united front agreement. This was done entirely at the Party's own initiative at a time when the other party was carrying on a bitter campaign against it. There could be no more genuine proof of the Party's earnest desire for socialist unity.

The agreement with the Red Trade Union Congress could not in the very nature of things have gone far. The two parties agreed on joint demonstrations and to 'cease fire'. Since we were not carrying on any war against Communist Party, the 'cease fire' clause had pertinence to the latter alone. As events showed, the Communist Party did not honour even this limited agreement. In its secret propaganda, its attacks on the Party continued; and even at joint public functions it showed little regard for the clause in the agreement that

[6] Rajani Palme Dutt (1896-1974); popularly known as RPD; Founder-member, Communist Party of Great Britain, 1920; and member of its Executive Committee, 1922-65; started *Labour Monthly*, 1921, and contributed 'Notes of the Month' for over forty years; Editor, *Workers' Weekly*, 1922-4, and *Daily Worker*, 1936-8; co-author of 'Dutt-Bradley Thesis' (1936) suggesting the formation of a United Front in India; publications include: *The Two Internationals*, *Modern India*, *Socialism and the Living Wage*, *Fascism and Social Revolution*, *India Today*, *Britain in the World Front*, and *India Today and Tomorrow*.

said that no party should utilise a joint function for partisan propaganda. We put all that down to the long sectarian tradition and practice of the Communist Party and hoped for better results in the future.

At this stage it would be advisable to keep in mind the wide difference that existed then between the Congress Socialist Party and the Communist Party. It should not be supposed that the Party thought an immediate unity with the Communist Party to be possible. The differences were too great for that. But the Party certainly believed that if unity was desirable and was to come in the future, it could be possible not by fighting each other but by trying to work together as far as possible. There is no doubt that had the Communist Party worked in the same spirit and really desired unity, there would have been a very different story to tell today.

The Communist Party was then, as it is now, a branch of the 3rd International. The Congress Socialist Party on the other hand, was and is an independent organisation. More than that: its very birth was in opposition to the line of the International. The Communist Party, following the latter, was outside the Congress and actively opposed to it. It had made attempts to launch organisations in rivalry to the Congress, such as the short-lived. Workers, and Peasants' Party and the still-born Anti-imperialist League. In contradiction to this line (which was the line of the 3rd International) the Party fully supported the Congress and stood for strengthening and developing it further as the instrument of national struggle. The Communist Party considered the Congress a bourgeois organisation which communists must shun and fight. The Party looked upon the Congress as a mass national organisation, which socialists must enter and develop along their own lines. The third fundamental difference was as regards the trade union movement. The Communist Party had split the movement (again following the dictates of its International) and formed its own miserable Red Trade Union Congress. It is hardly necessary to point out what would become of the trade union movement and workers' solidarity if every little party were to form its own unions. Workers in every industry and every factory would be split up into rival unions fighting among themselves. Yet, even this elementary Marxism was unknown at that time to our communist friends, and if one may venture to suggest, to the 3rd International too. Here again the policy of the Congress Socialist Party was totally different; and it was a truly Marxist Policy. The Party believed firmly in the unity of the trade union movement and from the start worked to that end. Till such time as unity was achieved, the Party joined hands with the All India Trade Union Congress. All unions formed by or under the control of the Party were to be affiliated to the All India Trade Union Congress. In selecting this Trade Union Congress out of the three organisations that existed, the Party once again showed the quality of its judgement, because it was the All India Trade Union Congress into which the two other organisations were later to merge. We shall instance one more important difference: it is regarding this very question of socialist unity which we are considering. The Communist Party believed in itself as the only true socialist party with a right to exist, and treated all others as enemies. The Party, on the other hand, stood for immediate cooperation among all the socialist groups and the eventual growth of a united socialist party.

During those days as now, the principal communist line of attack was that we were no socialists and had no understanding of Marxism. It was they who were the true interpreters of Marx[7] and Lenin. It is, therefore, of interest to note here that it was not very long before these self-appointed priests of Marxism were eating all their words and repudiating all the fundamental policies which they had been asserting with such half-educated cocksuredness. In less than two years they came running into the Congress, disbanded their red trade unions, joined the All India Trade Union Congress, and at least in words, accepted the objective of socialist unity. The Marxism of the Congress Socialist Party proved sounder than the parrot-like dogmatism of the Communist Party.

To resume our story. Due to the hostility of the Communist Party, the National Executive had, at the time of the first conference in Bombay, made a rule that no member of that party could be admitted into the Congress Socialist Party. This was a decision forced upon the Executive by the policy of the Communist Party itself. However, since the earliest days the Executive was determined to bring about a situation in which this ban would become unnecessary and through a process of infiltration and cooperation the two parties would soon become one. Therefore, the General Secretary of the Party and certain other important members of the Executive kept up during the subsequent months a continuous contact with the leaders of the Communist Party. These contacts were very useful to the Party's point of view. This position continued for a year. In the meanwhile the seventh Congress of the 3rd International met in Moscow and decided after eight years to reverse gears. It was, however, some time before the Communist Party of India officially changed its policy regarding the Congress, the Congress Socialist Party or the Trade Union Congress.

In January 1936 the 2nd Conference of the Party met at Meerut. There, acting on the report of the General Secretary, the National Executive unanimously decided to open the doors of the Party to members of the Communist Party subject to its supervision. It should be appreciated that this was entirely an unilateral decision taken at the Party's own initiative. It was based on the belief that important elements in the Communist Party accepted the main ideas of the Party and that by admitting them into the Party, we would be furthering the cause of socialist unity. However, officially,

[7] For biographical note on Heinrich Karl Marx see *JPSW*, Vol. I, p. 100.

the Communist Party still followed its old policy. And it should be mentioned that at the time when the Congress Socialist Party took such a revolutionary organisational step in the direction of unity, the Communist Party had advanced only to the extent of sending a representative to Meerut to study this 'left manoeuvre of the bourgeoisie' and submit a report!

It was not till several months later that the Communist Party on its side decided to grasp the proffered hand of comradeship of the Congress Socialist Party. That was at the time of the Lucknow Congress [1936]. That was a moment of great satisfaction to us. We thought that we were well on our way towards socialist unity. The Royists were already with us, and we hoped the communists too would now gradually come in, so that very soon, as in the course of joint work differences would wear off and mutual confidence would increase, the united socialist party of India would emerge into being.

It should not be supposed that we were unaware at this stage of the differences that still remained between us and the Communist Party; for instance, the difficulty about international affiliation. We, however, thought that as the movement grew it would be able to solve its problems as they arose, and that there would be no purpose served in trying to solve all possible problems at the start. A mature movement might find means and strength to overcome difficulties entirely beyond the resources of its childhood. Experience has shown that we would have been right in thinking thus only if all the other parties were equally serious and honest about unity.

However, after Meerut a large number of communists joined the Party. It was laid down at Meerut that they would be taken into the Party only with the express permission of the Executive in every case. But, in practice no permission was ever taken. The Executive was aware of this fact, but it did not take a very serious view of it because it did not wish to queer the process by stressing technicalities. This indeed was a great mistake. The communists in this way came into the Party under false pretences, and later when difficulties arose they were able to deny their membership of the Communist Party.

In course of time, as more and more communists entered the Party, disturbing notes began to be heard. During the whole of the latter part of 1936 and latter months, reports kept on reaching the Executive that the communists were doing fraction work within the Party and trying to capture its organisations. There were frequent complaints from Andhra. Outside the Party also the relations between our cadres and those of the Communist party were not very happy. Complaints came particularly from Cawnpore, Bombay, Calcutta, i.e. the labour areas. It was reported that the communists were found claiming that they would not permit any other party to entrench itself in the labour movement. One wishes, speaking parenthetically, that they had shown equal anxiety in preventing careerists and reformists from entrenching themselves there. One might go further, without closing the parenthesis, and point out that they have indeed always exhibited a strange adeptness in allying with such elements in the labour movement in order to keep out those socialists who did not belong to their church. Regarding the reports of fraction work, the National Executive did no more than warn the Provincial organisations to keep an eye on it.

After this situation had dragged on for months, there came in August 1937 a great shock to us which proved to be the turning point in our relations with the Communist Party. With that we reached the end of the second stage of our relations and entered the third. In this instance also, as in the case of the Royists, the initiative towards disruption came from the other side (i.e. the communist party in this case). The National Executive was meeting at Patna in August. At this meeting a statement of the Communist Party was read which caused a painful shock and great indignation. The statement was a secret document of the Communist Party and evidently meant only for its members. It said, in brief, that the Congress Socialist Party was not a socialist party, and that the Communist Party would never tolerate a rival party. It went on to say that the Communist Party was the only real socialist party, and that the Congress Socialist Party was to be developed merely into a platform of left unity.

It is necessary for members of the Party to fully appreciate the nature of the Communist Party statement. It set forth clearly the true aims of the Communist Party with regard to the Congress Socialist Party and explained fully all the latter policies of the former. It cannot but be regretted that the Executive at Patna disregarded the dangers that were thus exposed and, in the pursuit of its idealistic aims, committed an organisational blunder. The statement, in the first place, knocked the whole basis out of the Lucknow agreement between the Congress Socialist Party and the Communist Party. That basis was that both these were socialist parties which in course of time and following certain policies of cooperation would unite to form a single party. Without this basic assumption there could have been no meaning in the slogan of 'socialist unity'. If there was only one socialist party, as the statement pugnaciously asserted, where did the question of unity with *another* socialist party arise? In other words, the statement clearly showed that the Communist Party had not given up its monopolistic and sectarian attitude, and that it had really no faith in socialist unity. That slogan merely served it as a convenient device to enter into relations with the Congress Socialist Party and gain access to the positions it held. The statement clearly admitted as much, when it declared that the Congress Socialist Party was to be developed only as a platform—a platform dominated by the Communist Party. Further, when the statement talked of not tolerating a rival socialist party, it again gave the lie to the Communist Party's professions of unity. In what manner could the question of rivalry arise if both parties truly believed in unity? The statement thus made it clear, firstly, that the Communist Party did not believe in socialist unity, because it recognised no other socialist parties; secondly, that it wanted to destroy the Congress Socialist Party as a socialist party and capture it to be used as its open platform.

All this came as a great shock to the Executive and the indignation was unanimous. There were at that time four 'Trojan horses'[8] of the Communist Party on the Congress Socialist Party Executive. They too joined in the indignation (so that they might not give themselves away). Not a voice was raised in defence or mitigation of that statement. After a short discussion, the Executive arrived at the unanimous decision that in future no member of the Communist Party should be allowed to enter the Party. That was a mild, and as experience proved, a mistaken decision. Organisational and political considerations required not only a ban on their future entry but also immediate expulsion of the communists who had already been admitted into the Party. The Executive, however, was eager to avoid doing anything that might make the chances of unity more difficult; and it hoped that the action taken might induce the Communist Party to correct its ways. Also, it still hoped that there were important elements in the Communist Party who genuinely stood for unity. This too later proved to be a vain hope.

Thus, the next check to socialist unity after the Royist walk-out came from the Communist Party.

After August 1937, the situation steadily deteriorated, the Party feeling itself increasingly paralysed. For months it felt that there was no alternative to expelling the communists, and yet the Party hesitated to undo all that it had done before and to let go all the hopes it had so fondly cherished. Indeed, when it came to taking action, the Party continued to harbour and accommodate the communists. It was during this period that the General Secretary of the Party, by way of reorganisation, handed over to them the whole of the Andhra Party. This was in due course endorsed by the Executive.

The next landmark of importance in this depressing history is the Lahore Conference of the Party in April 1938. This Conference reinforced the conclusion to which the Party was being driven. At this time the Communist Party conveyed an astonishing note to the National Executive. It was a sort of comic anti-climax to Patna. The note categorically stated that the Communist Party considered the Congress Socialist Party to be a true revolutionary Marxist party, and believed that socialist unity could be brought about only by the unity of the two parties. This was only eight months after Patna. In eight months the Congress Socialist Party from being a left platform had become a revolutionary Marxist party. What progress we must have made to have so impressed the Indian branch of the 3rd International! No body was, however, taken in by this comic *volte-face* of the Communist

[8] Refers to Dinkar Mehta, E.M.S. Namboodripad, Sajjad Zaheer and S.S. Batlivala.

Party. The real purpose of the note was obvious to everyone, as it must be to the reader. The fact was that the Communist Party was in fright. Since Patna, feelings against the tactics of the Communist Party had been growing and a body of opinion was gaining in strength in the Party that the time had come when the communists should be shown the way out. They had too long been allowed, in the name of unity, to take advantage of the Party. The fact that M.R. Masani was Chairman of the Conference added to the fears of the communists. The latter have tried to denounce Masani as a communist-baiter. He, of course, was nothing of the sort. What angered and frightened the communists was his organisational competence and soundness. He disagreed with the communists violently, but was prepared for honest co-operation with them as between two independent parties. But he was the first to see through their game of disruption and capture, played under the cover of unity. He was therefore early to demand the wholesale expulsion of the communists from the Party, not as an anti-communist measure, but as a counter-measure to their anti-Congress Socialist Party and capture tactics. Experience has completely vindicated Masani's stand. But to continue, it was the fear that the Party Conference might not only endorse the Patna decision, but also go beyond it that led the communists to communicate that note to the Party. That they were wholly insincere was made abundantly clear at the Conference itself.

The Executive naturally did not take the Communist Party statement seriously, and the Conference endorsed the Patna decision. The Party, however, still held fast to the objective of unity, and it put forward the slogan of 'unity in action' as a preliminary process. The communist members were allowed to continue in the Party. The weakness of the Executive in this regard was reflected by the Conference. It was clear that the time had come to send the communists packing from the Party, but the Executive refused to face the situation. It had not much faith in the success of its new slogan, 'unity in action', but it clutched at it to save itself from taking an unpleasant decision. As a result, the Party embarked on a career of sheer drift which ended but recently.

It has been remarked above that the conduct of the communists at the Conference completely belied their solemn note. During the elections for the Executive, they made and put up an alternative communist list and voted for it *en bloc*. In other words, even while they talked and breathed unity they made a secret bid to capture the Party. Now, it is elementary politics that capture and unity politics are poles apart and contradict each other. But in the peculiar dialectics of the communists all contradictions are reconciled. It cannot be wondered therefore that they not unoften equate counter-revolution with revolution.

Some months after Lahore came another shocking evidence. A circular of the Communist Party fell into Comrade Masani's hands, who published it under the title *Communist Plot against the Congress Socialist Party*.[9] The circular laid down in detail the tactics to be followed by the communists to capture the organisations of the Party. Here was further evidence of the unity tactics of the Communist Party. For many comrades that circular was the proverbial last straw. Yet, the Executive again held its hands, and allowed things to drift. Now it was no longer the ideal or hope of unity that decided the Executive: it was just reluctance to face an unpleasant task. Those were dark days for the Party, when lack of decision created a good deal of confusion and weakness. The enemies of the Party did not fail to profit fully by it.

This drift and paralysis of the Party continued. There were only two ways out of the stalemate: either an immediate merger of the Communist Party and the Congress Socialist Party or the creation of a completely homogeneous Congress Socialist Party with all members of other parties immediately removed from it. In view of the experience already gained, there was little possibility of the success of the first alternative. However, as my opinion regarding the Communist Party died hard I mooted the question with the leaders of that party. It was obvious that without a common ideological basis a merger was out of the question. Therefore it was agreed to explore such a basis. But there was little progress made in that direction. In the meanwhile differences grew wider between the two parties in the field of day-to-day politics. Then came Tripuri,[10] and then Calcutta.[11] The Communist Party, lacking ballast and independent strength in the national movement, grew panicky and in order to satisfy its ambition to lead the Left ran widely after whoever declaimed loudest.

The first alternative was clearly an impossibility. But the Executive still lacked the courage to take recourse to the other. This policy of drift which was daily delivering the party into the hands of the Communist Party drove some of the leading members of the Executive[12] to resign. This produced great consternation in the ranks of the Congress Socialist Party, though it was welcomed by the Communist Party and its 'Trojan horses' and stooges.

In these circumstances a memorable meeting of the Executive was held in

[9] See Appendix 2 for text of *Communist Plot against the C.S.P.* by M.R. Masani.

[10] Refers to fifty-second session in the Congress at Tripuri (March 1939) where the C.S.P. under the leadership of J.P. had remained neutral *vis-a-vis* the Pant resolution expressing continued faith in Gandhi's leadership and refused to treat the controversy regarding the presidential election as a contest between the right-wing and left-wing of the Congress.

[11] Refers to the meeting of the A.I.C.C. at Calcutta (29-30 April and 1 May 1939) where Subhas Chandra Bose tendered his resignation from the presidentship of the Congress and Rajendra Prasad was elected in his place.

[12] These were M.R. Masani, Achyut Patwardhan, Rammanohar Lohia and Asoka Mehta.

Bombay in 1939, at the time of the All-India Congress Committee session. At this meeting practically every member, excepting those who belonged to the Communist Party, expressed the view that it was high time to check the drift and stop internal disruption. For this purpose, it was the overwhelming opinion of the Committee that all communists and others who belonged to any other party should be asked to leave the Party. After a long discussion, the question was left by the Committee to my decision as General Secretary. I did not feel happy at the prospect of precipitating a grave crisis in the socialist movement. I gave a sort of compromised decision. I fully accepted the ideal of a homogeneous Congress Socialist Party, but advised that communists who were already members of the Party should not be expelled, as that would lead to much bitterness and mutual destruction. I however emphasised that henceforth every attempt should be made to keep the control of the Party in the hands of genuine members, i.e. those who were not members of any other party. This decision was accepted by the Executive. Henceforth, the slogan was that of a homogeneous party. It was an advance over the previous position, but still suffered from not making a complete break from the policy that had led the Party into such a morass.

In practice, the Bombay decision, half-hearted as it was, found still more half-hearted application. In fact, it remained entirely inoperative till the declaration of the European War. And here we must record a remarkable, if also a regrettable, fact. It was after the Bombay decision that the General Secretary, acting on his own authority, allowed eight communists to be admitted into the Allahabad committee of the U.P. Party. To such lengths was the secretary of the Party prepared to go to accommodate the communists in the hope that they might reciprocate in the same spirit and a new chapter might be opened in the history of the socialist movement in this country. But it was all in vain. Every opportunity offered to the Communist Party was used against the Congress Socialist Party.

In September, 1939, came the European War. The War made no change in the policy of our Party as far as it related to socialist unity. We have traced above the development of this question upto the beginning of the War. We have seen how starting with enthusiasm for a policy of unity by bringing all socialist elements into the Party, we were forced step by step to give up that policy, and, finally, to arrive at the objective of a homogeneous Congress Socialist Party. The emergency created by the War and the possibility of wide-spread repression and of illegal functioning made it necessary to make certain organisational arrangements and also to give effect to the Bombay decision. Accordingly, soon after the beginning of the War small emergency committees were set-up in the provinces, and care was taken to see that they were homogeneous committees. The Communists were still within the Party. The Party was still ready for full cooperation with the Communist Party provided it was honest cooperation in actual work and not merely setting up of high-sounding committees.

As regards the Communist Party, soon after the War began its policy underwent a sudden change. It tore off its mask completely and stood as the sworn enemy of the Congress Socialist Party and of every other progressive organisation with which it had worked before, the Congress as well as the Forward Bloc.

It is necessary to relate just one incident to put this *volte-face* of the Communist Party in its proper perspective. In October 1939 a meeting of representatives of certain leftist organisations was held at Lucknow at the instance of Shri Subhas Chandra Bose. At this meeting a proposal was put forward by the representatives of the Communist Party and the other groups to form a sort of 'joint command' to conduct the anti-war activities of the various groups. The representatives of the Party opposed that proposal as impractical due to lack of sufficient political unanimity and mutual confidence. They made a counter-proposal: namely, that a 'common programme of work' be chalked out to be carried out by all the groups in cooperation with one another. This proposal was accepted in the end, and a seven-point programme was chalked out which was accepted by all the representatives present. With that the meeting ended, and it was hoped that since an agreement had been arrived at on the concrete nature of future work, there would be full cooperation at least between the parties that were represented at it. That meeting might well have proved to be of momentous importance. But it was not to be. We had reckoned without the Communist Party.

It was hardly three weeks later that a Communist Party thesis[13] appeared making a frontal attack on the Congress Socialist Party. With that we were back in the primitive days of 1934. To this day it has not been made clear what it was that led the Communist Party to declare war so suddenly on the Congress Socialist Party. Surely, between the Lucknow meeting and the early part of November when the Communist Party thesis appeared, or at any time before or after, the Congress Socialist Party had been guilty of no crime against the Communist Party. Only a few weeks before the Communist Party had agreed to carry out a common programme. It was demonstrating a strange method of doing it. Well, be that as it may, the fact is that in November, 1939, the Congress Socialist Party completely fell from grace, and since then has been subject to a most vicious attack. Indeed an early (1940) Communist Party document has already celebrated the demise of the Congress Socialist Party and examined in a learned Marxian manner, peculiar

[13] Refers to the statement of the Politbureau of the C.P.I. published in the *Communist*, Vol. II, No. 1, November 1939. For text of the Statement see Hari Dev Sharma, ed., *Selected Works of Acharya Narendra Deva*, Vol. I, pp. 292-314.

to the Communist Party alone, the reasons for such a lamentable—or, rather, happy—event. It is not at all an inconsistency if February 1941 number of the Communist Party organ threatens to publish a history of the Congress Socialist Party since Ramgarh. One may be sure that this will be only a spiritual history—the history of a ghost! It is only the ghost of the Congress Socialist Party that is playing on the Politbureau, and it must slay it on paper to be rid of the nightmare.

Why did the Communist Party suddenly start attacking the Congress Socialist Party and everybody else? There was a political reason. With the advent of War, the Communist Party discerned the approach of the revolution. At such a moment it did not want that any other party should be about to dispute the leadership of the coming historic event! It desired to appear before the masses—workers, peasants, students (above all students, mark you)—as the *sole* revolutionary party in the country. It could brook no competition, and when power came to be seized it wanted no shareholders at all. The Communist Party *uber alles*! It was a magnificent ambition, clearly in accord with the Marxism that the Communist Party understands. The natural corollary of the thesis of megalomania was that other parties must perish, i.e. their hold over the masses must be destroyed. Therefore, the scribes of the Politbureau set about filling up reams of paper with stuff hardly intelligible to the masses, well-versed as they are in the jargon of the learned writers. And lo and behold, the Congress, the Forward Bloc, the Congress Socialist Party have all disappeared into thin air, and the Politbureau is soon to be converted into the Council of Commissars!

A lovely dream from which there is sure to be a rather rude awakening. It will not be long before another learned thesis of the Communist Party painfully dilates upon the mistakes of this historic period!

To bring this story to an end. The Congress Socialist Party did not retaliate against the Communist Party offensive. It did not even expel the communists from the party for some time. It declared that, while it must criticise the mistakes of the Communist Party, it wished it no ill-will and was prepared to cooperate with it as a sister revolutionary party. It raised its voice against the disruption that was being caused to the socialist movement. But all these gestures were rejected with jeers, and the war on the Party went apace. At Ramgarh, when no other alternative was available, the National Executive, more than four years after Meerut, was compelled to expel from the Party all those who were either members of Communist Party or its agents. Thus ended a tragic chapter in the history of the Indian socialist movement. It should be made clear that in taking this decision the Executive was not launching upon any manner of campaign against the Communist Party. That decision was merely an elementary organisational measure, long-overdue, and expressed simply the idea that a party may have no one as a member who is a member or an instrument of a hostile party.

IV

Conclusions

The above history makes clear the effort made by our Party to bring about unity in the socialist movement and how they failed. Except for the earlier months, this problem of socialist unity was really a problem of the coming together of the Communist Party and the Congress Socialist Party. We have seen how the tactics of the Communist Party made that impossible. But it would be a mistake to blame the Communist Party for those tactics. They were inevitable. In the very nature of things the Communist Party could not have behaved otherwise. This was not clear to us before, otherwise our Party would have been much stronger today. But now that it is clear, every comrade must fully grasp its meaning.

The inevitability of which we have spoken is inherent in the nature of the international communist movement. The movement is not formed from the bottom upwards. The 3rd International is not an organisation of genuine working class parties or socialist parties that have developed in various countries, but a central organisation controlled entirely from above by the Communist Party of the U.S.S.R. with *branches* in the various countries. The 3rd International must have a branch in every important country (except those, such as Turkey, the government of which has a pact with the Russian government prohibiting the formation of such a branch). The Communist Party of India is such a branch. It cannot therefore unite with any other party and cease to be a branch. It is possible for the Communist Party to 'unite' with another socialist party only when the united party itself becomes a branch of the 3rd International—in which case unity is a misnomer or, when the Communist Party secretly works as such a branch within the united party hoping to capture it eventually—in which case again unity is a misnomer. Therefore, it is desirable once for all to give up vague talk of unity with the Communist Party. It is possible to unite with such socialist parties as are not sub-feudatories like the Communist Party but unity with the latter has no meaning. Its only meaning is that the Congress Socialist Party too becomes a branch of the 3rd International, i.e. it becomes a part of the Communist Party.

Here, the question arises: why does not the Congress Socialist Party affiliate with the Communist International, i.e. become amalgamated with the Communist Party? Is the Congress Socialist Party anti-Communist International or anti-Russia? It is neither.

But the question of affiliation is beset with grave and insuperable difficulties. The Congress Socialist Party is not a party transplanted from outside. It is a growth of the Indian soil. It was not inspired by any outside force. It grew and developed out of the experiences of the Indian people struggling for freedom. Its very formation was a protest and revolt against the line the 3rd International pursued in India. That initial fact was enough to instill into the Congress Socialist Party entire lack of respect for the wisdom and guidance of the International. Subsequent events did not improve mattes. Immediately after the formation of the Party, the Indian branch of the International, viciously attacked it. Leaders of the latter, including members of its Central Committee, rushed to denounce it as 'social fascist'. All this was not exactly calculated to draw us nearer the International. However, on our own initiative, we did attempt to draw nearer to the Communist Party, but were sorely deceived.

The International claims to be a leader of the World Revolution (though many working class parties in the world refute this claim and charge that the International has indeed betrayed the Revolution). As such, it was its duty to encourage and draw together all the revolutionary force, wherever found. Instead it has functioned as a narrow sectarian Church, supporting its own sect and calling curses upon the heads of all others. In the six years of the life of the Congress Socialist Party, in spite of its standing as a significant revolutionary force in the country, the International made no attempts to get into contact with it or help or encourage it in any way. On the other hand its Indian agents did everything possible to destroy it. Is it not more appropriate to ask the leader of the world revolution, why it failed to draw the Congress Socialist Party within its fold?

In this connection might also be urged the wide divergence between the policies of the Congress Socialist Party and of the International as applied to India. Past differences have been indicated above. Let us turn to the present position. The Communist Party, once again is ploughing its lonely furrow and has pitted itself against the Congress, the Congress Socialist Party, the Forward Bloc. It is condemning outright the satyagraha movement. In a recent publication it made fun of even such a serious thing as the disappearance of Subhas Babu. The Communist Party alone will create and lead the revolution. This is the policy of the International. The Congress Socialist Party is totally different. It stands still for cooperation between various groups; it does not oppose the satyagraha movement, nor the Congress. It criticises the inadequacies of the movement, its background of compromise, its future dangers, but cooperates with it, arguing that isolation with the national struggle (limited though it be) would be disastrous for the revolutionary forces. It at the same time works to develop the labour and peasant movements, with a view to precipitate a mass revolutionary struggle when the occasion arises. Thus, once again the Communist Party and the Congress Socialist Party, and therefore the International and the Congress Socialist Party are widely separated in their policies.

We might urge a last consideration. There is a large body of opinion, claiming to be Marxist, in the international working class movement which alleges that the Communist International is no more than a bureau of the Soviet Foreign Office, and that its policies are solely dictated by the exigencies of Russian foreign policy. Even such a sympathetic author as Edgar Snow[14] in his *Red Star Over China* echoes the same sentiments in his discussion of the relations between the Chinese Communist Party and the Communist International. The frequent and violent twists and turns in the policies of the communist parties throughout the world before and after the War lend colour to this view. Whatever be the truth, one fact is clear—that every communist party must follow the dictates from Moscow because Moscow alone knows what is good or bad for Russia. Now, the Congress Socialist Party, while recognising that the position and role of the U.S.S.R. must enter into every socialist calculation, is not prepared to follow dictates from anywhere. Moreover, affiliation with the International not only means following its dictates, but also being obliged to uphold any and every action of the Russian Government. We are not prepared for such a subservience.

The above consideration should make it clear why we cannot affiliate with the 3rd International. We should add that our attitude nevertheless remains one of utmost cordiality (inspite of the International's attitude of hostility) and however futile it may be the hand of cooperation will always be extended by us.

To return to the Communist Party. It might be asked why, if it did not believe in unity, did it agree to send its members into the Congress Socialist Party. For two obvious reasons. It might be recalled that for some time it refused to have anything to do with us. But when it was ordered by the International to change its policy and to enter the Congress it found itself faced with a serious problem. It had no contacts with the Congress, and, of course, it must become at once the leader of the national forces. It was here that it found in the Congress Socialist Party an ideal instrument. The Congress Socialist Party held a strategic position within the Congress. The communists were anxious to get into the Provincial Congress Committees, the Executive, the All India Congress Committee, possibly the Working Committee. With their own resources it was impossible for them to get anywhere near them. They were not four-anna members yet. Here was the Congress Socialist Party with its members even in the highest committees. 'Three cheers for the

[14] Edgar Parks Snow (1905-72); American journalist; correspondent, *London Daily Herald* (1932-41); Associate Editor, *Saturday Evening Post* (1943-51); author of *Red Star Over China*, *The Battle for Asia*, and *The Other Side of the River*.

Congress Socialist Party. Let us join it.' They did, and the Congress Socialist Party votes sent them as high as the All India Congress Committee and the Provincial Executives. In addition, being an open party, the Congress Socialist Party afforded a splendid platform for self-advertisement to these, till then practically unknown communists. What was the other reason for their entering the Party? It has been pointed out that in their view no socialist Party apart from the Communist Party had any right to exist. The growth of the Congress Socialist Party into an independent party was a danger to their monopoly. Therefore, they took advantage of the opportunity to enter the Party so as either to capture or break it up. These were the two purposes that brought them into the Party. But, in order to gain admittance; they had to accept the slogan of socialist unity, for, otherwise there was no reason why the Congress Socialist Party should have let them come in. So, behind the smoke-screen of unity, they worked out their plans.

The foregoing has made it clear that the whole idea of unity with a party like the Communist Party was misconceived and the fundamental difficulties were not understood. But apart from that the manner in which unity was sought to be brought about was itself a grievous mistake. It was very wrong to have admitted members of other parties into our Party. This was against all sound principles of organisation. The experiment should never be repeated. It cannot but lead to internal confusion and conflict. It should be kept in mind that nowhere in the world has an attempt to unite two parties been made by allowing the infiltration of members of one into the other. The Congress Socialist Party tried it and found it to be a disastrous experiment.

In this connection a point is often made in Party discussions. Why was the Communist Party alone able to do fraction work? Why could not we do the same? For two simple reasons. Communists had the opportunity of doing it, because we had given them a place in the Party. We had no such opportunity, because we had neither the desire nor the occasion to enter their party. Secondly, and this is the more important reason, fraction work is contradictory to unity. We believed sincerely in unity; therefore, the question of fraction work did not arise at all.

Since the decision to expel the Communists was taken, persistent propaganda has been carried on by the Communist Party to represent it as an anti-communist drive. It should be fully understood that there was nothing anti-communist in that decision. It was a measure of self-defence taken against the anti-Congress Socialist Party drive of the Communist Party. The communists had no place in our Party by right; they had been admitted for a specific purpose, namely, that of uniting the two parties. When the Communist Party turned into an open enemy of the Congress Socialist Party and started a vigorous campaign to destroy it, and when the communists within the Congress Socialist Party began to function openly as its enemies, trying to undermine its influence and solidarity, the least that the Party could do was to remove them from its membership. No party can afford to keep within its ranks members who are its open enemies. It should, however, be realised at the same time that the expulsion of the communists was in no manner an offensive against the Communist Party itself as an independent party.

With relation to the expulsion of the communists a question is often asked, sometimes inspired by communists, whether the National Executive was a competent body to take such a decision. Is not the Party Conference the proper authority to decide such questions? The answer is that the National Executive was fully competent to take the decision in question. Since the beginning of this matter, it has always been the Executive that took decisions regarding it. The decision to admit the communists into the Party was not a decision of any Party Conference, but of the Executive at Meerut. Had it been a Conference decision, only another Conference could have rescinded it. As it was, the Executive was fully competent to rescind it. There was a reason why this matter was kept strictly confined to the Executive. The Communist Party was and is an illegal party. Any question relating to it could not be taken to the Conference. It was only during the Congress Ministeries when a measure of civil liberties was enjoyed that the matter was first discussed with any measure of freedom.

In raising the question just discussed, it is the purpose of Communists to paint the Executive as an anti-communist body, and to suggest that if the matter had been referred to a Party Conference, the result would have been different. The history of our relations with the Communists, given in section 3, is enough to show to what lengths the Executive went to accommodate them. When the Executive at Meerut decided to admit them into the Party, it was under no pressure from the rank and file. Subsequently, when even after clear proof of their disruptive tactics, the Executive bore with them, it was again under no such pressure. When the Andhra Party was handed over to them, when even after the Bombay decision, eight communists were admitted into the Allahabad Committee, it was not in response to any clamour from the rank and file. When even today, inspite to the Communist Party crusade against the Party, the Executive offers it its hand of cooperation, it is not out of any fear of the rank and file. Nothing can be more ridiculous than this attempt of the Communist Party to try to put the members of the Party against the Executive.

Another common, and often inspired question, is: why should there be two socialist parties; is not Marxism one and indivisible? This whole pamphlet is an answer to this question. Yes, Marxism is one and indivisible. The important question, however, is, how is Marxism to be applied to a given social situation? In 1934 too Marxism was one. Yet the way the Communist Party and the 3rd International applied it, and the way the Congress Socialist

Party applied it, were poles apart. There you have the answer in a nutshell.

A Marxist never tries to understand a social fact by itself. He understands it historically and in relation with other facts. We all wish that there were only one Marxist party. But, if we wish to understand how in a concrete situation two Marxist parties came to exist, we must look at the matter historically. During the national struggle of 1930-4, there was a considerable radicalisation of the younger cadres of the Congress. By 1934 a coherent socialist group crystallised. Between this group and the existing group, i.e. the Communist Party, there was an impenetrable wall in the shape of the latter's attitude towards and isolation from the Congress. A new party was bound to be formed: the Congress Socialist Party thus came into being as a result of the mistaken policy of the Communist Party and the Communist International.

What happened after this second party was formed has already been described in detail. Since its birth this Party, i.e. the Congress Socialist Party, made attempts to create a single Marxist party. It failed because the Communist Party did not want unity. As a result of this historical process, there are still two parties in existence. The present differences between the two parties have already been discussed, as also the difficulty arising from the question of international affiliation. As long as these differences and difficulties last, there will continue to be two parties.

To many this would appear to be unfortunate as it does to me, but in the circumstances described in detail in this pamphlet it is equally clear to me that it is inevitable. I am glad about one thing that inspite of the misgivings of some friends we tried the experiment as was consistent with the attitude of a party which from its very birth endeavoured to bring about as close a cooperation as possible between all the Socialist groups in the country, if not actual unity. I can also say with confidence that if the other groups had also adopted a less sectarian attitude the result of our endeavours might have been different. Let us hope that some day, not in the distant future, it will be realised that the cause is greater than petty fractional or sectarian advantages.

Left Unity

Related to the problem of organisation is the problem of Left unity. It appears to me that there is a great deal of confusion regarding this subject. The question of left unity is one of the most vexed questions in the world. It is my view that the question, in the form in which it is raised, is insoluble. Left unity in the sense of unity of all left parties and groups is an impossibility. Those who talk of such a unity should first ask themselves why is there Left disunity to begin with. In other words, the question should be asked, why do separate Left parties at all come into existence. I think if that question were examined properly, it would be found that the same causes that first gave birth to separatist and sectarian tendencies would also prevent subsequent unification.

The experience of Left movements throughout the world shows that Left groups have not found it possible to unite or even to work together except on specific occasions and for short periods. This historical evidence has surely a lesson for us.

In our own country our experience has been no different. We made serious attempts on two occasions for Left unity. These attempts not only failed to achieve their object, but also left a trail of bitterness that still hinders work. Our past experience showed that while the C.S.P. sincerely opened its doors to Left and Socialist groups and extended its hand of friendship to them, they only sought in all that an opportunity to enlarge their respective influence, recruit members and build cells, 'bore from within', and to play other tricks that have been played all over the world in the name of Left unity.

Therefore, as far as I am concerned, I have no faith in so-called Left unity, and do not wish to experiment with it, any more. I think the far better course is for all Leftists to forget their little denominational enthusiasms and doctrinal fanaticisms, and to come into one wide, roomy fold and build a single party of Left nationalism and Socialism. Such a party today is the C.S.P. It is possible to find fault with it and pick holes in it, but it is far more fruitful to join hands, to rub off our ideological angularities and fit ourselves into one large pattern in which doctrinal differences might be subordinated to one broad and bold design of common objectives, common methods and a broad common ideology. If the Left and Socialist movement in India is to grow, it could do so not through the unsteady and uneasy combination of various groups, who even when combining must explain and justify their separate identities, who even while trying to work together must work to strengthen their respective organisations by fresh recruitment and partisan propaganda, but by the growth of one large single party. I cannot conceive that there is any other party in India that can fill this role except the C.S.P. I therefore appeal to all fighters [for Left unity] to make the C.S.P. their own. They have already done so to a very large extent. I appeal to the others also to do the same.

Local difficulties, difficulties of personal equation and old prejudices might stand in the way of some friends, but I should like to assure every fighter that as far as it may lie in our power, we shall see that these difficulties are removed from their way and the path left clear for them to cooeprate in building up a real powerful organisation.

32. Deoli Papers, 31 July 1941[1]

I

TO PRABHAVATI[2]

I sent you two letters last time mentioning therein that if you received those, you should reply to me with the hints—'All are well at the house of Babuni[3] both at Murar and Daltonganj'. When I received your letter from Khandwa without the above hint, I was a bit perplexed. On enquiry I found out that the fellow who promised to deliver the letter became afraid and could not deliver it but kept it with him. Afterwards he returned the letter when he was threatened by me, that is why I had to send for you again. You will have to proceed to Bombay with this letter. You should ask Purusottam[4] that he should write letters to me according to the instruction I mentioned in my letter. You should also grasp the method. Take a big old book with a thick binding, tear the binding off, place the letter there, get the book bound again and sent it.

Basawanji[5] and others can also do the same if they want to send any special news.

With two or three other books, a novel of Premchandji[6] should be sent. The binding of this book should contain the letter or the letter may be sent inside the binding of any other book and a mark of plus "+" should be made on its page No. 100 with pencil. I will open the binding of the book which will be marked with plus sign.

Basawan should be informed to go underground. While underground, he should recruit men for the Secret Party.

[1] Home Political Department, F. No. 43/96/41 (NAI). R.F. Craster, Superintendent of Deoli Detention Camp, in a letter dated 31 July 1941 (see Appendix 15 for text of the letter) to V.T. Bayley, Assistant Director of Intelligence Bureau enclosed the copies of certain letters and papers of J.P. seized during an interview with Prabhavati at Deoli on 29 July 1941. These letters were published by the Government in various newspapers in an abridged form (see the *Bombay Chronicle* and the *Tribune*, 17 October 1941). These later came to be known as Deoli letters.

[2] For biographical note on Prabhavati Devi, see *JPSW*, Vol. I, p. 41.

[3] Younger Sister of J.P.

[4] Purshottam Trikamdas. For biographical note see *JPSW*, Vol. I, p. 88.

[5] Basawan Singh (1909-89); one of the prominent Socialist leaders of Bihar, especially on the labour front; became a Cabinet Minister in Bihar twice for short periods; in between was actively associated with the J.P. Movement (1974-7).

[6] Dhanpat Rai *alias* Premchand (1880-1936); Hindi writer, known for his novels and short stories; participated in the Non-Cooperation Movement, 1921; started Saraswati Press, 1923, and *Hans*, a monthly journal, 1930; presided over the first Convention of All India Progressive Writers' Association in 1936; publications include: *Gaban*, *Godan*, *Karmabhoomi*, *Rangabhoomi*, and *Sevasadan*.

Financial help should be procured according to the old method. We cannot do anything except this. Sukulji[8] also agrees with the above proposal.

Secret Party will not be a separate body from C.S.P. but its name will be a different one.

Inform Ganga Babu[9] if the other programme (going outside) is not possible at this time, he should work as a joint Secretary for all India Party. He should tour in the provinces and carry on the office work.

We were on hunger strike for 4 days about which I mentioned something in my letter. Get it copied at Bombay and take it with you for Bapuji. There are three separate documents in this connection with this letter. Take the copies of all the three documents with you.

N.M. Joshi[10] M.L.A. (Central) visited this place. We gave him everything in writing. Ask Purusottam[11] to see him and take a copy for Bapuji. If he is not willing to give a copy to Purusottam, Bapuji can write to him for the same.

I came with this letter to hand it over to you but could not do so. That is why I am sending it again through the same man, if you could get this letter, tell me tomorrow in the interview that 'You had headache last night'. This will be a hint for me of the delivery.

If you meet Ghaffar Khan Saheb at Wardha, tell him that Hakim Abdussalam Khan Saheb,[12] President, District Congress Committee, Hazara, is here in Camp II. He is keeping good health but has got pain in his hand like suspected gout. Khan Saheb should send news of Salam Saheb to the latter's house that he is well here. He has got a special complaint. The letters

[8] Refers to Yogendra Shukla. For biographical note see *JPSW*, Vol. II, p. 257.

[9] Ganga Sharan Sinha (1905-87); one of the prominent Socialist leaders; Secretary, Bihar Socialist Party, 1931-4, Bihar Provincial Kisan Sabha, 1935, and Bihar Congress Kisan Enquiry Committee, 1935-7; founder-member, C.S.P., 1934; member, National Executive and Central Parliamentary Board of Praja Socialist Party, 1956-9, its Deputy Chairman, 1956, and Chairman 1956-9; member, Rajya Sabha, 1956-62, 1962-8, and 1968-74.

[10] N.M. Joshi (1879-1955); labour leader; joined the Servants of India Society, 1909; started the Bombay Social Service League, 1911 and was its General Secretary till 1953; member, Bombay Municipal Corporation, 1919-23, Indian Legislative Assembly, 1921-47; General Secretary, All India Trade Union Congress, 1925-9, 1940-8; delegate, Round Table Conferences, 1930-2.

[11] For biographical note on Purshottam Trikamdas (popularly called P.T.) see *JPSW*, Vol. I, p. 88.

[12] Hakim Abdus Salam Khan; well-known freedom fighter of North-West Frontier Province; associated with the Indian National Congress; son of Khan Nur Muhammad Khan, a landlord and chief of Achakzai tribe of Gulistan; an associate of Khan Abdul Ghaffar Khan; President, District Congress Committee, Hazara, 1939-40; arrested for anti-war activities and detained at Deoli Detention Camp, 1940-1.

which he writes to his home, from this place reach his home after two or three weeks. The letters in question are censored here as well as by the C.I.D. Frontier. This complaint should be looked into. Comments against this process should be published in the Frontier papers.

There is another complaint. No paper from Frontier is given to him for reading. If you do not meet Khan Saheb at Wardha, then get a chit sent to him by Bapuji.

II

OLD REPORT FOR P.T.

A. Situation Here

(1) *Political*

This Detention Camp is mainly meant for Communists. Therefore, Communists are naturally in larger number here than others.

There are two camps here: Camp I and Camp II. In Camp I are Security prisoners of class I and in Camp II are those of class II.

In Camp I there are 104 prisoners—mostly from the U.P. Of these 66 are in the C.P. consolidation. Among the remaining 38 are 8 C.S.P., 11 R.S.P. (Anushilan),[13] 5 H.S.R.A.[14] (Hindustan Socialist Republican Association), and 14 unattached and miscellaneous, e.g. Royist, Tagorite, Labour Party Forward Bloc.[15]

Of the 66 of the C.P. consolidation, about 35 were members of the C.P. before they came here. The others joined the consolidation here (before my arrival). Among those who joined are B.P.L. Bedi,[16] Tilakraj Chadha,[17] Kulbir

[13] Revolutionary Socialist Party; founded in September 1938, arose out of the Anushilan Revolutionary group. It is generally considered the largest party among the non-Communist or rather non-Stalinist Marxist parties in India. Its prominent founders were the convicts of the famous Chittagong Armoury raid, detained in jail until 1938.

[14] Hindustan Socialist Republican Association. Bhagat Singh and his group were the active members of this organization. It had its militant wing, viz., Hindustan Republican Army. Sukh Dev, Rajguru and Chander Shekhar Azad were included in the militant group along with Bhagat Singh.

[15] Forward Bloc; it was an offshoot of the Congress. It was founded by Netaji Subhas Chandra Bose when he resigned in April 1939 from A.I.C.C. He organized this party to serve as a common platform for all the left elements inside the Congress.

[16] B.P.L. Bedi (1909-); prominent political leader of the C.S.P. in the Punjab; President, Punjab C.S.P., 1937; Joint Secretary, All India Kisan Sabha, 1938; member, National Executive of the C.S.P., 1938; joined Communist Party of India while in detention at Deoli Detention Camp, 1940-1.

[17] Tilak Raj Chaddha (1914-98); prominent Socialist leader of Punjab; joined Naujawan Bharat Sabha, 1934; attended Meerut Conference (1936) of the C.S.P. as an observer on

Singh[18] and Kultar Singh[19] (the last two are Bhagat Singh's[20] brothers, and all the four were in the C.S.P. before. Re. Punjab comrades in both camps see below).

Among the leaders of the C.P. who are here are Bharadwaj,[21] Ajoya,[22] Mirajkar,[23] Ahmad[24] (!), (in the other camp is Ghate[25]).

---

behalf of the Punjab Socialist Party; along with Munshi Ahmed Din and Mubarak Saghar negotiated with the C.S.P. leaders at Lucknow in 1936 which resulted in the Punjab Socialist Party becoming the Punjab unit of the All India Congress Socialist Party; appointed Lecturer in Economics, D.A.V. Degree College, Rawalpindi, 1937; arrested in connection with anti-war activities, 1941; went on hunger-strike along with several other detanees under J.P.'s leadership in Deoli Detention Camp to force the Government to accede to their demands; released, 1946; elected to the Punjab Legislative Assembly while in jail, 1946; Chief Editor, *Bande Mataram*, 1946-7; resigned from the Congress and Punjab Legislative Assembly, 1948; left politics, 1956; Principal, Mukundlal National College, Yamunanagar, Haryana, 1958-79.

[18] Kulbir Singh (1914-); younger brother of Bhagat Singh; revolutionary leader of Punjab; member, Naujawan Bharat Sabha; elected General Secretary, Punjab Kisan Sabha, 1936; sentenced to nine months' rigorous imprisonment for anti-war activities in 1939; released in 1940 but again arrested and detained at Deoli Detention Camp; later transferred to Lahore Central Jail, 1942.

[19] Kultar Singh (1918-); younger brother of Bhagat Singh; revolutionary leader of the Punjab; arrested in 1929; participated in the Civil Disobedience Movement, 1930; associated with Naujawan Bharat Sabha, and Hindustan Socialist Republican Army; joined the C.S.P., 1934; General Secretary, Lyalpur Kisan Sabha, 1937; arrested for anti-war activities in 1940 and detained at Deoli Detention Camp; joined the hunger-strike led by J.P.; released, 1946; associated with the Kisan Movement in the Punjab.

[20] Bhagat Singh (1907-31); well-known revolutionary; Founder-Secretary, Naujawan Bharat Sabha, Lahore, 1926; arrested in connection with Dussehra Bomb Outrage at Lahore, 1927; released, 1928; organized Lahore Students' Union, 1928; attended meeting of Hindustan Socialist Republican Association, Delhi, 1928; threw bombs along with B.K. Dutt in the Indian Legislative Assembly on 8 April 1929 and was arrested; sentenced to transportation for life, 12 June 1929; accused in the First Lahore Conspiracy case, sentenced to death, 7 October 1930; hanged on 23 March 1931.

[21] Refers to R.D. Bharadwaj. For biographical note see *JPSW*, Vol. II, p. 245.

[22] Ajoy Kumar Ghosh (1909-62); a prominent revolutionary; associate of Bhagat Singh and Chander Shekhar Azad; jailed in connection with the first Lahore Conspiracy Case, 1929; acquitted, 1930; arrested again in 1931, released, 1933; joined the Communist Party of India, 1933, elected member of its Central Committee 1934, and of its Politbureau, 1936; joined the Editorial Board of the *National Front*, 1938; detained in the Deoli Detention Camp, 1940-1; jailed, 1948-9; General Secretary, Communist Party of India, 1951-62.

[23] S.S. Mirajkar (1899-1980); prominent Communist leader; participated in the Non-Cooperation Movement, 1921; founder-member, C.P.I., 1925; edited, *Kranti*, 1927; Founder-member and Secretary, Workers' and Peasants' Party of India, 1927; organized, Girni Kamgar Union, and general strike of textile workers, 1928; arrested in connection with Meerut Conspiracy Case, 1929, and released, 1933; re-arrested, 1934; went underground for a year; re-arrested, 1936, and released, 1938; member, Bombay Corporation, 1938 and 1957-8; arrested, 1939; detained at Deoli Detention Camp along with J.P., 1940-1; President, A.I.T.U.C., 1957-73; Mayor of Bombay, 1958-9.

[24] Refers to Dr. Z.A. Ahmed. For biographical note see *JPSW*, Vol. II, p. 187.

[25] Refers to S.V. Ghate. For biographical note see *JPSW*, Vol. I, p. 112.

Among the C.S.P. members are Gautam,[26] Jetley[27] and myself. You would not know the others (All the Bihar comrades excepting myself are in Camp II).

Among the R.S.P. are Jogesh Babu,[28] Keshava Sharma[29] and others.

The H.S.R.A. group is nothing much to speak of. Not good material.

In Camp II there are over 90 prisoners. Of these about 72 are in the C.P. consolidation. About 6 or 7 are non-political. There are C.S.P. members (Jogendra Shukla, Suraj Narayan,[30] Shyamacharan Bharathuar[31]). The others are independents or belong to other groups (Forward Bloc, Congress, Babar-Akali, Akali, etc.). Just as Camp I is predominantly U.P., so Camp II is predominantly Punjab.

Now, about C.P. consolidation. There are two important factors in it. One is that the (Punjab) Kirti-Kisan (Sikh Communal) Party here has merged itself with the C.P. (All the Kirti leaders are here). This is not the first time that the Kirtis have joined with the C.P., and one cannot be sure that this unity will survive the Camp. However, at least at present, they are together.

The second factor is that our Punjab comrades have joined with them.

[26] Refers to Mohanlal Gautam. For biographical note see *JPSW*, Vol. I, p. 88.

[27] G.K. Jetley (1905-50); prominent surgeon and Kisan leader of U.P.; belonged to Faizabad; appointed Surgeon in Kashi Marwari Hospital, 1928; resigned and joined the Civil Disobedience Movement, 1931; Secretary, Medical and Sanitation Department of Bihar Central Relief Committee, 1934; detained at Deoli Detention Camp, 1940-1, and joined J.P. in the hunger-strike; detained during the Quit India Movement, 1942-5; elected to the U.P. Legislative Assembly, 1948.

[28] Jogesh Chandra Chatterji (1895-1969); revolutionary leader; arrested in connection with the Kakori Conspiracy Case, 1924, and sentenced to transportation for life, 1927; released, 1937; undertook hunger-strike in jail, 1934, 1935-6; arrested again, 1937; joined the C.S.P., 1938, but left it soon to found the Revolutionary Socialist Party of India, and functioned as its secretary, 1940-53; detained in Deoli Detention Camp, 1940-1; went underground during Quit India Movement, 1942; arrested, 1942; went on hunger-strike in jail, 1946; released, 1946; Vice-President, All India United Trades Union Congress, 1949-53, and United Socialist Organisation, 1949; President, All India United Kisan Sabha, 1953-5; joined the Congress, 1955; member, Rajya Sabha, 1956-60, 1960-6, and 1966-9.

[29] Keshav Prasad Sharma (1907-); revolutionary leader from U.P.; associated with Anushilan Samiti, 1927; Secretary, U.P. Kisan Sabha, 1938; founder-member, Revolutionary Socialist Party of India, 1940, and member of its Working Committee, 1948; detained at Deoli Detention Camp, 1940-1.

[30] For biographical note on Suraj Narayan Singh see *JPSW*, Vol. II, pp. 222-3.

[31] Shyama Charan Bharthuar (1900-); revolutionary leader of Bihar; associated with the C.S.P.; arrested in connection with Gaya conspiracy case; imprisoned in Andamans 1933-7; undertook hunger-strike, 1937; detained at Deoli Detention Camp, 1940-1.

Saghar,[32] Mangeram Vatsa,[33] Richpal Singh,[34] Thakur Govind Singh,[35] Ram Kishen[36] and three others (who are not known to you) are in Camp II. Saghar has played the leading role in this affair. Our friend Kishori[37] also did his bit by leading them to understand that at Hazaribagh I was also thinking along the same lines! (By the way, Kishori has also joined the consolidation. About him more later.)

It is a pity that I could not reach Deoli a couple of months earlier. However, there is nothing in this picture that I have drawn that need alarm or depress you. Since I came I have been discussing things with the Punjab comrades. Only one of them, Thakur Govind Singh, is irrevocably lost. All the rest agree that their decision is not at all final and that only after their release would they decide after consulting their All-India and Punjab friends. Tilakraj, Richpal, Vatsa (all very important members) are disgusted with the C.P. and have already decided that after going out they would advocate total separation from the C.P. and oppose those of their comrades who might advocate merging with it. Kulbir, Kultar and at least two other comrades of Camp II are practically of the same view. I forgot to state Bedi's position. He has been

[32] Mubarak Saghar (1905-); a poet and a prominent leader of the Punjab C.S.P.; adopted pet name 'Saghar' for his poetry; established contact with Naujawan Bharat Sabha and organized its branch at Karachi in 1929; elected member of National Executive of the C.S.P. at Faizpur, 1936; arrested for anti-war campaign in 1940 and detained at Deoli Detention Camp; joined the hunger-strike led by J.P.; President, Punjab Kisan Panchayat, 1946; migrated to Pakistan (1947).

[33] Mange Ram Vats (1905-85); prominent leader of the Punjab C.S.P.; worked in the police department for some time; resigned to participate in the freedom movement; joined Naujawan Bharat Sabha, 1928; associated with the Hindustan Socialist Republican Army; imprisoned for six months, 1930; joined, C.S.P., 1934; General Secretary, Punjab C.S.P., 1936; detained at Deoli Detention Camp, 1941, and joined the hunger-strike led by J.P.; released in 1944 and interned in his village Mandothi district Rohtak for a year.

[34] Rachhpal Singh (1910-); prominent leader of the Punjab C.S.P.; arrested in 1929 in connection with a bomb thrown on Chinab Club, Lyalpur; joined Naujawan Bharat Sabha and became General Secretary of its Lyalpur unit, 1930; participated in the salt satyagraha and imprisoned, 1930-1; member, Provincial Executive of the Punjab C.S.P., 1934-40, and Karan Singh Mann Enquiry Tribunal, 1936; declared absconder in June 1940; later arrested and detained at Deoli Detention Camp, 1941; joined the hunger-strike led by J.P.; released, 1944 and interned in Lyalpur till 1946.

[35] Thakur Gobind Singh (1907-79); Congress Socialist leader of Moga, Punjab; joined the C.S.P., 1936; detained at Deoli Detention Camp and joined the hunger-strike led by J.P.; shifted to Gujarat Special Jail, 1942; released, 1943; later settled in Shimla.

[36] Ram Kishan Bharolian (1921-76); revolutionary leader of the Punjab; member, Naujawan Bharat Sabha and the C.S.P.; imprisoned several times during the freedom movement for revolutionary activities; imprisoned at Montgomery Central Jail and Deoli Detention Camp for anti-war activities; joined the hunger-strike led by J.P.; shifted to Gujarat Special Jail, 1942; released, 1945.

[37] Kishori Prasann Singh.

much impressed with Dange[38] and Ranadive[39] (who were transferred to Ajmer before I arrived here) and has made close personal friendships with the communists. Politically, his position is something like that of Saghar's. But whereas Saghar is deep, he is shallow, and seems to lack convictions. Saghar himself, while not wishing to make any definite commitment, does not seem to be very keen on what he has done. In any case, the majority of the Punjab comrades are definitely for leaving the C.P. consolidation after release. We have discussed the advisability of breaking away here, but have decided against it, at least till Munshiji[40] comes here (we have been expecting him daily). Those Punjab comrades who are definitely with me are anxious not to create a split in their group here, as, they think, that would prejudice their cause outside. Anyway we are waiting for Munshiji.

Now, I do not want this news to get round among Party members in the Punjab or elsewhere. I have given you this information so that you may use it to good advantage with the utmost discretion. How you will do it, I do not know. But you must be very careful.

A word about Kishori. He has proved himself to be entirely lacking in self-confidence. He joined the consolidation before the Punjab comrades. His sole explanation to me was that he did not like to be isolated! He also has assured me that his decision is not final. But, I do not trust him. He tells me one thing and the others another. He carries on propaganda on such lines as J.P. is holding on to the C.S.P. and is keeping it going only for the sake of leadership! He has tried hard to persuade Shukulji to join the consolidation. But Shukulji has been firm like a rock. I have come to maintain the highest respect for his integrity and robust political sense. Comrades in Bihar should be informed of Kishori's betrayal. But here also care should be taken that breaking of the news does not do more harm than good.

[38] S.A. Dange (1889-1991); prominent Communist leader; founder-member, A.I.T.U.C. and Communist movement in India, 1920; Editor, *Socialist*, 1922-4; imprisoned several times; member, A.I.C.C. 1928, 1929, 1936, Bombay Legislative Assembly, 1946-51, and Lok Sabha, 1952-62, 1967-71; President, A.I.T.U.C., Nagpur session, 1943; Founder-Vice-President, World Federation of Trade Unions, 1945; Chairman, C.P.I., 1962-81; expelled from C.P.I., 1981; formed All India Communist Party and elected its General Secretary, 1981; one of the founders and Chairman, United Communist Party of India, 1989; publications include; *Gandhi versus Lenin*, *India from Primitive Communism to Slavery*, *Mahatma Gandhi and History*, *Gadgil and the Economics of Indian Democracy*, and *Origins of Trade Union Movement in India*.

[39] B.T. Ranadive (1904-90); prominent Communist leader; joined the Communist Party of India, 1928, and was member of its Central Committee, 1934-5, 1943-8, and Politbureau, 1943-8, and its General Secretary, 1948-50; jailed several times; elected to the Central Committee and Politbureau of the C.P.I.(M), 1964; President, Centre of Indian Trade Unions, 1970-90; Editor, *Marxist Miscellany*, 1982-9; publications include: *India's Economic Crisis and its Solution*, *The Two Programmes; Marxist & Revisionist*, *The Devaluation Surrender*, and *Caste, Class and Property Relation*.

[40] Refers to Munshi Ahmed Din. For biographical note see *JPSW*, Vol. II, p. 199.

Before leaving the C.P., I should mention that their attitude and behaviour both are extremely hostile and extremely childish. When I came here they received me very cordially and Ajoy Ghosh proposed to me that I should also join the C.P.! You can well imagine the talk that took place between him and me. However, the interesting point in the talk was Ajoy's statement there were no leftists and no socialists. Therefore 'left unity' or 'socialist unity' has lost all its meaning now. He said that their present slogan was 'mass C.P.'. (One thing I was forgetting. Among the C.P. fellows in our Camp most of them are young boys who do not count at all outside. In Camp II most are old Sikhs of the Kirti.)

Coming now to the R.S.P. Their attitude before I came here was not satisfactory. They were also trying to recruit and therefore they were criticising the C.S.P. Only Dr. Jetley stood his ground firmly (i.e. in Camp I). There are no R.S.P. in Camp II).

Since I came here, however, their attitude has changed. I proposed to them that we must consolidate here, as well as outside. You will remember that I had a talk on similar lines with Pratul Babu[41] when I was out. In this connection, I am anxious to impress upon you that I believe it to be absolutely necessary to bring the R.S.P. into our fold. There is every possibility of it. In Bengal we cannot make any progress without this. I am saying so notwithstanding our Bengal friends. By 'bringing into our fold' I mean the R.S.P. merging with the C.S.P. and disbanding their group. This is possible on the following basis—the C.S.P. to be the legal name of the party, and there to be an underground wing functioning under an illegal name. I am now convinced that if we have to successfully stand up against the communists, we must have an illegal organisation and illegal activities. I want to suggest that contact and friendliest relations should be maintained with the R.S.P. in Bengal.

From the H.S.R.A. also, I have got the better elements (two of them) completely with us.

As far as camp life is concerned and classes, etc., all the groups and individuals except the communists are with us.

In Camp II also some independents have joined us. I conduct a class in the playground every morning for them and the C.S.P. comrades there. (Here I should say that the people in the two camps were not allowed to associate with one another. But since a month ago association has been allowed in the common playground—between 6 and 7 a.m. and 6 and 7.30 p.m. daily.)

[41] Pratul Chandra Ganguly (1894-1957); prominent revolutionary leader of Bengal; active member, Anusilan Samiti; arrested in connection with Barisal Conspiracy case, 1913; acquitted; again arrested and released, 1922; reorganized Revolutionary Party in Bengal; came in contact with Subhas Chandra Bose and became his close associate; served various terms of imprisonment during 1924-46.

Pandit Dhanraj Sharma is very hostile to the communists and comes to my classes. He is friendly to us here, but has his grievances against Avadheshwar[42] and other friends. He is, however, unhappy about the split in the Bihar Kisan Sabha and agrees that after release we must see that unity is again restored.

(2) Concerning life in the Camp

Generally speaking there is nothing much to complain of here. We live in Barracks in which there are four or five big rooms (8 to 10 seated). There are also a few smaller rooms (double and four-seated). (I am at present in one of the ten seated rooms.)

When I came there was a tense situation here. There were preparations for hunger-strike. Our people (including the R.S.P., etc.) were unanimous in their interpretation that the C.P. fellows were thinking of the strike entirely in terms of Party propaganda. They were feeling that they must do something to bring themselves before the public's eye. Because of this our people were insisting that they would join the strike only if they gave an understanding that unless the minimum demands (which must be agreed upon before-hand) were fulfilled, the strike would not be called off. The C.P. fellows merely wanted a demonstration and were not keen about the demands except some minor ones (which have been already conceded now). Therefore they would not agree to bind themselves to any serious fight. When I came I advised that before serving an ultimatum (for strike) negotiations must be carried on with the authorities. As a result of negotiations the ration allowance of -/6/- daily of Camp II was raised to -/9/-, the privilege of association between Camps I and II, extra clothing for summer, ceiling *punkhas*, etc., were granted. This took the edge off the strike preparation. In the meanwhile instructions were received from the C.P. headquarters outside that hunger-strike should not be started till schools and colleges open and the Central Assembly meets. That is, till their A.I.S.F. (All India Students Federation) and Mr. N.M. Joshi have their platforms ready at hand to tom tom their great 'struggle'. Suddenly the strike fever went down.

In the meanwhile certain events, explained in a separate note prepared for the press,[43] forced us to go on hunger-strike. In this the communists did not join with us. They did intimate to the authorities that they too would resort to hunger-strike, but this was when we had already gone without food for a day. Their demands were also lower-pitched than ours, and they withdrew their ultimatum (without going on hunger-strike) before we broke our strike. In this way they betrayed us and deliberately tried to weaken us. However,

[42] Refers to Awadheshwar Prasad Sinha. For biographical note see *JPSW*, Vol. I, p. 142.

[43] Separate note for Press; see Appendix 13.

the next day, i.e. on the 5th day we broke our strike when our demands were conceded.

To the short story of the strike (which had already been sent yesterday) you should add the following. On the 4th day of the strike our representatives were called to the office by the Superintendent—to discuss our demands. (They were: Professor Mota Singh,[44] Gautam, Jetley, Jogesh Chatterji). When no settlement was reached, the four were taken to another camp (which is at present vacant) and segregated from us. This aroused great indignation. The next day they were sent back and the other demands were conceded.

If possible, I shall enclose herewith a copy of our ultimatum, as well as a copy of our reminder[45] to *Govt. of India* in connection with our memorandum[46] sent long ago.

B. Suggestions re. Party Policy

(1) Russo-German War

The suggestion made in a separate note is entirely mine. Other friends, including Jogesh Babu, agree. But I do not press it. I had a talk with Saghar this morning. He is afraid that the line I have suggested would create confusion in the public mind. He thinks the line of the Punjab C.S.P. as published in the Tribune is better—namely, that we sympathise fully with Russia, but are helpless to do any thing about it owing to the policy of the British Govt. My suggestion is more in the nature of a political stunt. However, I leave it to you and the Executive to settle the line. I think you should call another meeting of the Executive. It at least helps to keep the Party together.

In this connection we must at least express publicly our sympathy with Russia. Can't you send an ambulance corps on behalf of the C.S.P. to Russia.

(2) Central Organisation of the Party

It appears that since you returned from Patna you have kept no touch with the Party there, nor sent them any money. If this is the case with Bihar, which today is the most active unit of the Party, contacts with other provinces must be worse. This is very bad. The Centre should function properly and you *can* make it function so. I suggest that Ganga Babu be made a joint secretary of the Party and be made to stay in Bombay. (I suppose the other scheme about him will have to be given up in the changed situation.)

[44] Master Mota Singh (-1960) Akali leader; founder-member, Shiromani Gurudwara Prabhandhak Committee; associated with the Ghadar Party; declared 'proclaimed offender' by the Government; arrested in 1922 and sentenced to five years rigorous imprisonment; associated with the Kisan Sabha; arrested and detained at Deoli Detention Camp, 1941.

[45] See Appendix 18 for joint letter of J.P. and others (reminder to the Govt. of India).

[46] Not traceable.

Financing of the provincial branches is essential. You must manage this some how.

(3) Party Propaganda

The international situation and the shift in the position of the C.P. should be fully taken advantage of to push our propaganda forward. This is a very fine opportunity and must not be missed. All of you must give your fullest attention to this task.

(4) General Political Policy

I read news of your withdrawal of the satyagraha pledge. I liked it. But you must do something to bring out the Party's independent political line in contrast with this farce of satyagraha. I have begun to feel very strongly that we must do something spectacular at this moment. We cannot do anything big. But we must make a political investment at this moment. It does not matter if most of you are sent to prison. In this connection, I have been feeling about Bihar that instead of just holding Kisan conferences, the comrades should launch a Kisan struggle in a selected area or do something in the nature of 'action' as distinct from agitation.

Apart from Bihar, even on an all-India basis, we must do something to attract public notice and arouse enthusiasm among the youth. Do think of something.

An underground wing of the Party must be organised under a separate name—Revolutionary Worker's Party of India or anything else. The Punjab Party, as you know, is doing its illegal work under the name of the Communist League and is publishing an underground organ called the Bolshevic. An underground all-India organ is necessary to attract the youth if for nothing else.

C. Technical Matters

It is a pity that none of you has tried at all to establish contact with us here. This is not difficult if you attempt. Ganga Babu has already spent some time here. He should be sent here again to make arrangements. He may go to Ajmer and take the help of friends there to establish contact with local people in Deoli. Some money is necessary for this and a little organisation. If someone in Deoli village agrees to act as liaison, the thing will become simple. Tailors, dhobis, cobblers from the village come inside the Camp almost weekly. Then there are ward boys in Camp Hospital. All these are poor people (and some of them may even be sympathetic). A little persuasion and money may do the trick. The Communists have their regular contacts.

Till regular contact is developed I am suggesting the following method. I would want a reply to this note. Take a book of fiction, have its binding opened and your letter inserted inside the binding and have the book bound again. Send the book along with a couple of other books. Let not the other books be fiction, so that I would know which binding to open. I shall write to you in the same manner, if possible.

I have some serious suggestions to make, which I would do only when the contact becomes perfect.

In the meanwhile, I would anxiously await the arrival of the fiction.

D. Miscellaneous

(1) Re. Sardar Kulbir Singh (Brother of Sardar Bhagat Singh)

I have written about Kulbir above politically. He is with us in reality. At present he is very ill and is in the Camp Hospital. He is suffering from acute gastritis with haemorrhage. He vomits several times a day and throws up blood every time. He has grown very week. The local hospital is wholly inadequate for his treatment. The Civil Surgeon, Ajmer, also saw him some time ago, but his treatment is also not doing him any good.

News of his illness should be published in the press. Particularly in the Punjab press. Immediately after receiving this letter, news should be given to the press. The news should be so given that it is assured publication.

You should also write to Sardar Kishen Singh,[47] M.L.A., Bradlaugh Hall Lahore, giving him this news. Don't make the letter alarming, but give him the facts.

(2) Re. Shukulji

Jogendrabhai was rather bitterly speaking of the manner in which all of us have neglected his family. You *must* make arrangements for the education of his son—Chakradhar. It would mean not more than Rs. 10 per month.

[47] Sardar Kishan Singh (-1951); social worker and revolutionary leader of the Punjab; prominent worker of Arya Samaj; one of the founders of Bharat Mata Society; participated in the agrarian agitation in the Punjab, 1906-7; escaped to Nepal in 1907 but soon arrested and imprisoned, 1907-9; participated in the Non-Cooperation Movement, 1921, Civil Disobedience Movement 1931, and individual satyagraha, 1941; member Punjab Legislative Assembly, 1937-45.

(3) Re. Dhanraj Sharma

Dhanraj Sharma is suffering from fistula and operation is necessary. He has applied for transfer to the Patna General Hospital, so that his people might be present. The Civil Surgeon, Ajmer, has recommended his transfer. Sharmaji wants that there should be some press propaganda about it. He also wants that Mr. Yunus[48] should be informed about it and should be requested to do the needful. Ganga Babu should manage this. Sharmaji also wants Sir Ganesh Dutt Singh[49] to be informed of this.

(4) Re. Classification of Bihar Comrades

The Bihar comrades when they were in Hazaribagh were all placed in Class I. Here they have all been put in Class II. There should be some press propaganda in Bihar about this.

III

NEW REPORT FOR P.T.

The 'Old Report' was prepared when Prabhavati came here last time. It was sent out in two instalments for being delivered to her, but the fellow who had agreed to do it funked it at the last moment. He first gave us to understand that he delivered both the letters. We were very happy. But when in Prabhavati's letter there was no mention of the code I had suggested I grew suspicious. Then we got at the fellow who had deceived us. He finally brought both letters back intact. We are sure that he had not given them to the authorities.

There is not much to add to the Old Report. There is, however, one good news. Munshiji, has arrived. His attitude is perfect. He is attempting to get the Punjab comrades out of the consolidation. We cannot say for sure what will be the result. Some are sure to leave the C.P. here. Others may leave when they go out. I have consulted Munshiji about your telling the Punjab comrades this news. He says at present nothing absolutely should be known to them. *Therefore keep all this information absolutely to yourself.* Send books and things to Munshiji. Write to him also. You must also keep the

[48] Muhammad Yunus; prominent Muslim leader in Bihar; leading lawyer of Patna; member, Bihar and Orissa Legislative Council, 1921-6 and 1933-5, and Bihar Legislative Assembly, 1937-45; leader of the Muslim Independent Party in the Bihar Legislative Assembly.

[49] Sir Ganesh Dutta Singh (1868-1943); leading lawyer and prominent landlord of Patna; Secretary, Bihar Landholder's Association, 1917-19; gave up practice, 1922; Minister, Local Self-Government, Bihar and Orissa, 1923-37; member, Bihar Legislative Assembly, 1937-9.

closest possible contact with the Punjab comrades and take a special interest in them.

N.M. Joshi was here with the special permission of Government. He came to find out facts about the Camp. A written statement was given to him on behalf of the whole camp concerning the memorandum sent to Government. (By the way, Government have replied to our memorandum rejecting all our demands except those already granted. See our reminder for the facts.) Those of us who were on hunger-strike gave Mr. Joshi a supplementary statement[50] concerning the strike. A copy is enclosed herewith for your information. There should be some publicity of the facts given.

IMPORTANT

I am enclosing one note to Sardar Sardul Singh Caveeshar[51] from Professor Mota Singh and three notes[52] from Munshiji to Comrades Mangaldas,[53] Nisar Ahmad and others. These notes should be sent to their destination with a messenger. Professor Sahib has written to Sardar Sardul Singh about the relations between the Forward Bloc and the C.S.P. Professor Saheb is a very leading figure among the nationalist Sikhs and he was a member of the Forward Bloc outside. Here he is very sympathetic to us. His letter must reach Caveeshar. Munshiji's letters are also valuable.

In this connection I have a suggestion to make. The C.P. attacks both the Forward Bloc and the C.S.P. Yet the C.S.P. and the F.B. don't join hands together. We let the C.P. exploit the C.S.P. against us. Why should we have allowed Mrs. Ranga[54] to join hands with the communists? Why can't you people get in touch with Caveeshar, Kamath[55] and others who may be well-disposed towards us and persuade them to join hands with them. The Bihar *Golmal*[56] (split in Bihar Kisan Sabha) should not be allowed to spread

[50] See Appendix 14 for joint letter by J.P. and others, copy of which was given to N.M. Joshi.

[51] For biographical note on Sardul Singh Caveeshar see *JPSW*, Vol. I, p. 159.

[52] See Appendix 16 for Mota Singh letter to S.S. Caveeshar. See Appendix 17 for Letter from Munshi Ahmed Din to Nisar Ahmed (three notes).

[53] For biographical note on Mangal Dass see *JPSW*, Vol. II, p. 263.

[54] Bharati Devi nee Velugu; daughter of Velaga Subbayya, well-known Kisan of Machavaran; married N.G. Ranga in 1924; worked for the uplift of the Kisans and encouraged women to participate in the Kisan Movement.

[55] H.V. Kamath (1907-82); entered I.C.S., 1930; resigned and joined the Congress, 1938; joined Forward Bloc, 1939, and was its General Secretary for some time; jailed for anti-war activities, 1940-5; member, Constituent Assembly, 1946-50, Provisional Parliament, 1950-2, Lok Sabha, 1955-7, 1962-7, and 1977-9, National Executive of P.S.P., 1956-70, and National Committee of Socialist Party, 1971-7; detained during the emergency, 1976-7; publications include: *Communist China Colonizes Tibet, Invades India*, *Principles and Techniques of Administration*, and *The Last Days of Jawaharlal Nehru*.

[56] The Bihar Golmal, refers to split in Bihar Kisan Sabha.

throughout the country. I suggest that you go to Lahore and see Caveeshar as well as others who may be helpful. My talks with Subhas Babu when I was out should be fully utilised for this purpose. The Anushilan or the R.S.P. should also be asked to help us in this matter. I think, if properly tackled, they would be very helpful. They have influence with the F.B.

The Bihar Kisan Sabha split was bad enough; the All India split makes me very anxious. Do let me know what the position is. Please send a full report.

I understand you had been to Wardha. I am anxious to know what talks you had there. What are the general political prospects?

What about the War? What course is it expected to take.

Tell Caveesharji or send him word that he should reply to Professor Sahib in the same manner as I have suggested to you. Let it be an old book on Sikhism.

VERY IMPORTANT

Before replying please read my letter carefully and make notes of the points which need replying. Then please prepare your report.

IV

TO GANGA SARAN SINGH (OLD REPORT)

TRANSLATION OF HINDI LETTER FROM JAYAPRAKASH NARAYAN TO GANGA SARAN SINGH OF BIHAR

Dear Ganga Babu,

You should try to take permission to see me.

The other programme will perhaps be useless at this juncture. Therefore you will have to work in all India concern. Central work is not efficient.

You all should pay great heed to the matter I have mentioned in this letter.

Basawan should work in Bihar Underground and he should do our work—recruitment for underground party and underground publicity. You are responsible for the financial help.

Whatever the method I mentioned in my letter, you should also follow the same and send your own letter with Purushottam's letter in the same book.

You must have a knowledge of many things of this place. You should try your level best to have regular contact from inside the Camp.

I take leave from you as I am tired of writing letters.

Please inform me about receiving both the envelops.

Prabha should mention in her weekly letter the following line—'All are well in the house of Babuni both at Murar and Daltonganj'.

There is no Marxist book here. Please send one copy of each from the books of Marx, Engels,[57] Lenin. Those books may be found in Bombay after due search. These books are necessary for the Class work here. You will have to smuggle some books here which are not allowed here—Keep this also in your mind. I sent a letter yesterday, you must have received it by now.

V

To,
The Home Secretary,
Government of India,
Simla [after 29 may 1941]
Through The Superintendent, Deoli Detention Camp, Deoli.

Sir,
I desire to draw your attention to a memorandum[58] that I submitted, along with my other Comrades here, to the Government of India in March 1941. Though a quarter of a year has elapsed since the Government have not found it possible or urgent, except for a few trifling things, to do anything about the grievances and demands that had been set forth in the memorandum. The only items out of fourteen that the memorandum contained, about which anything has been done, are: clothes, shoes, convict workers, and association with our friends in the B Camp. Even with regard to these the situation is not altogether satisfactory. While the number of convict hands has been increased, that number is still inadequate, and our demands for barrack attendants still remains unfulfilled. As for clothes, there is unnecessary delay in giving us the clothing that has already been sanctioned. Finally we are able to meet our Comrades of the II Camp only for fixed hours and that also in the playground. We are not allowed to go to each other.

The other eleven items among which are included all our vital and important demands, remain entirely unsatisfied. Even such an urgent matter as conditions in the Camp Hospital has remained largely unattended too. We have made repeated representations in this behalf to the Camp authorities but hardly to any purpose. It is reasonable to assume that Government have been kept informed of all these representations. If so, Government must

[57] Friedrich Engels (1820-95); German philosopher; lifelong friend of Karl Marx with whom he collaborated to bring out *Manifesto of the Communist Party* (1848); edited and translated Marx's writings; own works include: *Landmarks of Scientific Socialism*, *The Origin of the Family, Private Property and the State*, and *The Condition of the Working Class in England*.

[58] See Appendix 11 for joint letter by J.P. and others to Superintendant Deoli Detention Camp, 29 May 1941.

know that we have lost all confidence in the present Medical Officer[59] and have been pressing insistently for his transfer. But, though for the last two months we have been given plenty of promises, nothing has already been done in this most urgent matter. Nothing, therefore, exemplified better the indifference and callousness of the Government and Camp authority alike to our life and suffering here than this painful affair.

To take another rather simple question; the question of censorship of books and other literature. The British Government lose no opportunity to impress upon world opinion the fact that they are fighting for freedom and democracy. Yet, the Government of India, which is only an agent of the much advertised British Democracy, finds it necessary to deny us the freedom of reading even such a scientific work as Karl Marx's *Capital*. Such obscuranticism can be rivalled only in the banning of Darwin's[60] *Origin of Species* by Dr. Geobbals[61] in Nazi Germany. It must be known even to the Government of India that *Capital* does not preach the overthrow of the British Government. It is merely a scientific critique of capitalist economy, which has even in England today a few defenders. Another simple question that I had raised in the memorandum was concerning our daily food allowance. I had pointed out that the allowance of -/12/- was, particularly in view of the prices obtaining here, too inadequate for any decent standard of living. I had also pointed out that in 1932, when prices were substantially lower, detenus in this very Camp were allowed a much higher allowance.

Coming now to the vital demands that I had put forth before Government. To imprison us without trial is fascistic enough. To create invidious distinction among us by introducing the hateful principle of classification; to put our dependents and families to trouble and suffering by not providing for an allowance for their maintenance; to remove us from the provinces of our birth and residence, and thus to cut us off more severely [from them] then to deny us without cause the opportunity of earning our livelihood and yet not to provide us with a personal [allowance] so that we may fulfil our everyday needs. All these and many other disabilities mentioned in my memorandum are cruel, unjust and oppressive in the extreme. A person whose offence has been established in a Court of law, even though the law may not be expression of people's will, is expected to be prepared for a certain amount of suffering. In our case, who have been thrown into prison without cause, Government have, if they are at all guided by the principles of civilized administration,

[59] See Appendix 12 for joint letter by Mohanlal Gautam and J.P. to Civil Surgeon, Ajmer, 30 May 1941.

[60] For biographical note on Charles Darwin see *JPSW*, Vol. I, p. 137. His work *Origin of Species* was published in November 1859.

[61] Paul Joseph Goebbels (1897-45); German Nazi leader and politician; became Hitler's Minister of Propaganda in 1933 and continued till the end of the Nazi regime in Germany.

certain obligations and responsibilities. In our opinion, the least that Government can do is to discharge these responsibilities to grant the very reasonable and moderate demands that I and my other friends have set forth in their memorandum.

Finally, I desire to impress upon Government, particularly in view of the fact that already there have been so much delay, the necessity of expediting their decision on our memorandum.

I remain,

Yours faithfully,
J.P.

VI

REGARDING OUR POLICY CONCERNING THE WAR (OLD REPORT)

The invasion of Russia by Nazi Germany has introduced a very complicating factor into the present war. Now, both Britain and Russia will be fighting against Germany, their common enemy. Does this mean that our attitude towards this war should be changed? Let us examine this question a little closely.

Till the invasion of Russia, we had looked upon the war as an imperialist war. Among other things, we knew that Britain was fighting in order that it might continue to rule over and exploit India. Clearly, it was none of our duty to help in any manner in the perpetuation of our slavery. We were, therefore, opposed to the war and were endeavouring to utilise it to attain our own freedom.

The recent action of Germany against Russia has in no way modified this position. The interests of Britain in fighting this war are still the same imperialist interests. If Russia and Britain are facing a common enemy it does not mean that their interests are the same. Britain cannot in the very nature of things cooperate with Russia in prosecuting the war to identical ends. It cannot be foretold when Britain, in order to protect its interests, would retire from the fight, leaving Russia alone to continue it. It is quite likely that Russia, in order to gain time and save what it can, agrees to settle with Germany. In any case, if Russia desires to destroy Nazism, it must in the end depend upon its own resources and strength.

It should follow from the foregoing that to help Britain in the war is not the same as to help Russia. Help to Britain would only strengthen British imperialism, which would doubtless use this strength to further its own interests. In fact, this added strength might become a factor in enabling

Britain in reaching an independent settlement with Germany, and betraying Russia.

Therefore, the invasion of Russia cannot, in the least, affect our attitude towards Britain's war. Our opposition to it must continue, and likewise also our strength against British Imperialism.

The danger which Russia faces, however, is a question which as socialists it is our duty to seriously consider. With all its faults Soviet Russia is a giant fortress of world socialism and of the world proletariat. We cannot sit quiet when this fortress is under assault. But we shall not bring succour to it if we rushed to the aid of British imperialist forces. On the contrary, it would be a mistake to relax our attack on imperialism. To continue this attack as relentlessly as possible would itself be a service to Soviet Russia. But, the question remains, can we do anything to render direct aid to the Soviets, without helping in any manner British war efforts. The British Government have already announced that they are united with Russia in their common aim of destroying Hitlerism, and have offered all help to the Soviets. This opens up an opportunity for us to offer direct help to Russia, and, also incidentally, of putting British professions to test. Let us, accordingly, put it to the British Government that we are anxious to help Russia with men, money and materials, and that we desire to be given the opportunity to organise this help. We should further put it to them that if they are sincere about aid to Russia, our offer gives them an excellent opportunity to vindicate it. In making our offer, it should be made clear to them that our opposition to their own war would continue unabated, as would our struggle against their domination over India. The men that we would recruit and the resources that we would collect must be sent directly to the Russian front, to be used and commanded by the Russian forces.

If the British Government were to reject this offer, they would further expose their selfish imperial interests in this war and their insincerity towards Russia. This would help workers in Britain and the U.S.A., and other countries to determine their attitude towards the present British Government, and exert pressure on it to adjust its war policies to the interests of the people of Britain and other peoples threatened by Nazism.

VII

NEW REPORT, NOTE

The above was written when Prabhavati came here last time. Since then the situation outside has become clarified. Purushottam's statement was on correct lines, though a difference should have been drawn between the Anglo-German war and the Russo-German war. As far as Britain is concerned, the character of the war has not changed; but Russia is not fighting an imperialist war (That is why sympathy with Russia was expressed in your statement.)

I suggest strongly that you should call a meeting of the Executive which should issue a statement on the war. The only purpose in this would be to associate all the provincial parties with the statement. It appears that we are not following the same policy everywhere.

I do not think that it is advisable now to talk of sending volunteers, etc., to Russia. At least, we should not appeal to the British Government in that behalf.

Our attitude should be that we sympathise fully with Russia but are helpless to do anything about it. At the same time our opposition to Britain's war and our national struggle continues and all our class movements.

I have written above somewhere that the present is a good time to carry on an ideological war against the C.P.I. and the C.I. I suggest that two small pamphlets should immediately be brought out, entitled the C.P.I and the War and the C.I. and the War in which the twists and turns of communist policy should be fully exposed. The C.P.I. pamphlet should not be restricted to C.P.I. policy regarding the war, but should also deal with their general political policy in India. Both should be effectively written. All the past documents of the C.P.I. and the C.I. should be collected for this purpose. [I understand there was a special issue of the Communist, 4th issue (1940) most probably, which published the C.I.'s policies regarding war. It was a special International issue. This might be of some use. Molotov's[62] and Stalin's speeches also may be of use.]

We are anxious to know what the policy of the C.P.I. today is. The fellows here continue to talk of intensifying the national struggle, though at the same time they maintain that the character of the war now is anti-Fascist! From your statement it appeared that the C.P.G.B. had changed its policy and the C.P.I., if there is one, [is deliberating] on their new war policy. Send us other news about them. It would help us in our work here.

What about the Cawnpore strike? Was it our show? What has been its result? Good or bad for us?

Send us all such material that may help me in recruitment here. Send illegal matter in the manner I have suggested. Send a copy of 'Betrayal of the Left'.[63]

[62] Vyacheslav Mikhailovich Molotov, original name Skriabin (1890-1980); Soviet statesman and diplomat; participated in the rising of 1905; Editor, *Pravda*, 1912-17; Foreign Minister, 1939-49; and 1953-6; negotiated Molotov-Ribbentrop Pact, 1939; Minister of State Control, 1956-7; dismissed from the Presidium of Central Committee, 1957; Ambassador to Mangolia, 1957-60; Soviet representative to International Atomic Energy Agency at Vienna, 1960-1; expelled from party, 1962, reinstated, 1977.

[63] Victor Gollancz, *Betrayal of the Left*, London, 1941.

33. To Mahatma Gandhi, 28 October 1941[1]

Deoli Detention Camp
Deoli, Rajputana
28 October 1941

Dear Bapuji,
Loving salutations! Many thanks for your kind letter.[2] I have seen the letters[3] published by the Government but just now I do not want to say anything. I would be ale to talk about them only after my release. At present, we are faced with a different problem.

I have seen one of the statements[4] you have issued regarding those letters. It gave me much satisfaction; it only proves your greatness.

I was surprised as well as pained to know about Prabhavati. Our relationship was never based on harmony of thoughts, then why should she be so disturbed over my ideas? You may kindly make her understand.

You are, perhaps, aware of the situation here. It is useless for me to write anything about it, as the authorities would censor it.

Yours,
Jayaprakash

[1] *JP Papers* (NMML). Original in Hindi.
[2] Not available.
[3] Refers to letters in *Deoli Papers*.
[4] See Appendix 19 for Gandhi's statement.

34. To Mahatma Gandhi, 1 November 1941[1]

Deoli Detention Camp
Deoli, Rajputana
1 November 1941

Dear Bapuji,
Loving Pranam,
I hope you must have received my first letter.[2] The situation here is becoming

[1] Home Political Department, File No. 43/65/41 (NAI). Translation of J.P.'s letter to Gandhi in Hindi was sent to the Commissioner of Ajmer-Merware and a copy was also forwarded to the Deputy Secretary to the Government of India, Home Department by R.F. Craster, Superintendent of Deoli Detention Camp on 2 November 1941.

[2] Refers to J.P.'s letter to Gandhi dated 28 October 1941. See item no. 33.

very grave. Maxwell's[3] stubborn attitude shows the Government view. Under such grave conditions I request you to do one thing, that you should send Rajendra Babu or Pantji.[4] I would prefer Rajendra Babu. They should seek permission of the Government of India for an interview with me. The interview should be without interception of the Camp authorities. After understanding the situation of this place and also statement of Maxwell[5] in the light of our demand Rajendra Babu should go to Delhi and try to bring about the settlement.

If his efforts fail then we are determined to die.

I am rather interested in this matter simply because the Government is making a wrong use by publication of the recent letters and that enhances our responsibility.

I hope you will be well.

Today is our eleventh day. I am o.k.

Yours,
Jayaprakash

[3] Reginald Maxwell (1882-1967); entered Civil Service, 1906; Secretary to Government of India, Home Department, 1936; Home Member, Viceroy's Executive Council, 1938-44; Adviser to the Secretary of State for India, 1944-7.

[4] Refers to G.B. Pant. For biographical note see *JPSW*, Vol. II, pp. 243-4.

[5] In his statement to the Indian Legislative Assembly on 29 October 1941 regarding the hunger-strike by detenus in the Deoli Detention Camp, the Home Member, Reginald Maxwell stated that they were not being ill-treated, their demand for repatriation to their home provinces was not a demand for which 'any prisoner is entitled to go on hunger-strike' and their demand for uniform classification had no justification.

35. To Mahatma Gandhi [before 14 November 1941][1]

Thanks for the telegram.[2] Have explained the whole position to Sardar Mangal Singh.[3] Our demands are reasonable. Please excuse inability to discontinue the hunger-strike. May do what you can outside. Do not send Prabhavati.

[1] *Hindu*, 16 November 1941.

[2] For Gandhi's telegram dated 12 November 1941 in which he had asked J.P. and his fellow prisoners to end the hunger-strike, see Appendix 21.

[3] Sardar Mangal Singh (1892-1987); prominent Congress leader; jailed several times during the freedom struggle; took up the cause of Gurdwara Reform Movement; member, Congress Working Committee, 1923, 1925 and 1930; President, Central Sikh League and Shiromani Gurdwara Prabandhak Committee, 1926; member, Indian Legislative Assembly, 1934-46; fought against communal forces among Akalis during the 1950s and 1960s.

36. To Mahatma Gandhi, 18 November 1941[1]

Much pained at telegram[2] afraid you have not understood situation correctly repatriation not our only demand cannot fight afresh for remaining after repatriation therefore asking for two small assurances first provincial governments shall consider sympathetically demands already before India government second pending decision at least Deoli standard shall be applied never insisted on literal application Deoli standard in Punjab detenus are given C class treatment fail to understand how our position unreasonable both Joshi Mangal Singh considered it reasonable if you send someone shall convince him completely.

Jayaprakash

[1] Home Political Department, File No. 43/65/41 (NAI).

[2] Refers to Gandhi's telegram dated 17 November 1941 in which he had requested J.P. and his fellow prisoners to end the hunger-strike. For text of the telegram see Appendix 22.

37. To Jawaharlal Nehru, 7 December 1941[1]

Deoli Detention Camp
Deoli, Rajputana
7 December 1941

My dear Bhai,
Warmest greetings to you . . .[2]

I cannot but feel extremely happy at your being out when the country needs your guidance most. . . .[3]

You must have learnt about Narendradeva's health. One of his greatest failings is that he cannot take care of himself. And I am afraid he will become a permanent invalid unless he is properly looked after. What he needs most is not medicines but a long rest in a suitable place. No place in the U.P. or anywhere in the North will suit him. Some districts of Maharashtra, such as Satara, or places further South—Bellary, Anantpur—might be good for him. Even Gujarat might suit him. Left to himself, I am certain, he would vegetate somewhere in the U.P., or at the best Sri Prakasa[4] might take him to Benares

[1] *Jawaharlal Nehru Papers* (NMML).

[2] Two lines blacked out by the censor.

[3] Five to six lines blacked out by the censor.

[4] For biographical note on Sri Prakasa see *JPSW*, Vol. I, p. 61.

to his Sevashram. What we call *sankoch* will prevent him from asking any of his innumerable friends to do anything for him. I am therefore writing to you to take a particular interest in this matter and to pack him off to some suitable place. You must not leave this thing to his option. In this matter you must treat him as one treats a child. You may consult Bapu also in this connection as he has been taking a keen interest in Narendradeva's health.

I am well now and am slowly regaining my strength. Sethji[5] too is well and sends you his greetings. Gautam is down with malaria and is in the hospital. Other friends are well.

With Love,

Yours,
Jayaprakash

[5] Damodar Swarup Seth (1896-1960); prominent Congressman of U.P.; imprisoned in connection with Banaras and Kakori Conspiracy cases, 1915-20, 1925-8; General Secretary, Bareilly D.C.C., 1920, U.P.P.C.C., 1936, and later its President, 1946; imprisoned several times during the freedom struggle; member, National Executive of C.S.P., 1938; member, Constituent Assembly, 1946-50, and Provisional Parliament, 1950-2.

38. To Yusuf Meherally, 17 December 1941[1]

Deoli Detention Camp
Deoli, Rajputana
17 December 1941

Dear Yusuf,
It was the best news in months to hear of your release.[2] You are out at a very opportune moment; your guidance and leadership would be invaluable to friends outside.[3]

How is your health? I hope you have put on some weight. I hope Asoka too has grown stronger.

We are fairly well here, though none of us has gained his normal weight yet. As you know already, we are soon going to be repatriated to our provinces. I do not know if I would be sent to Bombay, the U.P. or Bihar. However, I expect to know very soon.

As soon as I am transferred from here I should like to see you if the Government permit you an interview. At present you have to apply to the District Magistrate, Allahabad, for interviews.

[1] *Yusuf Meherally Papers* (NMML).
[2] Yusuf Meherally was released on 4 December 1941.
[3] Two paragraphs deleted by the censor.

Please give my love to Minoo,[4] Asoka,[5] Purshottam,[6] Lilubhai[7] and other friends.

With love,

Yours,
Jayaprakash

[4] For biographical note on M.R. Masani see *JPSW*, Vol. I, p. 66.
[5] For biographical note on Asoka Mehta see *JPSW*, Vol. I, p. 122.
[6] For biographical note on Purushottam Thakurdas see *JPSW*, Vol. I, p. 49.
[7] For biographical note on Lilubhai (K.D. Merchant) see *JPSW*, Vol. I, p. 123.

39. To M.R. Masani, 4 January 1942[1]

Deoli Detention Camp
Deoli, Rajputana
4 January 1942

Dear Minoo,
It is nearly six months now that I received your refreshing letter. Since then one thing or another prevented me from writing to you.

I am afraid I completely wasted my time here and engaged myself in what you would call the little questions of the present. The books that you had sent to help in a 'little intellectual spring-cleaning' were returned at your request. Later I received one of them: Koestler's *Darkness at Noon*. I greatly enjoyed the book and found it most revealing and stimulating. It is just as well that you did not send back Drucker's book, because I had read it at Hazaribagh—a Patna friend had sent it.

You have not satisfied me. I did not say that the utility to the Socialist movement of one who believed in the 'new dynamic' was reduced to vanishing point. What I said was that one who went about preaching from every platform that Gandhiji's was the only way had a vanishing utility for the Socialist Movement. I cannot say if in your case the two things are the same. It is likely that you have accepted the new dynamic in toto—along with the lumber of trusteeship and divinity and the rejection of the class struggle. You would perhaps be interested in the following statement of Gandhiji's: 'God is the force among all forces known and unknown. Non-violence without reliance upon that Force is poor stuff to be thrown in the dust.' (*Harijan* 28 June 1940, p. 201.)

[1] *M.R. Masani Papers* (NAI).

As for the new dynamic, I have respect for it, and believe that it has invented a useful form of mass action which should be (as it has been to an extent) adopted in Socialist practice. But, as regards its theory I reject it as utterly unscientific and built up of hocus-pocus. That the man who uses it exercises great influence need not surprise us when we turn to other great men in history who have done likewise. Indeed till the rise of Marxism and outside of the practice inspired by it, men have been impelled not by scientific understanding, but by the blind (in the sense of uncomprehended) laws of their existence.

Returning to the new dynamic, I cannot have much respect for its underlying theory—which to me is the only thing that matters—when I see that two and a half years of war and the Cripps episode were necessary to bring Gandhiji where he should have been from the beginning—I refer to his attitude towards the war, the communal problem, the question of anarchy, etc. There is a chorus of approval from every side today of Gandhiji's present policy. But what even our socialist friends have failed to tell the people is that what Gandhiji is saying today is what the socialists had been saying all along. When Mahadeo Desai expresses surprise that the authors[2] of *The Communal Triangle* [1942] should have hit upon the same solution of the communal problem and the Indo–British problem as Gandhiji before even the Cripps mission was mooted, he merely expresses surprise at the superiority of Marxian sociology to that of Gandhism. No one has a right to be disillusioned with Socialism or Communism because of disillusionment with the Stalin regime. It would be the same thing as being disillusioned with Gandhism after the Congress ministries. I have no doubt that if the Gandhian State came into being, the Stalins of Gandhism inspite of their best intentions would make of it no better mess than Lenin's successor has done with the Soviet State. But no one on that account should have the right to be disillusioned with Gandhism itself. I am also not forgetting the fact that the very failure of the Stalin regime is adequately explained only by Marxist theory.

However, it is not my intention to argue with you. It is clear to me that when a person of your perspicacity and intellectual integrity has arrived at a conclusion, it would be beyond my capacity to influence his thought. I, therefore, accept your statement that there is no return for you to the old faith—whether of the orthodox or the protestant denomination. And it seems futile to dwell on the pang that that statement has caused some people.

But may I say that you have paid too careful an attention to my words rather than to the spirit which filled them. You will remember that I had said

[2] The reference here is to Asoka Mehta and Achyut Patwardhan, both prominent leaders of the Congress Socialist Party.

I did not want you to come back only in the interest of our party but also in the interest of the larger political movement. It is true I had never conceived of you as ever leaving the socialist movement so completely. But even I am not so vain as to believe that outside of the socialist movement there is no political life whatever, and I had conceived of you, when I sent you my fervent prayer, as playing a noticeable and an effective part in the larger politics of the land. Your faith in the new dynamic should itself compel you to throw yourself into the boiling cauldron of Sevagram. I believe the greatest moment of Gandhiji's life is approaching and the new dynamic is to rise to unprecedented heights. What better opportunity could their be for you to take the plunge? I am not giving up hope about your socialism, but we shall see about that later. I shall no doubt earnestly pray that the new dynamic should solve the social problem. Perhaps its younger devotees may find the way out. Be that as it may, it is what we do in the present that matters. For the rest, I do not think socialism is so unmindful of the question of means and ends as you seem to think. But the whole question of Socialist action depends upon understanding of the dynamics of Society, which is as different from Gandhian understanding as Chalk is from Cheese. But, as I have said, I do not wish to argue.

I shall conclude by saying that my prayer to you has lost none of its force—rather it has been strengthened—by what you have said and by your confession of faith.

This is to make a fervent and prayerful request. Will you not reconsider your decision? Can you conceive of a better opportunity to serve the people? You will say you are doing your bit. I agree. But, you can do much more than bits. There, you should agree.

I am not thinking of the Party alone in making this request. The Party of course needs you badly. Your clarity, your drive and your capacity for organisation would revolutionise the Party—would make it alive and vigorous. This is the finest possible opportunity for organising and developing the Party, for making headway among the masses, in the Congress and among the students. What is needed most is not policy—policy we have—but initiative and action. Here we entirely fizzle away as the backwoods of the Congress.

But I am digressing. In requesting you to come back, I have in mind also the larger politics of the country and even to an extent international politics. You were always the Party's link with Europe, particularly with Great Britain. This link should be forged anew. The voice of Indian Socialism should be heard abroad. Who else can make it heard but you.

I do not know your present views regarding non-violence. I do not think that those who believe in it like Lohia have no place in the Party but I think it is very wrong to pose the social question as violence vs. non-violence. To do that is contrary to Marxism and [is] unscientific sociology. I am writing this because the evolution of your thought in the direction of non-violence had worried me. If a Socialist went about teaching non-violence from platform and emphasising Gandhiji's way as the only way out, his utility to the Socialist movement would approach the vanishing point. I am myself not a blood-thirsty monster. But I regard the issue of violence & non-violence as a side issue. And I do this inspite of the murders in Russia or the colossal murders now going on. These murders would no more check the evolution of Socialism than the murders of the Thermidor[3] or the Napoleonic wars checked the evolution of Capitalism or the murders of the Inquisition checked Protestantism. Even the progress of Nazism paves the way to Socialism—paradoxical though it may appear. The only issue today on the stage of history is Capital vs. Labour. Whether the issue is decided violently or non-violently, if labour (conceived in its widest social significance) wins, a better world, a more peaceful and a more civilized world would be born. This is not determinism. I am basing my optimism and view of the future on an estimation of the conscious efforts of men, being made now and to be made in the future. The estimation further assures me of the eventual victory of labour.

The whole Party is ready to welcome you. Recent events have created deep faith in your political judgement and insight and comrades would receive you with open arms.

I have never known much about your personal affairs. I know there were certain difficulties, but I also knew that they were not the real reasons why you left active politics. I believe I would not be making a mistake in thinking that they would not be the real obstacles to your coming back. But there are no 'real' obstacles left. The road is clear for you.

Most of the reactions to the Russian tragedy have not impressed me. As I wrote before they lose themselves in the sands of Liberalism and Utopianism. I like however such a reaction as Lucien Laurat's *Marxism and Democracy*. It is constructive and it holds fast to Marxian moorings. The book is valuable—the only one of its kind in English. I doubt if there is any English knowing Socialist who is so deeply read in Marxism—not as propounded by a Church, but as it is: a living, developing social science and methodology. My enthusiasm for the book does not mean that I agree with all that it says. There are several questions which I should like to pursue further. Moreover, neither is Indian Capitalism well developed, nor is the working class mature.

[3] Thermidor—The name given during French Revolution to the eleventh month of the year in the Republican Calendar. The month fell in the hottest season of the year beginning July 19 or 20 and ending on August 18 or 19 according to the year. In 1794 Thermidor had witnessed the overthrow of Robespierre, bringing the revolution's radical period to a close, without reversing its basic concepts.

In that case Leninism in some form is inevitable for us. By the way, it appears from Laurat's exposition that there is a lot of similarity between Lenin's principles of organisation and yours.

I am digressing again. Let me return to my main purpose and repeat my request. Do come back. Apart from doing justice to yourself, you would render inestimable service. I am not discounting the possibility of your soon landing in prison. That might appear fruitless. But even that would be service—more valuable, more effective than what you are rendering by your present activities. May you rise to the occasion.

40. To M.R. Masani, 26 March 1942[1]

Hazaribagh Central Jail
26 March 1942

Dear Minoo,

I had been thinking of writing to you for sometime, chiefly to thank you for the periodicals you have been sending and to complain that you had not yet replied to my letter from Deoli. Could that letter have offended you, I often asked myself and the reply was not often in the negative. In the meanwhile there was a registered letter from the Stock Exchange P.O. and I knew your long expected letter had arrived. Later I was officially informed that a letter from you had been received which had been withheld. You can imagine how utterly exasperating it was for me. For the folly, the fascistic mentality of Indian officialdom, there could not be a better example. I cannot imagine that you, an old jail bird, could have written anything that was subversive and really objectionable, but the Government seems to behave like a nervous child which is frightened of shadows and the sound of fluttering curtains and the wind sighing in the canes. It is either that, or the fascist zeal of the bureaucracy to crush all freedom and all thought. I believe the restrictions on the mind in a German concentration camp could not be severer.

It would have been interesting to know what you had to say about my orthodox faith, though I doubt if the word orthodox describes it suitably. You know, I do not owe allegiance to the established Church, and in that regard I am a protestant, but yet my faith in the original doctrines of the founders remains unshaken, and I do not see any alternative. Much of the disillusioned thought of the present period merely dries itself up in the sands of liberalism. Lohia seems to think that an alternative exists in Gandhiji, but I do not find myself in agreement with him, not because I am not impressed with his sublimity but because of his utter impracticability. But I am not sure if I am not talking irrelevently. In the absence of your reactions to my

[1] *M.R. Masani Papers* (NAI).

last letter, I am really unable to judge what I should say, so, I better leave the matter where it is. You might, by the way, find out from the Bihar Government what exactly subversive they found in your letter and what could a person write about to a prisoner. Was discussion regarding ethics, or democracy or social philosophy or astronomy, let us say, harmful to the interests of the Government established by law etc. in this country?

I have yet another shocking news and an instance to give you about our Government's war for democracy. All the copies of the *New Leader* and the *Labour Action*, both legal papers and published legally in democratic countries have not only been not allowed to me, but have also been 'seized' in the interests of democracy. Your old friend,[2] now elevated to the War Cabinet is now at New Delhi. You might let him in into these secrets of the War for democracy and the Indian people's war.

The copies of the *New Statesman* that you sent have been allowed. You need not in the future send me this weekly, however, as I get it from Patna. Any other magazines or other periodicals that you may send, will be welcome. I shall be particularly obliged if you could send me some literature on the socio-economic-political changes taking place in the allied countries. I recently read a contribution by [illegible] that interested immensely.

Now, how about yourself? Have you produced anything new? I have re-read *Our India* after coming here and it interested me as much as when I read it the first time. Your book on the Indian Constitution I have not seen yet. The copy you sent me never reached me, kind friends having intercepted it on the way. What is your latest work about?

I understand Asoka has produced a work on the communal problem. I should like very much to see it.

Prabhavati wrote recently that you had been to Delhi to see Mehra. I hope she is well and enjoying her work. Radio work must be very interesting. If you write to her, do remember me to her and send her my best wishes. Pisi I hope has been able to cross the Alantic and is at Harvard now. I hope he returns without contracting the usual intellectual infection. I am afraid the pendulum must have again swung to Moscow on the campuses of America.

It is good that Yusuf and Asoka and Rao[3] and others are out. I do not

[2] Old friend refers to Sir Stafford Cripps (1889-1952); one of the prominent Labour leaders of Britain; became Leader of the House of Commons and member of the War-Cabinet in 1942, came to India to secure Indian support for the War (March-April 1942) again came to India with two other ministers as a member of the Cabinet Mission in 1946; Minister of Economic Affairs in 1947; Chancellor of Exchequer 1947-50. Publications include *Why This Socialism, Towards Christian Democracy, God in Our Work*, etc.

[3] Dr. V.K.R.V. Rao (1908-91); associated with the Congress Socialist Party in the forties; later acquired fame as an economist, became founder Director of the Delhi School of Economics and Institute of Economic Growth, Delhi, and subsequently Vice-Chancellor, University of Delhi; still later joined the Congress and became a Minister in the Government of India (1967-71).

know why none of them remembers me and writes to me. I feel awfully lonely here. The difficulty with me is that while I can receive four letters every week I can write only two—one of which has to be for Prabhavati.

How are you getting on with your work at the Tata's and your literary and public work, such as your radio talks. Have you published anything again, i.e. since your '*Our India*' [1940]? how is Lilubhai doing? Do remember me to him and give him my love. Also give my regards to Mrs. Merchant.

As you know we are soon to be repatriated—exactly when, it is not known. Anyhow it is a matter of not more than couple of weeks.

With love,

Yours,
Jayaprakash

41. To all Fighters for Freedom (1), February 1943[1]

Revolutionary Greetings

Comrades,

Let me first of all offer you and those comrades who have been made prisoners of war my heartiest congratulation on the magnificent battle already given to the enemy. Nothing like it ever happened or was expected to happen in this our long suffering and suppressed country. It truly was the 'Open Rebellion' envisaged by our incomparable leader Mahatma Gandhi.

The Rebellion, no doubt, seems to have been suppressed for the moment. But I hope you will agree with me that it has been suppressed only for the moment. This should cause us no surprise. As a matter of fact, had the very first assault been successful and had it completely crushed imperialism, that in reality would have been a matter for surprise. The very fact that the enemy himself has admitted that the Rebellion came pretty near destroying his power, shows how successful was the first phase of our National Revolution.

And how was the first phase suppressed? Was it the Military power of the enemy, his unmitigated reign of goondaism, looting, arson and murder that did the job? No. It is wrong to consider the 'Revolt' as having been 'suppressed'. The history of all Revolutions shows that a Revolution is not an event. It is a phase, a social process. And during the evolution of a Revolution, tides and ebbs are normal. Our Revolution is at present going through the period of low water so soon rather than rising to higher heights

[1] *Jayaprakash Narayan: To All Fighters for Freedom* published by Gopinath Singh, Lucknow, 1946.

and going from victory to victory, not because the superior physical force of the Imperialist aggressors intervened, but because of two important reasons.

Firstly, *there was no efficient organisation* of the national Revolutionary forces that could function and give effective lead to the mighty forces that were released. The Congress, though a great organisation, was not tuned to the pitch to which the Revolution was to rise. The lack of organisation was so considerable that even important Congressmen were not aware of the progress of the Revolt, and till late in course of the rising it remained a matter of debate in many Congress quarters whether what the people were doing was really in accordance with the Congress programme. In the same connection should be mentioned the regrettable fact that quite a considerable number of influential Congressmen failed to attune their mental attitude to the spirit of this 'last fight for Freedom'. The earnestness, the urgency, the determination that marked the attitude of leaders like Mahatma Gandhi, Dr. Rajendra Prasad or Sardar Patel failed to reflect in the minds and hearts of all congress leaders.

Secondly, after the first phase of the Rising was over *there was no further programme* placed before the people. After they had completely destroyed the British Raj in their areas, the people considered their task fulfilled, and went back to their homes not knowing what more to do. Nor was it their fault. The failure was ours: we should have supplied them with a programme for the next phase. When this was not done, the Revolt came to a standstill and the phase of the ebb began. This situation was created many days before the British soldiers arrived in sufficient numbers to push back yet further the receding waves of the revolt. What programme should have been placed before the people in the second phase? The answer is suggested by the nature of Revolutions. A Revolution is not only a destructive process, it is at the same time a great constructive force. No Revolution could succeed if it only destroyed. If it should survive, it must create an authority to replace the one it has destroyed. Our Revolution too having accomplished over large territories of the country the negative task of destruction, called for a positive programme. The people who destroyed the objects and means of administration of the foreign power and drove away its agents should have set-up in their areas their own units of Revolutionary Government and created their own police and militia. Had this been done, it would have released such an unprecedented volume of energy and opened up such a vast field for constructive work that the waves of the Revolution would have mounted higher and higher till—if the rising was countrywide—the imperialist power had been broken and the people had seized supreme authority throughout the land.

The lack efficient organisation and of a complete programme of National Revolution: these were two causes of the downward course of the first phase of the present Revolution.

The question now is what are our present tasks? First, to banish all depression from our minds and those of the people, and create an atmosphere of joy instead at the success achieved and of hope for success in the future.

Second, we must keep steadfastly before our minds and of the people the nature of this Revolution. It is our last fight for freedom. Our objective can, therefore, be nothing but victory. There can be no half way houses. The efforts that men like Rajagopalachari are making for the establishment of National government are not only fruitless but positively harmful inasmuch as they distract public attention from the real issues. There is no compatibility between the slogans of 'Quit India' and of a 'National Government'. Those who are running after the slogan of Congress-League unity are merely serving the ends of imperialist propaganda. It is not the lack of unity that is obstructing the formation of a national government, but the natural unwillingness of imperialism to liquidate itself. Mr. Churchhill[2] left no manner of doubt about it, when he declared recently that he had not assumed the office of the King's First Minister to preside over the liquidation of the Empire. He would be a foolish student of society indeed who expected empires to wither away of their own accord. Those erstwhile 'revolutionaries' who are attempting today to wish away the Indian Empire by the cataclymic force of humble memorials are making of themselves the most pitiable fools of history.

It is not the unity of all the important elements in Indian life, to quote the imperialist jargon, that is the need of the hour but the unity of all the national revolutionary forces. And these are already united under the flag of the Congress. Unity between the League and the Congress does not foreshadow the growth of these forces, but their absolute negation, for the League cannot conceivably tread the path of revolution and freedom.

The complete overthrow of imperialism, then, is our objective and we must keep this steadfastly in view. There can be no compromise on this issue. Either we win or we lose. And lose we shall not. Not only because we are determined ceaselessly to work for victory, but also because powerful world forces are drawing the doom of imperialism and fascism ever nearer and nearer. Do not believe that the formal results of this war settled laboriously at the Peace Conference would settle the fate of the post-war world. War is a strange alchemist, and in its hidden chambers are such forces and powers brewed and distilled that they tear down the plans of the victorious and vanquished alike. No peace conference at the end of the last war decided that four mighty empires of Europe and Asia should fall into dust—the Russian, the German, the Austrian and Ottoman. Nor, was the Russian, the German, the Turkish Revolution decreed by Lloyd George, Clemenceau[3] or Wilson.

[2] Winston Churchill (1874-1965); British statesman, soldier and author; Minister of War, 1918-21; Chancellor of the Exchequer, 1924-9; Prime Minister, 1940-5, 1951-5.

[3] Georges Clemenceau (1841-1929); French statesman; Premier of France, 1906-9, 1917-19.

Throughout the world where men are fighting, dying and suffering today, the alchemist is at work, just as he is in India, where he has already let loose a mighty social upheaval. Neither Churchill nor Roosevelt, neither Hitler nor Tojo[4] will determine the fate of the world at the end of this war. It is forces such as we represent that will fulfil that historic task. Can we doubt that revolutionary forces are stirring everywhere? Can we believe that millions of people are undergoing unutterable suffering without a thought for the future? Can we believe that millions are satisfied with the lies that their rulers daily feed them with. No, it cannot be so.

Having therefore definitely fixed our vision on the goal of total victory, we have to march ahead. What concretely must we do? What does a general do when he loses or wins a battle? He consolidates and prepares for the next battle? Rommel[5] stopped at El Alamein[6] after his great victory to consolidate and prepare. Alexander[7] too prepared and he turned his serious defeat into a resounding vicrory. Ours was not even a defeat. We really won the first round of the fight inasmuch as over large territories of the country the civil rule of the British aggressor was completely uprooted. The masses have now learnt from experience that the imposing edifice of the police and magistracy and law courts and prisons which goes by the name of British Raj is but a house of cards when they hurl against either collective power against any or all of them. This lesson is not likely to be forgotten and it constitutes the starting point for the next offensive.

Our third and most important task then at the present moment is to prepare for the next major offensive. Prepare, organise, discipline ourselves—these are our present watch-words.

The next offensive? When do we expect to launch the next offensive? Some people think that the masses will not rise again for the next five or six years. This estimate might be true of peace time but it does not hold good for

[4] Hideki Tojo (1884-1948); Japanese military and political leader; Premier, 1941-4; provoked U.S. entry into Second World War by ordering bombing of Pearl Harbour, December 1941; resigned after successive losses; hanged as a war criminal on 23 December 1948.

[5] Erwin Rommel (1891-1944); German Field Marshal; earned name 'Desert Fox' while engaged in North African desert warfare (1941-3); defeated by the British forces at El Alamein, 1942; implicated in a plot against Hitler and forced to swallow poison (14 October 1944).

[6] El Alamein, a village in North Egypt, west of Alexandria; was the site of decisive defeat of the German forces by the British in 1942 and marked the first significant Allied success in the Second World War.

[7] Field Marshal Harold Rupert Leofric George Alexander (1891-1969); Commander of the 1st Division, 1938-40; General, 1942, G.O.C. Burma, 1942, Commander-in-Chief, Middle East, 1942-8; Governor General of Canada, 1946-52; Minister of Defence, 1952-4.

a stormy war torn world of fast moving events. The savage tyrannies of the British fascists—the Linlithgows, the Hallets, the Stewarts and the myriads of others and their base Indian lackeys—may have compelled the people to lie low for the present, but they have nowhere converted them into friends of the oppressors. The whole countryside, where this British type of Nazi Hell was let loose, is seething with the most intense discontent, anger and thirst for revenge. The people have merely to understand that powerful preparations are afoot to take courage again and to enter the plans and schemes of the next offensive, with active, coordinated and disciplined work; it would be wholly favourable for the next assault. International events may come to our aid. Then there is Gandhiji's ever impending fast unto death, a constant reminder to us and to the people not to slacken, not to waver, not to rest on the oars.

The question of the next offensive is linked up with the question of the positive task of the Revolution—i.e., the establishment of the units of the Revolutionary governments. With the latter question is bound up the question of violence and maintainance of armed forces. I wish, therefore, to place before you my view on this question, as to my mind it affects vitally the future of our Revolution.

First of all, I feel I must say a few words about the noise the British authorities have made about the violence committed in the course of this Revolution. There was some violence indeed under extreme provocation, but it was remarkably little as compared with the magnitude of the Rising and the staggering manifestation of individual and collective non-violence. It is not realised, perhaps, that thousands of British and Indian employees of the foreign power were for some days literally at the mercy of the masses, who took compassion on their foes and spared them their lives and property. And what of the cool, sublime courage of those thousands of young and old who received the enemy's bullets on their chests with the flag of revolution in their hands and 'Inqalab Zindabad' on their lips? Have the British a word of praise for this godly courage?

In any case is it not remarkable that the British power which is soaked in violence, which is based on violence, which daily commits the most pitiless forms of violence, which grinds down millions of people and sucks their life-blood should make so much noise about the violence that others commit? How are the British concerned with what weapons we choose to fight them with? Have they pledged non-violence if the rebels adhere to it? Have they not already shot down thousands of our non-violent soldiers? Whatever weapons we use the British have only bullets for us and looting and rape and arson. So let them keep quiet as to how we fight them, it is our business entirely to decide that.

Coming to the question as it affects us, I would first remind you of the difference between Gandhiji's views on non-violence and those of the Working Committee and the A.I.C.C. Gandhiji is in no event prepared to depart form non-violence. With him it is a question of faith and life-principle. Not so with the Congress. The Congress has stated repeatedly during this war that if India became free, or even if a national government were set-up, it would be prepared to resist aggression with arms. But, if we are prepared to fight Japan and Germany with arms, why must we refuse to fight Britain in the same manner? The only possible answer can be that the Congress in power could have an army, whereas the Congress in wilderness has none. But *supposing a revolutionary army were created or if the present Indian army or a part of it rebelled*, would it not be inconsistent for us first to ask the army to rebel and then ask the rebels to lay down arms and face British bullets with bared chests?

My own interpretation of the Congress position—not Gandhiji's—is clear and definite. Congress is prepared to fight aggression violently if the country became independent. Well, we have declared ourselves independent, and also named Britain as an aggressive power; we are, therefore, justified within the terms of the Bombay resolution[8] itself to fight Britain with arms. If this does not accord with Gandhiji's principles, that is not my fault. The working Committee and the A.I.C.C. themselves have chosen to differ from Gandhiji and to reject his conception of non-violence as applied to the war. Nor was Gandhiji allowed by the British power to lead and shape this revolution; so, in following [our own] interpretation we should in no manner be false to him. We should only be discharging our duties in the light of our own reason. As far as I am concerned, I feel that I should be completely justified as an honest Congressman, without in any manner intruding my socialism upon the question, in repelling the British aggression with arms.

I should add that I have no hesitation in admitting that non-violence of the brave, if practised on a sufficiently large scale, would make violence unnecessary, but where such non-violence is absent, I should not allow cowardice, clothed in Shastric subtleties, to block the development of this revolution and lead to its failure.

With the implication of the last phase of the revolution clear in our minds, *we have to prepare, organise, train and discipline our forces*. In everything we do, we have constantly to bear in mind that ours is not to be merely a conspiratorial action. It is total revolt of the masses that is our objective. So, along with our immense technical work, we must do intensive work among the masses—peasants in the villages and the workers in the factories, mines, railways and elsewhere. We must do ceaseless propaganda among them and help them in their present difficulties, organise them to fight for their present

[8] Refers to the Quit India resolution passed by the A.I.C.C. at Bombay on 8 August 1942.

demands, recruit from them selected soldiers for our various activities and train them technically and politically. With training, a few may succeed where thousands failed before. In every district and taluka and thana, in every considerable factory and workshop or other industrial centres, we must have a band of militants, mentally and materially equipped for the next rising.

Then there is our work *in the Indian Army and services*. There is agitational and demonstrative work. There is work in the schools and colleges and in the market place. There is the work in the Native States and on the frontiers of India. It is not possible for me here to describe our preparations more concretely. Let it suffice to say that there is tremendous work to be done and work for every one. Much is being done at present, but vastly more remains to be done.

Who but youth can accomplish all this? Is it too much to hope that our students who have set such a brilliant record already will follow up their achievements and vindicate the promise they have given? It is for the students themselves to answer.

I should make it clear that preparation does not mean that fighting entirely ceases for the moment. No. 'Skirmishes', 'frontier activities', 'minor clashes', 'sniping', 'patrolling'—all these must go on. These are in themselves a preparation for the offensive.

With full confidence in the people and devotion to the cause, let us then march ahead. Let our steps be firm, our hearts resolute and our vision undimmed. The sun of Indian freedom has already risen above the horizon. Let not the clouds of our own doubts and disputes, inaction and faithlessness, obscure that sun and drown us in our self-created darkness.

In the end, comrades, I should like to say that it has made me inexpressibly happy and proud to be able once again to place my services at your disposal. In serving you, the last words of our leader, 'do or die' shall be my guiding star, your cooperation my strength and your command my pleasure.

42. To all Fighters for Freedom (2), 1 September 1943[1]

Revolutionary Greetings

Comrades,

Months back, soon after my escape from the enemy's prison,[2] I had the privilege of placing before you my views on our national revolution, as also certain suggestions concerning it.[3] Six months have passed since then, and

[1] *Jayaprakash Narayan: To All Fighters for Freedom* published by Gopinath Singh, Lucknow, 1946.

[2] J.P. escaped from Hazaribagh Central Jail on 8 November 1942.

[3] Refers to his first letter to all Fighters for Freedom. See item no. 41.

as the saying goes, much water has flown under the bridges. I think, therefore, that it will be fruitful to review the past months and to examine the present stage of our struggle.

I

After a close contact with the progress of the revolution for the past half year, I find no cause to change the views I had formed at the very beginning, nor do I find that the analysis made in my last letter requires any vital modification, except in one respect, not of a vital nature, yet important.

In December last it appeared to me that it might be possible within a few months for another mass uprising to take place. That rising has not yet materilalised, and it has to be admitted does not appear to be immediately imminent. The question naturally arises how this fact affects our present policy and the course of our struggle. In order to be able to answer this question, it is necessary to probe a little into this failure of the masses to rise again.

First of all, it seems to me that it would be a mistake to deduce from this that the spirit of the people has been crushed or that there is no fight left in them. The people never hated British Rule as they do today and were never more determined to be rid of it. A certain amount of demoralisation undoubtedly exists today but it is found largely, I do not say wholly, in the cities and among the higher strata of the society. In the countryside, the areas where the repression had the full sway, are far from having been cowed down; they are on the contrary filled with a burning desire for vengeance. At the first suitable opportunity they will rise and tear up British rule to pieces. It is rather the people of those villages who escaped British goondaism that sometimes show symptoms of fright and tendency to save their skin at any cost. But I believe these people too could be persuaded to march abreast of their brethren when the final hour approaches. The students who played a notable part in the first rising are, it is true, back at their schools and colleges. But from what I have been able to gather, they are far from being dispirited and will be ready to place themselves at the head of a rising. The growing severity of the food situation, the increasing hardships of living, and steadily failing real wages have not induced labour to look kindly at the so-called war efforts, and were another 'open rebellion' to breakout, labour's contribution to it might not be less, but more than it was in August-September last. The lower ranks of the police forces, though apparently won back to loyalty to the usurper regime, are far from satisfied with it and would prove much less reliable in the event of another rising than they did in 1942. The discontent among the officers and the ranks of the Indian armed forces has grown rather than lessened with the progress of the war; nor are the new schemes regarding salaries, etc., of the new C.-in-C. likely to allay it.

It may be asked why, if this picture be true, has not a second rising broken out, and why is it not even an imminent possibility. The reason, to my mind, is to be found in the intangible psychological factors. These factors are often unpredictable though it is one of the tasks of leadership to assess them properly. One of the essential conditions [for a mass uprising], though not the only one, is the rise of a belief in the mass mind that the ruling class or power is played out and at the end of its tether. The course of the world war in the months immediately prior to last August had been such that the Indian people had come to believe that the British Empire was crumbling and they had but to deal it a blow for it to totter entirely to the ground. At the present moment and for some time past, this psychological background has been absent, or rather altered so as to become an inhibiting instead of a stimulating factor. To all appearances the Americans seem destined to save the British Empire and piece together the fallen parts. As a matter of fact, the dissolution of the doomed Empire goes apace as certainly as ever and strange though it may appear the Americans are not without their share in it, for they cannot fail to acquire the first mortagage over the territories they liberate. But this process is not visible to the naked eye and so an inhibition is created in the mass mind.

This inhibition can be removed under two conditions: either when the international situation improves, that is, when it goes against the British Empire, or when an organised revolutionary force by dealing sustained and continuous blows at the enemy assures the mass mind that the British inspite of a huge army are powerless in the face of a rebellious India and arouses in it the hope that an uprising would possess a powerful leadership and a fair chance of success.

In August last not only did the war situation contribute to the creation of a suitable psychological atmosphere but also the fact that the Congress stood in all its power at the head of the people. The people had faith in their leaders and when the call went forth they responded with confidence and enthusiasm. Today these leaders are in prison, and they must present an appearance of helplessness to the people. Thus the second element in the creation of a mass psychology of the rebellion is also absent today.

But while it is not in our power to provide the first element, we can and should remedy the situation in respect of the second. A tendency is growing amongst fighters to take shelter from activity behind the idle complaint that the masses do not move, do not respond. This is defeatism. The masses cannot move till there is force in us to move them. They cannot respond, they cannot follow us till we are able by our activities, and the strength and efficiency of our organisation to win their confidence. The masses did their duty once. It was we who were found wanting. They shall do their duty again provided we do ours. In August last the masses had before their eyes the concrete power of the Congress and the leadership of Mahatma Gandhi. Today if they are made to feel that they are left alone, that there is no organised force in the country, which remains undefeated and continues the struggle, they would naturally sink down into despair and resign themselves to their *Kismet*.

The present, therefore, is a stage primarily, for the enlisted soldiers of revolution, the irreconcilable fighters of freedom, to act on. They must strengthen their organisation and carry ceaseless war unto the enemy. No suffering, no sacrifice should be counted too great; no controversy, no temptation, no false hope should deflect our course. All avenues of struggle are open to us. Whatever be our faiths and creeds, whatever our methods and weapons, our course is clear. We must keep on fighting. Whether we fight a year or ten years should make no difference to us. The Americans fought their War of Independence for seven years, the Chinese have just entered the seventh year of their war of liberation. We have just completed our first year of fighting. During the American and Chinese wars there were moments when all seemed to be lost, but the leaders and men held on, and victory was eventually with the Americans, as it will be with the Chinese. The present is far from being the darkest moment of our struggle, and yet weaklings and cowards have dared raised their voice. These are traitors to their country and we must chuck them out of our way and march on. Worst times may be in store for us, but let hardship and suffering not deter us but harden us. Then shall we be worthy of the people's confidence; then they shall respond to our call.

II

For some months past, particularly since the correspondence between Gandhiji and the Viceroy was published, a controversy has sprung up among fighters over the question of violence and non-violence. My views on this question have been clearly stated in my first letter to you and I still adhere to them. There is no need to repeat what I have already said, but I should like to say a word or two about this controversy. To me a controversy on this issue at this stage seems meaningless. Every fighter for freedom is free to choose his own method. Those who believe in similar methods should work together as a disciplined group. And the least that those who follow a different path should do is not to come in the way of one another and waste their energies in mututal recrimination. Where 'do or die' is the *mantram* of action, there is no room for recrimination whatever. Those who believe in non-violence may harbour the fear that those who practice violence might compromise the position of Gandhiji. That fear is unfounded. Gandhiji's adherence to non-violence is so complete, his position in respect to it so clear, that not a hundred thousand Churchills and Amreys will be able to compromise him.

Also, we must remember that whatever we do, however we try, we can never prevent British Statesmen, whether tory or labour, form telling lies; for lies are one of the central pillars of the Empire. Remember also that if there is violence in India, no one but the British Government itself is responsible for it.

Another controversy that has been started since the publication of the Gandhi-Viceroy correspondence is whether the present struggle was started by the Congress and whether it can be called a Congress movement. It has been claimed by some, who have gone so far as to suggest that a rump A.I.C.C. should meet to withdraw the Bombay resolution, that since Gandhiji and other Congress leaders were arrested before they could make a formal declaration of war, this struggle is not a Congress struggle at all. According to the logic of this argument no struggle, if the British were to arrest the leaders in time, could ever have the formal authority and sanction of the Congress. In that event the Congress would become a laughing stock. What is it that those who deny the authority of the Congress to the struggle would desire to have happened on the 9th August after the cowardly attack on our leaders? What do they think was the desire of Mahatma Gandhi and the Working Committee in the event of their arrest? Would the detractors of the present struggle have been happy if there had been no reaction of the leaders, if the country had calmly bowed its head before the Imperialist jack boot? Or was it expected that only protest meetings should have been held demanding the release of arrested leaders (as was advocated by certain erstwhile revolutionaries), and when they were not released, further meetings should have been held, till the audience became too disgusted to attend, after which the 'protestants' could have gone to sleep with a clear conscience? If this be so, where was the sense of that brave resolution and those brave words that were poured forth from the lips of the greatest in the land at the Bombay A.I.C.C.? If, on the other hand, this be not so, and if the people were expected to rise in answer to the British offensive, if indeed, the arrest of the leaders was a signal for a struggle, then where is the grace and fairness in decrying the present struggle as un-Congress and un-authorised? When you are on the war path, it is foolish to expect the enemy to allow you the leisure to complete all the formalities required by a peace-time constitution. It therefore appears to me to be mean and cowardly to attempt to show that the national struggle that started on the 9th August 1942 has not the authority and the sanction of the Congress.

It is a different matter when we turn to the question whether the programme of the present struggle was authorised by Gandhiji or the Working Committee. Here we are in the realm of facts and not principles and political ethics. And about the facts there is no dispute. It is well known that the working Committee had not prepared a plan of action but merely requested Gandhiji to assume command of the struggle. Gandhiji in his turn also had no plan of action. He had sketched the merest outlines in his address to the A.I.C.C.[4] That outline and his articles in *Harijan* were all that the people had before them and they formed the basis of that detailed programme which was prepared by those Congressmen who were left behind, and who hastily met in Bombay to lay the foundation of that 'illegal' Congress organisation which has functioned since then. That programme still is the framework of national struggle. There is no room for murder in it, nor for any form of violence to the person. If murders were committed in India—as they were—99 per cent of them were the acts of British fascists and hooligans and not more than 1 per cent were of an infuriated and sorely tried people. Creation of deadlock and paralysing and dislocation of British rule by all non-violent means was and remains the sheet-anchor of that programme and 'go to the fullest extent under Ahimsa', the star to steer it by. While it is true that there are some who in the name of non-violence are attempting to disown certain parts of the programme, which they had themselves sanctioned previously, and which even such a high authority as Shri Kishorilal Mashruwala[5] did not have the heart to condemn or ask the people to desist from, there is no doubt that the conscious basis of the programme which the Congress organisation have followed since August 1942 has been non-violence as interpreted by people in authority during this period. They who prepared the programme have never disowned the responsibility; and when the time comes they will no doubt appear before the tribunal of the Congress and receive its commendation for having discharged their duty at a most critical moment. Be that as it may, to fasten the August programme on Gandhiji is a piece of perjury of which only the British Ruling class can be capable.

III

In the past couple of months there has been in evidence a symptom which bodes greater mischief than these controversies. Since the beginning of the struggle there has been a group of Indians who have deplored the step taken at Bombay and attempted in their wonted manner to 'resolve the deadlock'. I do not think Congressmen were ever concerned about them, nor need they be now. Every time India launches a fight for freedom this group sets out to 'resolve the deadlock'. The fact that men like Shri Rajagopalachari,[6]

[4] Refers to Gandhi's speech at the A.I.C.C. meeting at Bombay on 8 August 1942.

[5] K.G. Mashruwala (1890-1952); exponent of Gandhian principles and political worker; editor, *Harijan* and other Navjivan group of weeklies, 1948-52; publications include: *The Purification of Life*, *The Foundations of Education*, *Revolution from the Roots* and *Gandhi and Marx*.

[6] For biographical note on C. Rajagopalachari see *JPSW*, Vol. I, p. 174.

Bhulabhai Desai,[7] K.M. Munshi,[8] whose rightful place was in the midst of fighters, have joined the association of saboteurs of the freedom movement, should make no difference.

But, as time passes and fighters are released from prison, some among them, a very few no doubt, show signs of fatigue and demoralisation. They too have taken up the slogan, 'resolve the deadlock', and different proposals to affect this are set afoot by them.

Firstly, it is highly disloyal of these Congressmen to initiate a policy of retreat when the generals are in the firing line. A real sense of discipline is tested in action. At the stage of discussion, criticism and difference of opinion are the law of democratic life. But at the time of action, particularly in war, the strictest discipline is necessary. And discipline requires in the present instance that every Congressman should remain in the firing line and give no thought to retreat or surrender. It is for the generals to consider these issues. Mahatmaji and Maulana Azad are in jail, but in the matter of peace and war the initiative is still with them, as it always is with either side at war. Mahatmaji could easily 'resolve the deadlock' whenever he wanted, by surrendering. He has not elected to do so. This means that he wants the fight to continue or, to put it at the worst, the deadlock to continue.

Secondly, let us go a little deeper into this question of the so-called deadlock. It would be conceded by everybody that ending of deadlock is not an end in itself. It must mean an advancement of the national cause; it must take us a step further towards the goal that is unalterably ours.

Keeping this in mind we may proceed to examine the ways to bring the deadlock to an end. There are three possibilities, either we force the British Government to concede our demands, or we surrender, or there is a 'negotiated peace' between India and Britain—a compromise. The first would mean a complete victory for India and could clearly be brought about only by the method of struggle. Those who have lost all hope of victory and feel suffocated by the stalemate and yearn for the freedom of the parliamentary play-acting have the option of surrendering. But they would thereby most effectively kill the Congress and extinguish the spirit of resistance for at least a generation. That would be a complete victory for Britain.

We are left with the possibility of a compromise, the superficial attraction of which draws many well meaning people into its snare and the path to which, as to a well-known place, is already paved with a great many excellent

[7] For biographical note on Bhulabhai J. Desai see *JPSW*, Vol. II, p. 209.

[8] K.M. Munshi (1887-1971); one of the prominent Congress leaders of Bombay; Founder and President of Bharatiya Vidya Bhavan, Bombay, member, Constituent Assembly (1946-9); Chairman Indian Law Institute, 1957-60; Agent General of Govt. of India in Hyderabad, 1948; Governor of U.P., 1952-7; One of the Vice-Presidents of Swatantra Party from its inception (1959).

intentions. A compromise implies give and take on either side. Now, the least gain on the side of the Congress can be the release of all those imprisoned in connection with the national struggle and restoration of the status of 'legality' to the Congress and its auxilliary bodies. The least that Britain can gain is removal of the terrible strain that British administration has to bear due to the continuance of the struggle. It is my conviction that in this sort of a compromise Britain stands to gain everything and the Congress to lose much.

Let us picture the implications of such a compromise. What would be the Congress position with regard to the war? Nothing has happened since August of last year to cause Congress to change its views on the war or to induce it to join it unless it is in a position to wage the war in the interest of the Indian people and on their behalf. On the other hand, an awful deal has happened in the past year that would make it impossible for any self-respecting Congressman to be associated in any manner, official or otherwise, with the goondas and cut-throats who rule India and let loose such a hell over the heads of the people—a hell the fires of which have not yet been extinguished. It is inconceivable to me how Congressmen can ever offer the palm to men who have murdered and pillaged and burnt and raped and tortured tender boys in the stillness of prison cells. For this reason and for the reason that Congress cannot accept office in the present circumstances without power, I cannot imagine that Congress would agree to work the 1935 constitution again. Congress had once agreed to work that constitution in order to wreck it, and had nearly wrecked itself in the attempt. That wretched fraud has however been most effectively wrecked by the war and, as the memorable statement[9] of Maulvi Fazal-Huq[10] to the Bengal Legislative Assembly showed, not a shred of Provincial Autonomy remains to hide the ugly nakedness of bureaucratic rule (Parenthetically let me remark that it is a pity that after so ably exposing the hollowness of Provincial Autonomy Maulvi Huq and other nationalist members of the Bengal Assembly, including those who sail under one or the other Congress flag, should persist in playing at futile parliamentarianism. To my mind the only manly and patriotic course

[9] Refers to the statement of Fazlul Huq at the opening meeting of the monsoon session of the Bengal Legislative Assembly on 5 July 1943 regarding the circumstances connected with his resignation as Premier of Bengal. In that statement he had charged the Governor with partisanship and violation of the Instrument of Instructions.

[10] Abul Kasem Fazlul Huq (1873-1962); one of the most prominent political leaders of Bengal and later of East Pakistan; member, Bengal Legislative Council, 1913-20, 1920-35; associated with the Congress in the early 1920s; formed Krishak Proja Party, 1936; Premier, Bengal, 1937-43; Leader of Opposition, Bengal Legislative Assembly, 1943. Advocate General, East Pakistan, 1951-3; Chief Minister, East Bengal, April-May 1954; Minister of Interior and later Minister of Education, Government of Pakistan, August 1955-March 1956; Governor, East Pakistan, March 1956, dismissed, April 1958.

open to them after that grim statement was to walk out permanently of the present Assembly and have recourse to extra-parliamentary methods to seek to overthrow the monstrous Herbert regime). To return to my point, Provincial Autonomy being what it is, it would be the height of political imbecility to expect the Congress to resuscitate that fraud by instaling its ministers again in the provinces. The Act of 1935 is dead and there is no going back to it: let this be well-understood. Nor can India live at peace again with those who have heaped unspeakable indignities and beastial cruelities upon her; let this too be well understood.

A compromise with such implications would put the Congress in a most embarrasing position. The Congress would be restored to 'freedom', but would continue to be opposed to the imperialist war and to all the measures,—economic and political—that the usurper power might adopt to prosecute the war in the interest of British Capitalism; it would be unable to take a hand in the administration of the country and to democratise in the least the ordinance, or to use the modern phrase, fascist rule. It would be helpless to eliminate, the sufferings of the people, to provide food for the hungry, cloth for the naked, shelter for the homeless. In short, if the Congress took its principles seriously it would find itself drifting into opposition to the usurper authority at every point, and thence the road to the prisons would be straight and short. The deadlock would have been resolved in vain.

The Congress would suffer another great loss. As soon as Mahatma Gandhi, President Azad, Pandit Nehru and others are out of prison the world would forget India. The pressure that the deadlock exercises over those who guide the destinies of the world would be suddenly relaxed and the Churchills and Amerys would go peacefully to sleep—rightly thinking that the Indian question was settled for the time being and would not become pressing again till the mad Gandhi took into his head to march his flock once more to the prison. Pandit Nehru released from jail might make statements which American correspondents might lap up with avidity, but there would be no strength behind those statements, despite the beauty and grace of their expression. Nehru in prison is a greater problem for the Roosevelts and Churchills than Nehru proliferating nobly worded statements and casting his spell over the envoys of great nations.

It might be suggested that the basis of compromise might be more advantageous to the Congress than that pictured above. Let us see what this basis can be. Britain is not prepared to offer anything more than the Cripps[11] plan[12]—that is, no power during the war and a fraudulent promise of it at its

[11] For biographical note on Stafford Cripps see *JPSW*, Vol. II, p. 95.

[12] Sir Stafford Cripps came to India on 22 March 1942 with the British Government's draft declaration on the basis of which he was to conduct negotiation with the Indian political parties and communities. The object of the British Government was therein stated to be the setting up of a Constituent Assembly at the end of the war with a view to the

end. The Congress rightly rejected the British offer, and no one in his senses would expect Congress to accept it today. The most moderate demands of the Congress, with which I personally am not in the least in agreement and which I doubt if the Working Committee would be prepared to father today, were placed in the hands of the 'devil's advocate' in April 1942. They were rejected by the British Government. How do those, who are anxious to break the stalemate, propose to enforce the minimum demands, supposing the Congress would be satisfied with them? Could anything but a struggle succeed? So, it appears that we are back to deadlock again.

The deadlock is thus inescapable. Its resolution, except on the terms of the Congress, spells disaster to the country. It however does not mean that we are static. We remain at war, we continue to resist, to exploit every shift in the national and the international position. The very continuance of opposition to the British Rule, the very fact that India's best men are in prison is a guarantee that India remains unbeaten, the spirit of resistance remains unbowed, that Indian question remains a crying world problem, that the subject peoples of Asia and Africa draw inspiration from India's struggle, that the working classes of Britain and the allied nations are constantly made aware of the nature of 'democracy' for which they are said to fight, that the possibility of a better post-war world is brought near, that India gains the leadership of the third camp of the common men of the world for whom neither allied nor axis victory holds any prospects of liberation and happiness. I shall, therefore, be content even if the deadlock continues till the end of the war. None can tell how long the war may last and what turn it may take and what forces it may release. The longer the war lasts the more the internal situation deteriorates, not only in India but in every country of the world. A turn in the war, the release of a new social force may alter the situation so completely in India that the deadlock may become the starting point of a great leap forward, whereas if we have gone back to 'normalcy' again the normalcy itself might become for us a deadly fetter. The deadlock is the best guarantee of our success in the future.

It might be urged that by keeping alive the deadlock we are playing in the hands of Britain, for Britain too desires that there should be a political deadlock in India. This is misreading of British policy. Britain does not desire a political deadlock but a political black-out. She wants to crush the Congress and still its voice, to break the people's spirit of resistance and will to freedom. A deadlock in which the power of the Congress grows, the spirit

---

formation of an Indian Union with Dominion status, with the option of secession from the Commonwealth. Those provinces which did not want to join the proposed Indian Union would be free to opt out of it and frame their own constitution or constitutions. Indian states could also do the same. The Congress did not accept the Cripps Plan as it did not provide for immediate transfer of power.

of resistance remains unbroken, the fight for freedom continues; a deadlock as a result of which British prestige and authority daily dwindle and those of the rebels grow—such a deadlock would defeat Britain's purpose and turn her weapon into an instrument of her own defeat.

IV

Closely connected with the above discussion is the question of National Government and Congress-League agreement. A National Government by all means. But the most amusing thing is that while Congress fights for such a government and suffers others merely talk. If a National Government is not the same thing as Coalition ministries under the Act of 1935 Act or a glorified Viceroy's Council, it cannot be won by holding conferences. The Congress left that fertile path years ago and if Communists expect to establish such a government by petitioning to their Imperial masters they are welcome to their toading. But they will achieve nothing but the ridicule of the people and the contempt of their paymasters.

The agitation for a Congress-League agreement as a precondition of National Government is not new, and there was no reason for me to touch upon it here. But the depression that has caught some Congressmen who have been seeking a way back to constitutionalism has led them anew into this barren agitation. Becoming weary of direct action, they are eager to fall back on this easy nostrum forgetting that the author of the agitation Mr. Rajagopalachari is still cooling his heels before the gates of Mr. Jinnah's mansion, and that Mahatma Gandhi's letter to the League leader[13] still remains undelivered. (Though we have had the rare fortune of reading the reply to an undelivered and unread letter.) I have for this reason considered it desirable to touch upon this subject briefly.

One is compelled to pay a tribute to the skill of British propaganda when one observes how intelligent men fall a prey to it. Either that, or one must acknowledge the depth of national degeneracy which we have reached. If British propaganda 'takes in' the innocent Americans (though even among them there are quite a few who see through it), one can understand, but when it bamboozles Indians you have to regard it as one of the world's wonders. Recent events in India have torn Britain's every pretence to shreds. Not even a fig leaf hides now the true shape and purpose of British Imperialism. Yet,

[13] Refers to Gandhi's letter to M.A. Jinnah dated 4 May 1943 from the Aga Khan Palace, Poona, where he had been detained since 9 August 1942. Jinnah, in his presidential address to the annual session of the Muslim League at Delhi on 24 April 1943, had invited Gandhi to write to him if he was 'even now willing to come to a settlement with the Muslim League on the basis of Pakistan'. The Government did not forward the letter to Jinnah.

there are Indians who believe and want their countrymen to believe that nothing but the absence of a Congress-League settlement stands in the way of India achieving her independence.

If the course of British policy in the past few months has established anything it is the grim British determination to hold on at any cost to their Indian Empire. If any point emerged with undimmed clarity from the Cripps negotiations it was the firm resolve of Britain not to hand over real power to India during the war, no matter what measure of unity was achieved in the country. Cripps stated categorically that even if the Congress and Muslim League jointly demanded a real National Government responsible to the people, it could not be granted during the war (And who was or is interested in British promises for the future?). In view of this clear statement of British policy, to agitate for a Congress-League agreement serves no other purpose but to lend strength and respectability to the lies which the Churchills and Amerys tirelessly peddle around the world. The agitation for Congress-League understanding becomes in these circumstances a part of the Imperialist offensive against nationalist India.

It might be asked: even if Congress-League settlement does not by itself compel Britain to grant India a National Government, would it not at least strengthen the forces of freedom and, as such, is it not desirable in itself and worth working for? The conclusion would be true were so the premise. But the premise is entirely untrue. In our country the only forces of freedom are those that are ready to fight and suffer for freedom The Muslim League during its entire career has not once taken the path of struggle and suffering, nor is it ready to take the path today. Indian cannot win her freedom without fighting for it. And when the Muslim League is not prepared to participate in the fight, a settlement with it in no way strengthens the forces of freedom. Pandit Nehru was not using empty words when he stated that it would have been easy any day to settle with the League were it prepared to join the struggle for freedom.

So much for the Congress-League unity. A word about the realpolitik of the League. It is necessary to grasp clearly that the League is in league with Britain. Mr. Jinnah is a deliberate traitor to his country, a Mir Jafar[14] of the present day. He believes that he can get what he wants from Britain. But Britain is not accustomed to handing over parcels of her Empire to its tools. There is no doubt that after she has made the full use of Mr. Jinnah she will throw him into the dustbin of discarded tools as surely as she had thrown others into it before, Mir Jafar including. Let Muslims remember that it is

[14] Mir Jafar (1691(?)-1765); installed by Robert Clive as the Nawab of Bengal after the Battle of Plassey (1757) where he played traitor by betraying Nawab Siraj-ud-Daula to ensure British victory; deposed, 1760; reinstated, 1763.

not the sons of Mir Jafar who rule Bengal today but the dirty kin of Clive.[15] Mr. Jinnah no doubt considers himself a very clever person, but for all his conceit and Fuehrerian attitudes history will show him to have been made a historic fool.

Mr. Jinnah wants his Pakistan. But, if he is serious about it, he must fight for it, he must make sacrifices for it, possibly die for it. But, there is the rub: it is exactly these things which Mr. Jinnah and his followers are never prepared to do. Therefore Mr. Jinnah shrieks his demand for Pakistan in the face of Mahatma Gandhi. But poor Gandhi is not in possession of Jinnah's sacred homelands. It is the blood-soaked heels of Imperialism that possess and trample upon them, that defile and desecrate them. The Congress can have no objection if Mr. Jinnah can take his 'homelands' from the British—at least a part of India would then be free. But he will not take them, for he is not prepared to pay the price. He, therefore, wants to get along by black-mailing the Congress. But in the end it will be Churchill who will have black-mailed Jinnah. If India is ever partitioned under the auspices of the mother of Parliaments it would be in the interests of Imperialism to bestow a separate freedom upon the so-called Muslim nation of Hindustan. Ulster does no good to the Irish, but it is a British thrust into the very heart of Eire.

League realpolitik is the ugly issue of imperialist machination and national treachery.

V

You probably know that Shri Subhas Chandra Bose has formed a free Provisional Indian National Government at Shonan (Singapore) which has been recognised by the Japanese Government. He has also organised an Indian National Army which is said to be growing rapidly. The events have some significance for us. Paranthetically, I may add for your information that one of the first act of the Subhas Government has been to offer to send us as much rice as may be required to feed the starving people of Bengal, but the British Government prefers to let the native vermin die.

It is easy to denounce Subhas as a quisling. Those who are themselves quislings of Britain find it easiest to denounce him. But nationalist India knows him as a fervent patriot and as one who has always been in the fore-front of his country's fight for freedom. It is inconceivable that he should ever be ready to sell his country. No doubt it is true that all the necessary resources of money and equipment that he has have been supplied to him by the axis powers. But, in the first place, the men he has in his Government and the National Army are Indians who hate British rule, and burn with a

[15] Robert Clive (1725-74); British soldier and statesman; Governor of Bengal (1765-7); generally regarded as the founder of British rule in India.

desire to free their motherland. In the second place, it is well to remember that the resources of all the fugitive governments of Europe which bask in the patronage of the United Nations come from those nations. Thirdly, no one can tell what concessions the requirement of global strategy may force a great power to make to a weak and prostrate nation. The conferment of 'Independence' upon Burma by the Japanese has received some advertisement and a report says that the Soviet Government has been so much impressed as to congratulate the Tojo Government upon their act of generosity. Be that as it may, there seems to be no doubt that the Burmese today enjoy much more freedom under the overlordship of a fascist state than they did under British democracy. Turning to Shri Subhas Bose, it is clear that he has permitted himself to accept aid from the enemies of his country's enemies in accordance with an age old political maxim—older than Machiavelli[16] and older than Kautilya.[17] In thus accepting help from a third party he may be deceived in the end, but there can be no question as to the honesty of his purpose and the scale of his resourcefulness. His success or failure in assisting his country to achieve her freedom will depend on the course of events over which neither he nor any other political leader of any country has much control.

Recognising the importance of the Shonan Indian Government and the National Army, I must emphasise that our freedom largely depends upon our own strength and resources. Hopeless inaction which feeds upon the hope of outside help is suicidal politics. No outside help by itself can free us. It is fantastic to believe that Subhas's Army, no matter how large, can defeat the allied armies in India. If any army can defeat them it may possibly be the Japanese. But, if the Japanese defeat the British in India, they would not quietly hand over India to us whatever the understanding between Tojo and Subhas. We must be ready in the event of an axis and allied clash in India to seize power ourselves. Only if you are ready to make this attempt can outside help such as Subhas's National Army be of value to us and Tojo be prevented from annexing India. It is difficult to say how for Subhas himself is conscious of this aspect of India's national strategy.

This brings me to the question, what should we do when the war enters our doors. British policy has made the average Indian so anti-British that he is prepared if not to welcome the Japanese, at least to remain indifferent to the Anglo-Japanese conflict. This indifference will be our death. We must endeavour to remove it and in its place develop a positive policy of action. In

[16] Niccolo Machiavelli (1469-1527); Italian statesman and political philosopher; famous for his works on statecraft of which the most important was *The Prince*.

[17] Kautilya, also known as Chanakya and Vishnugupta (300 BC); Indian philosopher and politician; adviser to Chandragupta Maurya; author of *Arthashastra*, a classic treatise on governance.

the areas where war is waged or which the Japanese occupy or where they infilterate, the foreigners, civil rule will weaken or come to an end. In these areas we must establish a Swarajya Government. In the name of this Government we must appeal to the retreating units of the Indian Army to stay behind and become the people's army. From this day we must prepare to establish such a government in the eastern provinces which in the course of time might embrace the entire nation. This preparatory work raises many questions which cannot be discussed here. It is sufficient to point out the broad policy and invite the fighters to it as well as the people generally.

VI

A word or two about the war before I conclude. The futile controversy about the character of the war still goes on merrily in the back waters of Indian life. The fifth columnists still insist—naturally enough—that it is a People's War. And those to whom controversy is the beginning and end of politics get terribly excited about it and argue with words and sometimes with blows. But the Indian people have no doubts about the nature of Britain's war and about those of their countrymen who support it. They do not require any longer to be told what Fascism is or that this is not their own war. British Fascism has revealed itself to them in all its horrid brutality in the last year. Those who rot in prison, those who lost their dear ones in the country-wide murder by which the British reestablished their 'law and order', those whose homes were burnt and looted, whose women dishonoured, those who starve and die like rats on the streets—all these people know too well what sort of a People's War this is. A British general laid the decapitated heads of the Shahzadas of the House of Babar on a tray and sent them to the last Mogul Emperor (Bahadur Shah Zafar), the father of the hapless princes as a gift from Queen Victoria. A century and a half later Tottenham[18] boasted to American correspondents that he had bought enough sandalwood to burn the remains of Gandhi. India knows of these deeds and of other black deeds that fill the period from the beginning to the end (for the end is near) of British rule and she does not need to be told by traitors, masquerading as Marxists, what Fascism is.

The war has entered its fifth year. The destruction of life and happiness that it has caused can never be repaired. The interests of the common man of both sides demand the war to end immediately. But it cannot be ended by Churchills and Roosevelts, Hitlers and Tojos. Even if they cried halt to the present butchery, it would only be to prepare new and more terrible weapons for more terrible butchery in the future. Allied plans for the post-war world,

[18] Richard Tottenham (1890-1977); Secretary to the Government of India, Defence Department, 1932-7, and Home Department, 1940-6.

of which the barest glimpse has been vouchsafed to the common man, picture the same old world of privilege, class and national tyranny, capitalist rivalry and chaos which brought two devastating wars in a generation and will surely bring a third.

The war can be truly ended only by the common people of the world. But their voice is stifled. Russia which could have become the champion of the common man has herself suppressed him at home and disowned him abroad by truckling to the imperialists and supercapitalists of Anglo-America. Labour throughout the world has become the camp-follower of the capitalist class and has thus sold its conscience and forfeited its leadership of society and of the new world.

In these circumstances India alone actively represents the aspirations and promptings of the disinherited and dispossessed of the Earth. India's fight for freedom is at once anti-imperialist (and therefore also anti-fascist, for Imperialism is the parent of Fascism) and a drive to end the war through the intervention of the common man. Neither allied nor axis victory is our aim, nor do we pin our hope on either. We work for the defeat both of Imperialism and Fascism by the common people of the world and by our struggle we show the way to the ending of wars and the liberation of the black, white and yellow.

VII

I have taken too much of your time and must conclude now. I have tried to show above that the only course open to us to follow with profit is to continue to fight. How should we fight?

I have already pointed out that the present is a stage at which primarily the determined fighters have to play their role.

The first thing that these fighters must do is to maintain and strengthen and widen their organisation. Without organisation no army not even a non-violent one can fight. Mass actions are generally spontaneous and the resultant of social forces, but there must be an organisation of a revolutionary elite to give shape and decision to them. The spontaneity of mass actions is also often the cumulative product of organised work among the masses by such an elite. In the recent history of our struggle there has been a marked indifference shown by leaders of the struggle to problems of organisation. The leaders, upon their arrest, have always left too much to the spontaneity of the people. No doubt, the relation of secrecy to non-violent action has been at the bottom of this indifference to organisation. Non-violence does not permit secret functioning. Yet, during a struggle organisation must be secret. I do not pretend to have found a solution of this dilemma. All that I can say is that till the authentic technicians of non-violence discover a solution, it is essential in the interest of work for even those who strictly believe in non-violence to deliberately compromise with their principle to the extent of admitting secret organisation. Even Mahatma Gandhi makes such compromises. But merely condemning secrecy and extolling upon work we do not solve the difficulty nor advance our cause.

Organisation then is the first item in the programme of our struggle. It is the basic guarantee of a struggle. In regard to this item, I must emphasise the prime necessity of keeping alive, and in trim, the illegal Congress organisations. These organisations are the sole unifying principle of our struggle. It is true they have no constitutional basis, but it is only through them that the Congress can function today and reach the people and fight the enemy. In several provinces these organisations are not functioning properly. The cause of such organisational weakness is rarely the lack of workers. More often it is inadequate funds and the absence of capable organisers. Neither of these is irremediable. The central directorate of the Indian National Congress has been trying to provide the provinces with at least their minimum requirements, and its attempts have not altogether been a failure. This is not the occasion nor the time to examine the role that India's wealthy have played in the present revolution. Here it is enough to comment upon the entire absence of perspective or vision in them. If they could see but a little way ahead they should easily realise that if the national movements were crushed, British capitalism, harassed as it would be by the problems of the post-war world, would give them no quarter whatever. Their self interest, therefore, dictated that they should invest wholeheartedly in the national revolution. But they have proved to be not only extremely selfish but also exceedingly small men.

However, the requirements for funds must be met some how and all those who can help should. In some provinces, such as the U.P., some of the ex-ministers (Congress) are out of jail. If they and other prominent Congressmen who have recently been released in various provinces do not do anything else, they should at least see that the financial requirements of their provinces are fulfilled. As far as the central organisation is concerned, financing of provinces must remain its most important job. To send out programmes and instructions without the wherewithal to carry them into practice can be no more than perfunctory and unreal fulfilment of duty.

The absence of capable organisers and leaders, who can create work and take work out of others, is more difficult to remedy. However, a partial remedy is that those few who are left should tour around, meet the other workers and discuss with them their practical problems and give them such advice and training as may be possible. Where by fortuitous circumstances there happen to be more capable men than necessary, some of them may be sent away to places where there are none or too few. New workers should be recruited, particularly from among students, and those who are being released from prison should be drawn back into the rank.

With funds, recruitment, and training, and wise use of available talent and experience, it should be possible to tackle our organisational problems.

To hold our organisation together in the face of repression is a part of the fight—but only a part. Every unit of our organisation must be in touch with the people. The link between the fighters and the people should not be allowed to snap. The link in one word is propaganda—spoken and written propaganda—leaflets, pamphlets, posters, radio broadcasts, mobile columns of fighters touring in the countryside, meeting and talking to the people. Distribution of literature is as important as its writing and production and equal care should be devoted to each task. Spheres of propaganda should also be carefully studied. Apart from sections of the public—students, labour, shopkeepers, peasants—we should see that our voice reaches the services, particulary the lower ranks of police and the army. Foreign propaganda should also form a part of our job.

Propaganda is not only propaganda but also a form of our fight; for, to work a radio centre, to issue an 'illegal' leaflet, to hold a meeting where no meetings are allowed, to say things which are 'illegal'—all this is defiance of the usurper power and a part of the fight against it. What more can we do? I believe, and I do not mind saying so publicly, that unless there is a shift in the international situation—a Russo-German Pact, a Sino-Japanese Peace, a measure reverse of British Arms, war on Indian soil—we cannot do anything big. I want fighters to be under no delusion. Only those who fight on without hope of immediate results will win victory. Others will fall out of the ranks, will prattle wise words and pose as statesmen, but history will know them as deserters, as men of poor faith and poorer courage, who foresook duty in the face of suffering. Many friends are depressed by the thought that the resistance on the scale that we can offer—either in the form of satyagraha and strike or as acts of dislocation—is ineffective. True. It is so in the sense that its volume is not large enough to bring British rule to a stand still. But, it is effective in another, no less necessary sense—it is effective propaganda, it keeps up the morale of the people, it keeps alive the hope of bigger action, it gives training to fighters, it keeps the visible forms of the struggle and impresses upon the enemy that all his repression has been in vain. It is effective in the sense that it is a preparation for ultimate affective resistance. Therefore, we must continue to offer resistance to the British power in every shape or form possible, in accordance with whatever creed or programme we believe in.

I would call this our minimum programme for the present—organisation, propaganda, overt resistance. In addition to this we have the whole wide field of preparation. Our work among students and labour must continue, our contacts with the army and the services must be maintained and developed, our preparation for dislocation must go on. Rising of the nature of that of the 9th August [1942], but on a bigger scale and better organised and directed, should be our goal. Our every effort should take us a step nearer that goal.

A word about the food situation. I need not say anything about its seriousness. That is well known and well understood. What is not well understood is that the only real solution of the food problem is a Swarajya Government. The British, partly by their incompetence and partly by design, have created this problem, and as long as they are here there is no alternative to starvation. Therefore, the fight for freedom is the real fight for food. But to say this is not enough. We must also have a fight for food as a part of the fight for freedom. At the present moment the only public reaction to the food situation is charity. Charity has its own place in a class society, and much as I hate it as a socialist, I readily acknowledge the humanitarian motive of those who have hastened to rescue the starving from death. It is a commendable public effort. But charity is not enough. It will not solve the problem. Fighters have therefore the job—their most important job in the circumstances—to create feelings of resentment and anger in the needy and the starving and to turn those feelings against the foreign power which is at bottom responsible for all this misery. Let the hungry create a situation in which normal British administration becomes impossible. Let us tell them—not only tell but help them to do it. In the rural areas we should prevent grains from being sent out and distribute stocks through village panchayats or similar agencies (taking care to keep away from Government or pro-Government bodies). Fighters, organised as guerillas, should seize grain from government depots and similar places and distribute them among the needy. Forcible seizure by Government of crops and grains should be resisted. In the cities and towns too the passivity and despair of the hungry and needy should be turned into resentment and anger and given concrete, active shape of demonstration and direct action. Fighters often ask me for a programme. Here is a vital programme which, tackled with imagination and courage, can convert the country into a seething cauldron in which the Empire can soon be boiled to death.

Speaking of organisation, I have referred only to the Congress. Those, however, who wish to go beyond the creedal limitations of the Congress naturally require a separate organisation to carry on their special activities. I have suggested a guerilla form of organisation for this purpose, and some progress has already been made in developing a guerilla movement. In the very nature of things I cannot be expected to say more about this matter—except perhaps this that my views in this regard have no difficulty in reaching the proper quarters and those interested in this work cannot have much difficulty in putting themselves in touch with the organisation that has been set-up.

With these words, Comrades, I close. I have analysed the present position without passion and laid my views before you without rhetoric or embellishment. It is for you to decide what is worthy of acceptance in them. You will ever find me at your command. 'Do or Die' remains my guiding star as it is yours. Let us, therefore, do or die.

43. To Students, 1943[1]

Dear Friends,
I cannot tell you how happy it makes me to be by your side in this, our last fight for freedom.

First of all I have to pay my humble homage to the memory of those young patriots whose cool, incalculable heroism and sublime martyrdom have written the most glorious page in the living History of our National Revolution. Their example shall ever remain an inspiration to us and a rebuke to those whole fail or falter.

Then I must offer you all my heartiest congratulations on the magnificent role you have already played in this great war of liberation. I do not mind admitting that I was one of those who had little hope from the student community. It seemed incredible that the glorious tradition of 1921should prove as barren, yet that was what appearances let me to believe.

It was therefore, with unbounded joy and pride that I followed from day-to-day, behind the sombre prison walls, your brave and unforgettable deeds. Nothing that we did in 1921 could equal the unexampled heroism of our student martyrs or the great contribution you have made to this 'open rebellion'.

But friends, this is not time yet to rest on our oars or to look back at our achievements. The question of the moment is not how much we have accomplished, but what we are doing in the present and what we are to do in the future. It is this question which I have to place before you.

The colleges opened a few weeks ago and you are back at your studies. If I were to tell you that this is no time for books and examinations, I should sound to you trite and common. But can a similar thought be trite for the young men of the Russian and Chinese universities, of Oxford and Harvard? It is common for you to be told by your guardians and teachers and convocation orators that a student's primary duty is to complete his studies: only then he may enter politics if he so desired, for he would be better equipped then to serve his country.

This is how men with static minds think. In normal times there is no question but that a student must above all study and develop his personality so that he might be a better citizen and serve his nation to the best of his

[1] *JP Papers* (NMML).

abilities. But there are periods in nation's life when the development of the individual has to be arrested so that the nation as a whole might live and grow, when deliberate sacrifice and immolation of the individual becomes essential for the community's advancement. Do you think that the students of China and Russia wait to complete their studies before they march to the battle fronts and lay down their young lives so that their countries might live? Do you think that teachers and guardians in those countries are allowed to expound views such as are daily dinned into your ears? Do you think that at Cambridge and Columbia young men are asked to complete their studies before joining up at the fronts?

No, friends, there are times when the individual must die so that the nation might live and civilization endure. The present is one of such times. We too must die, must suffer, must immolate ourselves now so that our nation might live and come into its own and our civilization might flower. Therefore, pay no heed to traitorous, cowardly words.

Then what should you do?

By your revolutionary action you forced the schools and colleges to close down. They are open again, and that is a defeat for you and us all. I am unable to say why you returned to your colleges. I hope you did not, at least, make a mistake about the nature of the present fight. It was not meant to be a momentary outburst or a demonstrative feat. It is a deadly serious fight which knows no end but victory. Make no mistake about that.

I am not sure how your minds work, but had I been in your position I would have deemed it an insult to my self-respect to return to school after the events of August. I can also assure you from personal experience that it is no handicap to education to miss a year or two of college. I not only missed a year during the non-cooperation movement of 1921, but also in America I had to stay away from college for months, sometimes for a whole year, in order to earn the wherewithal to pay for my education. And I am glad to tell you that I learnt as much, if not more, from my work outside the campus as inside it. Our educational system here is so artificial, so cloistered, so cut off from life that everyone of you should really gain and not lose if you were to leave college for a year and throw yourself into the whirlpool of national life.

Perhaps you were troubled with ennui after leaving college, not finding enough to do. But I cannot conceive of any one not finding something to do at the present moment, for there is such a vast deal to be done. I should go so far as to say that had you even stayed at home and tried a hand at farming or just taught children or cleaned up your village and taught people how to live, you would have served yourself and your country well. For one thing, you would have prevented your schools and colleges from reopening and thus saved yourself from helping in the enemy's task being accomplished; for another you would have added something to your education and done something useful for the community.

But the fact is that the schools and colleges have opened, I do not feel confident enough to ask you to leave them again and to force them to close down. I am not sure what weight my words will carry. But, in any case, I should like to leave you under no misapprehension about what you have done. By returning to these institutions you have been false to yourself and to your leaders and have injured the cause which you so brilliantly served at the beginning. The path of your duty is clear: whether you will follow it, only you can tell.

But even for those of you who continue at school or college there is much work. In a moment of weakness, perhaps, or imagining the revolt to have been crushed, you went back to college. But I hope you have had time to take stock of things. Nothing would be more wrong than to believe that the revolution has been crushed or that it has run its course. In my appeal *To All Fighters for Freedom* I have analysed the present revolution and pointed out its future course of development. I do not wish to repeat what I have said there, but just two points I should like to reiterate. The first phase of our revolution was a great success inasmuch as it succeeded in uprooting the British power from large tracts of the country. Its further development was checked not because the superior physical force of the enemy blocked its way, but because of our lack of adequate organisation and of a complete, conscious programme of revolution. This leads to the second point, namely, that the present task is clearly to prepare, organise and discipline our forces for the second and last major offensive. We have not much time before us and therefore we must not lose a moment.

In every field of preparation we need your help. We have to work in the villages and industrial centres, on the railways and in the mines, in the army and the services. We have to publish and distribute our literature, maintain our contacts and communications, we have to raise and train a militia and bands of technical workers for sabotage and similar activities, and we have to continue our present clashes and skirmishes with the enemy. A network of organisation, working under a co-ordinated and central command, is being built up. Through our existing contacts among you, we shall attempt to reach you and to entrust different duties to such of you as may be prepared to enlist in the army of the revolution.

Many of these things you can do while you study, and this, I feel confident you will do, as some of you are already doing. I have faith that when the time for the next offensive comes, you will be at the front of the battle again as you were in August. But in order that the offensive might this time completely rout the enemy it is essential that you took up seriously, and immediately, the work of preparation and organisation.

You have much work to do. Therefore, I shall not take much of you time now. You have given great promise, which nobody but you can fulfill. Remember, throughout the world youth is pouring out its blood in unmeasured quantities for causes good and bad. No cause can be greater, judged nationally or internationally, morally or materially, than the cause of the freedom of four hundred millions of people. By becoming the soldiers of the freedom of one-fifth of humanity, you will place yourselves in the front ranks of the international army of freedom, peace and progress. The key to the world's future lies in Asia and India is the key to Asia.

Therefore, march on comrades. Nothing but blood, toil and tears shall be our lot, but out of that shall emerge the freedom of our land and people—a Free India and therefore a new world!

Long Live Our Revolution!

44. To American Officers and Soldiers in India, 1943[1]

Friends,

I address you as one who loves America only next to his own motherland. I spent the best part of my youth in your great country and seven of my happiest years. I went there as a student and learnt much not only from its universities but also from its factories and farms where I worked as an ordinary labourer in order to pay my way through college. Having studied at California, Iowa and Wisconsin, I finally graduated from Ohio. There may be men among you from these Universities. To such of you I send my fraternal greetings.

I address you further as one who loves freedom and is prepared, as you are, to lay down his life for it. And also as a socialist who believes that under socialism alone can war be banished from society and our freedom secured, which your President has defined as major objectives of the peace that is to follow this war.

I address you also as a prisoner of war who has just exercised his right to escape from the enemy. I recently escaped from the Hazaribagh Central Prison, so that I may serve the cause of freedom more actively. The enemy—I mean the British Imperialist Government—has set-up a reward for my arrest, as if I were a criminal run away from justice. Surely, every one of you, if a prisoner of war and given the chance, would run away from your enemy's camp; and your comrades and your countrymen would rightly look upon you as a hero. I am no hero, and yet I am not a criminal. I wish merely to work for the freedom of my people.

[1] Towards struggle.

Too many men in the world are fighting and dying today for freedom. But I am afraid this word freedom has become too abstract—and devoid of substance, too undefined and vague. For me freedom is not an airy ideal to be talked about in radio broadcasts, but a concrete object. First of all and most of all, it means the freedom of my country—the freedom of our hundred millions of people from British Rule.

You are soldiers of freedom and you have been brought into close touch with my country. It is, therefore, essential that you understand and appreciate our fight for freedom.

You are all acquainted with Nazi lies. Dr. Goebbels has become synonymous with lying. But, perhaps, you are not acquainted with a far subtler and refined tradition of lying—imperialist lying, of which Churchill, Halifax,[2] Amery[3] & Co. are the brilliant present exponents. If you have bothered at all about India, you must have been told two tremendous lies. The first that Britain holds India down only to educate and train her in the art of Self-Government, and will continue to do so only until such time as she is able properly to look after herself. The second that Britain is prepared to free India immediately if Indians united among themselves.

No greater lies were ever uttered in history. But these are not lies like those of Geobbels, nor do they come from the mouth of insolent Nazi rulers. Therefore, they do not grate upon your ears. They have the prestige of ages and tradition, they have the gloss of British culture, they are mouthed by noble lords and aristocrats of wealth. Poetry and literature, learning and science have sanctified them until we witness today the strange spectacle of even the most emancipated British minds failing to transcend their limits.

It is an insult to the intelligence of any but a moron to say that imperialisms are founded to train 'backward' peoples in the art of self-government; empires, as you know, are founded to loot and to rob and to exploit. And the amount of British loot and exploitation in India would stagger even you who are accustomed to the astronomical figures of your national budgets.

Before Britain enslaved her, India was a free country. She did not have to learn the art of self-government from anybody. If at that moment the country was torn with wars, that was no more evidence of the unfitness of the people to govern themselves, than the much too frequent and far more bloody wars of Europe prove that the continent, with its islands, is ready to be taught a

[2] First Earl of Halifax, E.F.L. Wood (Lord Irwin) (1881-1959); British statesman; member, British Parliament, 1910-25; Viceroy of India, 1926-31; Secretary of State for War, 1935; Lord Privy Seal, 1935-7; Leader, House of Lords, 1935-8; Foreign Secretary, 1938-40; British Ambassador to U.S.A., 1941-6.

[3] Leoplod Stennelt Amery (1873-1955); British statesman; First Lord of Admiralty, 1922-4; Secretary of State for the Colonies, 1924-9, Dominion Affairs, 1925-9, India and Burma, 1940-5.

lesson in self-government by, let us say, the United States of America. First to destroy the freedom of a nation and then to claim to train the enslaved in the art of freedom, is such a process of historic perversion that only the master of empire-building can venture to father it.

And how have the British been training us in the art of self-government? They have been here now for 150 years. In less than that period your great country, after it freed itself from a similar tutorship of the same power, has been able to transform itself from a disunited collection of backward colonies into the mightiest and the most advanced nation of the world. You can see for yourselves what the British tutors have done to us in a longer period of time. Not more than ten per cent of the population is literate, not more than ten per cent of the economic resources of the country has been developed. Even during the three years of this total war you can see for yourselves what progress the country has made under British tutelage in production for war. This has been so scandalous that the Government of India did not even dare to publish the report of the American Technical Mission, which investigated under Dr. Grady,[4] certain matters of industrial production. So anxious indeed have the British rulers been for our progress, that every little progress—political, economical, educational—has been made in the teeth of their opposition and after great agitation and often bitter struggle. The bitterest struggle of all, and the last, is on to win our total emancipation from the British stranglehold.

Much has been made of the Cripps Mission and the Cripps offer. But what did Cripps offer? A so-called status of freedom that was hemmed in by important limitations at the end of the war and nothing—absolutely nothing—at present and till the war lasts. India is not interested in promises. She wants immediate freedom. To this the imperialist propagandists answer, 'We shall give you freedom if you but unite.'

First of all what justification can a nation have for keeping another nation enslaved just because it is divided? If two brothers fight, is a robber justified in entering their home and taking possession of it? The British are in the position of the robber. Suppose Hindus and Muslims do fight, does that justify the British in marching into our home and occupying it? The plea that if one robber did not take possession of a divided house another would, is an argument that appeals to robber minds alone. No decent man would burgle an unguarded house on the plea that if he did not, another burglar might do so.

But the argument is not even true. The British are not prepared to hand over real power—unity or no unity—into Indian hands. During the Cripps negotiations it was clear without any doubt, that even if there were complete

[4] Henry Francis Grady (1882-1957); Head of the American Technical Mission to India, March 1942; American Ambassador to India, 1947-8, to Greece, 1948-50, and to Iran, 1950.

unity in India, as the British conceive it, the rule of the Viceroy-in-Council could not be replaced by that of a cabinet, responsible ultimately to the Indian people. Sir Stafford Cripps made it plain to the Congress that if a 'National Government', were formed, the members of the government, would be free to resign if the Viceroy disagreed with policy. In other words, the measure of freedom the British Government was offering us—and the offer we are told still remains—was the freedom which the people's accredited representatives were to have to resign their office in case the Viceroy's will, representing the will of imperialism, conflicted with their own, representing the will of the Indian people! You can see what a tremendous lot of freedom that is.

The question of Indian unity has nothing to do with the subject. It has been raised merely to side-track the issue. The real issue is: is Britain prepared to liquidate her empire? The answer of the Cripps mission was a clear no. The same answer was repeated by Mr. Churchill himself, when he recently announced that he had not assumed the office of the King's First Minister to preside over the liquidation of the Empire.

The test of Britain's preparedness to free India is what she is prepared to do in the present, and not in the liberality of her promises. It is easy to make promises and war is just the occasion when the ruling class of every nation is most liberal with them. You know what happened to the promises made during the last war. No better fortune awaits the promises of the present war. If after the war we have a better world to live in, it will not be the result of the promises of the present rulers of the world, but of the efforts you and I—the common men of the world—will make and are making.

I shall give you two further instances to show the enormity of British lies. For this let us turn from the Government of India to the Governments of the Provinces. Much has been made by the British statesmen of the fact that several provinces of India are still being self-governed. But do you know what sort of self-government there is in these provinces? The Premier of Sind, Mr. Allah Bux,[5] was recently dismissed,[6] by the Governor[7] of the

[5] Allah Bakhsh (1900-43); a prominent leader of Sind; member, Bombay Legislative Council 1926-36; elected to the Sind Legislative Assembly in 1937; Chief Minister of Sind, 1938-9, 1940-2 (with short breaks in 1940 and 1941); nominated to the Viceroy's Defence Council, 1941; renounced his titles of Khan Bahadur and OBE and resigned from the Defence Council, September 1942; assassinated on 14 May 1943.

[6] Allah Bakhsh was dismissed by the Governor of Sind Sir Hugh Dow on 10 October 1942.

[7] Sir Hugh Dow (1886-1978); Secretary to the Government of India, Commerce Department, 1936-9; Director-General of Supply, and President of the War Supply Board, India, 1939-41; Governor of Sind, 1941-6, and of Bihar, 1946-7; Consul-General, Jerusalem, 1948-51; Chairman, Royal Commission on East Africa, 1952-4, and Council of Royal Central Asian Society, 1957-8.

Province. What was his offence? He renounced his title of 'Khan Bahadur'[8] and wrote a letter[9] to the Viceroy in protest against the present policy of the British Government in India. That was sufficient ground for a Governor to dismiss the Prime Minister of a Province who enjoyed the confidence of his assembly and his people. In the great province of Bengal, one of the ablest and most popular ministers, Mr. Syama Prasad Mookerji,[10] recently resigned his office in protest against the interference of the Governor with the administration of the province and with the policies of the Ministry. In a public statement,[11] he described Provincial Autonomy as a complete farce.

Now, the British say that they only require unity in India to give her freedom. Well, there was unity in Bengal and Sind—all communities were joined in supporting the ministers. If there were opposition parties, they were only such as must exist in any democratic system. Why was self-government not permitted in even these narrow spheres of provincial administration? No more proof, I hope, is necessary to show that Britain is not prepared ever to surrender her Empire willingly.

Under these circumstances what are we to do? India as a whole is opposed to Nazism and Fascism. The Indian National Congress and the Indian Socialist movement, as represented by my party, The All-India Congress Socialist Party, have declared it, times without number, that they remain everlastingly opposed to these brutal systems. Before the beginning of the war and before many of the so-called democratic nations had decided to take a stand against Fascism, both Nationalist and Socialist India lined up with

[8] Allah Bakhsh renounced his title of Khan Bahadur on 26 September 1942.

[9] In his letter to the Viceroy Lord Linlithgow dated 26 September 1942 Allah Bakhsh stated that the British wanted to continue their imperialistic hold on India and persist in keeping her under subjection, use political and communal differences for propaganda purposes and crush the nationalist forces to serve their own imperialistic aims and intentions.

[10] Syama Prasad Mookerjee (1901-53); Vice-Chancellor, Calcutta University, 1934-8; member, Bengal Legislative Assembly, 1937-42, and 1946; Working President, All India Hindu Mahasabha, 1940-4; Finance Minister, Bengal Government, 1941-2; Minister of Industry and Supply, Government of India, 1947-50, resigned in protest against Nehru-Liaquat Pact, 1950; formed Bharatiya Jana Sangh, 1951; member, Lok Sabha, 1952-3; publications include: *Leaves from a Diary*, and *Integrate Kashmir*.

[11] Syama Prasad Mookerjee issued a statement in Calcutta on 23 November 1942 in which he observed: 'My experience as a Provincial Minister for eleven months justifies me in stating, clearly and categorically, that Ministers while possessing great responsibilities for which they are answerable to the people and the legislature, have very little power, especially in matters concerning the rights and liberties of the people. The Governor has chosen to act, in many vital matters, in disregard of the wishes of the Ministers and has depended on the advice of a section of permanent officials, who are indifferent to the interests of the province.'

Republican Spain and Chiang's[12] Republican China against Germany, Italy and Japan. Had India been free then, she would, no doubt, have played a great part in that international crisis, and it is possible that her intervention might have even prevented this world war, or at least its spread to Asia. Free India and Free China would be a great guarantee against any aggression; and had these two ancient nations been free to work together, the history of our times might have been differently written.

But while we are consistent as total opponents of Fascism, we are also total opponents of Imperialism. We are not prepared to live any longer under its subjection, and we are determined to destroy it root and branch. At a time particularly when a world war is said to be fought to liberate oppressed peoples, we cannot but fight for our own liberation. We need offer no one any apology nor explanation as to why we long for freedom and why we fight to acquire it.

You may perhaps be troubled by the consideration that our fight with the British might weaken the United Nations' war against the Axis. If that is so, the responsibility is not only ours to consider the problem. It is for the United Nations also to give active thought to it. For our part, we do not wish to embarrass or create difficulties for the United Nations. But we cannot help if our war of liberation comes in the way. If it does, it is not our fault, but theirs. They claim to be fighting to restore freedom to humanity: why should the liberation of one-fifth of humanity come in their way? If the United Nations are truly fighting for the aims they profess, the Indian struggle for freedom should not hinder but help them. If it hinders them, it is only proof of the fact that the basis of their war is false; that there is dire discrepancy between their words and deeds, and ideals and practice. Our struggle would, therefore, render an incidental service to the United Nations by forcing them to bring their deeds to accord with their professions, thereby ensuring a juster Peace.

I, therefore, appeal to you as soldiers of freedom to supports us in our struggle for freedom. You can support us in three ways. First, by refusing to take any part in Britain's fascist war against us. Perhaps your Government itself has issued instructions to this effect. Secondly, by letting your countrymen, your leaders and your government know the real truth about India. You are in our midst and are in a position to tell folks on other side, the true state of affairs here. By enlisting the support of your country in our favour, you would further the great objective for which you are prepared to

[12] Chiang Kai-shek (1887-1975); Chinese military and political leader; emerged as the head of revolutionary Kuomintang in 1920s; led military expedition (1926-8) to unite China resulting in overthrow of Peking government; head of State of the Chinese Nationalist government in China, 1928-31, 1943-9, and in Taiwan, 1950-75.

sacrifice your lives. Third, by speaking to the British soldiers and officers and explaining to them the reality about India. The British soldier is a brave honest man, and if facts are placed before him, he would not fail to realise the justice of our cause. At present he is filled with intense prejudice and race-hatred and with ignorance about India. As such he harms himself and his cause as much as he harms us. Most of the British soldiers are common working people, and as such themselves the victims of their imperialist exploiters. It is essential for them to realise that our cause is their cause too, for unless the Empire is broken and destroyed, the British people themselves would not be freed from exploitation and poverty. In England there is much talk about a new social order after the War; and our soldier has faith in that future, but no new order can be built upon the old foundations of empire.

Therefore, tell the British men that if they are fighting for a better world, where wealth and opportunity, power and prestige, education and culture, and the good things of life shall be more rationally and equitably distributed, they are going about it the wrong way, if they shoot innocent women and children, burn and loot houses and try to crush, in other fascist ways, the greatest fight for freedom that ever stirred this old Asiatic continent. Tell them that we do not wish to fight them or harm them, nor do we wish any evil to the British people. We merely wish to fight the empire and destroy it, because it is the enemy of our freedom and happiness and prosperity. Tell them also that after we are free we shall march shoulder to shoulder with them in an assault on all kinds of oppression and brutality—Nazi, imperialist, capitalist. Only then we would build a New World Order. Tell them finally to open out their minds and to think for themselves. If they continue blindly and meekly to gulp down any propaganda that their rulers feed them with, they would have fought and died in vain, for their children would inherit the same vicious world of tyranny and inequality, poverty and misery, wars and armaments.

This, friends, is in brief my appeal. I hope it will find its way to your hearts.

Long Live the Cause of Freedom!
Long Live Indian Revolution!

45. To Home Secretary, Government of Punjab, Lahore, February 1944[1]

To
The Home Secretary,[2]
Government of Punjab.
Lahore

Sir,
I beg leave to bring to the notice of the Punjab Government certain facts and place before you certain of my grievances that arise from them. I shall first briefly state the facts.

I was arrested on the 18th September last year at Amritsar and brought the same day to this fort. After about a month of my detention here I was taken to the office where the officers of the Punjab, Bihar and Bengal C.I.D.s were present. I was informed that I would have to answer certain questions that would be put to me and make a statement regarding my recent activities. I made it clear to the officers present that I was prepared to answer any question that did not relate to my recent 'underground' activities, and as for a statement, I had no more to say than that I was an enemy of the British Empire of India (not of Britain or the British Commonwealth), that I was working for my country's independence and that I would continue to do so till either the object was achieved or death intervened. The interrogating

[1] This letter was published in *Inside Lahore Fort*, Socialist Book Centre, Madras, 1959, with the following note by J.P. under the title 'This was Lahore Fort':

This letter was written to the Punjab Government early in February 1944. My "interrogation" had been completed by then. As I was at that time a State prisoner the Home Secretary to the Provincial Govt. Mr. A.A. MacDonald, used to visit me every month. He came to see me first in the middle of December 1943 when he told me that the Punjab C.I.D. had given me up as "hopeless". It was then that I had asked him for permission to make a written complaint to the Provincial Government. He said then that he would think over the matter. When he came again he told me that I had permission to write to the Government whenever I wanted. But there was a further delay of a couple of weeks. For inspite of the Home Secretary's orders, I was not provided with the necessary writing materials till the beginning of February.

There was no formal reply from the Government to my representation: only Mr. MacDonald informed me, when he came to see me next, that my letter was "sent up", as I had wished, and was "sent down" again. That was all the notice that the Government of Lt. Col. Malik Khizar Hyat Khan took of a serious and earnest complaint made to it.

[2] Angus Alexander MacDonald (1914-65); Deputy Commissioner, Lyalpur, 1933-6, and Amritsar, 1936-41; Deputy Home Secretary, 1941-3; and Home Secretary, Punjab Government, 1943-7.

officers on their part made me understand that I was not to be let off till they had obtained from me the information they wanted.

In this manner my so-called interrogation began. Thereafter I was taken to the office everyday and made to sit there for varying periods of time. For the first few days the hours were not too long. Even so I pointed out to the interrogators that forcing me to sit in the office for hours together and repeatedly asking me questions that I had declined to answer was a form of harassment to which they had no right to subject me. I was told that I was in the hands of the Punjab C.I.D. and the question of rights did hardly arise. Gradually the hours of 'Interrogation'—in plain language harassment—were lengthened: from 8 a.m. to midnight. Often varied threats would be given to me in varied manners, some politely and mildly, some harshly and annoyingly. At this state I made vigorous protests and asked repeatedly but fruitlessly to be allowed either to talk to the Superintendent in charge or to write to the Government. It struck me as a remarkable system in which a prisoner could not even complain or petition to the Government which held him in custody; and I wish to bring this point to the notice of your Government with some emphasis, for in this system lie the germs of much mischief and injustice. To my mind, the right to petition should never be denied to a prisoner. I should mention here that about this time I made it clear to the interrogating officers, not in boasting but in all earnestness, that I was determined to risk my life, if necessary, but would not submit to their pressure. No one knows his powers of resistance but that was my sincere resolution and I did my best to persuade the officers to believe me.

The final stage in my harassment, which turned then into a form of torture, was to allow me no sleep during day or night. From morning I would be continuously kept in the office, then taken to my cell for an hour, brought to the office again for an hour or two, taken back for an hour again and so on till morning. The interrupted portions of hours that I got in my cell could hardly bring me sleep, for, just as I would be dozing off, the time would be up and I would be out again. On paper this process perhaps does not appear to be so torturous, but I can assure you in all honesty that when continued for days, it is a most oppressive and nerve-racking experience. I cannot describe it as anything but torture.

In the Second week of December this torture suddenly stopped, as did the 'Interrogation'. A few days later I was informed by you that my interrogation was over.

So much for the facts.

My grievance is that I have been tortured and treated in this fashion without any justification or warrant whatever. There is and there can be no moral or legal sanction for it. Even the all-sweeping ordinances do not permit such practices nor vest the police with such powers. A prisoner is a most helpless creature, and whatever his crime, civilisation safeguards against his ill-treatment. For his crime, he may be hanged if the law required it; as a prisoner, he may be punished according to prison rules, but he cannot be harassed and tortured for refusing to give information to the police. That a political prisoner should be so treated is still more reprehensible. Here I should like to draw the attention of the Government to another aspect of the matter, I have no desire to appear vain or boastful, but in order to make my point I must say that if the C.I.D. went so far with me it can be imagined how much further it can go with those who, perhaps, worthier than myself, are yet not in the public eye or do not hold any position in public life. That such people should be completely at the mercy of the C.I.D. without even the right to petition the Government is a state of affairs that should not be permitted to continue.

Suppression of political opponents is of the essence of Nazism and Fascism, torture of political prisoners their most characteristic feature. I am conscious of the argument that those who believe in violence as a political method, as I do, must be prepared to be forcibly suppressed. I grant that, but there are lawful means even for such suppression. A political revolutionary may be executed for his offences when found guilty by the established law, but he may not be put to any torture for the extortion of information. War is the deadliest, most brutal and violent form of political conflict. Yet a prisoner of war has certain rights and immunities which civilised society scrupulously respects. The same person who would be most mercilessly bayoneted to death on the field of battle would be immune from ill-treatment in the war prisoners' camp and would receive such amenities as the standards of the countries concerned and his own status would warrant.

The plea that the work of the Criminal Investigation Department must be carried on, and that in such work there is no room for human values or standards of civilised conduct is a type of excuse that can hardly be seriously put forth by an enlighteued Government, such as the Government of the Punjab, no doubt, would claim to be. If the C.I.D. cannot carry on its investigations without the use of torture it were better to replace it with a department that relied on brains and the science of detection rather than on primitive and vulgar methods. No civilised Government to my mind can be justified in lowering its standards of conduct just to enable its criminal (investigation) department, without skill and intelligence, to find facile means of success. It is laziness of thought and conscience to believe that investigation of crime is not possible without torture.

I, therefore, while harbouring no bitterness for those who interrogated me, for they were only carrying out orders, cannot but feel the deepest resentment against those who were really responsible for meting out such treatment to me. I have no idea who these were, but I cannot be persuaded to believe that the Council of Ministers which is the constitutional Government of the Province, could have sanctioned such a policy or permitted it to be persisted in had it been brought to its notice. My purpose in writing this letter is firstly to lodge my protest with the Government against the treatment I have received at the hands of its C.I.D. Secondly, I must earnestly beg of you to place this letter before the Prime Minister, so that he may personally look into this matter and put a stop to a policy of which, I have no doubt, he cannot approve but for which he is constitutionally ultimately responsible.

The least, if I may be permitted to suggest, that should be done is to allow every prisoner under interrogation to petition or complain to Government whenever he finds cause to do so; to require the Superintendent-in-charge to see every prisoner once a week or a fortnight and to allow an accredited non-official visitor to do likewise.

Begging to be excused for taking so much of your time.

I remain,
Yours faithfully,
Jayaprakash Narayan

46. *In the Lahore Fort: Random Jottings and Letters*, 1944[1]

[1] The items included here contain random jottings and letters by J.P. during his imprisonment in the Lahore Fort between September 1943 and January 1945. Most of them were brought out in a book form in 1947 by Sahityalaya, Patna, under the same title as mentioned at the head of this chapter. While working for this series we discovered the xeroxed copy of J.P.'s original handwritten manuscript. When checked with the book it was found that some items, for whatever reason, were not included in the book. These have been added here and carry asterisk mark to distinguish them from those which had earlier appeared in the book. On the other hand, one item—J.P.'s letter to Masani dated 8 February 1945—although included in the book has been excluded from the present chapter and placed in the chapter immediately after it as it was written in the Agra Central Prison to which J.P. had been transferred on 1 February 1945. On a similar ground the Preface to the book by J.P. written on 15 April 1947 will be found at the appropriate place in the chronological order.

I

RANDOM JOTTINGS

"Release the Congress Leaders!"[1]

At least on one point the Viceroy[2] and I agree. It would be barren to release the Congress leaders. It would be so from the point of view of the British Government because the released leaders would not be in a position to offer the cooperation that is desired in prosecuting the war. It would be so from the point of view of the leaders because they would not be able to carry on their activities without drifting again into prison.

Let us examine both these positions. The majority section of the Congress, as said by Pandit Jawaharlal and Maulana Azad, has pledged its fullest cooperation with the war efforts of the United Nations. And, as the Congress is a democratic body, its majority means the Congress itself. It would thus appear that the statement made above contradicts the position of the Congress. But on closer examination it would be clear that this is not so.

The British Government seeks the cooperation of the Congress, and the Congress, on its part, is desirous of giving this cooperation. Where then is the difficulty and the cause of the Indo-British conflict?

The difficulty lies in the terms of cooperation that are offered by either side. The British, on their side, made and repeat, the 'Cripps Offer', which is interpreted by them as a promise of independence to India after the war. I personally regard this as a fraudulent promise, but we shall not go into the merits of that question here, because that was not the issue on which the Cripps talks broke down, nor is it the main source of trouble between Congress and Britain. The Cripps plan had another part which dealt with the present constitutional status of India. To that part the spokesmen of the British Government rarely, if ever, make reference. And yet it is there that the source of the present conflict and the so-called deadlock lies.

British statesmen have tried to tell the world that Cripps failed because the communities in India failed to agree among themselves. Everyone in India knows how far from the truth this propaganda is. During the Cripps negotiations no occasion arose for the communities to agree or differ. The

[1] Undated, but seems to have been written shortly after 17 February 1944 when the Viceroy, Lord Wavell declared in course of his address to the central legislature that he saw no reason to release the Congress leaders.

[2] Archibald Percival Wavell (1883-1950); Commander-in-Chief of British forces in the Middle East, 1939-41; Commander-in-Chief, India, 1941-3; Viceroy and Governor-General of India, 1943-7; publications include: *The Palestine Campaigns*, *Allenby*, *Generals and Generalship*, and *The Good Soldier*.

break came when the British refused to transfer power during the war. The question, 'to whom should power be handed over?' never arose, because the party that held the power was unwilling to relinquish it.

The Working Committee of the Congress was prepared to let the question of the future status and constitution of India rest where it did, provided substantial power was transferred immediately to the representatives of the people. The Committee was further prepared to make all possible adjustments to enable the United Nations to prosecute the war on Indian soil according to their own strategy and requirements.

But Britain which is so gushing with promises of future independence, including separation from the British Commonwealth, was not and is not prepared to grant the limited 'independence' that the Congress seeks in the present—and seeks, as its resolutions . . . have repeatedly made clear, for the very purpose of arousing a national enthusiasm for the war.

Here then is the source of all the trouble: Britain wants India's cooperation on the strength of a mere promise without making any present concessions whatever. On the other hand, the Congress is desirous, nay, eager to offer cooperation but on the condition that substantial power be now transferred to Indian hands—if for nothing, to create the proper psychological atmosphere for the war, and as an earnest of Britain's sincerity to fulfil its promises.

As I said above, I do not wish to examine here the merits of Britain's promise. But there is one aspect of it that is germane to the present discussion: If Britain is really prepared to allow India, at the end of the war, to go so far as to separate from the British Empire and Commonwealth, why should it be so reluctant now to part with any power? The Home Member of the Government of India in his parting speech to the Central Assembly[3] remarked that the first thing that Mahatma Gandhi would do if he had power now was to negotiate with Japan. The Home Member knew that he was misrepresenting Mahatma Gandhi, but lies are the warp and woof of British propaganda about India, and the Home Member could not help himself. Mahatma Gandhi is a man of peace and a consistent pacifist. As such he would negotiate with

[3] Here the reference is to the speech of Reginald Maxwell, Home Member of the Government of India, to the Indian Legislative Assembly on 8 February 1944. In his speech he quoted a line—'If India were free she would have determined her own policy and might have kept out of the war. . . .'—from the resolution adopted by the A.I.C.C. at its meeting at Allahabad (27 April-1 May 1942) at the instance of the Working Committee, and added that it was 'only a camouflage of Mr. Gandhi's original draft—"If India were freed, her first step would probably be to negotiate with Japan"'. Gandhi's draft did contain this line (see Appendix 24 for text of Gandhi's draft). He had not attended the meeting of the Working Committee or the A.I.C.C., but had sent his draft resolution for the former's consideration. A revised version of the draft was adopted on 1 May 1942 (see Appendix 25 for text of this resolution).

the Allies as with any other belligerent; and in any case, would take up arms against none. He has his own method of defending his country and he would no less hesitate to use it against Japan as against any other aggressor who attacked India.

But Mahatma Gandhi's views on the matter have no bearing on the controversy between the Congress and Britain. Both the Working Committee and the A.I.C.C. have made it clear what Congress policy would be in relation to the war when a real national government was formed in the country. That policy is one of unreserved alliance with the United Nations in prosecuting the war. This aspect of Congress policy British propagandists have carefully tried to suppress. Because when it is kept in view the refusal of Britain to part with any power in the present, when they are prepared to surrender all of it at the end of the war, becomes inexplicable, and cannot but create the deepest misgivings and expose British policy to universal condemnation. Hence the necessity of lying.

It is clear that for imperialist reasons, and not for lack of Indian unity, Britain refuses to hand over any power during the war. As long as that refusal stands Congress non-cooperation too stands. From the British point of view, therefore, release of the Congress leaders would be clearly a barren event.

From the point of view of the Congress, release of the leaders—in other words re-legalisation of the Congress—would be no less fruitless. Immediately on their release the leaders and the Congress organisations would find themselves in conflict with British policy, with the authorities in India, with the Ordinances, and above all, with the prosecution of the war, which in view of British policy in India remains for this country an imperialist war. The only outcome of this conflict, unless Congressmen were to become politically sterile, would be re-imprisonment and re-illegalisation. What can be more barren than that?

It were better therefore that the Congress leaders, as also every true Congressman, continued to remain in prison. Not the least advantage of such a situation is that it will ever remain as a constant spur to the conscience of the so-called democratic world. When the war ends, so will the ordinance dictatorship and irrespective of whether the August Resolution existed or not, the leaders would have to be released. Their detention in the meanwhile is a sort of incubation period for the Congress during which its influence and popularity grow unseen. When peace comes to the world again, it will be time for the leaders to put British promises to the test. Then will the Congress return again to its position of Indian leadership and resume the initiative in the fight for freedom.

*The Problem of the Released Congressmen**

A large number of Congressmen are out of prison, and more are likely to be released in the course of time. At the same time Congress organisation remains illegal, the Working Committee, Mahatma Gandhi and other leaders continue to be imprisoned. In these circumstances, confusion, and even an element of demoralisation, are bound to exist in the ranks of those Congressmen who find themselves without the prison walls. The situation is made worse by Government's deliberate policy of releasing especially those who are weak of spirit and faith. It is difficult to say what strength the present 'underground' Congress organisations possess, but in any case it is not likely that they would be generally recognised by the recently released Congressmen as bodies to which they owed allegiance.

It appears that here and there attempts are being made to bring together such Congressmen as are at liberty and to evolve some programme of work. Without work the position, if not of the Congress, at least of these men and women would become insupportable and intolerable. Therefore, the present attempts to evolve a programme of activity are commendable as far as they go. But the question is what should this programme be, what is the duty of Congressmen at the present moment?

So for those who are in search of activity, the 'constructive programme' is the first that suggests itself. Relief work and the food crisis come next. But do these activities comprise the primary duty of Congressmen today? To my mind they most emphatically do not. The British Government, that opened the Pearl Harbour offensive on the Congress, is still on the war path and its offensive continues unabated. The August Resolution of the A.I.C.C. remains its main target. For Congressmen too that resolution should remain the guiding signal. If it is not possible for them to do anything effective in furtherance of the resolution, they should court imprisonment by merely reiterating it, singly or jointly, by mouth or in writing. Their primary duty is to stand solidly behind the Working Committee and Mahatma Gandhi and to demonstrate that they present as solid a front to the enemy as the latter does to India. 'Every Congressman to jail as long as Gandhi remains in jail' this should be their foremost slogan. Except for those who are or may be engaged in 'underground' work and those whose health compels them to keep out of active politics, every Congressman should by publicly re-affirming the August Resolution betake himself to prison. Any other form of activity would serve only to weaken our ranks and undermine discipline.

* 21-2 February 1944.

22 February 1944*
India Divided

Shri Rajagopalachari is reported to have said the other day that he did not care if India were divided into ten different parts, each sovereign and independent of the other. His immediate inspiration for making this remarkable statement was the recent Molotov amendment to the Russian Constitution.

Rajaji is too informed a politician really to believe what he has been reported to say. He apparently talks in this fashion with a view to remove suspicions that are harboured in certain quarters, and to pave the path probably for a rapprochement between the Congress and the League. But he is doing himself an injustice by pretending to believe that he can ever succeed in his efforts by making fantastic and over-reaching statements. The tragedy of Rajaji is due to a not uncommon fault of clever people: their proneness to discount the ability of the other fellow to see through their trick.

But let us take Rajaji at his word. India divided into ten states? Even a high school knowledge of Indian history should enable one to forecast the result of such a vivisection of this country. Vivisection obviously pre-supposes the existence of a widespread desire for separation. Given this desire and the fact of division and undoubted foreign influences of a conflicting nature, India would present a picture not essentially different from that which existed at the dissolution of the great empires of Indian history. The only outcome of such a confused state would be cultural and economic backwardness, political weakness and eventual subjugation again to a strong foreign power or to more than one power. In fact, if the desire for the division of the country came generally to be shared by the Indian people, freedom from present subjection itself would become impossible, and in the place of Rajaji's ten free states of India, there would be perpetuated the one undivided Indian Empire groaning under the heels of His Majesty John Bull. The forces that are working for the division of India are anti-freedom forces of slavery and between them and nationalist India no compromise is possible. To say that without such a compromise freedom could not be won is a self-contradiction. It is to underestimate grossly the strength of Indian nationalism.

Let us turn now to the recent Russian constitutional innovation. There is no doubt that the Molotov amendments will be seized upon by all sorts of quacks to popularise their own nostrums. But for those who are seriously considering the future constitutional development of India, the Russian experiment can be of very doubtful value. It is necessary to remember that

* The date mentioned in the book is 18 February 1944, but it is apparently wrong since his hand-written manuscript mentions 22 February 1944.

the so-called decentralisation has been introduced into the Soviet state structure not as a measure of internal adjustment but to answer certain diplomatic requirements of Russia's international relations that have arisen during the war and are expected to become more pressing in the post-war period. Internally there can be no question of loosening the central dictatorship of the Communist hierarchy. It is also essential, where Russia is concerned, to distinguish between theory and practice. In 1936 was promulgated the Stalin Constitution, which was tom-tomed throughout the world by the Russian fifth column as 'the most democratic constitution in the world'. And yet, it was in that very year that began the most brutal suppression of political dissidents—it would be wrong to call them even political opponents—that is known to human history. It may be safely presumed, therefore, that the new powers that have been devolved upon the constituent Republics of the Soviet Union are entirely for purposes of Soviet world diplomacy rather than real measures of devolution. There can also be little doubt that even while these measures of decentralisation were publicly announced secret administrative and party measures must have been taken to concentrate even more power in the hands of Stalin and his junta.

But let us, for argument's sake, concede that there has been a real devolution of power and political decentralisation in the Soviet Union. Does that justify any one to demand the partition of India? First, the recent Russian amendment leading to decentralisation in Russia has not *broken up* the Soviet Union and divided it into a number of *independent* states. As for the 'right' to secede, it is an old constitutional guarantee that exists since Lenin's time. But there is all the difference in the world between the recognition of the 'right' of separation and the actual fact of separation. As far as Russia is concerned, the nature of the Russian state has always reduced this right to a nullity. In India it is not as if the units that are prepared to join the Indian Union are seeking to *reserve the right* to secede if they find cause later to do so. What is demanded is an outright separation and division of the country. There is a world of difference between the two positions: the first presupposes a desire to stick together and make a serious experiment in joint nationhood, while the latter kills the very possibility of union by immediate partition. In every federal constitution of the world where the right of secession is guaranteed, it has a twofold basis: while, on the one hand, it provides the ultimate solution of intra-national conflicts, on the other hand, it rests on the ground that mutual goodwill and adjustment and the desire to pull together would ever make unnecessary the exercise of this ultimate constitutional right. I believe Congress would have no difficulty in guaranteeing this right to the federating units in India provided there was genuine desire to start as a united nation and to preserve national unity to the utmost extent possible. The Congress would do this precisely in the hope and belief that the experiment in united nationhood would soon remove suspicion and cement the bonds that naturally exist among all the sections of the Indian people. It can be appreciated how different from this is the position that demands immediate and initial partition of the country. To that the Congress can never agree.

Turning to Russia, the second point to note is that Russia is not just a conglomeration of independent republics, but a highly centralised union with a powerful and effective central government which has the means to check disruptive tendencies and prevent the dissolution of the Union.

Lastly—and this is the most important point—the Russian State is a monolithic state—that is, based on a single political party, the organisation of any other party being illegal and treasonable. In view of this one-party rule, and in view of the highly centralised structure of that party, all paper freedoms, rights and enfranchisements lose their meaning. Suppose Latvia is declared to be a member republic of the Soviet Union. Only the Communist party of Latvia would be allowed to function there, and all political, economic, cultural and social power would be centred in that party, or rather, its higher bureaucracy. But the Communist party of Latvia would not be an independent body; it would be a part of, and subject to, the All–Russian Communist party, with the Stalin–Molotov caucus at the top. In this fashion all the rights and freedoms that the Latvian Republic would be guaranteed by the constitution of the Soviet Union would be effectively shackled and hamstrung by this party mechanism and the suppression of all parties but the Communist party.

If we were to draw an Indian parallel, it would be of some such fashion as this. The Congress, let us say, is the only political party that is allowed to exist anywhere in the country. The Congress then rules in every part of the country and suppresses *by force* all other rival parties. At the same time this very Congress grants the right to the various units of the Indian Union to secede if they so desire! We have only to picture this state of affairs to realise what a far cry the Russian system is for us.

Whether the Russian system is good or bad is irrelevant to the present discussion. What is of value for us is to remember that here in our own country no one worth bothering about advocates a monolithic state or one-party rule; nor is such a thing possible here, nor with the exception of British rule does any central power exist in India. In these circumstances, can the imitation of the devices of the Russian constitution be anything but fatal to us?

The partition of the country is proposed as a solution of the minorities problem. But will the partition *solve* the problem? If we take the Muslims, for instance, and treat them as a minority, does the constitution of a state of Pakistan solves the problem of the Muslim minorities? In areas where it is proposed to establish Pakistan, the Muslims are the majority and not the minority community. Even in a united India those areas would be ruled by Muslim-majority governments and the Hindus and others would be the minorities there. It is true that the Muslim provinces would be in a minority at the Centre, but apart from that even in an undivided India they would constitute a sort of Pakistan, as far as provincial and local matters are concerned and would have their own minorities. In an independent Pakistan too the situation would remain the same, except for central affairs. On the other hand, in Hindustan (so-called), i.e., the part of India outside Pakistan, the Muslims would continue to be a minority community, both as regards provincial and national matters. Thus neither in Pakistan nor in Hindustan would the minority problem be solved, and the problem of the Muslim minority in areas where they are really in a minority would remain unaltered. It is clear, therefore, that the only object of Pakistan is to remove the Muslim-minority areas from the interference of a Centre where the Muslims do not constitute a majority. But this is a problem of which, given mutual goodwill, it should not be difficult to find a much less drastic solution. The necessity of finding such an alternative solution becomes all the greater when it is considered that a division of the country would weaken both its parts economically, politically and in every other way. After all, when Hindus and Muslims are going to live together both in Hindustan and Pakistan, it appears precipitate folly to divide the country.

We are aware that the Muslim League's claim for partition is based on the theory that the Muslims in India constitute a separate nation, and, as such, should have their own independent State. We do not think this claim would bear any scientific scrutiny. It may conceivably be possible to claim that the Punjabis, including Hindus, Muslims, Sikhs and others, or the Sindis including again all the communities living in Sind, constitute a separate nation from, let us say, the Bengalis or the Tamils. But no social scientist would support the contention that the Punjabi Muslims and the Bengali Muslims constitute one nation and the Bengali Hindus and the Punjabi Hindus do another. Mere religion has never formed, obviously not in Islamic lands, the basis for a common nationality. The Arabs and Turks are both Muslims by religion but they constitute two distinct nationalities. It is very difficult to define a nation, as the League of Nations Committee on the European national minorities demonstrated after an exhaustive examination of the question; but race, language, history, culture, religion, geography, tradition—all these go to create that intangible psychological product known as nationality. No one of these various factors by itself creates a nation. People of the same race constitute separate nations, as witness the Slavs: those with the same language do likewise, as witness the English-speaking or Spanish-speaking nations of the world; likewise with religion, as witness the Muslims who constitute so many nations. Nor must a single nation have a single language, race or religion, as witness the Swiss, the British, the Americans, the Canadians, the Chinese. If we take race, language, history, culture, geography, religion, tradition all together, then India forms one single nation much more truly and really than do the separate communities living in this country.

However, let us concede for the sake of argument that the Muslims of India do constitute a separate nation. Does it follow necessarily that they should therefore separate from the rest of the country and constitute an independent State? Is it not possible for two nations to live together within a common state? Does not history afford examples of such common statehood? Do not the Scotch, the Welsh and the English live together under one government, do not the German, the French and the Italian Swiss form one national state, do not the British and French Canadians live together, is not the great American nation the result of the mingling of all the nationalities of Europe, are not practically all the South American nations multi-national in composition? It seems highly illogical to demand a partition of the country merely because the Indian Muslims consider themselves to be a separate nation.

With the national minorities problem of European and other countries there has always been associated the phenomenon of oppression of the minority nationality by the majority. In India there is no such historical tradition. In fact, it was the minority community which was till recently the ruling power and the oppressed or otherwise was the majority Hindu community. It is true that a lot of dust was raised by the League about oppression of the Muslims in the Congress–governed provinces. But we do not think that the charges brought against the Congress ministries by the Pirpur Committee[4] would bear examination by any impartial tribunal. However, even granting that the charges were true, would the division of the country save the Muslim minorities in these provinces from the oppression of the Hindu community? The answer may be that if that oppression did not cease, Pakistan would retaliate by oppressing its own Hindu minority. But this remedy, if it can be said to be a remedy, would be available to the Muslim provinces even in a united India, for the Centre, whatever its nature, could never interfere in the internal administration of the autonomous provinces. Thus it would appear that Pakistan would solve none of the problems it seeks to, except the one of the relation of the Central Government with the Muslim-majority provinces. We could willingly admit this solution if it did not endanger the growth and development, prosperity and safety of

[4] The Muslim League appointed a committee under the chairmanship of Raja Syed Mohammad Mehdi of Pirpur (U.P.) in 1938 to enquire into the alleged atrocities on Muslims committed in the Congress-governed provinces. This became famous as the Pirpur Committee and reported that atrocities had indeed been committed on the Muslims in those provinces.

the whole country, including both or all its parts, and if no other solution were available.

The Muslim fear is that the Central Indian Government in which Hindus will be in a majority will dominate and interfere with the Muslim provinces, as with the others. There are two ways of removing this possibility. One is carefully to define and limit the powers of the Central Government and vest the residue in the Provincial Governments. If the minimum possible powers are left with the Centre, the possibility of its interfering with the provinces would be reduced to that extent. The next problem is to ensure that the powers that are vested in the national government are so exercised that no injustice is done to the Muslim community. To do this it is possible to provide for checks and balances. The Central Government, as all governments, would have two main functions—legislative and executive. Both the Legislature and Executive may be so constituted that the Muslims may have no cause to fear. At the same time a final guarantee may be constitutionally provided in the shape of the right to secede. The very existence of this right—of the possibility of its being exercised—would be a check on the majority.

These three measures should be enough to remove Muslim fears. At the same time they would preserve the unity of the country, which is the only guarantee of its future prosperity, development and power.

27-28 February 1944
Three Vital Aspects of the Constitutional Problem of India

There are three vital problems, each equally important, that are connected with the evolution of a constitution for India. These problems are: the problem of the Muslims, the problem of the States, and the economic problem. Certain aspects of the first have been considered already. Here we shall briefly touch upon the other two.

Broadly speaking, four different parties are involved in the problem of States: the people of democratic India (the so-called British India), the people of the States, the Princes, and the so-called Paramount Power. Generally speaking the first two would find themselves in one camp while the last two would like to hang together. The starting point of constitution-making for free India is the assumption that the British Power, at least in democratic India, has been brought to its knees and that a Provisional National Government has been constituted at the Centre, no doubt under the nominal sanctions of the present constitution, but with the explicit and clear understanding that it shall enjoy full power without any restriction or limitation by the present safeguards or the Viceregal prerogatives. It is further assumed that the main purpose of this Provisional Government shall be to supervise the creation of a new constitution, conduct elections and usher in the new government of free India.

Given this assumption, the role of British Power, as far as democratic India, is concerned, would be reduced to pulling wires behind the scenes. But in feudal India its role would still retain both its constitutional and real prerogatives as the Paramount Power. And as such democratic India would have to fight not only the shadow, which are the Princes, but also the substance, which is the Paramount Power. Thus in the constitution-making of free India not a little trouble will arise on account of the States.

To my mind democratic India's attitude to feudal India should be defined according to two basic principles: first, the States should be democratised politically as soon as possible, the position and status of the Princes to be determined by their peoples, second, the representation of the States joining the Indian Union should be on a popular and not a princely basis. No state should be allowed to join the Union that has not democratised or is not prepared to democratise its constitution. In any case, the representatives of a state—even if it is not fully democratised should always be elected by the people the franchise and the manner of election varying.

An objection to this proposal may be that under these conditions, no state, encouraged by the Paramount Power, would be willing to join the Union. It may be so to begin with—though it is questionable that when in democratic India the British power has been brought to its senses, the people in the states would be sitting idle. But, at any rate, this plan will guarantee the creation of a strong Centre of a genuinely national character. With such a government functioning at the Centre it may be possible soon to bring such political and economic pressure to bear upon the Princes—which pressure would be powerfully supplemented by the vigorous growth of the state's people's movement that is expected to follow in the wake of the constitution of the Free Indian Union—that they may soon be compelled to surrender power to their people, who would doubtless lose no time in joining the Union. I believe that the combined strength of the Paramount Power and the Princes would not be able to stand very long against the combined and rapidly growing strength of the Indian Union and the states' people.

By the economic problem I do not mean merely the problem of poverty or industrialisation or any such economic problem in the ordinary sense of the term. I use this term here in a much more fundamental sense, namely, the determination of the basic economic principles on which Indian economy shall rest in a Free India. Shall this economy be that of capitalism in which not only shall present economic enterprises and undertakings be owned and directed by private agencies for private profit, but also the entire economic development and future material well-being of the nation will be at the disposition of a handful of moneyed people pursuing the ends of selfish profit? Or shall the economy of the nation be a national concern under the control and guidance of the State? We believe that unless a deliberate conscious attempt is made at the very outset to bring the Nation's economic life under the guidance and control of the State, not only would that life be made to serve the ends of Indian capitalism, but soon enough would the State itself be converted into the latter's subservient tool. At the outset, the influence of Indian capitalism on national politics may not be too great, for the middle classes, which in India do not live far removed from the borders of poverty, preponderate not only in numbers but also ideologically. Therefore, the middle classes, if they are so minded, can prevent the capitalists from tying the country's economy to the wheels of their profit-chariot.

Within the Congress there is happily a lively awareness of this vital issue. Pandit Nehru, of course, is a proclaimed socialist. Mahatma Gandhi himself, whose voice may have decisive influence over this question, is known to favour the public ownership of large industries. The Congress is already committed to the State ownership or control of key industries, mines, railways, etc. Therefore, it is hoped that Congress, further impelled in this direction by the experience of the war, will throw its united weight very substantially in favour of national control of the country's economy. It is doubtful what attitude the other constituents of the political set-up, as brought into existence for the purposes of framing the constitution of free India, would adopt towards this vital problem. The representatives of labour would no doubt be fully with the Congress: indeed they would endeavour to take the constituent assembly much farther on the road to socialisation of economic life. The representatives of the states' people would also be wholly with the Congress. It is difficult to say what the attitude of the Muslim League would be. So far the League, though claiming to represent a community which is even deeper in poverty than certain other communities, and more exploited, has refused to express any opinion on this vital question, as on so many other equally vital questions. However, if the present leadership of the League persists there is little doubt that its influence would be largely exercised in the opposite direction. It might even take shelter behind religion in order to avoid facing this problem. It is likely that with regard to many questions, such as the agrarian, the League might insist on leaving them to the provinces to settle. The representatives of Indian capital may be more subtle. They are likely to admit State control in principle, but might endeavour to see that it is so put into practice that, first, the interests of profit do not suffer; second, the resources of the State are utilised to bolster up industries of which they continue to be the proprietors; and, third, that they are so able to insinuate themselves into the economic limb of the State that eventually they come to rule the roost. What other elements there will be in the Constituent Assembly it is difficult to say. But it is doubtful if they will be of any but a conservative character. The influence of British capital in India that may directly or indirectly be exercised over it will naturally be on the side of capitalist economy. In these circumstances the course of the Congress at the Assembly—provided its own attitude is of a progressive character as we expect it to be—would be one of considerable difficulty. And the fear would be far from unreal of the lukewarm sections of the Congress making of these difficulties an excuse for dropping progressive economic principles.

Conscious of such a political set-up in the Constituent Assembly, I wish to lay down the following proposals in respect to our national economy. The economic life of the nation may be thus divided: land, industry, trade, banking, transport, shipping, mines and forests.

The first economic principle that should be adopted is that the State is the owner of all the natural resources of the country. This principle would immediately and directly affect land, mines, and forests. These should be declared to be State property throughout the Indian Republic and no provincial or regional exceptions or reservations should be admitted in this connection. The proprietorship having been vested in the State, the next question would be about their exploitation. It is clear that it would be impossible for the State directly to exploit all the natural resources of the country. Land is the primary and often the sole means of livelihood for the overwhelming majority of the Indian people and whatever the merits of collective agriculture, there is no doubt that the peasantry would oppose any such move at the outset. The State will have, therefore, to settle most of the land with individual peasants, the rights of the holders being carefully laid down. The remaining lands should be turned to demonstrative and educative collective or cooperative farming.

It should be noted that by the simple measure of vesting the proprietorship of land in the State, we abolish the zamindari system (permanent or otherwise). This naturally raises the question of compensation to the present zamindars and taluqdars. If the Constituent Assembly that is visualised here were meeting after a successful mass revolution, this question of compensation would not have arisen. But in the circumstances we are visualising, the zamindars would be in a position to demand compensation and the Assembly would have to consider and admit their claim. We shall not go into the details of this question of compensation because we believe it is not difficult to prepare a scheme of compensation that will meet the needs of justice if not the avarice and greed of our zamindars.

Another problem more difficult and ticklish than the previous one that is connected with the question of land is that of the size of holdings that each cultivator should be allotted. At present there is a great disparity between the biggest and the smallest peasant holdings. It is clear that such a situation cannot be permitted to continue. An attempt towards equalisation of holdings will have to be made. To quieten peasant fears, it would have to be announced that their present holdings would be respected as far as possible and that only in extreme cases would redistribution and re-settlement be resorted to. I believe that roughly speaking 25 per cent of the present holdings will have to be redistributed. It should be understood that technically and for the purpose of regularisation under the new land laws, the whole land will have to be re-settled, but it is expected that in respect of 75 per cent of the holdings no disturbance or very little, would be caused. With regard to the rights that the holders may enjoy in their land, it may be left to the provincial legislatures to prescribe them in detail.

The problem would be simpler in regard to mines and forests. But here too the State may not be in a position to exploit all the available resources and, therefore, concessions and leases may be given under suitable conditions to private agencies. The question of compensation to the present mine-owners will also arise and may be settled according to the general policy of economic compensation.

We turn to industry now. Industry is of small, medium and large size and of a heavy (or basic) and light (or consumption-goods-producing) nature. All heavy or basic industry such as iron and steel and machine-making, should be not only under the control and management of the State, but also purely State property. Of the other industries that produce goods for consumption, those that are on a large scale, such as textile or jute, should also be nationalised. The other industries may be allowed to be run and developed as private enterprises, but there should be provision made for certain amount of State control with respect to prices (both of raw materials and finished goods), wages and production.

The second basic economic principle that I wish to lay down and that the Indian State should adopt if India is to become a real democracy is the principle that labour should play an effective part both in the affairs of the State and industry. We shall consider the relation of Labour to the Legislature and Executive elsewhere; here we wish to confine ourselves to its relation to industry alone. In all the State industries, Labour should play an *equal* part with the representatives of the State in running them and disposing of their proceeds. Private capital having been eliminated from them Labour and the State would be the only two partners in the State industries and they should share equal power in their conduct.

In the privately owned industries the rights of labour to organise, to collective bargaining, to strike should be guaranteed by the state. Minimum wage, hours of work, housing, provident fund, should be guaranteed and supervised by the State.

Turning to trade, I shall distinguish the classes of it: retail, wholesale and foreign. Retail trade would clearly be beyond the scope of the State's control, though the State should endeavour to encourage and patronise non-profit-making cooperative trading institutions. With regard to wholesale trade, particularly in commodities that are of common use or constitute necessities of life, the State, if not taking over the entire wholesale trade into its own hand should exercise such control as to eliminate or reduce speculation, cornering and undue profiteering.

With regard to foreign trade, the State should no doubt be the chief foreign trader and control drastically all private foreign trading.

Banking should be entirely nationalised and to save the poor man, either in the village or city, from the clutches of the money-lender, cooperative banks should be developed on a large scale.

Regarding transport, railways and airways must be completely nationalised. Road and river traffic may be allowed to remain, largely or in part, in the hands of private agencies. Shipping too should be completely nationalised.

This leaves a huge number of undertakings in the hands of private bodies. The State should discover means to regulate and control the activities as far as possible in the interest of the common good.

28 February 1944

It is amusing and a little saddening to find Hindu leaders exulting so much over the Viceroy's declaration[5] of the geographical unity of India. Sir Tej Bahadur Sapru[6] has done well to warn against unnecessary rejoicing over it.[7] It is a pity that Indian politicians who are not of the Congress attach such importance to the pronouncements of British politicians. It is a still greater pity that they do not realise the game that the latter have been playing. It is *naiveté* to distinguish between Linlithgow, Wavell, Churchill, Amery and the rest. The British have a settled policy with regard to India and all their politicians pursue this policy. The apparent changes in the language used by them are nothing but the torturous ways in which that policy is applied. Take this question of Pakistan itself. It is doubtless that British politicians

[5] Here J.P. was perhaps referring to B.S. Moonje's comment on the Viceroy, Lord Wavell's speech to the Indian Legislative Assembly on 17 February 1944 wherein he had declared: 'You cannot alter geography. From the point of view of defence, of relations with the outside world, of many internal and external economic problems, India is a natural unit.' B.S. Moonje commended the Viceroy for his 'frank, straight and direct language' in a statement issued on 18 February 1944 (published in the *Tribune*, 20 February 1944).

[6] Tej Bahadur Sapru (1875-1949); leading constitutional lawyer; Advocate High Court, Allahabad, 1896-1926; member, A.I.C.C., 1906-17; U.P. Legislative Council, 1913-16; Imperial Legislative Council, 1916-20; Law Member, Governor-General's Executive Council, 1922.

[7] Tej Bahadur Sapru in a statement issued on 20 February 1944 characterized the Viceroy's speech as at best negative and remarked: 'The Muslim League cannot feel happy, but I think it is a little too precipitate for the Hindus to rejoice in what the Viceroy has said about the geographical unity of India. India may not be physically divided, but politically and constitutionally may be divided still more.' *Tribune*, 21 February 1944.

have been behind this scheme. It was necessary to play up to the Muslims and to set them up as an obstacle to India's political progress. Therefore, Pakistan received encouragement—both open and unseen. The Muslims have largely served their purpose now and the British probably find that if they have to keep the Congress outlawed they must cheer up the Hindus somehow. So a new Viceroy is made to prattle about the geographical unity of India. The pity is that the poor fish for whom the bait is intended swallow it so easily. But it is wrong to attach any importance to this declaration about India's geographical unity. The same person who talked of this unity also declared that British Government still stood by the Cripps proposals; and it should not be forgotten that those proposals are based on the division of the country. Divide and rule is the cornerstone of British imperial policy and any Indian politician who forgets it makes a mortal mistake. There is no doubt that the more precarious becomes the British position in India the more eagerly they will turn to this policy.

23 March 1944

*The India Policy of the British Government is prolonging the War**

British war leaders from Mr. Churchill downwards have always announced that the war in Asia must wait till that in Europe has been liquidated. They have made no secret of the fact that the resources of the allies are not adequate enough to launch two major offensives—one in Europe and the other in Asia. This policy of dealing with the enemy piecemeal will obviously prolong the war—costing so much more misery to human kind.

The question may be asked, is it *necessary* to prolong the war in this manner, is it inevitable? Whoever looks at a map of Asia and understands the Asiatic problem must reply in the negative. The world has seen and applauded China's resistance to Japanese aggression. Inspiring as that resistance is, it may be asked if the Chinese would have fought equally bravely and undauntingly had they been living under the subjection of foreign rule. No one who is acquainted with the spirit that pervades a people's war can answer the question in the affirmative.

British spokesmen have been constantly singing the praises of India's war effort. But the British people and people elsewhere would be foolish if they believed that a free India fighting for her safety and independence and in willing support of her allies, would have put forth no more effort than what goes for India's war effort today. Four hundred millions of free people richly possessed of nearly all resources and materials of war, would have within two years been able to put in the battlefield such an army, backed up by such a solid home-front behind, that simultaneously with the offensive in

Europe, an offensive could have been launched in South East Asia that, supplemented by the South Western and Chinese offensives, could have pushed the Japs back to their island homes perhaps sooner than the conquest of the Nazi fortress in Europe.

In spite of four and a half years of war, the British have neither taken care to develop Indian agriculture, nor Indian industry in order to make India a real base for the war in Asia. It would have been clearly in the interest of military operations to do so, but economic self-interest and not military strategy, determines the policies of Government, which are fighting to preserve not human civilization as they claim but that system of profits which goes under the name of Empire—whether economic or political. The development in India of a heavy chemical industry and heavy machine industry (including the manufacture of locomotives, automobiles, many armaments, aeroplanes, etc.) would be opposed to British Capitalist interests now and after the war. So even if India's industrialisation were to bring the end of the war closer, imperialist interest puts a veto on it. The constitution of a Provisional National Government of the type desired by the Congress would have infused that spirit into India's 'war efforts' that could convert it from a mercenary war—looking from the angle of Indians participating in it—into what has come to be known as a people's war. But that again is opposed to imperialist interests, *ergo*, humanity must suffer, the war must be prolonged. What does it matter as long as the Empire is safe and profits continue to be made? After all is not the war being fought mainly to save profits and Empire?

23 March 1944

*So This is What We are Fighting For!**

Dealing with colonial responsibility Mr. Hull[8] said 'It should be the duty of nations having political ties with dependent people as mandatories, or trustees, or as other agencies, as the case may be, to help aspiring people to develop materially and educationally to prepare themselves for the duties and responsibilities of self-government and to attain liberty'. Reuter, Washington, March 21.

Someone in America said recently that the Atlantic Charter[9] was dead. Here is an autopsy performed on the corpse by one whom it may not be far

[8] Cordell Hull (1871-1955); U.S. Secretary of State, 1933-44; awarded Nobel Peace Prize (1945) for work leading to creation of the United Nations.

[9] The Atlantic Charter, hailing the right of the people to self-government, was issued in August 1941 by Franklin Roosevelt and Winston Churchill as a statement of their war policy. However, Churchill announced on 9 September 1941 in the House of Commons that it would not be applied to countries like India, but only to those territories which would be liberated from the yoke of the Axis Powers.

wrong to consider one of its joint-fathers. In the post-war world which Mr. Hull has pictured, there will be dependencies, mandates, trusts and other agencies for the subjugation of one people by another. And he has the impudence to tell the world that the duty of the Powers that may have 'ties' with such dependencies, etc., will be to help them towards self-government and material development. This is the same old pre-war world of injustice and sufferings and slavery and the same old imperialist excuse, without even the cautionary gloss of vague American idealism. It is remarkable that a descendent of the rebel colonists of one time should persuade himself to believe and invite others to share his illusion that a ruling nation can ever desire to help its dependencies to become self-governing and to develop their material resources.

28 March 1944

The Central Assembly has rejected the Finance Bill. In an otherwise dull political atmosphere, this news might create some interest. But everyone knows how barren and tedious such an event always is. The direct result of the officious victory will be, as heretofore, nill. It may be useful to speculate on its indirect fruits.

Is the Congress-League combination within the Assembly an augury of a larger agreement? To my mind the answer is in the negative. I do not think there has been a change of heart on the part of the League *vis-a-vis* the Congress. The time is not yet for such a change. Though to me it appears certain that it is bound to come sooner rather than later. The League's alliance with the Congress in the Assembly is probably the result of a pique. The Viceroy recently spoke of the geographical unity of India, thereby tearing a big hole in the standard of the League. Hence Mr. Jinnah's annoyance and his decision perhaps to show it to the Viceroy and the British Government that when provoked the League can cause much embarrassment and create no little difficulty.

Again, do the participation in the debate[10] of Mr. Desai[11] and the presence of Mrs. Sarojini Naidu[12] and Mrs. Pandit[13] in the gallery suggest a change in the policy of the Congress or the emergence of affairs like the old Swaraj

[10] Reference is to the debate on the Finance Bill in the Indian Legislative Assembly on 27 March 1944.

[11] Refers to Bhulabhai Desai. For biographical note see *JPSW*, Vol. II, p. 209.

[12] For biographical note on Sarojini Naidu see *JPSW*, Vol. I, p. 47.

[13] Vijaya Lakshmi Pandit, nee Sarup Nehru (1900-90); sister of Jawaharlal Nehru; participated in the struggle for freedom and was imprisoned several times; married Ranjit S. Pandit, 1921; Minister of Local Self-Government and Health, U.P. Government, 1937-9, and 1946-7; member, Constituent Assembly, 1946-9; Ambassador to Soviet Union, 1947-9, and U.S.A., 1949-52; member, Lok Sabha, 1952-4, and 1964-8; was the first

Party[14] or the 1934 Ranchi conference?[15] I think most emphatically that the answer to all these questions is in the negative. A number of Congressmen are out—among them legislators. They apparently think it futile to go back to prison and since inactivity is not good for the nerves and a little propaganda may not be entirely fruitless—they thought it best to attend the Assembly. I think the presence of the Congress Party there has no greater significance than that.

Nevertheless, it was wrong to my mind for Congressmen to have attended the Assembly. The more dignified and politically the more useful and effective method would have been completely to ignore the assembly and its collegiate debates. As for the problems of inactivity, if the released Congressmen could not think of any other useful plan of work to keep them busy, they could at least have spun eight hours a day. That should have kept them reasonably occupied, with not a negligible profit to themselves and the nation.

Finally a word about the debate. Mr. Desai's speech, at least as reported, is stale and flat. In some respects the Nawabzada's[16] words were more forceful and to the point. Mr. Desai spoke like an accused defending himself before a tribunal. This was a queer role to play for the leader of the Congress Party. Within the limits chosen by him he did not put his case as an able lawyer, with the result that the Finance Member[17] found it only too easy to overturn the structure he had built up—as also that of the Nawabzada's—by a neat little thrust of a much used weapon. Mr. Desai and the Nawabzada both demanded a national government, to which Mr. Raisman's natural and simple reply was 'unite and we shall get out'. Both the League and Congress leaders should have anticipated this reply and made it impossible for any Govt. spokesman to use it by showing that it was not the lack of Congress-League unity, but the reluctance, indeed refusal, of Britain to part with power that stood in the path of a national government. This was the easiest thing for them to do. By having failed to do so, they allowed the British side again to get away with their lying propaganda. Thus the net result of the debate from

---

woman President of U.N. General Assembly, 1953-4; High Commissioner to United Kingdom, and Ambassador to Ireland, 1955-61; concurrently Ambassador to Spain, 1958-61; Governor, Maharashtra, 1962-4.

[14] Here the reference is to the Swaraj Party formed in 1923 by C.R. Das and Motilal Nehru to carry on the struggle for swaraj within the Legislatures.

[15] This refers to the conference held at Ranchi in 1934 to revive the Swaraj Party.

[16] Liaquat Ali Khan (1895-1951); one of the most prominent leaders of the Muslim League and its General Secretary, 1936-47; member, U.P. Legislative Council, 1926-40, Indian Legislative Assembly, 1940-7; and Deputy Leader of the Muslim League in the Assembly, 1943-6; Member for Finance, Interim Government, 1946-7; Prime Minister of Pakistan, 1947-51.

[17] Jeremy Raisman (1892-1978); Director, Reserve Bank of India, 1938; Secretary, Finance Department, 1938-9; Finance Member, Government of India, 1939-45.

the point of view of international propaganda—and it had little value from any other point of view—came to be next to nothing.

9 April 1944
Thoughts Suggested After Reading Ch. 1 of The Crisis of the Modern World *by René Guénon, Luzac, London, 1942*

Till now I had been ignorant of René Guénon. So when I found an authority such as Dr. A.K. Coomaraswamy[18] saying that 'No living writer in modern Europe is more significant than René Guénon', my interest in him was immediately intense, and I turned to him with an eager mind. His Foreword and Chapter 1 have awakened a fresh desire to know him better. It would be better however to comment on his views after completing the book, here I shall only put down a thought that has been suggested by Chapter 1.

It is a common place to contrast Eastern and Western civilizations as spiritual and material in character. It is also a common place for us socialists to laugh down this facile comparison. To us the character of a civilization is a mathematical function of its industrial technique. And, therefore, for us neither East or West exists.

I fear that in combating facile interpretations of civilizations we have ourselves surrendered to what appears to me to be an un-Marxian outlook namely, the formalistic attempt to fit every civilization into the mould of production-technique. Cloths woven out of silk and cotton would be different in substance, texture, quality, feel, notwithstanding the identity of the techniques used for their production. The so-called Industrial Revolution, when regrafted on a society which had practically no or little history, no or little civilization, produced results that were bound to be different from the results that the development of such a technique would have produced in a country like India and China. If we liken Indian civilization to silk and Western European civilization to cotton, the cloths woven by the technique of steam and electricity out of both the materials cannot be identical in substance, texture, quality or feel.

Both East and West are therefore objective facts; and no matter how common place it may be to say so, it is true that the East has always laid a greater emphasis on spiritual aims and values of life, whereas the West, at least in its modern phase of civilization, has emphasised more the material

[18] A.K. Coomaraswamy (1877-1947); noted scholar and critic of Indian art and culture; spent most part of his life serving as a teacher in the U.S.A.; author of several well-known books, including *The Dance of Shiva*.

aims and values. However, recent Western dominance over the East, brought about by virtue of material superiority, has disturbed the Eastern balance of life, dulled its spirituality and whetted its material appetite. Speaking of India, it would be true to say that today Indian civilization has no distinct quality, no individuality. At the same time it is certain that India will soon be abreast of the West in the matter of techniques of production and the consequent material advancement. To many this appears to be a tragic destiny because it is felt that modern industrialisation would destroy the finer elements, the moral and spiritual qualities of our civilization. The sensitive Indian is naturally hesitant to exchange his soul for [material gains]. But, is this an ineluctable choice, is there no alternative? I venture to think there is and it is this that I conceive to be the historic task of our country to reconcile the highly developed material forms of existence with the finest human values of life. I do not see why we should assume that spirituality can only be associated with the spinning wheel and not with the ultramodern flying machine. When we are a free people, it should be our glory to demonstrate how man can 'exploit' matter to the fullest extent and yet maintain his ascendancy over it. The West seems to be on the point of being overwhelmed by the genie that it has let out of the jar of material forces, because it has forgotten the *mantram* that will kill the genie.

The East knows that *mantram* and therefore need not fear. If our spiritualism is not merely a social psychological product of a rural and simple civilization; if it is anything vital and permanent, it will conquer Western materialism and force it to serve the needs of the spirit of Man.

P.S. If, in our anxiety to save our civilization we attempt to oppose material development, we shall do so in vain; and, in the result, only add to the confusion of thought. Whereas, if, with confidence, in the essential values of our civilization, we welcome that advancement and reconcile it with our values, we shall gain an integration of the social mind that will become a conscious factor in the development of our civilization.

12 April 1944
*The Question of the Revision of Marx**

The thoughts expressed here and elsewhere may be construed by some to be a new tendency of 'revisionism'. This term usually implies a modification of the fundamentals of a system of thought and is distinguished from development. No philosophy, no science—if it does not claim supernatural origin—is ever final. Truth grows by ceaseless elimination of error. The ideas of Marxism did not reach their final shape in the writings of its founders and Lenin. An idea grows and develops just as a tree does. To deny the possibility of development in Marxism is to convert it from social science to religion, rather to orthodox religion. History has unfolded through various stages since Marx's time and the social and physical sciences have risen to higher levels of truth. All this knowledge and social experience must be assimilated and Marxism restated and brought up to date. Though, this is being constantly done in narrow spheres of thought, a genius of the order of Marx has yet to arise to perform the task as applied to the whole range of thought embraced by Marxians.

But while development is natural, revision is a deviation, because it shifts the very foundations themselves. A revision of Marxism can be attempted only by one who questions its fundamental ideas. I am not one of these, and therefore reject the need for revisionism. I admit at the same time that it is not always easy to distinguish revisionism from natural development, and vice versa. Particularly when partisan controversy and no scientific honesty dominates or dictates opinion, the task of separating the two becomes doubly difficult. Here I should like to point out another complicating factor. Socialists in Russia are in control of the agencies of organised society and therefore are in a position to *act*, whereas socialists elsewhere can only talk. Those who are in a position to act can do whatever they like, deviate as far from Marxism and Leninism as they please, revise them as radically as they may, yet if they continue to repeat the well-known formulas, to profess their orthodoxy, to do everything in the name of Marx and Lenin, they can claim to be loyal and orthodox followers of the faith—much in the manner of Hindus who, no matter how they act and behave, preserve their orthodoxy by laying up service to the authority of the Vedas and Shastras. Socialists outside of Russia are not in such a position; action is not their chief occupation. Discussion, argument, controversy are of primary importance to them; and it is not difficult for any of them to dub the other as a revisionist. This is still the easier for the actionist in Russia to do—no matter how radical a revisionist he may be himself, in fact. If we keep this aspect of the matter in mind, we shall be less inclined to be troubled by the ex-cathedra opinions of Moscow and its votaries.

12 April 1944
The Dissolution of the Comintern

The Comintern was dissolved by Stalin because it had become a nuisance and a cause of embarrassment to the Soviet Foreign Office. On the other hand, it had no utility for the Soviet in the form it existed. The leaders of Russia had long given up the objective of a World Revolution—at any rate, they were not interested any more in playing the role of directors of such a revolution. The Comintern had already been converted into a mere Russian fifth column and had been acting as such. But when in view of Russia's active alliance with the dominant sections of world capitalism, it became a source of embarrassment, the Stalin junta had no qualms in liquidating it. It was only another Bolshevik tradition liquidated. It was easy for Stalin to do so, because the disappearance of the Comintern did not imply the disappearance of the fifth column. Even when the Comintern lived and breathed, the various national communist parties were not so much under the control and supervision of the Comintern Secretariat, as that of the agents of the Russian Secret Service. The latter held the whip hand not only over the national communist parties, but also over the Soviet embassies and consulates the world over. These embassies and consulates and Secret Service (N.K.V.D.) organisations have not been dissolved with the dissolution of the Comintern. Thus, the control of Moscow over its far-flung fifth column has not in the least been affected by the assassination of the International. What could be more suited to Russian policy?

In these circumstances it would be a mistake to think that the national communist parties are not held any more in Moscow's leading strings. There has been no change in their relationship to Moscow and their claim to speak for the people of their countries is no less false today than ever before.

19 April 1944
Economic Planning and Political Decentralisation

Dealing with the problem of settlement with the Muslim League, I pointed out that full provincial autonomy with residuary powers and minimum agreed powers for the centre, together with some other constitutional devices might create enough self-confidence in the League leaders to enable them to join hands with the Congress. On the other hand, dealing with the basic principles of social organisation, I indicated that the economic development of the country would require to a very considerable extent State planning, control and ownership. For a planned economic development the necessity of a large measure of centralisation is obvious. If economic planning were to be left to the provinces, nothing but confusion would be the result. The problem, therefore, is to reconcile these two necessities—centralisation and decentralisation.

I believe a solution of this problem can be found in providing a 'voluntary' clause in the Constitution according to which the Provinces may voluntarily surrender to the Centre certain of their powers. In this manner a large bloc might be created where planning might have full scope and a chance of success. It is even likely that no province may, in that case, remain out of the planned *bloc*, because, in the first place, submission to planning would be voluntary and not compulsory, and secondly, the advantages of planning might be too obvious to allow unreasoned prejudice to stand in the way of united endeavour. While this may be more than a likely possibility, we must, however, be prepared to visualise two economic spheres in the country—one under central planning, the other with only provincial planning or none. In this case there would arise numerous, though far from insurmountable, difficulties as regards inter-zonal trading. These difficulties will have to be got over by negotiations between the Central and Provincial governments.

In this connection the following report of a speech of Lala Shankerlal (delivered as President of the Punjab Chamber of Commerce, *Statesman*, April 13th, 1944) is interesting. He recalled Sir J.P. Srivastava's[19] statement that post-war reconstruction was a provincial responsibility. This pedantic constitutional dictum of Government seems to ignore all realities. He referred to the Australian example and said that the constitutional difficulty had been overcome by individual states surrendering to the Federal Government their power in certain directions for a period of five years after the war so that a uniform policy could be followed in the whole country.

19 April 1944
The Place of the Village in Free India

Village self-sufficiency had been the basis of Indian Society in the past. Its political result was the civic and political isolation of the village. This was not, however, a situation peculiar to India. In every society, such as the European, for instance, where the village was more or less self-sufficient due to the backwardness of the means of production, a similar attitude of mind could be found to have existed. Wars were everywhere not the occupation of the people but of the *Herrenvolk*—the military caste of feudalism and its mercenary retainers. Consequently armies marched past everywhere, leaving the people largely indifferent—except perhaps where a village offered possibilities. The East was no more different from the West in this respect than in so many others.

Among our national leaders there are not a few who look back upon the largely vanished village-self-sufficiency as an ideal to go back to. I find myself in opposition to such a view. I believe that if free Indian Society and

[19] J.P. Srivastava (1889-1954); prominent industrialist; member, U.P. Legislative Council, 1926-36, and U.P. Legislative Assembly, 1937-46; Minister for Education, Finance and Industries, U.P. Government, 1931-6, and 1937; member, Viceroy's Executive Council, 1942-6, Constituent Assembly, 1947-9, Provisional Parliament, 1950-2, and Council of States, 1952-4.

Lucknow
8.1.40

Dear Yusuf,

You must have received my statement on the independence pledge. I hope it has appeared in the daily press also on that side. Subsequently, I issued another statement – just a small one – saying that ~~I had~~ there was no objection to taking the new pledge itself* leaving out the words that express belief in the constructive programme. I am enclosing a copy of the *statement.

I have prepared a circular on our present policy which I am sending to you in a separate cover. Please see that it is properly circulated among Party members and ~~to~~ sympathisers. ~~Extra~~ A good summary may even be published in the daily press there. It should be translated in Gujrati and Marathi ~~and~~ also. Let me also know what you, Minoo and Asoka think of it. The thesis is not ready, yet, but I shall have it ready in a few days.

I am going ~~to~~ on tour today for a fortnight. Please reply here. The letters will be redirected.

With greetings,

Yours affly.

J.P.

Facsimile of J.P.'s Letter to Yusuf Meherally.

Deoli Detention Camp,
Deoli, Rajputana,
28.10.41

प्रिय बापूजी,

सप्रेम प्रणाम।

आप का कृपा-पत्र मिला जिसके लिये अनेक धन्यवाद।

जो पत्र सरकार ने प्रकाशित किये हैं उन्हें मैं ने देखा है, लेकिन इस समय उनके सम्बन्ध में कुछ भी नहीं कहना चाहता। अपनी रिहाई के बाद ही उस विषय में बातें कर सकूंगा। इस समय तो हमलोगों के सामने एक दूसरा ही सवाल है।

आपने उन पत्रों के सम्बन्धों में जो वक्तव्य प्रकाशित किये हैं उनमें से एक मैं ने देखा है। उसे देख कर मुझे बड़ा संतोष हुआ; उस से तो आप की महानता ही साबित होती है।

प्रभावती का हाल जान कर मुझे आश्चर्य और दुःख दोनों ही हुये। हमलोगों का जीवनसम्बन्ध तो कभी विचारों की समता या एकता पर आधृत नहीं था, फिर उसे हमारे ख्यालात पर इतना परेशान होने की क्या आवश्यकता है। आप उसे कृपया समझा देंगे।

यहां का हाल तो शायद आप जानते ही होंगे। उस विषय में मेरा कुछ लिखना बेकार है, क्योंकि उसे तो अधिकारी काट ही देंगे।

आपका
जयप्रकाश

Facsimile of J.P.'s Letter to Mahatma Gandhi.

Deoli Detention Camp,
Deoli, Rajputana,
7.12.41

My dear Bhai,

Warmest greetings to you.

I cannot but feel extremely happy at your being out when the country needs your guidance most.

You must have learnt about Narendradevas health. One of his greatest failings is that he cannot take care of himself. And I am afraid he will become a permanent invalid unless he is properly looked after. What he needs most is not medicines but a long rest in a suitable place. No place in the U.P. or anywhere in the North will suit him. Some districts of Maharashtra, such as Satara, or places further South – Bellary, Anantpur – might be good for him. Even Gujrat might suit him. Left to himself, I am certain, he would vegetate somewhere in the U.P., or at the best Sriprakasa might take him to Benaras to his Sevashram. What we call [illegible] will prevent him from asking any of his innumerable friends to do anything for him. I am therefore writing to you to take a particular interest in this matter and to pack him off to some suitable place. You must not leave this thing to his option. In this matter you must treat him as one treats a child. You may consult Bapu also in this connection as he has been taking a keen & special interest in Narendradevas health.

With love,

Yours,
Jayaprakash

Facsimile of J.P.'s Letter to Jawaharlal Nehru.

18 February 1944

India Divided

Shri Rajagopalachari is reported to have said the other day that he did not care if India was divided into ten different parts, each sovereign and independent of the other. His immediate inspiration for making this remarkable statement was the recent Molotov amendment of the Russian constitution.

Rajaji is too informed a politician to really believe what he has been reported to say. He apparently talks in this fashion with a view to remove suspicions that are harboured in certain quarters, and to pave the path probably for a rapprochement between the Congress and the League. But Rajaji is doing himself an injustice by pretending to believe that he ~~will~~ can ever succeed in his efforts by making fantastic and over-reaching statements. The ~~fault~~ tragedy of Rajaji is due to a not uncommon fault of clever people: their proneness to discount the ability of the other fellow to see through their trick.

Facsimile of J.P.'s Jotting in Lahore Fort.

"C/o The Home Secretary, Govt. of the Punjab, Lahore.

My dear Sriprakasaji,

I am returning by registered post both the volumes of the Science of Social Organization. I have felt greatly uplifted by a study of this book and I find myself ~~so~~ in much greater sympathy with Babuji's views today than in 1935. I also realised with a most pleasant surprise how much in common Babuji has with Gandhiji. That is because both have grasped the basic values of our civilization and the central truth of life. May he live long to carry on and complete the good work which he has undertaken. Please convey to him my most respectful pranams.

I trust you are well and are finding life interesting. I am fairly well, and though life is always dull in ~~a jail~~ prison, I am keenly interested in my books. Please remember me to friends there.

With affectionate regards,

Yours

Jayaprakash.

Signature of censoring officer	Date	Name of sender
[illegible signature]	16.7.44	Jayprakash Narayan

Passed by Supdt. of Police C. I. D.

Facsimile of J.P.'s Letter to Sri Prakasa.

14.10.45 -78- ६.१०.'४५
7.4/34

प्रिय बापूजी,

चरणों में सादर सप्रेम प्रणाम।

प्रभा के हाथों आप का जो कृपा-पत्र आया था वह उसी समय मिल चुका था। अब तक उत्तर नहीं दे पाया था इसके लिये क्षमा-प्रार्थी हूं।

मैं ने तो प्रभा से सिर्फ इतना ही कहा था कि वह आप से पूछ ले कि जो पत्र लाहौर से सेवा में भेजा था वह मिल गया था या नहीं। मुझे दुःख है कि आपने पत्र लिखने का कष्ट किया। फिर भी पत्र पाकर आनन्द हुआ है।

यह सही है कि कुछ विचार-क्षेत्रों में खिंच कर आप के बहुत निकट आ गया हूं, जिससे मुझे अत्यन्त ~~प्रसन्नता~~ प्रसन्न हुआ हूं। परन्तु साथ ही इस बात का दुःख बना हुआ है कि मौलिक सिद्धान्तों के क्षेत्र में आज भी अपने को आपसे उतनी ही दूर पाता हूं जितना कभी भी था। और जहां तक कार्यक्षेत्र का प्रश्न है, मुझे ऐसा लगता है कि मेरा क्षेत्र दूर ही नहीं बल्कि नितान्त पृथक् ही हो जायगा। इधर प्रायः जितनी घटनायें हुई हैं उनके कारण तो मैं इस धारा में अपने को अधिकाधिक वेगवान् ही हुआ पाता हूं। अस्तु, जैसा आपने लिखा है जेल और बाह्य जगत की भावनाओं में अक्सर अन्तर पाया जाता है। मैं नहीं कह सकता बाहर जाकर किस दिशा को ग्रहण करने के लिये प्रेरित होऊंगा।

यों तो जेल मनुष्य के रहने का स्थान नहीं है फिर भी आपको विश्वास दिलाता हूं कि मैं न रो-रो के दिन ही गिन रहा हूं न यही सोच रहा हूं कि कोई तपस्या में लगा हूं। क्रान्तियों में कुछ का मरना कुछ का बरबाद हो जाना, कुछ का जेलों में सड़ते रहना

Facsimile of J.P.'s Letter to Mahatma Gandhi.

अनिवार्य है, इस में किसी प्रकार के सोच विचार का स्थान ही कहां है। अभी हजारों जेल में पड़े हैं — आगे भी हजारों पड़े रहेंगे। —

अब हमारे बाग़ के बासंती फूलों के म्लान पत्र पर कुम्हलाने की झुर्रियां पड़ चुकी हैं। उनकी जगह लेने को शीत ऋतु के (फूलों के) अंकुर मिट्टी के अंचल से झांक रहे हैं। और अब मेरा अधिक समय उन्हीं के भविष्य के निर्माण बीत रहा है और इन्हीं कल्पनाओं में कि मेरी इस छोटी दुनिया के किस कोने को कौन सा फूल आलोकित करेगा और किस क्यारी को अपने प्रकाश से ढक लेगा। — परिस्थिति इस बात का विश्वास दिला रही है कि अपनी कल्पनाओं का मूर्त रूप अवश्य देखने को मिलेगा। —

भय है कि इस बकवास से आप का समय नष्ट कर आपको नाराज़ ही किया होगा — इस दशा में क्षमा याचना करता हूं।

मैं यह नहीं चाहूंगा कि आप पत्रोत्तर देने का कष्ट करें। — आपका आशीर्वाद सदैव प्राप्त है इसी से सदा सुखी और संतुष्ट हूं। —

बम्बई में ज्वर हो आने का समाचार पत्र का लिखित था। आशा है अब स्वास्थ्य ठीक होगा। — आदरणीय सरदार साहब के चरणों में मेरा प्रणाम पहुंच सके तो सुखी होऊंगा। — पूना की चिकित्सा से उनका स्वास्थ्य सुधर रहा है यह राष्ट्र का परम सौभाग्य है। —

प्रभा पिछले मास १५, १६ को आई थी, फिर इस महीने के अन्त तक उसके आने की आशा है। —

मेरा स्वास्थ्य बिलकुल ठीक है, राममनोहर को ओरिएन्टल सोर नासिक सायनुसाइटिस से तकलीफ रहती है, लेकिन अब एक विशेषज्ञ की चिकित्सा से उन्हें लाभ है, यह भी सदा प्रयास कर रहे हैं। —

आपका,
विनीत

the Indian people are to prosper, are to develop a sense of common and cooperative life, if national unity is to become real, if the divorce from national politics of the mass of the people—which was such a glaring aspect of past Indian society—is to be removed; if parochialism and clannishness are to be banished; if the rigours of the iniquitous caste system—which flourished on the fertile soil of village self-sufficiency and family specialisation of labour—are to be destroyed; if democracy and self-government are to be made effectual—if all these objectives are to be achieved, the Free Indian State will have consciously to endeavour to break-up the remaining self-sufficiency and isolation of the villages and make them 'coherent economic units' in a united and inter-dependant national economy. It is necessary to add that the break-up of a self-sufficiency that is emphasised here does not mean that the village should be placed at the mercy of international markets and the city capitalist. Far from it. What I am suggesting is the village, as a fully protected economic unit (protected both by the State and cooperation in the village itself), not independent or self-sufficient but interconnected, according not to the blind laws of capitalist competition and exploitation, but to a national and regional plan.

Not only economically should the village become a unit in a larger whole, but also politically. It appears to me that if our political life is to be rehabilitated, the village must become once again a self-governing unit in a very real sense of the term. In fact, unless this is done the village cannot perform the economic functions envisaged here. In the field of politics, if our political institutions are to strike deep roots and command basic loyalties, if they are to be the faithful expressions of our corporate existence, the village panchayats must be revived in all their glory and with all their old authority.

I conceive the panchayats as exercising revenue, executive, and judicial authority. With regard to the first, I have to make a suggestion which seems to me [likely] to simplify many tenancy and agrarian problems and at the same time to lay the foundations of an agricultural system that might enable us to combine the best of both the ancient and the most modern systems. One of our fundamental laws should vest the ownership of all land in the State. As the supreme land-owner, the state should settle certain areas of land to every village, taking into account the total land available, the size and needs of the village and the quality of the land, and assess the corresponding revenue. The land should then be divided among themselves by the villagers acting through their panchayats. For this distribution of land the Provincial Government should lay down rules for the guidance of the panchayats, the rules taking into account present proprietory rights. The panchayat there collects the revenue and pays it to the State. It may have to be provided that below a minimum acreage holdings would be revenue-free and above the minimum there may be a graduated scale of assessment. Periodically the State should review the settlement and assessment and revise them if found necessary. Through the panchayats, the State should control the production of grains and their disposal. Transfer of land outside the village should be illegal unless specially sanctioned by the State.

In the sphere of economics, the panchayat should also look after co-operation, marketing, credit and handicrafts. Regarding development of village industries it would be necessary to prohibit the import of manufactures that compete with handicrafts as also to prevent large-scale industry within the country from infringing on their sphere.

With regard to executive functions, the panchayat should have certain police powers, and the task of keeping certain records.

With regard to the third sphere, i.e., judicial, the panchayat should have power to try civil and criminal cases. In certain types of disputes, such as land boundaries, the decisions of the panchayat should be final. Legal procedure in India is so complicated and expensive that a real attempt should be made to simplify it and bring justice within the reach of the poorest. Panchayats, as the lowest courts, functioning right on the spot and in a position to find out the truth by immediate and intimate enquiry, should be made one of the most important means of simplification of law and justice in India.

30 April 1944
*Mr. Jinnah's Stalingrad**

Earlier this month when Mr. Jinnah had come to Lahore some writer in the local press had said that the League Fuehrer was likely to meet his Stalingrad in this the heart city of Pakistan. This eventually has proved to be so. Mr. Jinnah has been defeated, but it may be interesting to ask whose has been the victory. Is it the Unionist Party which has been victorious? As I have watched this controversy from the seclusion of my cell, it has been made increasingly clear to me that the laurels of victory should really go to the British—the British steel-frame of the Province, with the Governor[20] at its head. When Mr. Jinnah left Lahore after his first visit at the beginning of the month, the issues had been left undecided. Undoubtedly those who were pulling wires behind the scenes knew what the ultimate issue was to be. But the public was in no way certain. Whatever the wishes of the Muslim members of the Punjab Assembly, vocal Muslim opinion seemed to be behind

[20] Bertrand James Glancy (1882-1953); Political Adviser to the Crown Representative, 1938-41; Governor of the Punjab, 1941-6.

Mr. Jinnah. Then the Governor spoke at the opening of the War Exhibition,[21] and twice during his speech he made it clear to the people of this Province and to all others concerned that the British power was solidly lined up behind Lt. Col. Malik Khizar Hayat Khan[22] and the Unionist Ministry. The issue of Mr. Jinnah's endeavours, when he returned again to resume them, was no longer in doubt.

The question may well be asked why did the British suddenly decide to oppose and finally thwart such a valuable tool as Mr. Jinnah. The answer to my mind is two-fold.

First, the Muslim League had dared to act as a naughty child in the Central Assembly and had caused not an inconsiderable embarrassment by its fleeting association with the Congress. As I have pointed out elsewhere, the League was driven into making that Assembly gesture largely by the Viceroy's reference to India's geographical unity. The British on their part, no doubt decided to have a show-down with Mr. Jinnah as soon as an opportunity offered itself. Such an opportunity came in the Punjab almost simultaneously with the Delhi gesture. The British wanted to show to Mr. Jinnah that they could deflate his Fuehrerian paranoia whenever they liked, so he better not go too far out of hand. That lesson has no doubt been driven home and we may look forward in the future to more docile politics from the League as far as the British are concerned and perhaps to a few more Big Brothers being turned upon the Congress.

Incidentally, it seems the British are losing their cunning, for it was rather maladroit for the Governor to come out so openly in support of the worthy Malik and his ministry. On the other hand, it is possible that it was found necessary to do this to rally the loyalist forces—the spoken and unspoken hints of the Deputy Commissioners having been found to be inadequate.

The second cause of the Punjab show-down was perhaps the British fear that if the ministry of the Province came to be too directly controlled by Mr. Jinnah, they might not find it as pliable and governable as it has been so far. When the war ends and the time comes for a reshuffle and a re-deal the British will have ample opportunity to look at their hand and decide the bid. For the time being, they propose to hold on to the cards they hold.

This reading perhaps conflicts with British policy in Bengal There we saw a British Governor deviating so far from British ways as to break the rules of cricket in order to bring into office a Muslim League ministry—the

[21] This refers to the War Services Exhibition opened at Lahore in the second week of April 1944.

[22] Malik Khizar Hyat Khan Tiwana (1900-75); prominent Unionist Party leader of the Punjab; member, Punjab Legislative Assembly, 1937-47; Minister of Public Works, Punjab Government, 1937-42; Premier of the Punjab, 1942-7.

very thing they have prevented in the Punjab. Why? The answer lies in the difference between the political layouts in the two Provinces. In Bengal the ministry in power—or, more truly, in office had proved to be difficult to handle and was far less pliable than a ministry of the League was expected to be. In the Punjab the situation was just the reverse. And therefore British policy too here has been the reverse of that adopted in the Eastern Pakistan.

Finally, it may be asked if Mr. Jinnah's discomfiture is going to be the cause of a split in the ranks of the Punjab Muslim League. I do not think so. I believe Mr. Jinnah will quietly eat the humble pie and as far as the public is concerned some face-saving device will be found to preserve Mr. Jinnah's prestige on the one hand and prove the Punjab Premier's subordination to him (in all-India politics, for instance) on the other.

7 May 1944
Friends of the Soviet Union

I read yesterday of a conference of the Friends of the Soviet Union. It struck me as very odd—this conference of the Friends of the Soviet being convened by Indians at such a time. I wondered what I should have done had I been free and invited to the Conference? I think I should have sent some such reply: 'Shall attend conference if and when the Russians organise a Friends of India Society and convene its conference'. I know the so-called friends of the Soviet Union would have howled me down as an enemy of the socialist Fatherland and a fascist. But one has learnt to ignore such howls and barks.

It seems to me that, if there is any country in the world today that needs friendship of other countries it is India, and also that if there is any country in the world today that is expected by virtue of its professions to render such friendship, it is the Soviet Union. But not even the feeblest voice has been raised there for India, in spite of the boundless injustice that India has suffered during this war at the hands of one of the Soviet's principal allies. China, much weaker militarily and diplomatically and never claiming to play the role of a saviour of peoples, was courageous and honest enough to raise her weak but clear voice for India. But not so Russia, the professed leader of the oppressed and downtrodden.

Yet our Indian Friends of the Soviets must run about organising conferences. Well, let them. There are some people whose only role in politics today is to run about, shouting: 'Stalin be praised, Stalin be praised'.

Friends of the Soviet Union, it is interesting to reflect, were organised throughout the world when Russia was a great revolutionary crusader and in constant danger of being attacked in one way or another by the capitalist nations of the world. Russia's position is very different today. Russia is no longer the crusader she once was and it would be egregious folly to copy all that she says or does. Uncritical propaganda for Russia is likely now to do more harm than good. Secondly, Russia has become a great military power and an ally of the greatest capitalist powers on this earth and can be left to look after herself. I think a Friends of China Union is more appropriate than the one announced in the press. Adult Indian politicians should look at the world with Indian eyes and not through glass eyes made in Moscow or anywhere else.

P.S. I should like to add a postscript to say that no Friends-of-This-or-That Society should be formed in our country unless at least some people in this-or-that country are prepared to form in their home a Friends of India Society.

8 May 1944
Gandhiji's Release

In recent years perhaps nothing has rejoiced and relieved the country as Gandhiji's release.[23] I too share in this rejoicing, but entirely on the ground of Gandhiji's health and well-being. India, if not the whole of Asia, needs Gandhiji today and will need him tomorrow as never before and as nothing else. That he may live in health and undiminished strength of mind and body is the prayer of millions of Indians and many more millions of other peoples of Asia.

I do not, however, rejoice at the prospect of a settlement with Britain as a result of Gandhiji's having been restored to freedom. I do not want such a settlement during the war, because I believe that any settlement in the present conditions and on terms that these conditions will naturally determine, will do no good to the cause of India's freedom. I do not for a moment expect that Gandhiji will arrive at any settlement that is not of benefit to the country and, therefore, to my mind no settlement is actually going to materialise. However, it would have been better if Gandhiji had been kept in prison (i.e., if he had not fallen ill) till the end of the war. He would have been in a stronger position then and the risks and drawbacks of a war-time settlement would have been absent. I have explained elsewhere why I am opposed to a war-time settlement and there is no need to repeat my views here.

But due to his illness Gandhiji is free now, and whatever be my own views regarding a settlement, a serious attempt is going to be made for it. Therefore, keeping aside my own prejudices, it may be well to examine what the prospects are for a resolution of the 'deadlock'.

Let us take the British side first. What may be their desires and plans? They, no doubt, would like the opposition of the Congress to be withdrawn, but would they also like Congress cooperation? I am not so sure that the

[23] Gandhi was released from the detention camp at the Aga Khan Palace (Poona) on 6 May 1944.

British are very keen about Congress cooperation; not because they are doubtful about its value for the war-effort, but because they are afraid of it. First, they know that Congress would not be willing to cooperate unless substantial power—indeed all power except military direction of the war—is transferred from Britain to India. This they are not prepared for. Churchill cannot preside over the Empire's last rites. I believe the British might have agreed to hand over this power had they known that it involved merely constitutional and formal changes. But they know the Congress and they cannot forget that, when the Congress takes power, it means to wield it. There is no hoodwinking the Congress with jobs and positions. No, Congress cooperation is too costly a bargain for the British and they would do nothing on their part to remove the obstacles in its path. The position that the British would welcome most is the 1940 Congress position (before individual satyagraha was launched):[24] that is, the Congress, though not an ally, is also not an enemy. As I look ahead I see the British manoeuvring to bring the Congress to that position back again. That would be disastrous for the Congress. Far better that the Congress remained in prison till the end. The British would no doubt make a great show of renewing the Cripps' offer and of their eagerness for a settlement, but below the surface they will set at work all their cunning to prevent it.

What about the Indian side? Excepting the Congress all other parties have been eager for a settlement with Britain. The Muslim League have repeatedly demanded that the British should leave the Congress alone, intransigent as it is, and hand over to the League and others who may care to come in at the deal-out. The British Government have naturally ignored all such demands, as accepting them would have been a sort of *gunah be lazzat*.

The question, therefore, is, will the Congress and, in the present conditions, Mahatma Gandhi be prepared to settle with the British? I think Gandhiji would be quite prepared to restate his terms for an agreement as set forth in the famous Bombay resolution and would also draw the attention of the world to the fact that the resolution in question was not in itself a call to war, that it was first a statement of the terms of a compromise failing which it left power to him to launch a mass struggle so as to vindicate the nation's cause. To the re-stated terms the British will say 'no', or rather they will say that they cannot consider them as they are not supported by other sections of the Indian people, particularly the Muslim League.

Then, we are led to the second question: will Gandhiji and Mr. Jinnah come together and reach an agreement? I believe on the side of Gandhiji there is all the desire and willingness to do so, but I doubt if Mr. Jinnah will respond. So far, Congress-League talks did not make even a beginning

[24] Individual satyagraha was started on 17 October 1940.

because the League insisted on treating the Congress as a representative of the Hindu community and the League as the sole representative body of the Muslim community. I am afraid Mr. Jinnah will once again raise this initial obstacle, because he does not think he can get such terms from the Congress as from the British. But I should add that if the Punjab experience has at all embittered him against the British and accordingly if he does abstain from creating any initial difficulty and therefore if negotiations do actually start, there will not be any insurmountable difficulty in an agreement being reached between him and Gandhiji. After all, raising of that primary and insurmountable difficulty only meant that Mr. Jinnah was determined not to come to terms with the Congress. Otherwise there was no sense in creating it. However, as I have said above, if serious negotiations do actually start between him and Gandhiji, I see no reason why they should not bear fruit. I have a feeling that once Pakistan is reduced to definite terms, vivisection of the country will not be found to be necessary. I think it is possible for Mr. Jinnah to have quite a satisfactory Pakistan and at the same time for Gandhiji to have one undivided India. But to the question if Mr. Jinnah will be agreeable to talk seriously, my answer still is seventy-five per cent no.

If, therefore, there is no agreement between the Congress and the League, British propaganda will be vindicated and the release of Gandhiji will prove to have been a blessing for the British Government. Accordingly, it is most essential to be very cautious about starting negotiations with Mr. Jinnah. To my mind, Gandhiji should on no account launch upon any such conversations till he is given reasonable proof by mediators that his overtures will find response. If, on the other hand, no such proof is forthcoming, Gandhiji and all his well-wishers and nationally minded persons should proceed in such a manner that the British do not again get an opportunity to throw dust into the world's eyes by advertising our disunity. Rather, steps should be so taken that the real intention of Britain is brought out, i.e., her intention not to part with power. Gandhiji should say that he would produce national unity—as he would undoubtedly be able to do—within a fortnight if Britain agreed to hand over complete power here and now and not after the war. It should be said on behalf of the Congress that it is useless to discuss the sharing of anything unless the thing sought after is within one's grasp or is soon to be. The merit of this approach—even if it would be otherwise fruitless—is that it would bring out Britain's real game in India and strengthen the cause of Indian freedom here and abroad. This in itself would not be a small gain.

9 May 1944*

This is what the *Times* (I believe the *London Times*, because it [the report in an Indian newspaper] does not say that it is the *New York Times*) says on Gandhiji's release:

Whether Mr. Gandhi is more or less dangerous as a prisoner than he was as a free man may long be debated. His tremendous power is of moral order which could at all times pass the sentry lines and go about the country. Mr. Gandhi wished to drive the British as rulers out of India yet showed no rancour against individual Englishmen. He professed to see no great stake at issue in this and yet was willing to permit British troops to defend frontiers and outlined a campaign of non-cooperation with the Japs in case they invaded the country. He proved himself a selfless ascetic and a shrewd politician. To millions on India's crowded plains he has been a symbol of a long future as well as past.

These comments of the *Times* show that the British when they are inclined to see the truth do it well and say it graciously. The pro-Japanese, mischievous Gandhi has become a saint once again. Well, we hope this change in the tone of London's most influential paper reflects a change in the outlook of the British ruling class towards India, be that change only temporary and designed to serve an end.

10 May 1944
Gandhiji's Release (Contd.)

There are two other points in regard to Gandhiji's release which should be noted. A point which bears upon Congress-League agreement is that the Congress is prepared to leave the issue of Pakistan for post-war consideration if it is found necessary to do so in the interest of a war-time agreement with the League and the formation of a national Government. I believe this was made clear at the time of the Cripps talks. This attitude of the Congress should make a Congress-League settlement exceedingly easy if Mr. Jinnah were at all keen about it.

The other point is in regard to the August Resolution. Government have made such a lot of fuss about it. I think Gandhiji should point out that all this fuss has been beside the point and in the nature of a smoke-screen for a set policy of repression. The August Resolution has two parts: one ideological or explanatory and the other practical or operative. With regard to the first part, which is nine-tenths of the Resolution, it may be pointed out that it merely explains authoritatively the position of the Congress with respect to the war and British policy in India, and lays down the conditions on which the Congress might enter into an alliance with the United Nations, and demands the transference of the necessary political power. With respect to this part it may be stressed that neither can the Congress change these fundamental views which have been repeatedly set forth in many Congress declarations nor can their expression be justifiably sought to be suppressed.

As regards the second part of the Resolution, Gandhiji may point out that while it charged him to launch a mass movement of civil disobedience in certain events, effect was not actually given to it. Indeed, no effect could be given to it till attempts had been made by negotiation with the British Government to secure satisfaction of the demand expressed in the first part of the Resolution. Therefore, it is difficult to understand what is meant by withdrawal of the August Resolution. If it means the repudiation of the fundamental Congress position in relation to the war, not a moment's thought need be given to it, as the Congress cannot give up its very life-breath. If it means, on the other hand, withdrawal of civil disobedience, the demand is ridiculous because no civil disobedience was actually started by the Congress, the outburst of civil resistance and other anti-British activities were only in the nature of a reaction to the sudden arrest of the Working Committee, Gandhiji and other Congress leaders. In these circumstances, the withdrawal by Gandhiji or the Working Committee of something which they did not start is meaningless. Whatever anti-British activity there is would automatically cease if the Government released all Congressmen and established the *status quo* as in August 1942.

The demand for the repudiation of the August Resolution may have yet another meaning. It may be intended to ask the withdrawal of the 'threat' of civil disobedience which is held out in the Resolution. This is a childish demand. It means that the people of India are to have no sanction behind them when their representatives sit around the table with the representatives of the British Government, particularly when the other party has a large army, a whole system of ordinance rule and other dictatorial powers. It means that India would achieve her freedom merely on the strength of the sweet reasonableness of her plenipotentiaries, their command over English, and other virtues. Whether the threat of mass action is expressed or implicit, it is ever present by virtue of the very nature of Indo-British relationship. Non-violent mass action has been the foundation of Congress power since 1921, and whether it is expressly mentioned in a resolution or not should be immaterial to those who have to accept the Congress for what it is.

It, therefore, seems to me that all this fuss about withdrawing the August Resolution is merely British humbug and a political excuse for the continuation of the deadlock.

13 May 1944
Gandhiji's Release (Contd.)

The British like to be told how they blunder along and finally arrive, despite the studied mess they make of things and affairs. They positively revel in their blundering, for does not an amused, critical but admiring world tell them how finally they emerge from every crisis with their feet firmly planted on *terra firma*?

The Government of India communiqué stressed with a trace of over anxiety the fact that Gandhiji had been released solely on ground of health. One wonders if Gandhiji's illness really gave the British one more chance to pull out of another of their blunderings and land on solid earth with but a few bruises and scratches and a smile of self-satisfaction on their lips, and, most important of all, with a face kept perfectly intact. Next to the Chinese, the British probably attach more importance to face than any other people; and can it be doubted that Gandhiji's illness enabled them as nothing else could to save their face?

The situation in which the British found themselves was none too comfortable for them. India continued to be sullen, and economically things did not look too bright. In spite of all propaganda a considerable part of the world remained critical, even hostile, to British policy in India. The Congress seemed to be far from dead as election results showed, Gandhiji continued to be the centre round whom all Indian politics revolved. Meanwhile, the Japanese had invaded India and the Japanese propaganda drive must have been causing some anxiety. As in the case of all security prisoners, Gandhiji also must have been presented with a charge-sheet to which he must have returned altogether too uncomfortable a reply. Some day that reply would be published and the world would know how Britain continued to keep in prison a man who was not put to any trial at law and who professed the noblest possible ideals of democracy, peace and international brotherhood. No, the situation was far from comfortable for Churchill, Amery & Co. Not that they were prepared even then to do anything to remedy the situation. At this very psychological moment came Gandhiji's illness as a golden opportunity for the British to get out of their self-created difficulty.

Twice in recent years Gandhiji's health broke down seriously in prison. At the time of his Harijan fast[25] he was believed to be practically at death's door when he was set at freedom. Last year, again during a fast,[26] death closed in on him but the British were content to look on and let him die. This time, however, he has been released, though from press reports he does not seem to have been anywhere near death's premises. A sudden forth-springing of solicitude for the condemned rebel's life, particularly when that life was not in any great danger, hardly squares with recent British policy. The conclusion is, therefore, forced upon one that the real reason for his release is political. Having taken the first step without making any commitments whatever, the British can well sit back and watch developments. If they suit their policy they can take the other necessary steps without any sense of

[25] Refers to Gandhi's fast in 1933 (16 August to 22 August) in protest against Government decision not to grant all the facilities for Harijan work in the Yeravda Jail where he was imprisoned.

[26] Refers to Gandhi's fast in 1943 (10 February-2 March) in protest against Government propaganda that the responsibility for disturbances after the passing of the Quit India resolution and arrest of leaders was that of the Congress.

embarrassment. If not, well Gandhi may go back to his dreary Wardha and vegetate.

At least, that is what the British would like him to do. But they hardly know their Gandhi. That restless soul will vegetate nowhere—in or out of prison. His release is a golden opportunity not only for the British but for Gandhiji also and there can be no doubt that he will make golden use of it to serve whatever purpose and policy he may have at present.

16 May 1944

*Underground Europe Calling**

This seems to be a remarkable book by an Austrian socialist, formerly editor of the Vienna *Arheiter Zeitung*. The book is published in 1942, and yet it talks of the Russian armies hurling the Germans back to their own frontiers, indeed even occupying Berlin.

Oscar Paul believes that a German defeat is bound to produce a European revolution, limited by two factors: the attitude of Soviet Russia and of British-American policy. Leaving aside the question of what modification these two factors might produce in the European revolution, he proceeds to analyse its native character. According to him it should be characterised both as a national and social revolution—the countries of the West and North where democracy and social legislation was advanced emphasising the national aspect more than the social while the countries of the East and South and Centre reversing this emphasis, but both aspects being present in every country under German occupation today.

As regards the social aspect he makes the following interesting points:

Taking the countries of the Centre, East and South first (Austria, Czechoslovakia, Poland, etc.) he points out that along with German political domination, much of the industry, mines, forests, banks and other resources have passed into German *ownership*. After the overthrow of Germany where will the ownership of these economic undertaking and resources vest? Will a new set of capitalist owners (the old having been killed, dispossessed, appalled or having left) be created or will the State take them over? The answer seems to be clear. Take Poland. He points out that practically the entire former ruling class has been wiped off? Will the return of freedom to Poland create a new ruling class or will the peasants and workers and the humble middle classes come into their own? Even in the countries of the West and North, where the Germans have not formally confiscated industrial concerns etc., it is found, as in France for instance, that the class of collaborators with the Nazis is generally drawn from the big industrial and capitalist sections.

* J.P.'s comments on *Underground Europe Calling* by Oscar Paul, London, 1942.

In France it is the first 200 that are the pillars of Vichy. The question naturally is, when upon liberation the people of France rise up against the man of Vichy, will they treat kindly with the economic collaborators—the upper 200!

Again, in the freed countries the first problem will be food. Will the starving stand by and see the more affluent get away with their parties, dinners and limousines? Then there will be terrible unemployment immediately upon the secession of hostilities.

The natural result of all this is a move—on to social revolution?

Summing up this section he says: "But one thing is true: the existence of various States in various stages of revolutionary process, with varying degrees of adaptation to the making of a new international order and shaping of a common European destiny—this will present the revolution with its first crucial problem" (p. 39).

17 May 1944
The 'Economist' Discovers Truth

A few days ago I remarked how perfectly the British comprehend the truth when they wish to do so. But the truth that sits at the heart of the British Empire is so hideous and monstrous that no Briton dare look into its face too long or too often. Therefore they must need varnish and paint that monstrosity so that it may become decent enough to look at and to exhibit in the imperial window-case.

The *Economist* has accomplished such a dressing up of the truth in an article on Gandhiji's release, reproduced in the *Tribune* of yesterday.

First, it has been pointed out that the real reason behind Gandhiji's release is political. But when this political motive is analysed, we witness all the tortuous processes of reasoning that lying must adopt. It seems that in the ultimate analysis Gandhiji's release is a counterblast to the 'Tata Birla Plan'. It has been pointed out that the rich capitalists of India have so long been the power behind the throne in the Congress but they have now been thoroughly disillusioned or disappointed with the 'politicians' and have made a bid by publishing the Plan to take a direct hand in affairs and occupy the throne themselves. Further, they want to industrialise the country quickly and in order to do this they are determined to give the go-by to democracy and the noble principle of laissez-faire in business, and are plainly and unabashedly seeking to establish a sort of capitalist dictatorship over India. Gandhi, on the other hand, is known to be an agrarian in economics and an advocate of handicrafts, and, in politics, a liberal democrat. What more natural for the British, therefore, than to release Gandhi so that he might foil the attempt of Indian capital to capture the Congress and establish over the country a capitalist dictatorship? Younger Congressmen and Mr. Rajagopalachari among the older ones are expected to come to Gandhiji's aid!

Surely, the editor of the *Economist* is not so foolish as all this, nor so ignorant of Indian politics. But the threat to British capital is so great from any real scheme—capitalist or socialist—of Indian Industrial development that the mouthpieces of British capital must blare forth lies, raise false alarms, fetch up smoke-bombs and do everything else that might save the interests of British capital in India. As a part of this offensive the *Economist* has thrown a hint to those sections of British Labour that have been rather sympathetic to Indian freedom that they might ask themselves if in the name of freedom they would like to hand over 400 million helpless people to the exploitation of a handful of Indian capitalists. No doubt, that section of British Labour—the dominant section at the present time—that is as zealous a champion of the Empire as Churchill and Amery, will draw strength from the lesson that the *Economist* has endeavoured to teach them.

The *Economist* has also attempted to draw the Muslim League in its trail. It has shown that the League too stands if not for democracy, also not for the type of capitalist rule and exploitation adumbrated in the Plan. Moreover, the League is opposed a hundred per cent to the rich Hindu industrialist class, i.e., the Tatas, Dalals, Mathais, Ispahanis, Haroons, Daoods, Currimbhoys, Saits, all of whom are of course Hindus! A well-informed journal like the *Economist* cannot be ignorant of the committee appointed by the League to prepare a scheme for the industrial and economic development of Pakistan, but truth, Sir, is a hobgoblin of little minds who have never ruled empires nor ever will.

17 May, 1944
Underground Europe Calling

I have just finished this very valuable book. I propose to read it once again, for I cannot keep the book, it being a library volume kindly sent by Kamalashankar. I am afraid I shall also have to take down rather extensive notes. Today I wish to make only two remarks.

The book is addressed mainly to the British Labour movement, and the author plainly states at one place that who except the British Labour Party can be expected to understand and support the revolutionary implications of a Europe slowly being released by the allies from the death-grip of Nazism? I believe Oscar Paul is under a serious delusion. I do not know what sort of stuff the mass of British Labour is, but one has come to know its leadership rather well. It is not national prejudice for me to say that the test of British Labour leadership was India, and in this test the leadership failed miserably, proving itself to be merely the tail of the British capitalism. Can the same group of men be expected to behave with any independence with regard to

Europe or to apply to it the principles of socialism on which their party ostensibly rests? I am afraid the answer is a clear no. Their attitude towards the European revolution that Oscar Paul rightly expects to sweep over re-liberated Europe will be determined fundamentally by British national interests, which are plainly capitalist and imperialist. Whatever be the stand of British Labour in regard to losing [domestic?] affairs, in all international matters they will be essentially with the British ruling class—unless a miracle happens in Britain and British Labour becomes a real revolutionary and Socialist force—but this does not seem decidedly to be an age of miracles, not in Britain at any rate.

No, the European revolution, I am afraid is not going to get much support from the allies, either from the West or East. Stalin, I think, is not going to change and he is most decidedly going to attempt to make the European revolution at least in the Eastern countries—to order, i.e., no revolutions at all.

There is only one hope. If the European revolution succeeds in crossing national boundaries and of itself becomes a vital, powerful force, too strong to be dictated to or starved out or bribed over, it may win through and compel both East and West (i.e. Russia and Britain-America) to reform and uphold it. But is it not hoping too much. All really depends upon how strong the European underground is and what are its thoughts.

The second remark I wish to make is that I find Oscar Paul's point of view to be so much similar to my own, and possibly to that of the C.S.P., that I feel encouraged to hope that in the post-war world the Indian socialist movement may find it possible to be associated with a real international social movement. The question is how much Oscar Paul represents the new socialist outlook in Europe, also how far I represent the socialist movement in India—whether confined to the C.S.P. or not. We shall know when the war ends.

19 May 1944
Gandhiji's Release (Contd.)

It strikes me that irrespective of Congress-League agreement or settlement with the British Government, the Japanese invasion of India may offer Gandhiji such a wide and vital scope of activity that he may be able to turn his August defeat into a resounding victory and also present to the world a course of action which might have a profound influence over international relations. From the beginning of the war Gandhiji has been insisting on non-violent resistance to aggression. The Congress, no doubt, disagreed with him and a situation arose when a serious split in its ranks appeared imminent. But apart from the resignation of Khan Abdul Gaffar Khan from the Working Committee, the threatened split matured no further, though it was widely known at that time that if the Congress assumed responsibility or an armed defence of India, Gandhiji's ideological followers in the Congress, such as Dr. Rajendra Prasad, Acharya Kriplani, Dr. Profulla Ghosh[27] and, of course, Badshah Khan would leave the Congress, though they would offer no resistance to the Congress policy of violence.

It seems to me that Gandhiji's opportunity has at last arrived with the Japanese on Indian soil. Leaving aside the problem of a political settlement for the Working Committee to solve—if and when the Committee are in a position to do so—Gandhiji may well ask the British Government to be allowed to organise a non-violent resistance to the Japanese invasion. For this he may not even ask for a release of his associates, which in dignity he ought not to do: he may only gather together those who have already been released and issue a general appeal to every Indian to join his colours on certain strict terms. In this plan of resistance to the aggressor, Gandhiji, of course, will not cooperate with the British and the United Nation's war against Japan: he will indeed leave Lord Mountbatten's[28] plans alone. All he would ask for is to be allowed to go to the villages of Assam, East Bengal and Orissa to organise his battalions of passive resisters to the Japanese offensive. If Gandhiji is able to do this he would succeed in giving such a demonstration to the world of his principle of non-violence as would not only add a crowning chapter to his life's work but also open up a new path of hope for the world that is foundering today in human blood.

There seem to be two difficulties, however. One is Gandhiji's health. In order to organise such an army of passive resisters and to lead them to 'battle', Gandhiji must become at least 20 years younger. Can he, yogi as he is, perform this miracle? Who can tell? It seems to be extremely difficult, but not altogether impossible, not for Gandhiji.

The second difficulty is this: in view of recent and present British policy in India, will Gandhiji feel called upon to undertake such a programme? Among other things, can he ever trust the British to leave him full freedom to develop his plans which can never succeed under the limitations of ordinance rule. Gandhiji is not likely to launch upon what will undoubtedly be his greatest experiment in an atmosphere of mass mistrust and hatred of

[27] Prafulla Chandra Ghosh (1891-1983); joined Anushilan Samiti of Dacca, 1910; taught at Presidency College, Calcutta, 1919-20; participated in the Non-Cooperation Movement, 1920 and imprisoned; Secretary, Bengal P.C.C., 1921; participated in the Civil Disobedience Movement, 1930, individual satyagraha, 1940, and the Quit India Movement, 1942; member, West Bengal Legislative Assembly, 1947-62, and 1967-8; Chief Minister of West Bengal, 1947-8, and 1967; left politics, 1969; publications include: *History of the Congress from Nagpur to Lahore*, *Indian National Congress*, and *Mahatma Gandhi As I Saw Him*.

[28] Lord Louis Mountbatten (1900-79); first Earl Mountbatten of Burma; Supreme Allied Commander in South East Asia, 1943-6; Viceroy of India, March-August 1947; Governor-General of India, August 1947-June 1948.

the British on the one hand and British mistrust and oppression on the other. It seems to me that Gandhiji can never undertake such a stupendous task unless he has the whole people behind him in the first place, and a government, in the second place, that is if not cooperative at least not obstructive. As long as present British policy continues in India, can even Gandhiji ever hope to rally the people around him for the purpose in question and also can he ever expect that the imperialist government will leave him in peace to develop his weapon and his plans? One must reluctantly answer both these questions in the negative. It seems inescapable that only a free people can resist aggression, whether violently or non-violently. A people that is already bound down in slavery can do little of either effectively. It has to fight on two fronts and combine as best as possible resistance to aggression with resistance to pre-existing slavery. That has been our lot since the war began and remains so today.

19 May 1944
*Gandhi-Jinnah Agreement?**

Yesterday the local *Inquilab* had a leader on the possibility of Gandhi-Jinnah agreement. The *Inquilab* in spite of its name is a pro-British paper and professes loyalty to both the League and the Unionist Party, or at least, the leader of the Party, Lt. Col. Malik Khizar Hayat Khan Tiwana (an impressive name, by the way). In the recent League-Unionist controversy, the *Inquilab* naturally was with the Punjab Premier.

Such being the paper's character, I turned hopefully to the editorial expecting to find a unionist presentation of this case. But the *Inquilab* proved to be too loyal to the formula: 'With Mr. Jinnah outside the Punjab, with the Unionist ministry inside it.'

The editor began by saying that no one would be happier than him if Hindu-Muslim Unity was at last brought about. Then he proceeded to point out how attempted negotiations failed to make a beginning in the past due to the demand that the Muslim League should be recognised as the sole organisation of the Indian Muslims and the Congress as an organisation solely of the Hindu community. Then strangely enough the editor proceeded by laboured argument to support this demand, and ended up by saying that no settlement or even negotiation was possible unless Gandhiji accepted that demand.

It made me sad to read this editorial. One had hoped that after the tragic events of these war years and the fruitless manouverings of Mr. Jinnah, we shall see the end of merely obstructionist tactics and that a serious attempt will be made at least to find out if an agreement is at all possible.

The demand of Mr. Jinnah that not only the League should be accepted as the sole representative body of Indian Muslims, but also that the Congress should convert itself into what Mr. Jinnah should like it to be is a pre-posterous demand, and is, no doubt, made only to obstruct every attempt at a settlement. That there are other organisations of Muslims in India than the League is clear enough, but for the purposes of negotiation it may be conceded that the League shall be taken to speak for the Muslims. This may even be facilitated by a previous understanding to this effect with the other Muslim bodies. But that Mr. Jinnah should insist on defining not only the character of his own body but also that of others with whom he may want to talk is so patently absurd that it hurts one to find that any sensible person should approve of it. Since its birth the Congress has embraced all the communities of India and worked as a purely national body. Today it is no less national than ever before, embracing men of all communities who are agreed upon certain aims and means. When Mr. Jinnah demands that the Congress should go to him as spokesman only of the Hindus, he in effect denies the right of the people of India, irrespective of communities to form political associations. He wants that there should be only communal political parties, communal trade unions, communal student organisations, and so forth. Only a step from this is communal government, communal armies, communal police. If this demand of Mr. Jinnah were to be accepted it would prove to be an eternal blight for Indian political life and development. What objection can Mr. Jinnah have to negotiate with the Congress—i.e. if he accepts the need for an agreement with it as the most important political body, let him negotiate with it as with one of the important bodies. The Congress surely never demanded to be considered as this or that. It is quite content to be what it is and to be accepted for what it is. If Mr. Jinnah is at all persuaded to believe that it is desirable to settle with the Congress, it is obviously the most natural thing to take the Congress as it is and find out by getting down to brass tacks if an agreement is possible. Surely, the Congress on its part, has repeatedly made attempts for a settlement.

It is a pity that even such quarters as the *Inquilab* who profess their deep anxiety for Hindu-Muslim unity lose sight of these obvious questions. Either, this is due to mental laziness or it shows that the League is not yet ready to settle with the Congress. There is of course, a third possibility—the hand of the third party, the enemy of both Indian Muslims and all other Indians. How far the *Inquilab* is a pawn in the British game of Indian chess, it is difficult to say, but it is not altogether impossible that it should be such. The paper surely is eloquently pro-British.

20 May 1944
*Hindu-Muslim Unity (Contd.)**

I find my suspicions of yesterday fully confirmed. Yesterday again the *Inquilab* had a leader on Gandhi-Jinnah agreement. That leader could very well have been written by the editor of the London *Daily Mail*. It presents the British case perfectly, only wrapped up in Muslim or rather League colours. The recent remarks of Lord Halifax in New York in the course of which he made incidentally a reference to 'this selfless, saintly man' meet with the *Inquilab's* enthusiastic approval.

In short, the paper says India cannot win her freedom unless the Hindus, the Muslims, the *rulers* of the Indian states, and all the other communities and interests come together and produce a united political demand. One wonders how India travelled from 1858 to the Act of 1935. However the paper goes on to say that Mahatma Gandhi has so long only deluded the public with sweet words without making a serious attempt to bring about real unity; that he did this because he always thought in terms of Hindu power and Hindu dominations; that if he is now serious about unity he should forthwith accept Pakistan, thereby not only achieving Hindu-Muslim unity, but also Indian independence. One wonders again why should it be Gandhi's role alone to bring about unity in India. Let it be granted that Gandhi is an obstinate old man, dreaming of Hindu raj. Leave him alone therefore, and let Mr. Jinnah, a great patriot and lover of freedom as he is, proceed to call together the rulers of the States, the Hindu Mahasabha, the Akali Dal, the European merchants and all other communities and interests (leaving the Congress aside) and hammer out a national agreement. Surely, the Congress will never stand in the way of any such attempt. But let us turn to the *Inquilab*. The greatest Englishman that ever lived, said something about the unsubstantiality of a name. Surely, a rose is sweet under any name. In like manner British propaganda stinks equally whether it calls itself the Civil and Military Gazette or the Revolution.

27 May 1944
Maurice Hindus[29]

Since I finished *Russia Fights On* I have been wanting to make a comment or two. Maurice Hindus in this book may strike one as a very subtle Stalinist propagandist, who frankly admits Stalin's mistakes and his monstrosities, only to lead his reader to love and admire the more the Russian Vozhd. But I don't think there is any conscious subtlety of this sort in Maurice Hindus; at any rate, not in this book. His attitude towards Stalin and the Russian ruling clique is to my mind determined by a much simpler emotional factor. Hindus was born a Russian and his entire attitude towards present-day Russia is produced by a nostalgic nationalism. The fact that Russia and America

[29] Maurice Gerschon Hindus (1891-1969); An American journalist and writer of Russian origin; author, among others, of *Russian Peasant and Revolution*, *Humanity Uprooted*, *The Great Offensive*, and *Mother Russia*.

are allies makes his Russian nationalism compatible with American citizenship. Hindus is just everlastingly grateful to Stalin for making Russia within twenty years a first class military and industrial power. The deeds of the Red Army have washed away all the sins that Stalin and his junta might have committed—for, mind you, Hindus does not concede all that Stalin's critics say, though he does most of it.

This is why *Russia Fights On* is such a paradoxical book. Hindus, whatever else he may be, gives the certain impression that he believes in the democratic way of life. And though he is not a socialist, he could not be unaware that a socialist society should be far more democratic and humane than the type of democracies that exist today. Yet, he recounts story after story of Stalinist oppression and retrogression without caring to question their need or their place in a socialist society. He pours scorn enough over foreign radicals and communists who went to Russia as to a pilgrimage, and returned disillusioned to write about the dream they lost. These were all faint-hearted, make-belief idealists who could never understand realities and never allowed the glories of the Red Army to dissipate their petty doubts and soft scruples.

Yes, there were purges, those who had hidden vaults of gold were tortured; the kulaks were mercilessly destroyed; inequality of incomes has increased instead of decreasing; there is no democracy in the Communist Party which is ruled by a junta; in matters social such as education, marriage, divorce, there has been a great reaction; and many other things said about Russia and Stalin are true; but what of it? Can't you see the exploits of the Red Army, the courage of the guerillas, the resistance and endurance of the home front? What more do you want? Let squeamish democrats wail and squeal. For me Mother Russia is everything. And she lives today and shall live tomorrow and Fascist hordes shall never subdue her—thanks to Stalin, the worthy son. Therefore, whatever others say I say 'Stalin be Praised'.

For Maurice Hindus, the over-grown Russian peasant lad, all this may be satisfying enough and simple enough. But can those who have a serious concern with problems of social and political organisation ever accept the view that the Red Army and Russia's fighting strength must justify and vindicate all Stalin's follies, brutalities and vulgarisations of socialism? I am afraid not. They must ask whether all those things were essential, whether there were no other alternatives, whether Russia would not have been stronger instead of weaker if they had been followed, whether the history of Europe during the last twenty years and the history of this war itself could not have been different and far more satisfactory if Russia had followed different policies, whether Nazism could not have been prevented from winning in Germany and whether in that case Fascism could have become the danger it came to be, whether the Spanish Revolution should have failed, whether the Labour Movement, both in its national and international aspects, could not have been united or at least better integrated—all these questions and many more they must ask. And I am afraid some of their answers may not be to the liking of Russian nationalists, whether naturalised in the United States or born and bred in India.

8 June 1944
Mr. Roosevelt Prays to God

It is reported that President Roosevelt offered prayers to God, to bless those who 'this day have set out upon a mighty endeavour', that is to say upon the deliverance of France and of Europe. In the course of the prayer the President says: 'They (i.e. the soldiers of the Allies) fight not for lust of conquest. They fight to let justice arise and tolerance and goodwill among all Thy people. . . . Help us conquer the apostles of greed and racial arrogance.' Finally he asks God to 'lead us' to a peace 'that will let all men live in Freedom'.

Having succeeded so long in duping their people, the leaders of this war, Axis or United, have been encouraged to believe that they could also succeed in duping their God. What God will do in the future may be left to the servants of God to speculate upon. What He has done in the past and is doing today, millions and millions of His suffering creatures, famished, diseased and dying, know only too well.

The Allies, says Roosevelt, fight not for lust of conquest. No, they fight for the lust of their *past* conquests (recall Churchill's declaration about the liquidation of the Empire). They also fight for the world's trade, for the world's oil and rubber, for the world's myriad raw materials. Roosevelt wants God to help him crush the apostles of greed and racial arrogance. Yes, God should do that, but spare those who force Negroes to travel in separate compartments, eat in separate restaurants, live in separate quarters, pray in separate churches, who deny them positions in business and government, who deny them positions even in that very army which is to crush the apostles of race arrogance. He should also spare those who do not want coloured peoples to buy property and settle in 'white' areas, who steal the land from the native African and pen him down 'within narrow strips of inferior and disease-filled soil'; also those who want a whole continent, of which they occupy but a tiny fringe, reserved for Whites; also the Burra Sahibs of the East, who have been exemplary specimens of racial equality and goodwill.

Finally, Roosevelt asks God for a peace in which all men will live in freedom. Here also God should distinguish between men and men. He should preserve men of North and South and Central Africa, of Near and Far and Middle East, of South East Asia, from the evils of freedom, for freedom in their case would only mean chaos and anarchy. Therefore, men of India, Burma, Malaya, Java, Sumatra, Indo-China, HongKong, Korea and the coloured men of the whole of Africa must not be free. So God's will will be done.

16 June 1944
All Our Tomorrows

This is a remarkable book by the author[30] of *Insanity Fair*, *Disgrace Abounding*, and *A Prophet At Home*. I have not read his other books which judging from the present one must be worth reading if for nothing else at least to gain an insight into current English history.

Reed writes with vigour, more vigour than one finds in many an English writer of the present generation, and is always in dead earnest. He hates cant and faces truth boldly as he sees it. Above everything he is a real English patriot, for his patriotism is not that false political commodity which is peddled from the conventional platforms to which politicians pay homage and which hides the selfish interests of the British ruling class. He loves England fervently and the English people, the common English people. His book is addressed not to the politicians or the great political parties but to the common man (and woman) in England—the miner, the mechanic, the soldier, the bus driver, the waitress, the clerk, the farmer. There is a note of despair in his appeal for, though he believes in the common man, he feels that if he does not awake in time, all would be lost, even victory in this war, of which he is now assured.

15 July 1944
Gandhiji's Present Position

Due to censorship here I have not been able to read all of Gandhiji's statements and letters. I do not, therefore, have a complete picture before me of what is in his mind today. However, judging from whatever I have been able to read, it appears to me that he has once again set out on the other half of his two-fold policy. As the British have a two-fold policy, that of repression now and concession again, so Gandhiji too has a two-fold policy, which is nevertheless a composite whole and follows a single unswerving goal. The two parts of his policy are direct action when the situation is ripe for it; and negotiation, temporising, constructive work when that is not possible. Clearly the present is not a fit time for an upsurge of direct action. August 1942, on the other hand, was eminently fit for it. But British prescience out-manoeuvred Gandhiji then, and nobody can blame him today if he is trying in his own way, as he

[30] Douglas Reed (1895-1976); British author and journalist; publications include: *The Burning of the Reichstag*, *Insanity Fair*, *A Prophet at Home* and *All our Tomorrows*.

alone can, to repair the wreckage caused by British policy in 1942 and regain the initiative for the Congress in Indian politics. Whichever turn Gandhiji's policy takes, there can be no question that he pursues the same, unchanging goal—the independence of the country. After the events of 1942 not even the most fiery revolutionary should doubt this.

In concrete terms, Gandhiji seems determined to bring about an Indo-British settlement, and to that end he has put forth demands (in the Gelder talks)[31] that are, in his own words, not as high as those of August, 1942. He has done so because, as he himself says, conditions today are not the same as they were in 1942. Writing on this point, the *Tribune* of today says:

> There are some who suggest that the change in Gandhiji's attitude is due to the change in the war situation and because the war has taken a turn for the better, from the point of view of the Allies, he has descended from the high horse he was riding. Assuming for argument's sake that this was so, why should not the Government take advantage of the change and put an end to a state of affairs which was a perpetual challenge to their professed aims? For our part we know that the changed attitude of Mahatma Gandhi is due not so much to the war situation as to the internal circumstances in the country, the arrest of the Congress leaders, the disturbances which broke out after it, the ruthless methods adopted by the Government in suppressing them, the famine in Bengal and the acute suffering and distress produced among the people because of rising prices and dwindling supplies. If, under the circumstances, Gandhiji felt that it was the duty of the Congress to accept even a restricted measure of responsibility for the government of the country, why should any one blame him or seek to attribute unworthy motives to him?

It seems to me that the *Tribune* is rightly interpreting Gandhiji's mind. Personally, I do not think an Indo-British settlement at this time would be of advantage to India. I also thought we had crossed the Rubicon in 1942 and whether we or Pompey won, there was no turning back for us. However, if I were free today, I think I would have desisted from saying or doing anything to hinder Gandhiji. We fought in 1942 and after and we lost—though only in the sense that we failed to reach the goal. But the experience the country went through then did raise it to a higher level of political strength and consciousness. We did go forward and not backward, but not forward enough to reach the goal. Only in that sense we failed. Today, when Gandhiji himself is out and has decided to pursue a certain course of action, it is not for us to obstruct. If he succeeds in his attempt we can wait and see what result it produces. On the other hand, if he fails, he will have come on top, wiped off the effect of British repression and cleared the way for future action.

[31] This refers to Mahatma Gandhi's interview to Stuart Gelder, correspondent of the *News Chronicle* (London) on 11 July 1944. Gandhi told Gelder that he realised that the situation had changed since 1942 and he would be satisfied with the formation of a national government to function as a cabinet and in full control of civil administration and defence. The Allied Forces would be allowed to carry on their operations on Indian soil, but the expense of the operations would not be borne by India.

22 July 1944
The Bricks of Society

In the conditions in which the vast majority of our people live, it is natural that our first thought should turn to the means to secure their material well-being. The greater part of humanity shares with us the woes of poverty and misery and, therefore, in the west as well as in the awakening countries of the East, such as China, the most dominant social problem is the problem of poverty or, broadly speaking, the economic problem. Undoubtedly, first man must live and, therefore, those conditions have first to be created in which he can live happily, i.e., as far as happiness can be derived from the satisfaction of material needs.

But in laying the foundations of the Indian nation and the future free society of India, it is not sufficient to pay attention to the material aspects of life alone. The human aspect, though not urgently demanding our present attention, is perhaps even more important than that of material well-being. The human aspect, which I have in mind, goes beyond the question of social relationship which indeed will be largely, if not wholly, dictated by the nature of the economic organisation; it goes beyond that of education and art and culture. That aspect goes deeper than all these and is their basis, viz., the character and the type of men that we shall rear in a free India. We socialists have suffered from a good deal of fatalistic thinking on this point. We have, no doubt, always conceived of man in a socialist society as an educated, developed, dutiful, good member of society. We probably never had a clear conception of these virtues, but we believed complacently that when economic life had been socialised and acquisitiveness and exploitation removed from society, man in the course of the social process would evolve automatically into a paragon of virtues. But recent experiences have shown that there is as much need of fixing targets and assuring planned progress towards them in the field of character-building of a nation as in the economic field. Indeed, it seems doubtful if the economic and political gains can become permanent without a concurrent development of the human material. On the other hand, even if those gains do become stable, is there much value in creating a society of prosperous but brutalised men? If in the course of socialisation of economy and political dictatorship, or in the course of any other process of development that aims at material happiness, man becomes insensitive to cruelty, an intellectual automation, a moral coward; if lying, deceit, dishonesty, hatred, instead of meeting with universal condemnation, and therefore being liquidated, are exalted into a principle of state-craft and party-management, all who are not drunk with power must be seriously concerned about the wisdom of such a one-sided development.

What I wish to drive at is that political freedom and economic regeneration and prosperity should not be the only two aims of our nation-builders. A nation is made up of individuals, so it should also be our aim to so mould the character of every individual that we become eventually not only a nation of prosperous but also of good men. Clearly, this is not merely a question of education, though education must be the chief instrument of character-building. The question is of discovering and establishing those basic values of life which should determine the principles of education and govern the entire corporate life of the people and their relations with other peoples. According to Dr. Bhagvan Das,[32] in the view of Manu and the ancient law-givers and seers, all human activity should be organically and consistently related to the well-ascertained and clearly-defined objects of life. The ascertainment of these objects, however, took the ancient seers into the domain of metaphysics and they developed the Science of the Self (*Atma-Vidya*) as the basis of all the sciences and as a compass to guide man on the ocean of life. But here a great obstacle will face us. Apart from the validity of the assumptions of *Jiva* and *Brahma* and therefore of *Atma-Vidya* or *Brahma-Vidya*, we have in our country several religions and consequently several varieties of metaphysics. And, though great minds of all religions point out the essential unity underlying them, the mass of the people is most reluctant to seek unity in the varied religious practices. Therefore, it seems to me that, important as the question of essential and basic values of life is, we would be putting our finger into a hornet's nest if we proposed to go to metaphysics and the 'science' of the supernatural to discover those values. It may be left to the various religions to discover them in the light of the teachings of their own scriptures and to inculcate them into their followers. But the State or the Nation, though concerned primarily with the secular aspects of life, cannot ignore the task of character-building of the citizen. The citizen of free India must be a good man, no matter what may be his religion, occupation and station in life. I believe it is possible without, on the one hand, plunging into the multitudinous seas of religious differences, and on the other, without restricting ourselves to any one school of philosophy allowing the materialist as well as the idealist full scope for participation in national education and character-building, to agree upon the basic values of life that should inspire all human relationships in our society and be the corner-stone of our education, the common platform of all political parties, the matrix of our economic life.

[32] Bhagavan Das (1869-1958); an eminent philosopher; founder-member, Central Hindu College, Varanasi, 1898, Banaras Hindu University, 1916; later served on the Senate, Syndicate and other academic bodies of the University; founder-member, Kashi Vidyapith, 1921, and its first Chancellor and Professor of Philosophy; member Indian Legislative Assembly, 1934-8; works include: *The Science of Emotions, The Science of Social Organisation or The Laws of Manu in the Light of Atma-Vidya* (3 vols.), *Mystic Experiences, The Essential Unity of All Religions, Samanvya, Prayojana and Purushartha.*

Among socialists there is not a little confusion over public and individual morality. Marx and the other great socialist writers laid bare the historical connection between reigning moral standards and class relationships in society. In doing this they had little difficulty in showing that moral codes are usually psychological devices for the preservation of the rights and privileges and enjoyments of the dominant classes in society. But thereby they did not mean to suggest that in socialist society, which shall have no ruling class, there should be no public or individual morality. They did perhaps put too much faith in the automatic growth of socialist morality, which, being free from the taint of being a hand-maiden to class oppression, would be superior to all moral codes, except perhaps to those that obtained in the idyllic days of primitive communism. I have indicated above that this expected automatic growth of a new morality is at best too tardy and there seems to be real need here for the socialists to lay down the essential virtues of the social, therefore, ideal man. It seems to me to be unreasonable to plan with meticulous care the production of pigs, for instance, but to leave it to blind social forces to produce man. Planning and conscious direction of every aspect of life is implicit in a socialist society, and in the sphere of morality, as in others, can we plan without a definition of the objectives, the targets? In other words, socialists must fix *a priori* the moral standards and concepts of their society, modifying and developing them as social progress goes apace.

Apart from the question of socialist morality, or the code of morals that shall be suited to a socialist society, when the founders of socialism pointed out the relativity of morality, as of truth, they never meant that there was no such thing as morality at all. While Engels brilliantly demonstrated the relativity of truth, he made withering fun of those who asserted that there was nothing at all that was true. Likewise with morality. Though moral codes have a direct relation with the class nature of society, it does not follow that there is nothing that can be considered moral. It is a different matter that certain types of manifestly immoral behaviour, such as killing or deceiving or lying to the enemy, have been considered by the socialist fathers as of inevitable necessity in the class war and therefore permissible in that sphere. But thereby killing and lying do not become moral virtues, which may be glorified into eternal revolutionary principles. Even the most uncompromising revolutionary socialist must consider lying and killing as immoral, to be resorted to only for the sake of the revolution. I am aware that according to Gandhiji one may not use immoral means even in a virtuous cause. I admit that his is the nobler path. I am also conscious of the warning that Russia has given us all. We have seen that those who used lying and killing as means of the Revolution became so habituated to them and were so debased by them that they did not hesitate to use them as means either of personal aggrandizement or party factionalism or state management, dispensing with party and social democracy. Notwithstanding all this, I am not prepared to reject the use, within limits, of immoral means for moral purposes—if for nothing else, because I do not possess the requisite moral strength to do otherwise.

Returning to the fundamental values of life ours is a country of great diversities, but to my mind there is a very large and essential unity that characterises us as Indians. This unity is not in the outward forms—obviously—but in those essential matters which go to determine human character. It should not be difficult anywhere in the world to tell an Indian—no matter to what religion or caste or territory he belonged—from men of other nationalities. A common history and a common geography have moulded us all into a common nationality, which is as distinct as any in the world. I therefore make bold to assume that it would not be at all difficult for the leaders of our country, irrespective of differences of party or programme, secularly to determine the common values and virtues and aims of life which should inspire and govern all the secular aspects of our individual and national life.

1 August 1944
Enemies of Freedom

A Patna report (*Tribune*, 1.8.'44) says that consequent on Gandhiji's recent statement on underground activities,[33] the Bihar Provincial Satyagrah Council has been dissolved. This is natural enough. But what does not appear to be equally natural is a further report of a meeting of Gaya Congressmen which expressed the view that activities such as sabotage were the 'work of people who were enemies of the freedom of India and were out to discredit the leadership of Mahatma Gandhi'. Something similar seems to have been said in a pamphlet circulating in Purnea, claiming to speak on behalf of local Congressmen.

It makes me sad to reflect on this inglorious end of 'the last fight for freedom'—a fight, which, it now appears, the Congress never started, though thousands of poor fools died in the course of it and many more thousands lost their homes and properties and yet many more thousands lost their 'freedom'. They were enemies of the freedom of their country anyway, so what does it matter?

Violence, it seems, is a terrible sin, but only when used against British rule. For, don't you see how Mahatma Gandhi himself is straining his utmost to have a 'National Government' established, at the command of which hundreds of thousands of Congressmen—the young ones, of course—will

[33] See Appendix 27 for Gandhi's statement dated 28 July 1944.

shoulder a gun and march forth in the shadow of fluttering tricolours to murder and mutilate the brutal Jap and the bestial German? That would be violence too but not sinful, for, were it so, how could Gandhiji himself be so anxious to make it possible for Congressmen to commit sin?

Gandhiji is a deadly dialectician and there is no doubt he could make any intelligent person understand his logic. The trouble is I have no intelligence.

But even I cannot help noticing that during former attempts to set-up a National Government, first made by Sardar Vallabhbhai Patel and Shri Rajagopalachari, then by Jawaharlalji and Maulana Saheb, Gandhiji was, at least, not personally involved. As such he was in a position to preach his doctrine of unalloyed non-violence from his high, unsullied pedestal. But this time—third time during the war—that such an attempt is being made in the name of the Congress, Gandhiji in his own person is endeavouring with all his heart and soul to have a national government formed in this country. No doubt, he still protests that for himself he is a hundred per cent man of peace, and says that after the national government has come into being he will retire from active direction of Congress policy, or such part of it as may relate to that government. This is as if Gandhiji were to drag Jawaharlal out of prison, put a gun into his hand and tell him 'now go and shoot the Japanese, I do not personally approve of it, but since you were always so keen on the United Nations and China, here is your chance; take it and be damned'. (I mean all of it, except the last two words, which may be taken as my own humble contribution to the resolution of the deadlock.)

There is something, it seems to me, in what Mr. Jinnah said the other day about Gandhiji's various personalities or 'capacities'. It is conceivable that Gandhiji may explain all that he is doing by saying that in attempting to resolve the deadlock, he is not acting in his personal capacity, but is trying, as far as humanly possible—one of his favourite phrases—to interpret and express the mind of the Working Committee and the Congress generally, as he feels he is bound to do. The Congress is in prison today largely due to his policy and so, he might say, it is incumbent on him to interpret the Congress and act accordingly.

That is dialectics for you—Hegelian, Marxian, Gandhian.

Inspite of my deep love and reverence for Gandhiji, he sometimes bewilders me. But as I said a few days ago, I would not, if I were free, obstruct him, and for the reasons I gave then. I like less and less what he is doing, but as on last Friday, I think, Churchill, Amery & Co., will not let me down. There does not seem to be any danger of a national government being actually formed in war-time and, therefore, there seems to be no cause to worry. In fact, in these circumstances, whatever Gandhiji does to bring about an Indo-British settlement is bound to develop the country's political consciousness and stimulate the already pervasive anti-British feelings. A few years after the war, we shall see what we shall see.

4 August 1944
*Jail Journey**

Jim Phalen is an Irish revolutionary who was sentenced for life by the British. His father and grandfather were in British prisons too. Though *Jail Journey* is autobiographical, Phalen has written very little about himself. So the book has created in me a powerful desire to know more about him. He seems to be an extraordinary man and an extraordinarily powerful writer. I doubt whether anything as raw and alive and vital has appeared in the English language in recent years.

Jail Journey is a description of the life of prisoners in three British prisons: Maidstone, Dartmoor, and Parkhurst, on the Isle of Wight. Britain is a leader of modern civilization and *Jail Journey* is a sad commentary on modern civilized society. It is not Phalen's purpose to point out the evils of an evil system so as to enable kind-hearted people to institute jail reforms. He merely lifts, or rather tears up, the veil that surrounds prisons in this self-satisfied modern world and enables all who have eyes to see what man makes of man. Those who will look at that picture will reach only one conclusion: a British prison is a factory where man is turned into a mindless animal and where ultimately every human attribute is pressed out of him. That is the distilled essence of British penology at work.

Whether Phalen's book will create a revolution in penology it is too much to say, but his struggle against a soul-less, animalised system will remain a rare human epic of modern times.

I also believe that he has added a few words to the English language, such as 'Madam de Luce' and 'mix'. I do not mean that these words will find their way into the Oxford dictionary, but they will nevertheless have a wide and increasing use. A hundred years later the Oxford lexicographer might include them in his time-honoured circle.

One of the books I would like very much to read at present is the *Life*.+

4 August 1944
Make This The Last War

This is an English edition of the book published first in America in 1942. Julian Huxley[34] writes the Introduction. Straight is an editor and Washington

* Jim Phalen, *Jail Journey* (London, 1940).

\+ *Life*, an earlier book by Jim Phalen.

[34] Sir Julian Huxley (1887-1975); British biologist and author; contributed to the early development of the study of animal behaviour; first Director General of UNESCO, 1946-8; works include, *Heredity East and West* (1949).

correspondent of the *New Republic* and 'is now training to be a pilot in the U.S. Army Air Corps'. As a student he lived in England and travelled in Europe, Russia, Africa and India.

Straight is a wide-awake economist and has written a brilliant book. But, unfortunately, brilliant books do not seem to affect the progress of humanity. As the Allied Powers approach victory, many of the hopes that burnt so brightly in the hearts of men like Straight are already turned to ash. The United Nations Ltd., is nearing liquidation and the Atlantic Charter has shrunk to the dimensions of the English Channel. The author has referred again and again to India as a test-case. The result of that test is no longer in doubt. Both Capital and Labour in Britain are agreed that India must remain the bulwark of the British Empire and of British domination over Africa and Asia that it has always been. Even in 1943 the result of the test was known. Julian Huxley, who inherits a great name, wrote in the Introduction in regard to the colonies and India in particular, 'he (i.e. the author) seems to me not to be aware of some of the aspects of the problem, or of the constructive new policies that have been taking shape in Britain in regard to India in 1943'. Has not somebody said: 'Scratch a Briton and you will find a Tory?' Huxley, I believe, is one of the bright lights of the British Left or whatever they call themselves. And, at the very moment when British rule in India revealed itself in its darkest shape, this celebrated scientist discovered 'constructive new policies' taking shape in regard to India! Lest the reader should think that Huxley is referring to the Cripps proposals which probably Straight did not know about when he wrote his book early in 1942, I hasten to inform him that he will find a penetrating analysis of the Cripps fiasco on page 142. I shall quote just two sentences: "*Yet the Cripps Plan was cast in the classical mould of meeting a present crisis* by promising reforms at a future date and reserving present powers to the Viceroy. It was not based on an appreciation of the true impact upon India of the fall of Singapore and the extent to which Indian demands had shifted from the assurance of a constituent assembly in the future to the granting of immediate participation in the war effort". So much for constructive new policies and 'left' British intellectuals.

Straight's suggestions can be compressed under three large heads: (i) a federation of Europe, (ii) liquidation of empires and imperial economics, (iii) setting up the United Nations as a world organisation of cooperative economy, pledged to democratic ways of life, and to which other nations could be admitted on fulfilment of certain conditions. These are very large objectives and there is no hope that any of them will be realised in the manner Straight visualises them. A European federation may be brought about by the European people themselves if they are united enough and clear enough about their aims. But such a federation must arise against the wishes of the Allies, including Russia. I do not think Russia would want a strong Europe, federal or otherwise. England and America would try to set-up France and

Italy on their legs. Russia would try to bolster up the Slav nations near her frontier. Central Europe I believe, would again be left as an amorphous mass, with only Czechoslovakia as a crystallised agent, friendly equally to Anglo-America and Russia. In any case, a European federation does not seem to be even a remote possibility.

Liquidation of empires and imperial policies cannot come from the top, that is, on the volition of the imperial powers which one should remember include the U.S.A., which has not inconsiderable economic empire in Central and South America. The empires will no doubt be liquidated, but in a different manner. The spearhead of that process would be, as it is even today, India. China's regeneration, if it is allowed full scope by America after the war, will be the second powerful nail into the coffin of world empires. Further, the freedom movement in the Islamic countries of the Middle East, mainly of the Arab peoples, would be a third blow to the empire in Africa and Asia. India must try to link up all these forces to hasten the process of imperial liquidation.

As for the United Nations, it is just a tremendous hoax. The post-war world is going to be dominated by Anglo-America and the United Nations will be only the band boys. Certain institutions of economic cooperation may be created, but their real objects will not be those that Michael Straight sets before him.

No, the prospect is distinctly gloomy and we might as well prepare for World War No. III, unless—and this is a very big condition—unless the European Revolution bursts forth with a force sufficient to sweep away the Old Order in Europe clean into the Atlantic.

5 August 1944

A Revolution is Disowned Because it Failed

For many weeks now, since Gandhiji made his comments on the August movement, a great bitterness has been gnawing at my heart. I know it is fruitless to be embittered and, perhaps, I take things too seriously. Perhaps my fundamentally socialist way of looking at things leads to my being so completely possessed with political issues of the moment. Anyway, I just cannot shake off this bitterness that daily eats deeper into my being. I cannot say if in the end I should not find myself bidding good-bye to Congress politics to dedicate myself entirely to the labour and socialist movements, such as they may be.

I feel bitter because I find we have been badly let down—not I personally, because I openly preached violence and was, therefore, prepared in the event of failure for severe censure and ex-communication. But, thousands, rather lakhs, of Indian patriots, have been let down.

That Gandhiji should dissociate himself from violent activities, should even condemn them, was natural; and nobody can have any justification for expecting him to do otherwise. No one can feel any bitterness on that score. But all that happened after August 8, 1942, was not violence. By far the greater part of those moving events was a non-violent mass demonstration—swift, elemental, cyclonic. Nothing like it had happened in 1921, 1930 or 1932. Great deeds of heroism, of non-violent heroism, were performed. They deserve to be made immortal in song and national history. But, I fear, they will rather be treated as ugly spots disfiguring the purity of the Congress name and flag. Already, those who performed deeds of sabotage have been condemned as enemies of their country's freedom. Those thousands of unknown soldiers of independence who participated in the stirring events of 1942 did not stop to consider whether the upheaval that caught them in its surge and flung them onward was technically, in accordance with the niceties of political formulae, a Congress movement or not. It was sufficient for them to know that their leader had declared an 'open rebellion', that before he could give the call he was arrested with his colleagues of the Working Committee, that the entire Congress was outlawed and sought to be suppressed. They answered the (technically ungiven) call, and not for a moment did they doubt that the Congress willed them to fight. And what a fight they put up! How many lives were lost, how many villages ruined, looted and burnt! What unspeakable horrors they faced! But they endured all in the faith that they had done their duty.

That they erred is possible: they did no doubt err, judged from Gandhiji's unapproachable standards. But, because of those errors, is the Congress justified in disowning them and their struggle? It is true Gandhiji has praised their courage and patriotism, including the courage of those who are no more to receive his praise. That is the least that Gandhiji and the Congress owed them. But they owe them much more. What the Congress in sheer fairness owes them is to acclaim their struggle as its own and to receive with gratitude both the poison of their errors and the glory of their deeds. A frank, unashamed, identification with the people in travail—that and not cant and hypocrisy (at the worst) and ratiocination (at the best) is the obligation the Congress bears the people. Those who would churn the ocean must be ready to drink the poison with the nectar.

But Gandhiji has disowned the people's struggle, not only because it was tainted with violence but also because the Congress had never formally 'started' a mass struggle. That even a 'Congress' struggle, started duly after the fulfilment of all ceremonial technicalities, may also at some stage become tainted with violence, is a possibility that cannot at any time be ignored. But such contamination and impurity cannot convert the whole movement from a Congress campaign to just a mob outbreak. The violence may be condemned but the struggle as a whole may not be disowned. In the same manner, it appears to me, the struggle of 1942 cannot be disowned on grounds of violence.

As for the argument that the Congress had never formally launched a mass struggle, the argument, of course, is true. The A.I.C.C. had appointed Mahatma Gandhi the sole leader and had asked him to initiate and lead a mass struggle when he should find it necessary. But before Gandhiji was able to do anything about it he found himself in prison. These are facts and nobody can deny them. But I have asked before and ask again: what were the people expected to do in such a condition? Surely not to lie supine under the boot of the British, just because Gandhiji was not offered an opportunity to lead them personally into battle. It was the duty of Gandhiji and the Working Committee to have considered such a possibility and to have forewarned the people about the course of action they should have followed in that event. But if Gandhiji and the Working Committee failed in their obvious duty, expecting a super-human forbearance and magnanimity from the opponents, should the people too have failed in their obvious duty? If they had, not only would that have broken the heart of our leaders, but also made the Congress the laughing stock of the entire world. The people took care not to let down the Congress. Is it fair then for the Congress, just because the people made a few mistakes—and that too because their leaders had omitted to give them timely guidance—to turn round and disown the people's travail and suffering and to tell the world that it takes no responsibility for them at all?

Furthermore, is it strictly true that the leaders omitted to tell the people anything about their duties in the event of their arrest? I seem to remember the Congress President eloquently asking every Indian in such an event to become his or her own leader. Is it fair, then, to disown those who did become their own leaders and followed the call of the Congress? Had they succeeded, the Congress would have got the credit: when they failed should not the failure too be that of the Congress? Does any one believe that the people would have done anything, had they known that the Congress had given them no call to fight? After reading Gandhiji's statements I think the fairest thing would have been for him and the Congress President to have frankly told the people on the night of the 8th of August that if by any chance they were to be removed from their midst on the morrow, absolute peace was to be maintained, nor a leaf was to stir, not a blade of grass to turn, the nation's normal course of life was to run on unaltered.

Some may think that I am just being morbid and making an unnecessary fuss over this business of 'disowning'. After all, what difference does it make if a particular movement is described as a Congress movement or merely as a mass disorder? Well, may be I am making an unnecessary fuss, but it does seem to me that no one likes to be disowned by his family or excommunicated by his community. In history many have preferred death to being put out of the pale.

I shall wait and see if the Working Committee too, like Gandhiji, throws its gallant soldiers overboard. I shiver at that tragic possibility.

7 August 1944
Three Books

I read yesterday and today three little books that Minoo had sent: *Tomorrow* (edited by Raja Rao[35] and Ahmed Ali,[36] Padma Publishers): *Talking to India* (George Allen and Unwin): *Gandhism Reconsidered* (Dantawala, Padma).

A few words about these. First, Dantawala's pamphlet. I believe the main argument of Dantawala was already coming to be fairly shared even before the war by Socialists in India, at least by Congress Socialists. I had a brief talk, perhaps in 1938, with Professor J.C. Kumarappa[37] at Wardha about these problems. After that talk I had formulated certain general ideas which I had on several occasions shared with various friends, and even placed before small meetings of co-workers. I had spoken to Gandhiji also about them who had asked me to stay at Wardha and work out the details along with Prof. Kumarappa, but unfortunately I never got the time to do so. The main idea I had formed then was of large-scale industries (in the spheres of production that are, as Prof. Kumarappa said, by their very nature large-scale) under State ownership and management and a countrywide network of cooperative cottage industries: both dovetailed together into one economic whole. Professor Dantawala's pamphlet covers a wider field and makes a very valuable contribution to current political and economic thought. But he seems to have been in a hurry. The questions he deals with and the suggestions he makes are of vital importance to a country about to choose its future mould of life. Most books are written around a single, simple, central theme. Dantawala has at least half a dozen themes, which are all central but far from simple. He should develop his themes, and write so that an average Indian reader, who reads English and is interested in these questions, may

[35] Raja Rao (1909-); writer; went to Europe to do research in literature; wrote and published stories in French and English; after living in France for some years moved to the U.S.A.; wrote *The Cat and Shakespeare*, *The Serpent and the Rope*, *Kanthapura*; received Sahitya Akademi Award for *The Serpent and the Rope*; co-edited *Tomorrow* along with Ahmed Ali.

[36] Ahmed Ali (1912-); writer; one of the founders of Progressive Writers' Movement; author of *Twilight in Delhi* and *Ocean of Night*; also published four volumes of short stories in Urdu; co-edited *Tomorrow* along with Raja Rao.

[37] For biographical note on J.C. Kumarappa see *JPSW*, Vol. I, p. 126.

understand the problems and the solutions or analyses he offers. As the book stands, only the upper layer of even the Socialist workers can appreciate it or understand it enough to agree or disagree with it. Why should he, for instance, assume that everyone has read Burnham's[38] *Managerial Revolution* and understood the problems it deals with? Further, his treatment of agrarian exploitation in relation to Gandhiji's thinking is unjustifiably too brief. Did he forget the eternal refrain, 'India is an agricultural country?' What is the Gandhian solution of this myriad-processed exploitation? Take again that quotation from Nym Wales; it sums up beautifully one of Dantawala's (or Gandhism's) central themes. But he should explain and illustrate it at adequate length before his average reader will understand all its implications. I think he will render a great service to his country if he gave six months to rewriting his pamphlet, which in many parts is no more than synoptic, into a book say, ten times larger.

The gentlemen who thought they were 'Talking to India' were talking largely to themselves or to the shadowy shapes of their own minds, or to Ahmed Ali, Mulk Raj Anand[39] etc. (which is the same as talking to themselves). There is little in these 'literary talks' that would interest India, much less inspire her. It never seems to have occurred to these talkers, some of whom seem to expect a great deal from this country, to give her something more solid than words—words at best are sounds, but these words are hollow sounds, vapid, toneless, false.

Here is, for instance, Mr. Mulkraj Anand "...We too, have been part of a vast cultural awakening which witnessed not only the blinding spectacle of a great renaissance of the spirit, but the education of the people through mass literary campaigns, the training of men in the art of physical defence against oppression and aggression. When, for instance, the Indian writers recently resolved to tell the people by word of mouth or through the newspaper, of Japan's intentions with regard to India, they were evidencing to the same heroic spirit as possessed you and our brother writers in China." I do not know of any mass literary campaigns, though when the Congress Ministry functioned, a serious attempt was made for adult literacy. These literacy campaigns, however, were promptly liquidated as soon as power reverted to the hands of the British governors. Mass literacy and imperialist rule do not

[38] James Burnham (1905-87); Professor of Philosophy, New York University, 1932-54; Editor of *National Review* for many years; publications include: *A Critical Introduction to Philosophy*, *The Managerial Revolution*, *The Struggle for the World*, *The Coming Defeat of Communism*, *Containment or Liberation*, *Suicide of the West*, and *The War We Are In*.

[39] Mulk Raj Anand (1905-); writer and critic; associated with B.B.C., 1942-5; Tagore Professor of Literature, Punjab University, 1962-5; author of several novels, short stories and critical essays, including *Untouchable*, *An Indian Prince*, *Morning Face*, *Confession of a Lover*, and *The Bubble*.

hold together, a fact which Mr. Anand might have mentioned for the enlightenment not of his Indian listners, but his British friends. Where he learnt about the training of men in the art of physical defence is a puzzle. Perhaps the British Ministry of information or the India Office supplied him with this Madam de Luce* or perhaps the *People's War* of his Indian communist friends. But the statement that takes the prize is about 'the heroic spirit' of the Indian writers 'who recently resolved to tell the people' etc., etc. Who and what these Indian writers are we know. Japanese *intentions* had no doubt to be exposed: but it never occurred to those 'heroic' writers to expose British *deeds*. Perhaps they had never heard of these *deeds*—how could they as they were not listed on their folios of 'International Information'. Perhaps they were not concerned about them. After all, Chimur, Balia, Bhagalpur, Midnapore were not so near as Hankow or Cracow. Or perhaps it required too much heroism to talk about British deeds in India. After all, it is not too pleasant to vegetate in an Indian prison, when you could be talking on the All India Radio or writing nicely-worded exposes of Japanese intentions. Gandhi and Nehru too wrote about Japanese intentions, but they also wrote and talked about certain other things, and look what happened to them.

Here is again Mr. R.R. Desai talking: "For instance, when it was reported that the Nazis had levelled to the ground a whole village in Czechoslovakia as punishment for aiding the assassins of Heydrich, there were many who said this report was a fabrication, or that the account was perhaps just partly true. Of course, at a distance of six thousand miles things look different; the reactions would have been different if this massacre of the menfolk and the wholesale deportation of women and children had taken place in the village not of Lidice, but shall we say of Lalpur."

That is just the trouble. A distance of six thousand miles makes such a lot of difference, you know. Now Mr. Desai is gravely concerned about Lidice, as every human ought to be and, I am sure, all Indians would be if they know about it. But the Lalpur, not Mr. Desai's imaginary Lalpur, but the real ones—and there were many of them—are six thousand miles away from London and the B.B.C. And that makes a difference. One may just ignore them and forget all about them. A few Chimurs, a few hundred burnt and looted villages in Bihar and U.P. and Bengal: a few women raped, a few breast bitten off, a few children shot in the back, a few others shot in the chest while their unflinching hands held little fluttering tricolours—all these; what do they matter, since they are six (or is it seven?) thousand miles away

* I must explain this term. 'Madam de Luce' or just 'Madam' is a term used by prisoners in Britain, as Jim Phalen writes in his *Jail Journey*, to signify untruth, humbug and cant rolled into one. I do not apologize for using the term because I like it and hope it will soon be in common use. [Note by J.P.]

from London and the glorious fight for liberty and freedom? I may add that Mr. Desai at least, if not his British colleagues, should know that distance never blinded India unlike some other countries. India's heart went out in sympathy when humanity suffered under the tyrant's heel—to Abyssinia, to China, to Spain, to Czechoslovakia, to Russia. No, it is the fog in London that obliterates everything more distant than your nose.

Here finally is a specimen out of Five Specimens of Propaganda: "To those who say that Japan will set Burma or India free, the best answer is: 'why then have they not set free Korea and Formosa, which they have had in their power for so long?" Yes, that undoubtedly is the best answer, and to any man with intelligence a crushing answer. But the trouble is there are others too who talk of fighting for freedom and one may ask them also with equal force, why do they not free India "which they have had in their power for so long?". This answer, however, would appear to the B.B.C. and its intellectual talkers to be beside the point. Don't you know India is a very complex problem: there are all those minorities to be protected and those innumerable elements in its political life to whom Britain owes very special responsibilities? What madness to talk about freeing India? Did I become His Majesty's first Minister . . . mumbojumboabracadabra . . .?

Tomorrow is not a very exciting picture of international culture. I was not much impressed by the reproductions from the foreign writers. The purpose of some of these writers seems to be not to express themselves, but to disguise their meaning by cunning tricks with words. I think anybody who really had something to say would say it simply and, may be, beautifully if he also understood beauty and had learnt to express it. I find neither beauty nor meaning in some of the pieces collected. But that is my fault.

Raja Rao's *Javni* is a good story and should read very well in Kanada. But in English, well, I don't know if the language does not fail utterly to do justice to what he wants to say. I cannot say how Conard did it, nor how some in our own country do it, but it seems to me that a foreign tongue, i.e., any tongue we have not spoken in childhood, is a poor medium for creative writing. Our creative writers would do greater justice to themselves and enrich greatly the literature of their country if they could give up the temptation of writing in English. In a foreign tongue we can but copy ideas, style, life; we can never create, innovate, experiment. Tagore is a second rate English poet, but in Bengali, he is a colossus—unapproached and unapproachable.

10 August 1944
Hindu-Muslim Unity?

If any one told a Congressman that the Congress was a Hindu body, he would rightly feel indignant. Yet, Congress leaders, other public leaders, nationalist editors, constantly talk of a Congress-League settlement as a settlement between the Hindu and Muslim communities. Why this confusion?

The reason, to my mind, is that following the cue of the British, we have been led to look upon the lack of unity in India as disunity among the communities. We talk endlessly of 'Communal Unity' and equate it with national unity. This, of course, assumes that all political life in India is organised on communal lines, which obviously is not the case. Then, why don't we stop to analyse this muddle and state the position in clear terms?

Some weeks ago, in the course of my comments on Dr. Abdul Latif's[40] book [*The Cultural Future of India*] I had pointed out that there are two parallel developments in India—one the organisation of political and economic and cultural life on a national basis, the other the organisation of such life on a communal basis. Examples of the first type of organisations are the Congress, the Liberal Federation, the All-India Trade Union Congress, the States People's Conference, the Federation of Chambers of Commerce and Industries, the Student's Congress, the Unionist Party and the Bangiya Krishak Proja Party. Examples of other type are the Muslim League, the Hindu Mahasabha, the Muslim State People's Conference, the Muslim Chamber of Commerce, the Muslim Student's Federation, and the Akali Dal. Of these two, the national type of organisations have been by far the stronger, but recently fed by various adventitious circumstances, the second type has been growing in strength. There has never been any conflict, though there has been difference of opinion, among the first type of organisations. The conflict really is between the national and the communal forces in our national life. A settlement between the Congress and the Muslim League is not to be a settlement between Hindus and Muslims, but between national and communal ways of life. The ideal thing, of course, for our national growth would have been for the national tendencies and forces to gather such strength that communalism would have been dead. But the existence of a third party makes this impossible and an urgent need is felt now for an understanding between these forces. If such an agreement has become necessary, let it be brought about, but let us not misunderstand and misrepresent the character of this development. I wish this could be made clear to the country by someone at this time. Will Gandhiji himself make it clear or will he blur the issues in his eagerness to reach an agreement?

[40] Syed Abdul Latif (1889-1971); noted educationist and political thinker; Professor of English, Osmania University, Hyderabad; President, Academy of Islamic Studies and the Institute of Indo-Middle East Cultural Studies, Hyderabad; author among others of *The Concept of Society in Islam*, *The Mind Al-Quran Builds*, and *Reorientation of Islamic Thought* and *The Cultural Future of India*.

15 August 1944
The Disowned Revolution: Another Sidelight

Last night I read Louis Fischer's[41] *A Week with Gandhi*. The same sincerity and genuineness that one finds in his *Men and Politics* are stamped on every page of this little book. To a foreign reader it reveals Gandhi, or a part of him. To an Indian reader it no less reveals Fischer. Such men are a bridge between nations, but unfortunately they are so few that the bridge never gets completed.

In connection with what I wrote about a revolution disowned, the following conversation between Gandhiji and Fischer will bear reproduction.

"Well", I asked, "how do you actually see your impending civil disobedience movement? What shape will it take?"

"In villages," Gandhiji explained, "the peasants will stop paying taxes. They will make salt despite official prohibition. This seems a small matter; the salt tax yields only a paltry sum to the British Government. But refusal to pay it will give the peasants the courage to think that they are capable of independent action. Their next step will be to seize the land."

"With violence?" I asked.

"There may be violence, but then again the landlords may cooperate."

"You are an optimist," I said.

"They might cooperate by fleeing," Gandhi said.

Nehru who had been sitting by my side, said:

"They might vote for confiscation with their legs just as you say in your 'Men and Politics' that, as Lenin put it, the Russian soldier voted for peace with his legs in 1917—he ran away from the trenches. So also the Indian landowners might vote for the confiscation of their land by running away from the village."

"Or", I said, "they might organise violent resistance."

"There may be fifteen days of chaos", Gandhi speculated, "but I think we could soon bring that under control."

"You feel then that it must be confiscation without compensation?" I asked.

"Of course," Gandhi agreed. "It would be financially impossible for anybody to compensate the landlords."

"That accounts for the villages," I said. "But that is not all of India."

"No," Gandhi stated. "Working men in the cities would leave their factories. The railroads would stop running."

[41] Louis Fischer (1896-1970); famous journalist and author; American Correspondent in various countries, particularly Russia, Spain, and India; wrote mainly on Gandhi and Soviet Russia; publications include: *Stalin* and *Hitler, Men and Politics* (an autobiography), *A Week with Gandhi*, *Gandhi and Stalin*, *The Life of Mahatma Gandhi*, and *Gandhi*: *His life and Message for the World*.

"General strike", I said to myself. "I know", I said aloud, "that you have in the past had a large following among the peasants, but your city working-class support is not so big."

"No", Gandhi acquiesced, "not so big. But this time the working men will act too, because, as I sense the mood of the country, everybody wants freedom, Hindus, Moslems, untouchables, Sikhs, workers, peasants, industrialists, Indian civil servants, and even the princes. The princes know that a new wind is blowing. Things cannot go on as they have been. We cannot support a war which may perpetuate British domination. How can we fight for democracy in Japan, Germany and Italy when India is not democratic? I want to save China. I want no harm to come to China. But to collaborate we must be free. Slaves do not fight for freedom." (90-2)

That was Gandhiji's mood in June 1942. It was a mood which reflected the mood of the mass, and the two acted and reacted on each other. General strike, non-payment of taxes seizure of the landlord's estates, a short interregnum of chaos! What a picture of a red-blooded revolution! Later, the mass, suddenly become leaderless, put a few crude strokes of this picture on history's canvas. For that the mass has been disowned. No one had authority, we are told, to function in the name of the Congress. A few thousand arrests were supposed to have extinguished the Congress, or, at least, isolated it from the people. Were the threads so slender that bound the Congress and the people together? The people were evidently expected to create, all of a sudden, as if out of a magic basket, another organisation which could inspire them and symbolise for them their yearnings and hopes as did the Congress! History records no such magic. If there was anything, any organisation, any name, that in August 1942 meant to the people, freedom and suffering and struggle, it was the Congress. Nothing could take its place, therefore, nothing *did* take its place. No matter how many times that struggle is disowned and by whom, it will ever remain in history, with all its faults, a part of the Congress struggle for Indian freedom.

16 August 1944

There is another point of interest in Fischer's book which I should like to note here in connection with what I have written above. It is clear from the conversations recorded that, as early as June 1942, Gandhiji was expecting to be arrested and he told Fischer that he was 'ready'. This is an astounding piece of information. Gandhiji was talking of open rebellion; in June he said he was 'ready' to be arrested. The question is: had he got the people ready? He Had not—not till August 8, at least. I do not know what to make of this. Everybody knows that Gandhiji is ever ready to turn his footsteps to prison. He needs barely half an hour's notice to pack up his kit. But a responsible leader, thinking of launching upon his life's last and greatest campaign, is not 'ready' for prison till he has told his followers what they should do when he is gone. It seems to me that both Gandhiji and the Working Committee owe an answer to the nation as to why on the 8th of August they left it entirely unprepared and completely ignorant of any programme of action that might have been in their mind. I doubt, however, if the nation will have the courage to put them that question. In any case, I know that the answer, charged with great moral and mystic weight and bursting with self-righteous complacency, will be that it is not in the nature of non-violent technique to lay down in advance the forms of struggle.

16 August 1944
"Restrictions" on Released Congressmen

In one of his conversations with Louis Fischer, Gandhiji told him how he came actively to oppose British rule in India, and incidentally discovered the method by which India could be made free. Gandhiji described to Fischer how he was prevailed upon to go to Champaran in Bihar, how an order was served on him to leave the district and how he decided to disobey the order:

> That day in Champaran became a red-letter day in my life. I was put on trial. The government attorney pleaded with the magistrate to postpone the case, but I asked him to go on with it. I wanted to announce publicly that I had disobeyed the order to leave Champaran. I told him that I had come to collect information about local conditions and that I therefore had to disobey the British Law because I was acting in obedience with a higher law, with the voice of my conscience. This was my first act of civil disobedience against the British. My desire was to establish the principle that no Englishman had the right to tell me to leave any part of my country where I had gone for a peaceful pursuit. The government begged me repeatedly to drop my plea of guilty. Finally the magistrate closed the case. Civil disobedience had won. It became the method by which India could be made free. Elucidating his action Gandhiji said, 'What I did was a very ordinary thing. I declared that the British could not order me around in my own country.'

This is a simple and beautiful description of the birth of civil disobedience in India—an event that became a turning point in the country's history. But, after twenty-five years of precept and example of civil disobedience, it is unfortunate that even Congressmen have not grasped its basic principle: that the foreigner has no right to order us about in our own country. Punjab Congressmen seem to be the worst offenders in this respect. A large number of Congressmen have been 'released' here in recent months, but most of them have been placed under various restrictions. As far as I know, everyone of them is meekly obeying them. I find it humiliating that Congressmen should do so. It is far better to be in prison than voluntarily to agree to carry out British orders as to one's movement and activities. The whole thing goes against the very fundamentals of the Congress. No wonder the Congress is no moral force in this province.

In extenuation of the guilt of these Congressmen, I might say that this tradition of submitting to restrictive orders has been established by the revolutionaries. Both in Bengal and the Punjab a large number of revolutionaries submitted, as a mater of course, to such orders. But it would not do for Congressmen to imitate the methods of the revolutionaries. The latter do not fight with civil disobedience as a method. Their forms and principles of fight are different. They see no reason why they should court imprisonment. When a revolutionary chooses to live under restricrtions, he has usually two motives. Either he hopes to disappear underground in course of time, or he thinks he would be able to do more for the cause with the little freedom he enjoys than when he is denied all freedom in prison. If he follows the second course, he finds himself sooner or latter in prison again. If he does neither of these things, he has ceased to be a revolutionary and is merely living on his past.

A Congressman may not follow the revolutionary's reasoning. He cannot go underground, at least not in normal times (If he does, of course, the stigma of obeying orders does not attach to him). Secondly, he cannot further any Congress programme when he is denying the very first principle of the Congress and undermining the very moral plane on which the Congress must function.

Therefore, it seems clear to me that the Punjab Congressmen, or Congressmen anywhere, who are living under government-imposed restraints must refuse to do so, and go back to prison. If nobody accepted such restraints, they would not be heard of any more.

18 August 1944
As You Were!

I wrote in my note of August 1: "I like less and less what he (i.e., Gandhiji) is doing, but as on last Friday, the day of the last parliamentary debate on India, I think, Churchill-Amery & Co., will not let me down. There does not seem to be any danger of a national government being actually formed in war time, and, therefore, there seems to be no cause to worry." Any such cause for worry has, at last, been finally put beyond all doubt. This morning's *Tribune* publishes the latest declaration of British policy on India in the shape of further correspondence between Gandhiji and Lord Wavell. It has now been made clear, without even the vaguest shadow of doubt, that the British Government are not prepared during the war to make the slightest transfer of power to India in any field whatever and under any circumstances. Self-blinded hopefuls like Mr. Rajagopalachari have always believed and asked others to believe that, once the Congress and the League come together, the formation of a national government would become inevitable. Mr. Rajagopalachari has slowly been blossoming into a prophet, and many things may be pardoned him. But unfortunately for him and his followers, his prophecies have all been going away. For some years now he has been speaking in mysterious accents—prophets must be mysterious—of a national government being born in just a couple of months. But his couple of months have grown into a couple of years, and now they have grown into eternity.

The British Government have now made it clear that, even if all the elements in Indian political life including the States, came to a common understanding, no change in the Viceroy's powers could be made during the course of the war. That is, even if India were to rise as one man and demand a national government—be it only in the sphere of civil administration—the British would shoe that demand firmly into the ocean. After all, there are enough white soldiers in India, as once Mr. Churchill recalled with satisfaction, to take care of all the consequences.

Leaving men like Mr. Rajagopalachari aside, I cannot understand how or why Gandhiji ever thought that the British, who refused to part with any power when they had their wind up after Singapore and Rangoon, would agree to do so now when they had the war situation well in their hands. Or perhaps I do understand. I think Gandhiji never had any illusion about it, even when he decided to stoop to conquer. But, he probably wanted to clear the deck and remove the cobwebs from the minds of the C.R.'s and Saprus and Sastris before taking other steps. He might have thought that, unless he 'climbed down' and made an attempt to settle with the British—an attempt that would be considered by every honest Indian as reasonable—he would be hounded at every step by cries 'intransigent', 'unreasonable', 'settle now', 'national government', and so forth. World opinion too might misunderstand him. So, I think, he decided to go to the farthest limit possible to meet the British so that no doubt might remain anywhere as to his anxiety for a settlement; so that every one with the least intelligence might see for himself what the real obstruction to a national government was. If this was Gandhiji's intention, he has fulfilled it to the fullest extent. Now, the whole world can see that it is not Indian disunity that is in the way of Britain transferring power to India, but British determination to hold all power in their own hands even in the face of the completest Indian unity. All cobwebs have been swept away and even Mr. Rajagopalachari has no fine-spun yarns left to clutch at, nor even a pinch of dust in his political bag to throw into the eyes of his fellow countrymen.

Now, Gandhiji can go ahead, whatever his course of action, without being pursued at every footstep by distracting cries and strident noises. The question is: what can be Gandhiji's future course of action. It is clear that during the course of the war, there is no possibility now of putting any mass pressure—in the form of mass civil disobedience—upon the British for enforcing the demand for national government. Even if the Congress were made lawful again—which is doubtful—and if the leaders were released, the possibility of mass action must be ruled out. The only course of action left to Gandhiji is carefully to nurse the wounds of the nation and bring it back to health and vigour, and bide his time. Soon after the war, his chance will come. Part of this process of national rehabilitation will be settlement with the League, and the growth of national unity, conceived not as an agreement between communities, castes and classes, but as the growth of nationalism. It is slow patient work, but there is no alternative before Gandhiji. A joint Gandhi-Jinnah demand for a national government will have no more than propaganda value; neither would the British yield, nor would Mr. Jinnah agree to fight the British. In fact, Mr. Jinnah's refusal to fight might torpedo the entire negotiation that Gandhiji is to carry on with him. Gandhiji is not likely to take the recent description of British policy as a settled fact and he might press Mr. Jinnah to join him in unsettling it, but the League leader is not expected to do so. He will ignore the war-time issues and concentrate only on a post-war settlement. Gandhiji has a difficult task before him. But even if Mr. Jinnah chooses to sacrifice the interests of his country and the Muslim community and refuses to join Gandhiji in demanding immediate power, and thus if the negotiations are terminated, the country would not have the same sense of loss and failure as it would have had if the recent British declaration had not been made. So, even in the case of failure of his negotiations with Mr. Jinnah, Gandhiji might feel less cramped in pursuing his chosen course of action. I wish all power to his elbow.

20 August 1944
The Problem of Congress-League Settlement

I have been feeling for some time now the need of integrating my thoughts on the problem of Congress-League settlement. I have, in the past months, expressed views on this subject which appear contradictory. Writing on this problem in February of this year I said, "In every federal constitution of the world where the right of secession is granted, it has a double aspect: while, on the one hand, it provides the ultimate solution of intra-national conflicts, on the other hand, it rests on the ground that mutual goodwill and adjustment and desire to pull together would ever make unnecessary the exercise of this ultimate constitutional right. I believe the Congress would have no difficulty in guaranteeing this right to the federating units in India, provided there was genuine desire to start as a united nation and to preserve the national unity to the utmost extent possible. The Congress would do this precisely in the hope and belief that the experiment in united nationhood would soon remove suspicions and cement the bonds that naturally exist among all the sections of the Indian people. It can be appreciated how much different from this is the position that demands immediate and initial partition of the country. To that the Congress can never agree." Writing in the middle of July last, I said again, "The underlying principle of Rajaji's formula[42] is contained in the Delhi resolution[43] (of the Working Committee of the A.I.C.C.). That resolution explicitly admitted the right of territories in India to self-determination. That same general idea has been put in concrete shape by Rajaji and no Congressman can take objection to it."

There is an obvious contradiction between these two views. First, let me clear up the position of the Congress in this regard. I do not have before me the resolution of the Working Committee which conceded the right of self-determination to territories; therefore, it is not clear to me in what circumstances that right was conceived to be exercised. As far as I remember the resolution, it went no further than merely stating that the Committee could not oppose the right of any territorial unit to claim self-determination. This might mean, at least, two things: first, that this right was to be exercised after the free Indian state had come into being, second, that it was to be exercised before the establishment of free India. There is a great difference between the two. In the first case, we start as a united nation, with one common constitution, framed jointly: we make a serious attempt at living together, and only in the event of failure of the experiment of joint nationhood does a territorial unit exercise its right to separate. In the other case, the country is partitioned, probably under British aegis, two or more separate constitutions are framed separately and India starts as two or more national states. I find it difficult to believe that the Working Committee had in mind the latter meaning when it framed its resolution at Delhi.

If the Working Committee conceived the exercise of the right of self-determination in the manner described in the first case above, the contradiction between my views expressed in February and July is resolved.

So much for the position of the Congress. The question before me is, irrespective of the Congress view of the matter, what is my own view of it today? I have followed rather carefully the present controversy over Rajaji's formula. I am to some extent acquainted with Muslim communal opinion in the Punjab, through the columns of the *Inquilab*, *Ehsan* and *Shabbaz*. I have found no cause to change the opinion expressed in February last. And if the Working Committee meant to allow a territorial unit of the country to separate *before* the united Indian state had come into being and an experiment in living together had been made, I am opposed to that resolution. Further, if

[42] See Appendix 26 for C. Rajagopalachari's formula.

[43] Refers to the resolution on the Cripps Plan, containing the draft proposals of the British Government, adopted by the Congress Working Committee at its meeting at Delhi, 29 March-11 April 1942. For text of the resolution see Appendix 23.

Rajaji's formula implies the same procedure, I am opposed to it also. I am prepared to go no further than conceding the right to self-determination *after* the United States of India had come into being, and after a certain specified period had elapsed during which every part and section of the country and the people had a chance freely to fashion their lives in common with other parts and sections.

The question is: what happens if the Muslim League did not accept that position? I do not for a moment believe that the League would agree to such a proposition: but I also never believed that our entire future progress was dependent on an agreement with Mr. Jinnah. I have described Mr. Jinnah elsewhere as Mir Jafar of his day. I still stick to that description. He is a conscious traitor to his country, and it is foolish to expect him to agree to anything that would be good for the country.

Some people are obsessed with the League's popularity with the Muslim masses. I do not believe that nationalist Muslim opinion can never become a force in the country, or that the Congress itself can never win the affections of the Muslim masses or its intelligentsia. The eagerness of those who want to come to terms with Mr. Jinnah at any price is largely induced by their anxiety for the immediate establishment of a national government. I do not think there is any possibility now, short of a national revolution, of any such government being formed in war-time. As for a national revolution, it is not reasonable any more to place it within the range of war-time possibilities.

To my mind, our present task is to prepare for a post-war showdown with the British. All our present actions must suit that future task. I am not suggesting that Gandhiji should not meet Mr. Jinnah. That business has already gone too far now to cry a halt. It would have been better had no attempt been made in that direction, but now the only thing to do is to go with it to the bitter end. But in the negotiations Gandhiji should not go beyond agreeing to Muslim majority areas exercising their right of self-determination *after* freedom had been achieved, and the United Indian state had been formed. Mr. Jinnah would reject that, naturally. But the negotiations would have fulfilled their purpose if Gandhiji could succeed in getting down on paper the League's exact demands. Then the Congress and patriotic Muslim bodies could go to the Muslim masses both with Gandhiji's offers and Mr. Jinnah's demands. That clarification would, I believe, give a starting push to nationalist Muslim opinion.

Mr. Rajagopalachari talked the other day of bloodshed and civil war if Mr. Jinnah were not placated. On a different occasion he told Mr. Savarkar[44]

[44] Vinayak Damodar Savarkar (1883-1966); sentenced to transportation for life, 1910; for association with the revolutionary movement and imprisoned in the Andaman Islands, 1911-21; brought back to India and kept in Yeravada, Nasik and Ratnagiri Jails for three years; released, 1924; President, Hindu Mahasabha, 1937-42; arrested in connection with

that it was easy to talk of maintaining the unity of the country through civil war, but would the British allow it? One may ask Rajaji, following his own logic, would the British allow Mr. Jinnah to wage civil war? To that Rajaji might reply, "No, the British would not do that either, but then we must be prepared to have the British perpetually as our masters." That exactly is the trouble. Rajaji thinks, probably quite honestly, that unless we placate Mr. Jinnah, we can never hope to drive the British out of our midst. I do not agree with him. Looking back at the last fourteen years of our national history, it seems to me that the Congress never properly prepared for a mass struggle. All its civil disobedience movements, except perhaps the one started in 1930, were haphazardly begun and without much preparation. My short acquaintance with the actual functioning of the Congress in 'peace' times has led me to believe that the Congress has been losing touch with the masses. If we leave aside such bodies as the A.I.S.A.,[45] and the A.I.V.I.A.[46] which are non-Congress in constitution, or at least are non-combatant bodies, the Congress has no programme of work which puts it in daily and constant touch with the people. My experience is that Congress committees devote the greater part of their time and energy to elections—Congress elections and elections to local bodies and provincial legislatures. It is my firm conviction that if the Congress gave itself, say, five years to an intensive preparation for a struggle through constructive and educative work among the masses, and introduced vigour and energy into its organisation, it might be possible to launch a struggle that would sweep all opposition away and bring the British to their knees. I believe if this were done and, further, if an understanding were reached with such bodies as the Muslim Majlis and Jamiat-ul-ulema, we should succeed in rallying a large section of the Muslim masses and intelligentsia, to the banner of freedom and nationalism. I believe further that if this were done, Mr. Jinnah's leadership would be no more than a deflated balloon, and the march of events would leave him gasping by the roadside.

Indian nationalism has not become such a spent-up force that it must lose all hope and commit suicide. Mahatma Gandhi is evidently impatient. But, I do not think he agrees with Mr. Rajagopalachari that we cannot rid ourselves of British rule without an agreement with Mr. Jinnah. His sturdy faith in Indian nationalism is, I believe, still as sturdy as it was in August 1942. Therein lies hope—hope that Gandhiji would not, like a despairing man,

---

Gandhi Murder Case, 1948; acquitted, 1949; arrested under Preventive Detention Act and released, 1950; publications include: *The Indian War of Independence*, *Hindutva*, *Kala Pani*, *Moplah Rebellion*, and *The Story of My Transportation for Life*.

[45] All India Spinners Association: see *JPSW*, Vol. I, p. 145.

[46] All India Village Industries Association: founded by the Indian National Congress in 1934 for revival and encouragement of dead or dying village industries. J.C. Kumarappa was authorized to form the Association.

such as Rajaji who even sorrows over our failure to accept the Cripps' proposals, barter away Indian nationalism by giving Mr. Jinnah all that he may want. Gandhiji has still his last fight to fight with the British.

I should add that, if I too had despaired of Indian freedom without placating Mr. Jinnah, I would not have hesitated to give him all he wanted. Some people are fond of asking: "Will you have two Indias—both free, or one India, slave?" I do not think these are the alternatives. I do not believe that without division of the country, we cannot be free. In fact, knowing Mr. Jinnah and the League, in case we accept Pakistan, I fear, we shall have both division and slavery.

I shall conclude with a few words as to why I am opposed to the division of the country before we have made a serious attempt to live together in a united and free India. I think such division will solve none of our present problems and will create others, more serious than those existing today. The Muslim states are bound to be British protectorates, the Muslim communal leaders themselves asking for that status. This would mean the existence of the third party on Indian soil, which will be a source of great worry to the Indian nation. I have no prejudice against the Muslims. If the political unity of the country were maintained I would be prepared to go the farthest limit to assuage their fears of what is termed as Hindu domination. I love my country and do not care if its 400 millions are Muslims or Christains or Hindus. But I do care whether or not they are free and happy and prosperous. I believe firmly that before long they will be free and happy, and not long after, prosperous too.

24 August 1944
Political Planning

In the previous note I remarked upon the haphazard manner in which national struggles had been launched by the Congress in the past. For quite a while now a thought has been taking shape in my mind, of which the above observation is but a part. I have been in rather close touch with Congress activities since 1930. As I look back at the last fourteen years, the impression grows in my mind that the Congress never worked according to a plan. It had, of course, its constructive programme. But that was to keep the rank and file engaged and give the people something to bite at. But, in the matter of higher policy, the leadership merely drifted—or so it seemed to me. It lived from hand to mouth, as it were, and from day-to-day. As events came, it adjusted itself to them as best it could. But it never did such a thing, for instance, as to set a goal which it should reach, say, in three years, and then work towards it, keeping the initiative always in its hand and forcing events to follow in its wake. Such a basic political plan never seemed in the past to inspire Congress work.

This defect, I think, should be removed if in the future we are to be more successful than hitherto. When the war is over and ordinance rule comes to an end and the Congress is free to function 'normally', the leaders must draw up a basic political plan for the succeeding years. They should anticipate events—world events and the events at home—and in that light and in the light of resources and energies available, a master plan should be laid down which should determine Congress work in the years to come. This plan need not be placed before the people, or even the entire Congress, but it must nevertheless be present in definite shape in the minds of the leaders. Let us say, the goal is to prepare the country within five years for mass civil disobedience in order to enforce finally the national demand. The minimum requirements for that action should then be determined and the Congress organisation so set in motion as to fulfil these requirements in the given time. This does not mean that the Congress, having fixed upon this master plan, should refuse to be drawn into any negotiations whatever. But whatever other course we may have to follow to suit rising exigencies, the under-current of all our activity must flow unchecked and undiverted to that central goal. When this is not done, we get lost in the immediate diversions, and when these lead nowhere we feel frustrated and become paralysed for action. If Gandhiji sees the Viceroy, for instance, all hopes are centred on that, and when his talks bear no fruit, we are made impotent with impotent rage and despair. Then again, when Congress ministries are bundled into prison again, we find ourselves unprepared to move, indeed even ignorant of the very direction in which we should move.

If after the war we repeat this mistake, we shall deserve to wallow in our slavery for another quarter century.

24 August 1944
The Liberation of Paris

It is a great day today. Paris has been liberated. The mother of revolutions, the heart of European culture, rises from the dust again. Paris, resurrected is Europe resurrected. The world asks today, when will the Swastika, be banished from Paris, cease to wave over Europe? For me that is no more an important question. Today I ask Pairs if her resurrection means also the resurrection of liberty, fraternity and equality, or merely the resurrection of an empire and the system of profit and privilege. Will Paris, risen from the dust, allow Syria and Lebanon and Algiers, and the millions in the East to rise from the dust? Will the resurrection of Paris mean the resurrection of the people of France, or only of the two hundred families—old or new? Will France be ruled by her people or by the liberators and their Quislings? These questions I ask Paris today. On their answer depends the fate of Paris herself and France, and Europe and the world. Will the Red Cock crow again from the cradle of revolution? Who can tell? Paris can.

30 August 1944
Indian Economics

I have just finished the first volume of Jather[47] and Beri:[48] *Indian Economics*. A little earlier I had read Wadia[49] and Merchant:[50] *Our Economic Problem*. I also remember to have read Kale's[51] *Indian Economics*. There appears to be a long list of books bearing the same or similar titles. All these books, at any rate those that I have read or seen, follow the same stereotyped pattern with minor variations as to the arrangement of chapters or inclusion of the latest statistics. They all start with a description of the country's area, population and resources. Then they plunge into a fragmentary presentation of facts concerning population, agriculture, industry, banking, trade, etc. These are little more than historical surveys and digests of the reports of various Royal or other Commissions and Committees, official statistics and past controversies. The picture that the reader gets of Indian Economics after reading all this material is disjointed, patchy and unharmonised. He gets no understanding of Indian economy as a whole and its place in the modern world. What the reader wants is an organic, whole picture of Indian economic life, and he expects his economists to enable him to grasp its central facts and principles, without being led through a maze of material which merely dissects the disconnected limbs of that life. A detailed study of Indian industry and agriculture is of course important, but first we must understand Indian economy as a whole and in relation to the wider world.

[47] G.B. Jathar; educationist; served in the Indian Educational Service; Principal, Elphinston College, Bombay, 1940-3, and Karnatak Education Board's Arts College, Dharwar, 1946-7; author of *Indian Economies, Introduction to Economics*, and *Elementary Economics* (the last two in collaboration with S.G. Beri).

[48] S.G. Beri; economist; served in the Bombay Educational Service; Professor of Economics, Sydenham College of Commerce and Economics, Bombay, 1941-5; besides *Indian Economics* also co-author with G.B. Jathar of *Introduction to Economics* and *Elementary Economics*.

[49] P.A. Wadia; economist; Professor of Politics and Economics, Wilson College, Bombay, in the 1930s; author of *Our Economic Problems*, *The Bombay Plan—A Criticism* (in collaboration with K.T. Merchant).

[50] K.T. Merchant; economist; Professor of History and Economics, Elphinstone College, Bombay, in the 1930s and 1940s; author of *Our Economic Problems*, and *The Bombay Plan—A Criticism* (in collaboration with P.A. Wadia).

[51] Vaman Govind Kale; educationist; Professor of History and Economics, Fergusson College, Poona, 1916-21; member, Council of State, 1921; author of *Indian Economics, Gokhale and Economic Reforms, India's War Finance and After-War Problem, Currency Reform in India*, and *Indian Industrial and Economic Problems*.

Take, for instance, the question of the relation of Indian economy to British economy and British rule. At least during the last 150 years Indian economy has grown or languished or withered in the context of that relationship. Now, an average Indian reader, and I am not excluding the students who sit at various University examinations, would like to know exactly what that relationship is and has been, how it has affected and shaped our economic life, what influence it has today and how it is exercised, and what course it is likely to follow in the future. No volume of Indian economics that I know of deals with these questions in an integrated manner. True, we read references to various British interests resisting or imposing this or that economic policy, but the subject as a whole is nowhere thought worthy of adequate treatment. Yet, this relationship with Britain—economic and political—has been the very matrix within which Indian economy has been formed or deformed. I suspect that most of our economists themselves have not studied this problem from the standpoint of their country. The result of any such study is bound to be that Indian economy must be freed from the type of relationship that it has had with Britain so far. For most of our academic economists it must be rather difficult to state this conclusion in their writings. Some of them may even argue that academic study of problems, economic or otherwise, must be kept severely away from politics. Those who may advance such arguments should give up the teaching and writing of economics. They might study the waves of the sea or Indian bird life, but not Indian economic life. Those who do not appreciate the importance of the study of the very mould in which the economy of their country has been cast, do not begin to understand the A.B.C. of economics. Their talents are obviously better employed elsewhere.

1 September 1944
Indian Economics (Contd.)

Further, as I have said above, our economists should describe our economic life as a whole and not piecemeal. I know this is easier said than done. The temptation to follow the beaten track, to lump together disjoined chapters and call the medley Indian Economics is too great, because it is much the easier course to follow. I am hardly competent to say how *the* book on our country's economy should be written. A scholar who is not only a complete master of his subject but who also has a historical perspective and originality and synthetic ability, who does not approach the subject in the so-called detached academic manner but who has identified himself with his country and is deeply concerned with its future, who, while not a propagandist, is yet courageous enough to state the truth as he finds it, and, not the least, who looks at economic life not in isolation from other aspects of life, that is who has a wide social outlook, may succeed where others have failed.

A real organic work on Indian economics written under existing circumstances must also relate the present with the past. This is sometimes attempted in the existing text-books but again in the same disconnected manner. For instance, in a chapter on land revenue we might be told what kind of system existed during the 'Mogul' or the medieval period or how the ancient Indians smelted iron ore. This is extremely unsatisfactory. Indian history is too long to be summarised within a few pages; yet if we have to understand the present, we must know the outstanding facts about our past. A detailed study of economic life at various periods of our history is a subject that properly falls within Indian economic history. It is a study that may not be exhausted even in hundreds of volumes. Yet in an organic work on Indian economics, it seems to me necessary to describe, as briefly as possible, the economic organisation during certain representative periods of our history. No doubt, great care should be exercised in presenting the picture of the past. Not details, nor merely the highlights, but the main outline of the whole should be given, and while the picture should not be emotionally coloured, it should be dealt with sympathy and the understanding that comes from identifying oneself with one's subject. The next step should naturally be to describe the disintegration of Indian economy during the period of British conquest and British rule. Then one may show the lines on which regeneration of our economic life has been attempted and the trends and successes and failures that have marked this period. This would include a description of our present economic life in its national and international setting. Finally, one may end up with the prospect in view and the policies and measures necessary for a complete regeneration. Such a presentation of Indian Economics would be much more meaningful and purposeful to the average reader and the university student than the texts current, and might become a powerful instrument for the economic regeneration of the country. After this grounding, the reader, including the student, may follow up with a detailed study of any branch of Indian economy that he may be interested in.

I may add that it is true that every Indian economist will not present the same organic picture of Indian economy. But there is nothing in that to grieve at. It is natural and can only contribute to a better understanding of our problems and to more considered national judgements.

Most of the material for writing such a book on Indian economics is, I believe, available. Only the point of view, the organic composition, the capacity to get out of the beaten track are lacking. There are, several economists in India at present who, given the urge, are competent to fulfil this task. May one hope that some of them will put their hands to it?

1 October 1944
Today's 'Tribune'

A lump rose up to my throat and the eyes grew dim as I read Professor Einstein's[52] tribute to Mahatma Gandhi. What a beautiful tribute, how beautifully expressed from the world's greatest philosopher-scientist! "Generations to come, it may be, will scarce believe that such a one as this ever in flesh and blood walked upon this earth." The world's greatest prophets might envy, if envy can ever be in the nature of prophets, these words of homage.

On the same page an Englishman, who is too candid to use his proper name and writes as 'Candidus' makes scurrilous attack on Gandhiji. Reading it I was reminded of the Hindustani idiom about spitting at the moon.

There are two other items of news that are encouraging. In a statement Mr. [A.K. Fazlul] Huq says: "I do not agree with Mr. Rajagopalachari that the Mussalmans of India have lost a great chance simply because Mr. Jinnah and Mr. Gandhi will not come to some settlement. The failure of Mr. Jinnah should not be considered to be the failure of the Mussalmans of India." Mr. Huq is proposing to call a conference of Muslim political organisations to consider the situation. The other item is a statement by the President of the Jamiat-ul-Ulema, Maulana Saiyed Husain Ahmed Madani.[53] The Maulana describes Pakistan as impracticable and injurious to the Mussalmans.

The trouble with Mr. Huq and with the nationalist Muslims generally is that they are neither well-organised, nor persistent in their efforts, nor always consistent in their opinions. Mr. Huq particularly has been swinging from one extreme to the other. He speaks today like a real nationalist; yet it was he who moved the Pakistan resolution at the Muslim League session at Lahore in 1940, and it was he who for a number of years went about the country making the most offensive and the most reactionary communal speeches. Since he was ousted from the league by Mr. Jinnah he has swung to nationalism. But even during this period he has not done anything whatever, apart from making an occasional statement, to rally nationalist Muslim opinion or to educate the communal Muslims. The other nationalist Muslims of the Azad Muslim Conference[54] type have lacked faith, self-confidence

[52] Albert Einstein (1879-1955); eminent physicist; developed the theory of relativity; awarded Nobel Prize for Physics for work on photo-electric effect, 1921.

[53] Husain Ahmad Madani (1879-1957); Islamic theologian and scholar; teacher, Deoband Seminary; assumed leadership of Jamait-ul-Ulema-i-Hind, 1919; participated in the Khilafat, Civil Disobedience and Quit India Movements and imprisoned in 1922, 1930, 1932 and 1942; was opposed to the two-nation theory.

[54] Azad Muslim Conference, an organization of nationalist Muslims, which held its conference at Delhi from 27-30 April 1940 under the presidentship of Khan Bahadur Allah Bux, ex-Premier of Sind. The Conference condemned the scheme of Pakistan, calling it impracticable and financially untendable.

and persistence. Instead of launching a bold campaign to win over the Muslim masses, they too have lately been only shouting the slogan of Congress-League unity. The communist Muslims have largely been responsible for the lack of independent action on the part of the Azad Muslims and for converting the Azad Muslim Conference into a platform for demanding Congress-League unity. Whereas this conference should have boldly challenged the League, it ended up by lending indirect, but strong, support to it.

It is often said that to the Muslims religion is everything. I do not believe this. If this were so, the Muslims would be more influenced by the fatwas and opinions of their Ulema than of their politicians, nawabs, knights, khan bahadurs and such others. It does appear rather strange to me that though the Ulema of India, to their great credit, have been consistently nationalist, the League has succeeded in carrying the Muslim masses with it. Between Maulana Hussain Ahmed Madani and Mr. Jinnah, there is no question as to who is the greater representative of Islam, yet it is the latter who is the Quaid-e-Azam and not the Maulana.

I think the real situation is something like this. Politics in India is largely a middle class affair—the middle classes of all communities. For the Muslim middle class, as for all other middle classes, it is not religion that is important, but jobs, power, position. Naturally over this class the Ulema have little influence. The Muslim masses on the other hand are truly religious, but the Ulema cannot reach them. In the field of politics it is the middle class that has the organs of public opinion in its control. The Ulema are poor, the nawabzadas are rich; the Ulema are not learned in English, the knights are; the Ulema being anti-British cannot join the Viceroy's cabinet, the job-hunters can; the Ulema do not know political manoeuvring, the lawyer-politicians thrive on it. The result of all this is that while to the Muslim masses religion is everything or nearly everything—not forgetting their bread—it is not the Muslim divines who become their political leaders, but the vocal middle class for which religion—except in personal life—is largely a cloak.

2 October 1944

A Few More Books

Kamalashanker has sent me 'For Whom the Bell Tolls' by Ernest Hemmingway.[55] I don't think I have read anything of Hemmingway's before. In this book there are a few 'stills' from the movie of the same name. I may describe the book itself as a still from the Spanish Civil War. It describes the incidents of three days at a Republican guerilla centre in some mountains on

[55] Ernest Hemingway (1899-1961); American novelist and story-writer, works include: *The Sun Also Rises*, *A Farewell to Arms*, *For whom the Bell Tolls*, and *The Old Man and the Sea*; awarded Nobel Prize for Literature, 1954.

the fascist side. The main character is Jordan, an American Professor of Spanish, whose grandfather was a Republican officer in the American Civil War.

The interest of the book is more human than political. Jordan's soliloquies, though sometimes tiresome, reveal to us Jordan the man. Jordan is no revolutionary, and though he admires the discipline of the communists, he is no communist and no dialectician. He is an idealist, who loves liberty and hates fascism, an idealist who is calmly prepared to lay down his life for his cause. Jordan does make that sacrifice, and, in fact, till I reached the last pages of the book I was not inclined to attach much significance to it and Jordan's sexual transports with Maria did not seem to me to be such an extraordinary affair as to deserve so many pages of warm description. Jordan's leave-taking of Maria, his cool acceptance of death, his matter-of-fact fight to the last are such intense moments of living that they seem to empty death out of all its contents.

Pablo is nearly Jordan's rival for the hero's place in the work. Pablo is no hero, however. He is a guerilla leader turned gangster. That act of his of shooting to death his fellow guerillas at the blowing of the bridge can hardly be matched in its calculated and completely unscrupulous selfishness by any gangster, dead or alive. One hopes that Pablo was not a representative type of the Spanish guerillas. Hemmingway himself does not help us much on this point, though it is true that his other guerillas are not mean or unprincipled. Pilaw, the woman of Pablo, is a strong character and a great unlettered psychologist. Her success in enabling Maria to collect herself out of her disintegration was an achievement which the cleverest psycho-analyst might envy.

For the rest, through these human screens, Hemmingway allows us a dim glimpse into the tragedy of the Spanish debacle. The disorganisation of the Republicans; the fake propaganda-made leaders and the heresy-hunting of the communists and their machinations; the made-up Passionaria legend—all that is there in glimpses. But they do not form the central theme of the book.

Hemmingway has no thesis which he is anxious to peddle. I think he is concerned mainly with telling us what the Spanish Civil War was like. But to do this he does not write history, nor does he discuss politics. He merely takes a few people who played a part in it—not a publicized part, but an ordinary part—and shows what they did, how they did it and, above all, what they thought and felt. The result—a three days' still from a three years' passionate struggle—gives us an insight into that European tragedy which is in many ways deeper than what the carefully worded histories give us.

Hemmingway writes simply, without affectation. But though he has simplicity, he rarely, if ever, achieves beauty. In fact, for beauty of expression and thought there is nothing in the book to match John Donne's[56] words printed on a fly-leaf: words which suggest the Book's title: "No man is an *Iland*, intire of it selfe: every man is a peace of the *contient*, a part of the *maine*; if a clod be washed away by the *Sea, Europe* is the lesse; as well as if a *Promontorie* were, as well as if a *Mannor* of thy *friends* or of *thine owne* were; any mans *death* diminishes *me*, because I am involved in *Mankinde*. And therefore never send to know for whom the bell tolls: it tolls for *thee*."

The last book of which I wish to write today is Erich Fromm's[57] *The Fear of Freedom*. It is easily the most valuable book I have read here so far. I have not been able to understand the enthusiasm of some for psycho-analysis. A few biological urges and their suppression, inhibition or sublimation have been made the corner-stone not only of individual but also of social psychology. To me all this had more the appearance of magic than of science, and I always looked, if not upon Freud,[58] upon Freudians with grave suspicion. For me, Behaviourism gave a far more satisfactory account of human psychology than the subconscious, the libido and the rest of the magic terms.

It was, therefore, very refreshing to read Fromm who appears to be not only a psychologist and psycho-analyst of the first order, but a social thinker of the same merit. It is true that he finds Behariourism inadequate. But, in the first place, his criticism does not apply to such theoretical behaviourists as [A.P.] Weiss who never look upon the relationship between the individual and society as passive, or passive on the part of the individual and active only on the part of society; in the second place, I am in agreement with Fromm's criticism in so far as it applies to Behaviourists like Waston[59] who emphasise only the social or enviormental conditioning of the individual and ignore the dynamic adaptation that the human organism makes to the environment.

The central theory of Fromm's psychology is that human psychology is the result of a dynamic adaptation of the human organism to society. Human nature is neutral, but life has an urge to grow and expand and find fulfilment. It is this urge that is at the root of the dynamism that he emphasises. Fromm has great respect for Marx and is impatient of those who misrepresent or

[56] John Donne (1571-1631); renowned English metaphysical poet; works include: *Holy Sonnets* and *Devotions*.

[57] Erich Fromm (b. 1900); American psychoanalyst; works centring on problems of man in industrial society, include: *Escape from Freedom* (1941), *The Fear of Freedom* (1942) and *The Sane Society* (1955).

[58] Sigmund Freud (1856-1939); Austrian psychiatrist and pioneer of psychoanalysis; stressed importance of dreams in psychoanalysis; author of *The Interpretation of Dreams*, *Totem and Taboo*, and *The Ego and the Id*.

[59] John Broadus Watson (1878-1958); American psychologist; one of the founders of the Behavioural school of analysis, emphasizing the study of responses to stimuli; writings include *Animal Education*, *Behaviourism*, and *Ways of Behaviourism*.

misunderstand him. Marxists have often overlooked the dynamism of the human organism and have emphasised only the role of society and social forces in moulding human psychology. We should be thankful to Fromm for his corrective, by which he has brought us nearer to Marx, for Marx was always conscious of the creative or active principle in human nature. He could not be the revolutionary he was, unless he recognised that not only history made man but also that man made history—a phrase common to both Fromm and Marx.

Fromm in this book, however, is not concerned with expounding his central theory. He is rather concerned with applying it to the problem of freedom. He has done a most brilliant job of it. Starting from the feudal age in Europe he traces the evolution of this problem to the present day. He shows that in the typical feudal order man—every man—was tied up to society by certain definite bonds. Thus while his freedom was in many ways restricted, he did not feel alone in the world. When, however, those ties were broken up, man, while he became free *from* external bolds, also was left alone. The growth of monopoly capitalism has increased man's isolation and helplessness, which give rise to what Fromm calls the authoritarian character-structure. Using older psychological language, he calls this character-structure maso-sadistic. It is this psychological make-up of modern man in every industrialised society—and not only in the fascist countries—which makes *possible* (this is not to say inevitable) the rise of fascism. I shall not go into the details of Fromm's analysis, as I have decided either to appropriate Minoo's book or to buy a copy as soon as I go 'out'. I should, however, make a note of Fromm's conclusion. He says that the remedy of this malaise of the social mind is not reversion to the 'primary' bonds of feudal society which gave a sense of wholeness to man's life, but progression into a state of democratic socialism (his own phrase) in which impalpable agencies will not 'manipulate' man and in which man will not be buried in the mass and will live an affirmative, cooperative life. Fromm is conscious that socialisation of production means bureaucracy and manipulation of the individual and he points out that the solution of this problem is one of the major tasks of the present. A balanced system of centralisation and decentralisation must be evolved so as to reconcile large-scale social planning with freedom for the individual.

22 October 1944
Prof. Brij Narain & Mr. Jinnah

I have great respect for Prof. Brij Narain,[60] both as an economist and as a man with a keen sense of public service. As a writer he is refreshingly free

[60] Brij Narain (1889-1947); eminent economist; Professor of Economics, Sanatan Dharma College, Lahore, 1917-47; murdered by a frenzied mob during communal riots in Lahore, 1947; author of many books on economics.

form academic 'detachment'. I like him for that. He is frankly partisan, as everyone who has anything vital to say must needs be. But partisanship is not malice, and sometimes the learned professor says thing which betokens malice. Today's *Tribune* publishes the first instalment of a series by him on the 'Bombay Plan'. I have no quarrel with the main argument of this article. Indeed, as a socialist I enthusiastically support it. Our own approach to the communal problem has been identical with that of the learned professor.

But there is in this article an attitude towards Gandhiji that appears to me to be instilled with malice. Opposition to Gandhiji I can understand, as I have myself often been opposed to him and as, am afraid, I may again. But malice is bad. Prof. Brij Narain quotes the following sentence from one of Mr. Jinnah's letters to Gandhiji: "It is for you to consider whether it is not your policy and programme in which you persisted which has been the principal factor of ruin of whole of India." The professor adds: "If a single individual is responsible for ruining the political life of the whole country, it is Mahatma Gandhi." This is an astounding statement for anyone to make. That an eminent Indian economist should make it, makes it a hundred-fold astounding. What, if not malice, can prompt one to say such things?

Prof. Brij Narain's charges against Gandhiji are that by reviving the ancient Indian cult of *ahimsa*—to which the Professor thinks the country owes her loss of independence—Gandhiji rendered great disservice to the cause of Indian freedom; and incidentally, by thus basing his politics on an exclusively Hindu ideal, he kept the Muslims away from the national movement. The second charge is that Gandhiji has turned the attention of the country to ante-diluvian economics—the economics of village self-sufficiency.

Before I take up these charges, I should like to point out that the professor must be anxious for some reason to throw bouquets at Mr. Jinnah. He has quoted Mr. Jinnah with great appreciation and has gone on to amplify his meaning. But the quotation was quite unnecessary, for Mr. Jinnah did not mean what the professor had to say. Let me remind the professor that whatever Mr. Jinnah and the nawabs and knights of the Muslim League might say on the issue of non-violence as a theory, if these windbags ever took courage to fight the British for Pakistan or anything else, they would take up not the sword nor the rifle but the method of non-violence and would follow meekly in the footsteps of the much-maligned Mahatma. As for the constructive programme, there too if ever the League undertook any kind of day-to-day work among the Muslim masses, that work will not be the manufacture of bombs or tractors but some sort of imitation of that much-laughed-at constructive programme. The League has always imitated the Congress and here too it will do the same.

As for the professor's charges they are not new. I do not agree with them as they have been stated, much less with the spirit behind them. I am no believer in non-violence. But I do not think that by teaching the unarmed Indian people the method of civil resistance, Gandhiji has done a disservice to the country. On the contrary, I consider this to have been his greatest service to the nation. Those of us who consider it feasible to use violence in our struggle for independence could never have hoped otherwise to drive such large masses of people in open opposition to the foreign power. I believe everyone who accepts the method of violence understands that in the existing conditions a movement and organisation based on this method can only be secret and for a long time restricted to a chosen few. The mass awakening and the mass resistance that Gandhiji has brought about are therefore of the highest value for the fight for freedom.

Furthermore, it is futile for those who believe in violence to blame Gandhiji. If we have failed,, it is not because of Gandhiji, but because of our own shortcomings and the weakness of our movement and organisation.

As for the argument that non-violence kept the Muslims away from the Congress, it is neither historically true nor logically so. Large masses of Muslims have always been with the Congress and are with the Congress. The recent growth of the League has nothing to do with this non-violence which men like Maulana Azad, Khan Abdul Ghaffar Khan and Maulana Husain Ahmed Madani do not consider foreign or repugnant to Islam. To explain the recent estrangement of a section of vocal Muslim opinion from the Congress on the basis of non-violence is not only to oversimplify a complicated problem but also to distort it.

As for the economics of Gandhism, I am surprised that the learned professor should still be repeating the same old controversial cliches and be unaware of the recent developments in Gandhiji's economic thinking. I do not say that Mahatmaji's economic views are now entirely acceptable to me, but I think that the day has definitely been left behind when one merely cracked a few jokes at the spinning wheel and village self-sufficiency and called it a critique of Gandhism. A re-examination, as that made by Dantawala, for instance, should be seriously considered by all thinking men. But in doing this preconceived notions will have to be kept under control.

In this same article the learned professor quotes another passage from Mr. Jinnah's letters to Gandhiji: "We are a nation of a hundred millions, and, what is more, with our distinctive culture and civilization, language and literature, art and architecture, names and nomenclature, sense of value and proportion, legal laws and moral codes, customs and calendar, history and traditions, aptitude and ambitions—in short, we have our distinctive outlook on life and of life. By all canons of International Law we are a nation."

"The words ring true. They cannot be dismissed as nonsense," says the professor and here again he is throwing quite undeserved bouquets at Mr. Jinnah. The words not only do not ring true, they are utter nonsense. First, if we grant that in respect of all those things that Mr. Jinnah has enumerated the hundred million Muslims of India—the Pathan, the Bori, the

Khoja, the Moplah, the Jat, the Rajput, the Bengalee—are one and distinct from other communities in India and, therefore, a nation we will have to grant that all the Muslims of the world, the Arabs, the Turks, the Afghans, the Iranians, the Chinese, the Javanese, too, constitute one nation. But that would obviously be absurd. By virtue of common religion, Muslims do share certain values of life, but that common factor does not make them all one nation. All that Mr. Jinnah says in that eloquent passage is that Muslims, because they follow one religion, constitute a nation, a proposition which the history of Islamic nations so completely refutes. The Christians, Catholics and Protestants, share many common values and standards or life, but that does not make them all one nation.

Furthermore, is Mr. Jinnah's statement true in fact? Do the Bengalee, the Moplah, the Pathan and the Khoja have common language, race, literature, art, names and nomenclature, architecture, customs, history, calendar, aptitude, ambition and tradition? Anyone who knows the Muslims of Malabar, Bengal, Bombay and the Frontier cannot but say 'No' to this question. Again is the Bengalee Muslim radically different from the Bengalee Hindu—to take only one example—in such matters as language, literature, dress, manners and customs, history, race, tradition, ambition, names and nomenclature, architecture, calendar, aptitude and so on? No one who knows the people of Bengal will say that that Muslims and Hindus are different from each other in these respects, or that they differ much.

I have said above that I have no quarrel with Professor Brij Narain's main argument that if we emphasise common economic interests, stress the problem of a planned economic development of the country, we shall succeed better in fighting the two-nation theory and communal separatism. He concludes today's article with these words: "There will be little talk of partition if planning were better understood in our country."

I do not wish to damp the professor's enthusiasm. I was myself at one time under the influence of that facile assumption. But experience has taught me, and I hope others, that mass psychology is not so easily susceptible to economic motives and appeals as one assumes, particularly when other powerful factors of an emotional nature held it in their grip. The professor thinks that the communal problem is one of correct understanding. This is a naive view. The professor does not seem to be fully aware of the sinister motivations of Pakistan. Mr. Jinnah and his knights understand fully the problem and purpose of planning, and they are determined to do their best to foil and obstruct it. I invite the professor to read with care the speech that Dr. Sir Ziauddin[61] will soon deliver in the Central Assembly in opposition to

[61] Ziauddin Ahmed (1878-1947); educationist; member, Sadler Commission, 1917; appointed the first Pro-Vice-Chancellor of Aligarh Muslim University, 1920; its Vice-Chancellor, 1935-47; elected to the Indian Legislative Assembly, 1930; publications include: *Systems of Education*, *Systems of Examination*, and *Indian Railways*.

the 'Bombay Plan'. The League gentlemen know that economic planning in India means a united central state for the whole country. Therefore, in their eyes planning is a scheme of Hindu domination which they must fight tooth and nail. That a planned development of the country as a whole would mean far greater prosperity and happiness for the Muslims of 'Pakistan' than what Pakistan separated from the rest of the country can ever hope to create is an argument that has no value for the League even though it claims to represent the Muslims.

There is no magic solution of the communal problem. Neither the economic nor the political approach is sufficient in itself. Both approaches, as well as social and cultural approaches, are necessary and even then the task will be a heavy, uphill task. I wish Professor Brij Narain every success in his endeavour to tackle the problem from his own specialised point of view.

25 October 1944

A Visitor Comes To My Cosmos

It was a great day for Europe when Paris was liberated. But Europe is far away and beyond my world. A sealed-off, walled-off, barred and bolted, fifteen-by-twelve bit of space—that is my world set in a cosmos of similar planets. A cosmos that is not of God's but man's creation; a cosmos presided over by disconsolate kites, shrieking and watching, watching and shrieking: a cosmos where nothing ever happens; that is, nothing happens that the eyes can see except perhaps Churchill's love affairs with his assortment of females—three black ones and one black and white, from whom he is reputed to have descended. Churchill is the local tom-cat. No, it was not spite that inspired me to call him thus. It was his face that only lacks a cigar to equate it with that other famous face that is the hope of Europe—of that Europe that is utterly dead but is frantically trying to live.

Yes, nothing happens in my cosmos that meets the eye. Yet, there are things that do happen here—things that neither I nor the sun's eye can see. but while walls can shut off sight, ears can see through them. So, sometimes as the sun goes down and darkness falls over men's deeds, I hear both the howls of the captive and the thudding of the ogre's blows—the ogre who rules over this cosmos. No, the ogre is not an individual. He is like Brahman—all-pervasive. He is a spirit—the spirit of a system, a system that makes brutes of men.

When I hear those howls, a great many things happen to me. I find myself turning into a brute—a raging, tearing, brutal vengeance wells up within my being. I fight hard to keep my humanity. It is difficult, very difficult, and I am not sure I quite succeed.

Such is my microcosm. Europe, and its hopes and fears, are far away from me. The liberation of Paris was a great day—but for Europe. For me, as long as this ogre lives and rules—can there be happiness? And yet a great thing happened today—that nearly made me forget this evil Brahman of my cosmos. I was sitting at my table reading *Thorofare* and pretending to be a human being and a citizen of the world, when I heard the cell lock being opened. I thought it was some routine affair, still I rose and went up to the door, and whom did I see but Rammanohar,* his eyes twinkling as ever through his glasses? Was it a dream or magic? Yet, there he was, solid enough to be real—though thinned somewhat. It was a great moment for me—greater than the liberation of Paris or Europe. The walls of my cosmos were shattered for the moment, and I was no longer a captive in the grip of the ogre, but a human being, transported to the human world.

So, things—real things that happen in the real world—do happen in my cosmos too—even though they take thirteen months in happening. I wonder how long this illusion of reality will last!

7 November 1944

Planned Economy & Democracy

Minnoo's pamphlet, 'Cooperative in a Planned Economy,' is rather disappointing—not on account of what he says but for what he leaves unsaid. That planning involves centralisation and bureaucracy, and curtailment, if not total suppression, of democracy is granted on all sides today. The problem is to reconcile planning with democracy. It is clear that in the course of this reconciliation, both planning and democracy as we know them today will have to undergo important modifications. But we have to be careful that those modifications do not alter the essential character of either of these social institutions. That seems to be a difficult task, and till now no adequate solution is in view.

Minoo considers industrial cooperatives, forming a possible basis of planning from the bottom upwards, as a solution. This does not seem to be an adequate solution of the difficulty. Planning from the bottom cannot replace planning from the top. Both would be necessary and the relation between the two may not be an easy matter for coordination.

Furthermore, it is futile to consider any kind of economic planning without considering the necessary and suitable political forms with which it must be associated. No one seems to be giving thought to this problem in this country,

* Rammanohar Lohia was taken to the Lahore Fort in May or June 1944. He was tortured there for months and after they had finished with him and given him up as hopeless they brought him suddenly to my cell one day as my new companion. Thereafter he was brought to my cell practically daily for an hour every day, till we were both transferred to the Agra prison. [Note by J.P.]

though economic plans are galore. The problem of political power and of political institutions is far more serious than one of drawing up economic plans for this or that period of time. The actual planning is a matter for experts, but the social direction and significance of it are a matter of politics.

Minoo would do well to work out this problem. He naturally dislikes the totalitarian political system, based on a single ruling party. We all dislike that system. But what do we propose to put in its place? That system is well suited to planning from the top, whether productive property is owned by the State or by private corporations. In our country we do not want private corporations owning large-scale productive property. We want all such property to be the property of the State or of other public and social bodies such as municipalities and village panchayats. Alongside, we want co-operatives of small producers and of cultivators. What can be the political system that can smoothly pull such a train of economic institutions? It is true political forms cannot exist without their corresponding economic forms. We have visualised the economic forms. What political forms correspond to them? Will there be more than one party? Surely, that seems to be obvious enough. But will the parties be based on individual membership or on the cooperatives, workers' unions and village panchayats? If on both, what will be their relationship? In the executives and legislatures will the corporate bodies be directly represented, or indirectly through the political parties that might exist? What will be the form of the executive and legislature from the bottom upwards? How will power be distributed between them? These and a host of other questions will have to be put and answered before this dilemma of planning and totalitarianism is solved. In our country the ignorance and backwardness of the masses will ever be an incentive to totalitarian tendencies. This will further complicate our task. I hope Minoo will not stop with the slogan of 'planning from the bottom'.

8 November 1944
Marshal Stalin

Marshal Stalin's speech to the Supreme Soviet on the occasion of the twenty-seventh anniversary of the Russian Revolution will be read by socialists throughout the world with consternation and sorrow. That speech could have been delivered almost in the same words by Churchill or Roosevelt. I am acquainted to some extent with Stalin's devices to cast Russian life and thought in the mould of nationalism. But I was not prepared to find him present a view of internationalism that is such a complete negation of all Marxian fundamentals. Perhaps this was due to my lingering faith in Stalin's socialism, for it should have been clear to me that a Russian nationalist could not but look at the world from the standpoint of Russian nationalism.

Stalin was telling the Supreme Soviet how war could be avoided in the future, because it was not enough to have just won this war. He said, replying to his own question, that there were two kinds of nations in the world: peace-loving and war-loving. In the first category came Britain, America and the U.S.S.R., in the other Germany and Japan. Such being the international layout, the remedy was simple: first, the aggressors, that is, the war-makers, must be disarmed—militarily, economically and politically; second, the peace lovers must set-up an organisation for safeguarding peace, and at the disposal of the controlling body of this organisation must be placed a minimum armed force sufficient to nip aggression in the bud, wherever it made its appearance.

Any one who understands the nature of war—and the causes of aggression—will laugh at such a conception of war and peace and of international relations. A socialist will shed tears over it—at least he will want to. Stalin, the head of a professedly socialist state, talks like the imperialist and capitalist rulers of the world. All that Marx and Lenin taught about the nature and causes of war and the means of peace has been forgotten and the oppressed of the world betrayed.

I wonder how the Stalinists will embroider and embellish these apostatic words of the successor of Lenin.

2 January 1945
Petition to the Lahore High Court,

[Note by J.P.: This is the third petition I had made to the High Court on 2-1-45. It was heard on 31st January 1945 and I was transferred from the Lahore Fort to Agra Central Jail the next day. The petition, of course, was rejected on the ground that, as the Central Government had informed the court through the Assistant Solicitor-General, who was present at the hearing, that the Government had decided to transfer me to an ordinary jail outside the Punjab, and, as the charge of maltreatment and torture related to incidents that took place more than a year before, the court saw no reason to entertain the petition. The presiding Judge went further and remarked that the purpose of the petition had been served inasmuch as I was to be transferred soon to an ordinary prison. The purpose, however, had not been served at all. My main purpose in petitioning to the High Court was to bring out the dark and sordid facts relating to maltreatment of detenus in the C.I.D. Fort, Lahore, and to make it possible for a court of law to examine those facts and pronounce a judicial verdict. The Lahore High Court, however, proved to be too much under the thumb of the Provincial Executive, for it refused to take notice of the serious complaints made by me and Dr. Rammanohar Lohia, whose *habeas corpus* petition too was rejected the same day by the same court. The Provincial Government on its part had promulgated a special ordinance prohibiting any news of the hearing from being published in the press. In the

court itself nobody except High Court advocates and barristers were allowed. For the rest the petition will speak for itself.]

To
The Hon'ble the Chief Justice*,[62]
High Court of Judicature,
Lahore.

Your Lordship,
At the risk of causing annoyance to Your Lordship, I beg again to make the following submissions with regard to my habeas corpus petition which was disposed of by Mr. Justice Munir[63] on 4.12.44. Before I proceed to make my submissions I should like to express my thanks both to Your Lordship and Mr. Justice Munir for the rehearing of my petition which had been rejected once before.

(1) It is my misfortune that even at the second hearing, though I was represented by my counsel, my case failed to be presented correctly due to the fact that I had refused to instruct my counsel within the hearing of the police. It appears that I was under a misunderstanding and so was Mr. Kapoor,[64] my counsel. I understood from him that even if the Court refused to permit me to instruct him without the police listening in, I would

* This is the third petition J.P. had made to the Lahore High Court on 2 January 1945 (the texts of his two earlier petitions could not be found anywhere). J.P.'s purpose in filling these petitions was to draw the court's attention to the brutalities to which political prisoners like him were subjected in the Lahore Fort so that those who were taken to that place after him could be saved from them. However, the concerned judge failed to take note of it and rejected the petition on the ground that the Central Government had informed the court that J.P. was soon to be transferred to an ordinary prison outside the Punjab (he was actually transferred to the Agra Central Jail the next day). The judge went on to remark that J.P.'s purpose had been served by the Government's decision. Although he was happy to be transferred to an ordinary prison, the remark of the judge pained him, for as mentioned earlier, his purpose had not been to seek transfer or any other kind of redress for himself.

[62] Arthur Trevor Harries (1892-1959); Judge, High Court, Allahabad, 1934-8; Chief Justice, High Court, Patna, 1938-43, Lahore, 1943-6 and Calcutta, 1946.

[63] Muhammad Munir (1895-); Judge, Punjab High Court, 1942-8, and its Chief Judge, 1948-54; Chairman, Pakistan Pay Commission, 1948; and Court of Inquiry constituted to inquire into the Punjab disturbances of 1953, its report published in 1954 came to be known as Munir Report; author of *Principles and Digest of the Law of Evidence*, *Constitution of the Islamic Republic of Pakistan*, *Islam in History*, and *From Jinnah to Zia*.

[64] Jeevan Lal Kapoor (1897-1982); advocate, Lahore High Court, 1922-47; President, District Congress Committee, Lahore, 1930-1; imprisoned for participating in the Civil Disobedience Movement, 1930, Judge, Punjab High Court, 1949-57, Supreme Court of India, 1957-62; Chairman, Law Commission of India, 1961-8, and member, Delimitation Commission, 1963-6, and Minorities Commission, 1965-6, India.

get a chance again to interview him and instruct him if I then wanted to do so under the conditions prescribed. I had thought then that I would take advantage of that opportunity as a second choice and make the best I could of it. It is not clear from the Court's order why a second chance was not given me, even though Mr. Kapoor seems to have asked for it. Perhaps the language of the affidavit, which was rather categorical, was responsible. I wonder if the layman's language does not say things more clearly than legal forms of expression. However, I regret very much that I was unable in the end to instruct my legal adviser, with the result that my case could not be presented in the manner I wanted and to my better advantage. But I should like to make it clear that I am not making a grievance of it.

Here I should like, with Your Lordship's permission, to explain why I refused to proceed with my interview with Mr. Kapoor. Firstly, I was under the impression that a prisoner had a right under the law to see his legal adviser alone, or, at least, without any officers of the state being within hearing distance. I wanted to exercise that right. There were two other considerations. The learned Judge writing on this point observes, "Whatever information the petitioner had to give to Mr. Kapoor could only have been intended to be publicly communicated to this Court and could well have been given within the hearing of the police. I do not see any real reason in the petitioner's not letting the police hear what they were bound to hear a few days later." I submit that this is a very partial view of the matter. Let me describe the situation at the interview: there were two police officers present and there was a police short hand writer sitting beside me. It was clear that whatever I or my counsel said, or the parts of it that interested the police, would be taken down verbatim. The whole affair looked more like a prisoner making a statement before the police than consulting his legal adviser. Now, when a defendant or complainant meets his lawyer, he does not merely lay before him facts that would be stated in the open court later, but also discusses all the points of his case. There are weak as well as strong points, there are pros and cons of every point, there is the manner of presentation of the case. All this requires a free and frank discussion between him and his lawyer. I too wanted to discuss frankly my points in all their aspects and seek and give advice. But this was impossible with the police officers listening in and the stenographer taking notes. Such a thing would be impossible anywhere in this country, but specially so in this province, where the state of civil liberties is so low and where the 'all-powerful Punjab C.I.D.' is such a terror even to the law-abiding citizen.

There is a third point in this connection which I wish to urge. My counsel after receiving instructions from me was to argue my case before the Court and the Crown Counsel; the Advocate-General was presumably to attack it. Now, if all the details of my instructions to Mr. Kapoor, including the notes of our discussion, were to reach the hands of the Crown Counsel before

Mr. Kapoor had a chance to appear in the Court, would it have been considered giving me and my counsel a fair deal? I do not think there was anything to prevent the police from supplying a copy of the notes taken at my interview to the acting Advocate-General. I regret very much that these aspects of the question were not considered by the learned Judge.

(2) The second part of my submissions relates to certain facts incorrectly stated in the judgement on my petition. I do not know who supplied these facts to the Court. If it was my counsels, they are obviously not to blame because they could not have known them correctly. If, however, it was the Crown, I do not see why it should have been thought necessary to mislead the Court. Perhaps it is not vital to my case to correct these facts; yet it seems proper to me that the Court should be correctly informed.

I have never denied that I escaped from the Hazaribagh Central Prison in Bihar, but this was in the company not of one other prisoner but of five others. Further, this was not in 1943 but in November 1942. I was arrested at the Amritsar railway station as I was travelling by the Frontier Mail from Delhi to Rawalpindi, and the date was the morning of September 18, 1943. It is stated in the judgement that I was arrested at Lahore on August 19, 1943, presumably under Rule 29 of the D.I.R., and on September 22 my detention was converted into one under Rule 26 of the D.I.R. The facts concerning my arrest are wrong; I do not know if the facts relating to my detention are true, because no orders were served on me at that time. Further, I am not a member of the Congress Working Committee, nor was I when I escaped from the Hazaribagh Prison. In fact, except for a brief period in 1936, I have never been a member of that Committee. I am particularly anxious to correct this information, as I do not wish the Working Committee or the A.I.C.C. to be in any manner associated with my recent activities and views.

In this same section, I should like to narrate the succession of Government orders as they were served on me. The first such order was that of the Chief Secretary[65] to the Punjab Government asking the I.G. (or D.I.G.) Police to retain me in the Lahore Fort as a prisoner under the Bengal Regulations of 1818. This was about the middle of November, 1943, i.e., as it now appears to me, only a few days after Mrs. Purnima Banerji[66] moved her application.

[65] Frederick Chalmers Bourne (1891-1977); entered I.C.S., 1920; Secretary, Electricity and Industries Department, Punjab Government, 1934-7; Deputy Commissioner, Lahore, 1937-40; Secretary to Home Department, the Punjab Government, 1940-1; Chief Secretary to the Punjab Government, 1941-5; Governor of Central Provinces and Berar, 1946-7; Governor of East Bengal, 1947-50.

[66] Purnima Banerjee (1911-51); freedom fighter from U.P.; sister of Aruna Asaf Ali; participated in the individual satyagraha, 1941 and Quit India Movement, 1942; elected to the U.P. Legislative Assembly and Constituent Assembly, 1946.

I know nothing of the previous orders under Rules 129 and 26 of the D.I.R. The second order to be served on me was again an order of Mr. Bourne, directing this time that I be detained there as a Security prisoner. This was the order of July 1st, 1944, mentioned in the judgement. As for the order of Mr. Sahay,[67] Jt. Secretary, Home Department, Government of India, I have no knowledge. Some time later, an order of the Central Government of August 24, 1944, signed by Mr. Tottenham,[68] was served on me directing that I be detained here in pursuance of an order already said to be in force under clause (b) of sub-section (1) of Section 3 of the Ordinance III of 1944 and sub-section (4) of Section 3 of the same. The last order to be served on me was a few weeks ago and was dated November 30 and made by Mr. Tottenham directing that order No. III/4/43 M.S. of 27.6.44 shall continue in force.

Thus far for the orders. Here I should like to bring to Your Lordship's notice a curious fact about the first order to be served on me. As I have stated already, this order, placing me in the category of a State prisoner, was served on me about the middle of November, 1943. I do not exactly remember the date, but I am certain that it could not be later than the early part of the third week of November. I was made at that time to sign the order paper in question and I believe I also put down the date. Months later, when it was finally decided by the Punjab Government (or may be the Central Government) to make available to me all the privileges to which a State prisoner is entitled in this Province, Mr. Robinson,[69] Superintendent of Police, visited me on February 1, 1944, in order to communicate to me the Government's decision. I was informed, among other things, that I should get a monthly allowance of Rs. 50 and that the arrears of this allowance beginning from the date I was made a State prisoner, would also be paid to me, plus an initial payment of Rs. 50. He said that the sum in arrear, together with the initial amount, came to Rs. 125, which would be credited to my account. At the moment I did not stop to examine the figure he mentioned. Later, when I did my own calculation, the sum in arrears appeared to be Rs. 175 (initial payment Rs. 50, plus Rs. 25 for half of November, plus Rs. 50 for December and Rs. 50 for January). When I raised the matter with

[67] Bhagwan Sahay (1905-); Joint Secretary, Government of India 1944-5; Commissioner, Food & Civil Supplies, 1946-9; Chief Secretary, U.P., 1949-51; Chief Commissioner Himachal Pradesh, 1951-2; Chief Commissioner Bhopal, 1952-4; Ambassador to Nepal, 1954, etc.

[68] Sir George Richard Frederick Tottenham (1890-1977); Secretary, Government of India, Defence Department, 1932-7; Additional Secretary and Secretary, Home Department, 1940-6; retired, 1948.

[69] W.D. Robinson; joined police service, 1927; appointed Central Intelligence Officer, Punjab and Delhi, 1939; Assistant Director Intelligence Bureau, 1941; Superintendant, 1942; and Senior Superintendant, Delhi, 1944.

the local officer-in-charge, he told me that the official figure had been computed as from the middle of December (i.e., initial payment Rs. 50, plus Rs. 25 for half of December plus Rs. 50 for January). When I pointed out to him that I was made a State prisoner about the middle of November, he naturally admitted the incorrectness of the official figure, but appealed to me, on grounds that he did not make clear, not to pursue the matter. I was not at all concerned about the fifty rupees, and there being no reason to attach any significance to the matter, I, of course, dropped it.

Looking back, however, it is clear to me that somebody had a definite motive in letting it appear that I was made a State prisoner not soon after Mrs. Banerji's application in the Lahore High Court, but much later, or possibly there was a different motive. But without the assumption of a motive of some sort, it does not appear that it could have been worth Mr. Robinson's while to be made deliberately to deprive me of a paltry sum of Rs. 50.

Here I should further like to draw Your Lordship's attention to the rather strange fact that, whereas the dates of all the orders served or not served on me, including the alleged order of September 22, 1943, have been disclosed to the court and mentioned in the judgement, the date on which the order under the Bengal Regulations was made was apparently not stated, for it finds no mention anywhere in the present judgement.

I cannot say if this curious fact has any importance in relation to the subject-matter of my petition. I have stated it for what it may be worth. I should like again to say that I am not in the least concerned about the fifty rupees involved and wish to lay no claim to them.

I am unable to judge if this narration of facts in nay manner affects the findings of Mr. Justice Munir. That is for Your Lordship or the learned Judge himself to determine and for my counsel to argue, if any new point for argument does arise.

(3) Coming to the main part of my petition, namely, the legality or otherwise of my detention, I must say I have not the least competence to discuss the matter. Yet I should like briefly to state my case. Before I do so I should like to express my satisfaction that the Court rejected the Crown's contention that no order made under Ordinance III of 1944 came within the jurisdiction of the courts.

My counsels, in the absence of any instructions from me, have tried to present the case as best they could on the basis, I presume, of the information contained in my previous petitions. They attacked the order of my detention on two grounds, namely, that the authority making the order was not competent to do so; secondly, that the order was made for a *malafide* purpose. The first ground was rejected on the presumption that authority must have been delegated to the Joint Secretary to the Government of India to make such orders. The presumption may be right, probably it is, but there is no positive proof for it. The second ground was rejected on the basis that there was no reason to presume that interrogation was the sole purpose of my detention, and further, that in any case there has been no interrogation after December 10, 1943.

My own case briefly put is as follows. I freely admit that, according to the law forcibly imposed over this country, my activities, both before and after my escape from prison, would be found to be aimed at disturbing the public order and interfering with the effective prosecution of the war. That I consider these activities to have been in the best interest of my country. It is a political view with which the law and the courts, as they exist here, have no concern. And I do not raise this question here, except to draw attention to it in passing.

In view of this, when I was arrested and detained, I never doubted that it was, as the phrase runs, with the purpose of preventing me from acting so as to disturb the public order and prejudice war efforts. It never was, nor is, my intention to seek release, or interference of the courts with my detention, on the plea that the charges against me were or are false. Yet I have caused Your Lordship and the Lahore High Court some inconvenience by making two petitions already, to which I am adding by writing a third.

My reasons even today, at least partly, are the same as were briefly indicated in my first petition. At the time Mrs. Purnima Banerji had moved her application I had no knowledge of it, nor did I know that I had myself a legal right to move an application under section 491 to prevent the illegal and intolerable treatment to which I was then being subjected. I had, however, on numerous occasions in the course of the so-called interrogation, expressed a wish to write to government about the matter, which I was not allowed to do. Indeed, looking back it seems to me that even if I had wanted to make a habeas corpus petition, I would have been disallowed, as I was disallowed to complain to Government. I believe it is only after the Pardiwala[70] case that it has become possible for the prisoners in distress in this province to seek the protection of the law by means of a habeas corpus application.

It was months after Mrs. Banerji's application had been disposed of that I came to know vaguely about it, though its full purpose I have learnt only

[70] Homi Rustomji Pardiwala (1906-2001); Bar-at-law, M.L.A. Bombay; member, Indian Students' Association in Great Britain and London Branch of Indian National Congress; practised at Bombay High Court; took keen interest in the Labour movement and organized a number of trade unions in Bombay; arrested in August 1942; released in early 1943 and organized the Bombay Legal Defence Committee for political prisoners; arrested again in November 1943 in Lahore where he had gone to file an application for the release of Jayaprakash Narayan; released shortly after as a result of general revulsion at his arrest while working as a lawyer.

from the present judgement of Mr. Justice Munir. But I had learnt this much that her petition was dismissed because when the Bengal Regulations were applied to me, section 491 ceased to have jurisdiction. So when early in July I was converted again into a Security prisoner, I naturally suspected that the order under the Bengal Regulations was a hurried device to cloak some kind of illegality about my detention during those days. And the purpose of my petition made in the spirit of assisting the law was that the matter be investigated. In fact, in my second petition I had gone so far as to state that it was quite likely that current orders regarding my detention had been regularised. Yet I had pointed out that it was necessary to find out if there was any irregularity at an earlier period. The irregularity I had in mind was of the type dealt with in the first point of my counsel, namely, that the order of my detention was not made by the proper authority or in accordance to the rules prescribed in the ordinance. This question still remains undecided, because the attack of my counsel was concentrated upon the order of June 27, 1944 of the Central Government.

Mr. Justice Munir in his judgement writes: "When the petition came up for hearing on 17th December 1943, it was contended by the learned Advocate-General that since the petitioner was being detained under the Bengal State Prisoners Regulation, the Court by reason of sub-section (3) of section 491 of the Code of Criminal Procedure had no jurisdiction to entertain the application and that on that ground the application should be dismissed. This contention succeeded and Mrs. Purnima Banerji's application under section 491, Criminal Procedure Code, was dismissed on 23rd December, 1943. These words themselves show that the Bengal Regulations were pressed into service only to defeat the application of Mrs. Banerji. This was either because there was an illegality involved in my detention, or, as now appears more probable to me, knowing the purpose of that application, because I was not being treated according to law, which fact the Government was afraid of being brought to light. In either case, the order under the Bengal Regulations was in the nature of a ruse meant to hide an illegal act, and I for one am anxious to explore every available aid of the law to right that wrong. That the wrong was committed more than a year ago, cannot by itself right it, nor, on that account, can the law refuse to take notice of it.

Coming now to the *malafide* point, while I agree with the judgement of the court that extortion of information was not the sole purpose of my detention, I do hold that the purpose of detaining me in the Fort was certainly to extort information, and as such malafide. The learned judge has remarked upon the length of time that intervened between my arrest and the beginning of my interrogation. Firstly, the period of time was not so long as it has been supposed, because I was arrested on September 18 and not on August 19. Thus it was just over a month after my arrest that the interrogation started, and this period was necessary to collect all the relevant records as more than one provincial government, apart from the Centre, was concerned. In fact, when the interrogation opened, there were officers of the Bengal and Bihar C.I.D.'s present in addition to those of the Punjab C.I.D. Secondly, the reason that the interrogation stopped on December 10 was not that the *malafide* intention of the Government had undergone a sea-change, but, in the first place, it was my own attitude, that is to say, my refusal to give the information desired; in the second place, it was the panic created in the Executive by the fact that Mrs. Banerji's petition had been admitted by the High Court which threatened to bring to light damaging facts. The reason again why the interrogation was not resumed later was, firstly, that the police did not expect to get anything out of me, and, secondly, the fact that I had in the meanwhile complained against the interrogation to the Home Secretary to the Punjab Government and to the non-official visitor, Nawab Muzaffar Ali Khan—both of whom saw me soon after I was made a State prisoner—and had also made a written complaint to the Punjab Government. Therefore, I maintain that one of the intentions, clearly a *malafide* intention of detaining me in the Fort was extortion of information regarding my activities and the national struggle that had begun on August 9, 1942. And this brings me to the fourth submission that I have to make.

(4) I have shown that my detention in this Fort was *malafide*, inasmuch as the purpose was to extort certain information. I wish now to submit that, apart from this aspect of the matter, my detention here has been with a view, indirectly and vindictively, to inflict additional punishment on me, not in the least incidental to mere detention. The conditions of imprisonment in this Fort are such that, aside from willful ill-treatment, of which I have had no cause to complain for the past some months, and, as compared with conditions in the jails, they constitute by themselves a severe form of punishment. This fact was brought to the notice of the Government by me some months ago, yet they refused to transfer me to a jail, presumably on the ground that no jail in the country was safe for me. This was a ridiculous plea, and I have naturally been driven to the conclusion that, whatever be Government's future intentions, their insistence on keeping me locked up in this Fort was prompted by the motive I have spoken of above. I am aware that it has been held that Government have power to determine the place and conditions of a security prisoner's detention. Without denying this fact I maintain that this power is not open to unlimited interpretation. That there must be recognised standards to limit this power, and that the limitations must be such as to require a Security prisoner, who is not under any punishment under the law, but is merely 'detained' by executive order so as to be prevented from certain activities, to be kept under reasonable conditions of comfort and well-being. To remain locked up alone for fifteen months day and night, except for an hour morning and evening for exercise, and to be deprived of all company for the greater part of this period are forms of hardship and punishment that

are not incidental to detention, nor known anywhere in the jails and detention camps, except as forms of punishment for prison offences and they cannot fall within the recognised standards of which I have just spoken.

(5) I come now to the last part of my submissions. I have stated above and in my previous petitions that between October 20 and December 19, 1943, I was subjected to harassment and torture. I shall first state the facts briefly. In this connection, I can do no better than quote from the letter I had written to the Punjab Government, through the Home Secretary in February last:—

I was arrested on the 18th September of the last year at Amritsar and brought the same day to this Fort. After about a month of my detention here I was taken to the office where officers of the Punjab, Bihar, and Bengal C.I.D.s were present. I was informed that I would have to answer certain questions that would be put to me and make a statement regarding my recent activities. I made it clear to the officers present that I was prepared to answer any questions that did not relate to my recent 'underground' activities, and, as for a statement, I had no more to say then that I was an enemy of the British Empire in India (not of Britain or the British Commonwealth), that I was working for my country's independence and that I would continue to do so till either the object was achieved or death intervened. The interrogating officers on their part made me understand that I was not to be let off till they had obtained from me the information they wanted.

In this manner my so-called interrogation began. Thereafter I was taken to the office every day and made to sit there for varying periods of time. For the first few days the hours were not too long. Even so I pointed out to the interrogators that forcing me to sit in the office for hours together and repeatedly asking me questions that I had declined to answer was a form of harassment to which they had no right to subject one. I was told that I was in the hands of the Punjab C.I.D. and the question of rights did hardly arise. Gradually the hours of 'interrogation',—in plain language, harassment—were lengthened: from 8 a.m. to 5 p.m. to 10 p.m. to mid-night. Often varied threats would be given to me in varied manners—some politely and mildly, some harshly and annoyingly. At this stage I made vigorous protests and asked repeatedly but fruitlessly to be allowed either to talk to the Superintendent-in-charge or to write to Government. It struck me as a remarkable system in which a prisoner could not even complain or petition to the Government which held him in custody; and I wish to bring this point to the notice of your Government with some emphasis, for in this system lie the germs of much mischief and injustice. To my mind, the right to petition should never be denied to a prisoner. I should mention here that about this time I made it clear to the interrogating officers, not in boasting but in all earnestness, that I was determined to risk my life if necessary, but would not submit to their pressure. No one knows my powers of resistance, but that was my sincere resolution and I did my best to persuade the officers to believe me.

The final stage in my harassment, which turned them into a form of torture, was to allow me no sleep during day or night. From morning till 12 p.m. I would be continuously kept in the office, then be taken to the cell for an hour, brought to the office again for an hour or two, taken back for an hour again and so on till the morning. The interrupted parcels of hours that I got in my cell could hardly bring me sleep, for just as I would be dozing off the time would be up and I would be brought out again. On paper this process perhaps does not appear to be so torture-some, but I can assure you in all honesty that when continued for days it is a most oppressive and nerve-racking experience. I cannot describe it as anything but torture.

In the second week of December this torture suddenly stopped, as did the 'interrogation'. A few days later I was informed by you that my interrogation was over.

These were the facts, my Lord, and they have never been contested or denied by Government. I shall proceed now to quote further from the same letter, because what I said then is relevant to my present purpose. I said:—

My grievance is that I have been tortured and treated in this fashion without any justification or warrant whatever. There is, or can be, no moral or legal sanction for it. Even the all-sweeping ordinances do not permit such practices not vest the police with such powers. A prisoner is a most helpless creature, and whatever his crime, civilization safeguards against his ill-treatment. For his crime he may be hanged if the law required it, as a prisoner he may be punished according to prison rules, but he cannot be harassed and tortured for refusing to give information to the police. That a political prisoner should be so treated is still the more reprehensible. Here I should like to draw the attention of the Government to another aspect of the matter. I have no desire to appear vain or boastful, but in order to make my point I must say that, if the C.I.D. went so far with me, it can be imagined how much further it can go with persons, who perhaps worthier than myself, are yet not in the public eye or do not hold any position in public life. That such people should be completely at the mercy of the C.I.D. without even the right to petition to Government is a state of affairs that should not be permitted to continue.

Suppression of political opponents is of the essence of Nazism and Fascism and torture of political prisoners their most characteristic feature. I am conscious of the argument that those who believe in violence as a political method as I do must be prepared to be forcibly suppressed. I grant that, but there are lawful means even for such suppression. A political revolutionary may be executed for his offences when found guilty by the established law, but he may not be put to any torture for the extortion of information. War is the deadliest, most brutal and violent form of political conflict. Yet a prisoner of war has certain rights and immunities which civilized society scrupulously respects. The same person who would be most mercilessly bayonetted to death in the field of battle would be immune from ill-treatment in the war prisoners' camp and would receive such amenities as the standards of the countries concerned and his own status would warrant.

This is what I wrote then, and I have repeated these words for Your Lordship's consideration.

There remains another aspect of this matter. During the interrogation it was suggested to me that the police had to do their work and that in such work there was no room for human values and civilized conduct. The plea was unworthy of any civilized government or its police. But, even granting that human values and decent conduct did not have a place in police work, at least such work must be in accordance to law. My point is that the treatment meted out to me which I have described above was not lawful.

Before concluding this section I wish to suggest to Your Lordship that the D.I.R. and the ordinances have converted this Fort into a paradise for the police. A prisoner who is brought here is completely insulated from the world outside: he does not have to be produced before any magistrate or other court; the police can keep him here as long as they like and do with him what they will. I have personal knowledge of three cases—

those of Mr. Indra Prakash Anand,[71] Mr. Jayachand Vidyalankar[72] and Dr. Rammanohar Lohia—in which similar, or even severer, treatment was meted out. I am sure there must be hundreds of others cases. I wonder if Your Lordship as the highest guardian of justice in this province cannot offer protection in some manner to these unfortunate victims of the police, or rather of the Government.

I shall now sum up the submissions I have made. I submit

(i) that certain facts stated in the judgement are incorrect and that certain other facts that I have stated may affect the finding of the learned Judge;
(ii) that when I was hurriedly made a State prisoner, there was either some illegality about my detention which the Government were unwilling to have examined by the High Court, or it was sought to prevent the fact of my illegal treatment from being brought to light;
(iii) that my detention in the Fort was and is *malafide*;
(iv) that I was subjected to unlawful treatment, that is to say, to harassment and torture, between October 20 and December 10, 1943.

My prayer is that under section 491, Criminal Procedure Code, or any other suitable section of the law, I be permitted through my counsel to present these points in Court so that decisions may be made regarding them. With regard to my last submission, I have two further prayers, namely, that Your Lordship may initiate such proceedings as may be necessary to bring to book those guilty of unlawful conduct; secondly, that I may be permitted to sue the Crown for the illegal treatment I received at the hands of its servants.

In order that I may seek the advice of, and instruct, my counsel, Mr. Jiwanlal Kapoor, Advocate, with regard to these points, I pray that I be allowed to interview him under such conditions as Your Lordship may deem suitable. I pray further that a copy of this petition may be made available to him so that he may take such steps in regard to it as he may find advisable.

[71] Indra Prakash Anand (1912-); freedom fighter and prominent industrialist based in New Delhi; a close associate of J.P.; arrested on 30 September 1943 and imprisoned in Lahore Fort along with J.P.; released in November 1945; joined Thapar Group in 1946 and rose to the position of Executive Director; Chairman, Holding Trustees, Gandhi Smarak Nidhi, New Delhi since 2001.

[72] Jayachand Vidyalankar (1898-1977); a revolutionary from Punjab; associated with the Anushilan Party; historian; taught at National College, Lahore; Bhagat Singh and Sukhdev were his students; later taught history at Kashi Vidyapith and Bihar Vidyapith; arrested in April 1943 and detained at Lahore Fort, later shifted to Campbellpore Jail; released, April 1946; publications include: *Hamari Aaj Ki Ladai Aur Hamara Kartavya*, *Bharat Bhoomi Aur Uske Nivasi*, *The Language and Script Problem in the Panjab*, and *Bharatiya Krantimargi Rashtriya Vichardhara 1920 Ke Baad*.

Begging to be excused for taking so much of Your Lordship's time,

I remain,
Your Lordship's
Most truly,
Jayaprakash Narayan

II

LETTERS TO M.R. MASANI

8 February 1944

Dear Minoo

Accept my belated congratulations [on being elected as Mayor of Bombay]. I would not have been so tardy had it been possible earlier to write. I hope inspite of the obvious handicaps you are finding your work interesting. I have no doubt it will also be fruitful and add to Bombay's betterment. You have my utmost good wishes.

You will naturally be anxious to know all about me, but I am afraid I cannot tell you much. I have to be content to say that* as you may know I am classed now as a State Prisoner under the Bengal State Prisoners' Regulations of 1818. I get a daily diet allowance of Rs. 3 and a monthly allowance of Rs. 50 for sundries. I may write three letters a week and receive newspapers and books with the usual censorship safeguards.*

I am afraid I am going to give you a lot of trouble with regard to books. Prabha and most other friends being in jail, you will have to shoulder most of the burden of supplying me with intellectual fare. I wish to concentrate for the time being on Indian economics and the constitutional future of India. Both subjects are in your line and for the present I leave it to you to make a selection of a few books and send them as soon as you can. Later on, I shall make more specific demands.

I used to be a member of the Royal Asiatic Society's Library, Bombay Branch. Will you find out from them if they received the books that I had left at Hazaribagh and if they would take the risk of renewing my membership? If they received back the Hazaribagh books, my transit box would be with them. If they decline to renew my membership, please claim the box on the strength of this letter and keep it with you. If otherwise, send me their membership form and leave the box with them.

I am deliberately not writing to Yusuf, for I do not wish to trouble him when he is so ill. But please give him my love and tell him that though I am

* Blacked out by the censor.

a Godless person, I nevertheless offer devout prayers for his early and complete recovery. I shall write to him as soon as you advise me that I may do so.

With love,

Yours,
Sd/-Jayaprakash
c/o D.I.G., Police, C.I.D., Punjab
Lahore

Mr. M.R. Masani,
Mayor, Bomaby Municipal Corporation,
Bombay.

Lahore
16 March 1944

Dear Minoo,

I had nearly despaired of hearing from you or any others to whom I had written; so you can imagine my happiness when your letter came on the 4th of this month. It was the first letter that I received in reply to the several I had written. My happiness was still the greater when I read of the books that you had sent—all of which I received in due course. Till these books came, Shakespeare,[73] along with the Ramayan and the Gita, was my only reading, and while I agree with Longfellow[74] about 'the great poet who foreruns the ages, anticipating all that shall be said', our present world has got tied up in so many complicated knots that, though in essentials there is really nothing to add to the poet, yet the details, which in a world of superficial values have become almost more important than the essentials, have gone a little beyond his ken. So your books were a feast to me and I fell to them with a shameless voracity. 'The Imp' I found absolutely delightful and parts of it I read twice. Andre Maurois'[75] writing retains its charm and delicacy in spite of the translation. The theme may be a little outdated, as when compared with the horrible reality of the present expressed by Koestler;[76] yet I cannot help wishing that there were more Madame la Guichandies in this understanding or perhaps hypocritical world. Koestler was perhaps better in 'Darkness at Noon' and he seems to be taking Freud much too seriously. An ounce of

[73] William Shakespeare (1564-1616); famous English poet and dramatist; writings include: *Richard III*, *Henry V*, *Julius Caesar*, *Antony and Cleopatra*, *As You Like it*, *All Is Well That Ends Well*, *Hamlet*, *Othello*, *King Lear*, *Macbeth* and *The Tempest*.

[74] Henry Wadsworth Longfellow (1807-82); American poet; well known for lyric and narrative poems; works include: *Evangeline*, *Song of Hiawatha*, and *The Courtship of Miles Standish*.

[75] Andre Maurois, originally Emile Hertzog (1885-1967); French writer; wrote *Les Silences du Colonel Bramble* and several other books.

[76] Arthur Koestler (1905-83); Hungarian born novelist and essayist; settled in Britain in 1940; his works include *Darkness at Noon*, *Spanish Testament* and *The God that Failed*.

truth that Freud possesses has been exaggerated by a certain type of intellectuals and artists into a ton of science....*

I am well and, since the books arrived, usefully employed. As for you, yes, work always agreed with you. May you ever be overworked! When you write, don't fail to say how yourself is getting on. Give my love to friends whom you may meet.

As a matter of caution, I should like to add that nothing that I write to you or other friends should get into the press or be made public in any manner. I should not fancy being denied the privilege of writing to you or others.

I had forgotten all about Shridharani.[77] His book is good stuff for America, and he writes well, sometimes brilliantly. But why place him along with Conard[78] or even Lin Yu Tang?[79] Whoever has done it must be either over-anxious to encourage him or singularly lacking in feeling for style—Conard, one of the finest masters of English prose!

With love,

Yours truly,
Sd/-Jayaprakash

Mr. M.R. Masani,
Mayor, Bombay Municipal Corporation,
Bombay

* Blacked out by censor.

[77] Krishnalal Shridharani (1911-60); writer and journalist; arrested for participation in Dandi March, 1931; member, A.I.C.C., 1933; resided in the United States, 1934-47; author of a number of books including *My India, My America.*

[78] Joseph Conrad (1857-1924); English novelist; works include: *Lord Juri, Typhoon,* and *Victory.*

[79] Lin Yutang (1895-) Chinese author and philologist; Editor, *Academia Sinica*, 1929-33; inventor of Chinese indexing system; author of *My Country and My People, The Importance of Living, Moment in Peking, With Love and Irony,* and *A Leaf in the Storm.*

21 April 1944

Dear Minoo,
It is an eventful day for me here when books arrive. Such a day was when I received the fifteen books, pamphlets and magazines that you have been so kind to send me. These will keep me busy for some time, though it seems you have inclined towards the lighter side a little too far this time; but I have no doubt I shall enjoy them immensely—the thrillers as much as *The Agaria.* Of course, the first thing I did was to read through your pamphlet [Socialism Reconsidered]. I do not know if you will feel happy or begin to doubt your sanity, if I tell you that I nearly agreed with you hundred per cent! Well, the world does change, doesn't it?

Here are the titles I have received: (1) *The Agaria*, (2) *Socialism Reconsidered*, (3) *Planning of Science*, (4) *Four Day's Wonder*, (5) *Our Admirable Betty*, (6) *The Documents in the Case*, (7) *Greek Tragedy*,

(8) *Scenes of Clerical Life*, (9) *The Problem of Population*, (10) *Tariffs and Industry*, (11) *Private Worlds*, (12) *Confessions and Impressions*, (13) *Marcus Aurelius*, (14) *The Indian Council of World Affairs*, (15) *Film India*. Isn't that all you sent?

When will you write or have you written already?

What news of Yusuf?

That was a ghastly accident in the docks, wasn't it?

I am fairly well,

Yours with love,
Sd/ J.P.

c/o The Home Secretary
Govt. of the Punjab
Lahore
6 May 1944

Dear Minoo,

In all these months there has been only one letter from you; and I believe I must have written thrice already. It is very unlike you to neglect your correspondence and I rather wonder what may be the cause. In any case, do you mind dropping me a few words as soon as you get this? By registered parcel I am returning the following twelve books: (i) *Scenes of Clerical Life*; (ii) *The Agaria*; (iii) *A Time for Silence*; (iv) *There We shall hear singing again*; (v) *Private Worlds*; (vi) *Our Admirable Betty*; (vii) *Confessions and Impressions*; (viii) *Four Days' Wonder*; (ix) *Chronicles of the Imp*; (x) *War and Indian Economy*; (xi) *Marcus Aurelius*; (xii) *Planning of Science*.

Please let me know when you have received them. You will perhaps want me to say something about these books. I shall do so briefly in the space available. George Eliot[80] I rather found heavy reading, with tiresome asides to the gentle and discreet reader and as tiresome descriptions of men and materials. Her style too I found dull something like a slow, turgid river, deep perhaps, but looking at us with a serene, uninteresting face. In style I prefer something like the sparkling, bubbling, jumping stream, catching the rainbow in its spray, and laughing—everlastingly laughing. Ethel Mannin[81] has movement and the trembling stream's joy of living, but her spume catches no rainbow. With her views I agree largely, though not sharing her enthusiasms

[80] George Eliot (1819-80); famous English novelist; works include: *The Mill on the Floss*, *Silas Marner* and *Middlemarch*.

[81] Ethel Mannin (1900-); English journalist and novelist; author of *Marth*, *Sounding Brass*, *Crescendo*, *Ragged Banners*, *Men are Unwise*, *The Pure Flame*, *Rose and Sylvie*, and *Julie*.

equally. Bertrand Russell[82] was my god too in my undergraduate days at Wisconsin, and I have always considered him, if not the best, the most emancipated mind of the century. But recently I had to move him down a peg or two and was deeply sorry to have to do so. By the way, did not Mannin marry Reginald recently? Other comments must wait till the next week. How is Yusuf now? I am fairly well and hope that you are none the worse for the sweltering heat of your Urbs Prima. With regards,

Yours,
Sd/- J.P.

[82] For biographical note on Bertrand Russell see *JPSW*, Vol. II, p. 97.

c/o The Home Secretary
Govt. of the Punjab
Lahore
11 May 1944

Dear Minoo,
This is just to complete my brief comments on the books I have returned to you. Elwin[83] has done a careful piece of ethnological work. I cannot say more than that about it. If *The Agaria* is not as interesting as one expected it to be, it is Agaria's fault and not Elwin's—they seem to be a most uninteresting people. Again, if I find the book lacking in certain respects, it is only because it is intended to be a supplement to *The Baiga*. At any rate, those aspects of Agarian life that Elwin has dealt with, he has done with great competence and equal sympathy and understanding—the ethnologists' most essential qualifications. *Our Admirable Betty* and *Four Day's Wonder* were most amusing. Sergeant Zehedee won my heart outright and in the *Four Days' Wonder*, Hippo's younger brother, the artist, I liked best. *Marcus Aurelius* was poor poetry and rather faded philosophy—the palest reflection of the Gita, I thought. I do not imagine Phyllis Bottome[84] intends it but the impression that her *Private Worlds* gives is that psychoanalysts are as helpless

[83] Verrier Elwin (1902-64); anthropologist and author; Chaplain of Merton College, Oxford, 1927; lived in Bombay Presidency as member of Christ Seva Sangha, 1927-32; among aboriginal tribes of Central India, 1932-46 and 1949-53; Deputy Director, Department of Anthropology, Government of India, 1944; Advisor for Tribal Affairs, North-East Frontier Agency, 1954; member, Scheduled Tribes Commission, 1960-1; publications include: *Leaves from the Jungle*, *Myths of Middle India*, *The Art of the North-East Frontier of India*, and *The Tribal Art of Middle India*.

[84] Phyllis Bottome (1884-1963); English writer of novels and short stories; books include: *Level Crossing*, *Danger Signal*, *Mortal Storm*, and *London Pride*.

in understanding and ordering their emotional and inner life as laymen, perhaps more so. In any case, whereas normal individuals discover their loves for themselves, it seems brilliant psychiatrists must be brought together by other equally brilliant psychiatrists. The scientists of Britain in their planning of science seemed to be hopelessly burdened with the past and too timid to venture upon the mysteries of the social order, without ordering which no planning whatever is possible. Well, I can go on endlessly talking about the books and their character, but must stop now and give you my greetings. I am anxiously awaiting your letter.

Yours truly,
Sd/- J.P.

c/o The Home Secretary
Govt. of the Punjab
Lahore
2 June 1944

Dear Minoo,
It was a great pleasure to have your letter after long last. I had begun to imagine all kinds of things. But the flu—from which I hope you have fully recovered—and the accident explain everything, and now I hope to hear from you oftener. I have written to you rather frequently in recent weeks, and some time back I also returned twelve books out of the two lots you had sent me. In some of the letters I had made brief comments on things that I had read—including your two pamphlets—and I should like to know whether you were allowed to read them.

Regarding the literature you send, the supply is adequate to the demand, but only quantitatively. As I wrote you in my first letter, I wished to devote my time especially to Indian economics and Indian constitutional problems. On these subjects you have sent me very little material. You ask me if I want any particular books. In my letter of 16th March, to which you have replied, I had given a list of 8 or 9 books which I wanted. I shall be obliged if you send me some of them.

It was good to know that Yusuf has been able to leave the Nursing Home. I wrote to him last week.

I share your feelings entirely about 'the general jubilation', as you have termed it.

I hope you are keeping well. My health is O.K. The sciatica, though ever present, is not active. I *have* gained in weight, as you have been informed, and may gain a little more, for I am not trying to stop it yet.

With love,
Yours,
Sd/- J.P.

c/o The Home Secretary
Govt. of the Punjab
Lahore
24 June 1944

Dear Minoo,

I was very happy to get your letter of June 4 and to know that you have now received all my previous letters, including the comments, and the parcel of books that I returned. I was also glad to know that you liked my comments and so did some others. I have not yet received the new lot of books you have sent, but there is no doubt, I shall do so in course of time. By the way, I find from your list that you have again failed to include the kind of books I want most. Will you remember it next time?

Kamalashankar has also been good enough to send me books from time to time. I have been particularly interested in two of his books: *Underground Europe Calling* and *All Our Tomorrows*. The latter is an impassioned work of a genuine English patriot, with a patriotism of the grand, unselfish, Shakespearean type. One hopes fervently that Douglas Reed's appeal to the common man of Great Britain to shake off his spiritual nihilism and reclaim that democracy which he has allowed to slip out of his fingers succeeds. If such a miracle happened, what a day will dawn over Europe and the many continents of the world! But is this an age of miracles, Minoo? I am well. Don't get ill again. It is a bad habit.

Yours, with love,
Sd./ J.P.

P.S. You may write as often as you please and so may other friends. There is no fear of the limit of letters I may receive every week being exceeded.

c/o The Home Secretary
Govt. of the Punjab
Lahore
5 August 1944

Dear Minoo,

Your letter of July 12. I hope you found Dindugal pleasant. But why Dindugal of all places? I never knew it was a health resort. Anyhow, I hope you are fully restored to your normal health.

As I have been made a security prisoner again, my books are rationed now—10 a month. I have therefore been able to read only five of the lot you sent with your letter of 4th June. I shall return that lot as soon as I have read the remaining books. The last lot of ten books which you sent with your letter of July 12 must have been received at the office, but naturally it will be some time before I get them.

You ask if I am writing something. Well, I did intend to do a little serious writing, but it just does not seem possible. Nobody's fault, I believe, but without adequate material I do not see how can I get a start and keep going. So I write occasionally either to amuse myself or to organise my thoughts when I feel agitated. All of it is of no use except for myself.

As for getting chubby-faced, well, I would have hated that, but under the present dispensation, no danger of it remains.

Well, cheerio,
Yours,
Sd/- J.P.

Minoo, Prabha wants you to send her a few English books that she can read. She was reading sometime ago your *Our India*.

c/o The Home Secretary
Govt. of the Punjab
Lahore
12 August 1944

Dear Minoo,

I wrote you last week. I am writing again to say a few words about the books you sent. I have also to thank Mrs. Naidu, Shanti Kumarji for the good wishes they sent through you. Do give them all my very best regards and tell them that it made me very happy to be remembered by them. I hope Zub's wife has completely recovered now and their baby is grown into a charming little lady. Does she speak only American or also Urdu?

Among the books (I have got only nine of them yet) I liked *Jail Journey* best as a piece of writing. I doubt if anything as raw and alive and vital has appeared in the English language in recent years. . . .*

. . . *Plato's Mistake* I found delightful, and, in a different way, also *Prelude for War*. 'These animals are the property of Mr. Kane Lukes'—that was delicious, I thought. I won't mind having the *Saint Omnibus* around me. More in the next.

With greetings to you all,

Yours,
Sd/- J.P.

* Blacked out by the censor.

c/o The Home Secretary
Govt. of the Punjab
Lahore
17 August 1944

Dear Minoo,

This is the third one in three weeks. I hope you are not bored. I am returning nine of the books you sent me on June 4, namely: 1. *Jail Journey*, 2. *Make This the Last War*, 3. *The International Development of China*, 4. *Prelude For War*, 5. *Plato's Mistake*, 6. *Tomorrow*, 7. *Talking to India*, 8. *A week With Gandhi*, 9. *Uncle Sam's Empire. Tomorrow* is not a very exciting picture of international 'culture'. I was not much impressed with the reproductions from foreign writers, the intention of some of whom seems to be not to express themselves, but to disguise their meaning by cunning tricks with words. I think anybody who had really something to say would say it simply, and may be beautifully, if he also understands beauty and had learnt to express it. I find neither beauty nor meaning in some of the pieces collected. But that is my fault. Raja Rao's 'Javni' is a good story and should read very well in Kannada. But in English—well, I don't know if the language does not fail utterly to do justice to what he wants to say. I cannot say how Conrad did it, nor how some in our own country do it, but it seems to me that a foreign tongue is a poor medium for creative writing. Our creative writers would do greater justice to themselves and enrich greatly the literature of their country, if they could give up the temptation of writing in English. In a foreign tongue, we can but copy ideas, style, life; we can never create, innovate, experiment. Tagore is a second-rate English poet, but in Bengali he is a Colossus—unapproached and unapproachable. . . . 'Uncle Sam's Empire' has been misnamed—so it seems to me. The booklet is rather a bird's-eye review of the Old World discovering and despoiling the New than an elucidation of the title it bears. . . . You are going to have rather exciting days in Bombay in a short while. Let us hope the prayers of millions are at last heard and granted.

With love,

Yours,
Sd/-J.P.

c/o The Home Secretary
Govt. of the Punjab
Lahore
2 September 1944

Dear Minoo,

Do you know your last letter was dated July 12 and this is September 2? You can't say you have been to busy or that the rains have stopped you from writing! There was another friend who volunteered to write every fortnight, but he seems to follow not earthly but cosmic time. . . . Well, I have really nothing new to say except that I thought I should complete my comments on your books. I should like particularly to compliment Dantawala on his very thoughtful contribution to current social thought. But why was he in such a hurry? Most books, including the best, are written around a single central theme. Dantawala has half a dozen themes which are all central but far from simple. He should develop his themes, and should not assume that the reading of his readers is as wide as his. I think he would render a great service to his country if he gave six months to rewriting his pamphlet, which in many parts is no more than synoptic, into a book, say, ten times larger. . . . The gentlemen who thought they were 'talking to India' were talking largely to themselves or to the shadowy shapes of their own minds or to Ahmed Ali, Mulk Raj Anand . . . etc. etc., which is the same as talking to themselves. There is little in these 'literary talks' that would interest India, much less inspire her. It never seems to have occurred to these talkers, some of whom expect a great deal from this country, to give her something more solid than words. Words at best are sounds, but these words are hollow sounds, vapid, toneless, false. . . . By the way, I have not heard anything yet of the books you sent with your letter of 12th July. You may write to the D.I.G. and find out. Of the previous eleven books, I have already returned nine; Dantawala's book I have kept with me; and the eleventh, your friend Fielden's[85] *Begger My Neighbor*, was probably considered objectionable because I did not get it. You may write about that too and find out.

With the best thoughts to you,

Sd/- J.P.

[85] Lionel Fielden (1896-1974); Controller of Broadcasting in India, 1935-40; Director of Public Relations, Allied Control Commission, Italy, 1944-5; works include *Beggar My Neighbour*.

c/o The Home Secretary
Govt. of the Punjab
Lahore
29 September 1944

Dear Minoo,

Your letter of August 9 reached me on September 9! I was greatly distressed that there should be such delay. I replied a few days later, but, as I understand now, the letter was not allowed to pass. So I am writing again. I understand you wrote me another letter on September 4, but that too has not been passed. Try again.

No, I was not too ill to write. In fact, I wrote you several letters last month. I can only hope they have reached you now.

I have been given five of the ten books that you sent in the last lot. The rest I'll get after I finish these. I shall return the books after I have read them, though I may keep one or two. Erich Fromm's *The Fear of Freedom* is easily the most valuable book I have read here.

I hope all is well with you. I am so so.

Cheerio,
Yours,
Sd/- J.P.

c/o The Home Secretary
Govt. of the Punjab
Lahore
21 October 1944

Dear Minoo,

Your letter of Sept. 19. Yes, you have 'put the record right', as you say, even though I have not received all your letters.

Yes, I did fall for Phyllis Bottome's *Heart of A Child*. It is like some cool Himalayan stream that cleanses you right through.

Will you please send me a list of the five books you sent with your letter of Sept. 6? I shall be able to keep track of them better then.

It was very kind of you to think of my needs. But, in the first place, even security prisoners here do get a monthly allowance of Rs. 20. Secondly, I have at present enough private cash for my requirements. I may pinch an occasional book or two of yours, but more than that there is nothing that I want just now. However, I thank you very cordially for your enquiry.

With the best thoughts for you,

Yours,
Sd/- J.P.

c/o The Home Secretary
Govt. of the Punjab
Lahore
11 November 1944

Dear Minoo,

(1) I have returned the following books to your address: (i) *How India Pays for the War*; (ii) *Why Pakistan and Why Not*; (iii) *Planning for India*; (iv) *Fear of Freedom*; (v) *Trial of Mussolini*; (vi) *Protective Foods*; (vii) *Thorofare*; (viii) *Towards Zero Hour*; (ix) *Polish Conspiracy*; (x) *Genghis Khan*; and (xi) *India since Cripps*. I am keeping your pamphlet

on 'Co-operatives in a Planned Economy' and Coupland.[86] Sir Manilal Nanavati's[87] book I'll return in a month. I have taken the liberty of sending *Heart of a Child* to Prabha, who will return it to you after reading. There was a tenth book in the lot which included Coupland and other titles, but you had forgotten to tell me its name 'I just forget what was the tenth', you said. That unnamed book I never got. You may enquire in the proper quarters . . .* Remember me to friends there and give them my greeting.

With love,

Yours,
Sd/- J.P.

P.S. Prabha wants me to thank you for the books you sent her. She can't write to you, because she may write only to her nearest relations.

[86] Reginald Coupland (1884-1952); British historian; held Beit Professorship of Colonial History, Oxford, 1920-48; appointed to Royal Commission on the Superior Civil Services in India which included a visit to India, 1923; publications include: *Britain and India*, *The Cripps Mission*, *Indian Politics*, *The Future of India*, and *The Constitutional Problem in India*.

[87] Manilal B. Nanavati (1877-1967); economist; joined Baroda State Service in 1904; Revenue Commissioner, 1932-3, and Naib Dewan, 1934-5, Baroda State; Deputy Governor, Reserve Bank of India, 1936-41; President, Indian Society of Agricultural Economics, 1941-59; publications include: *Report on the Agricultural Indebtedness in the Baroda State*, *Rural Life Problems* and *Report of the Industrial Development in the Baroda State*.

* Blacked out by the censor.

c/o The Home Secretary
Govt. of the Punjab
Lahore
9 December 1944

Dear Minoo,

Your letter of November 8 reached me on December 6! The next day arrived the five book you sent with the letter, for which thanks. I read the *Stories of Rural Bengal* yesterday, but did not feel very enthusiastic about them. Some of the writers do not seem to have an intimate knowledge of their material. *Rural Bengal as seen from Calcutta* might be a better title for some of these stories. I am sure I'll find the other books more interesting. I am glad you have sent me Burnham's books,—I was rather anxious to read them.

You mention having received my letters of Sept. 29 and Oct. 21. I think I wrote you two more letters—of one I am certain in which I told you the names of the books I have returned, and also something about some of the books. I do hope you received that letter as also the books. I have finished Sir Manilal Nanavati's book and I shall be returning it with the latest lot. Sir Manilal and Anjaria[88] have done a most valuable piece of work, though I think some of the measures they advocate, even as first step, do not go far enough. I shall be obliged if you send me a copy of the promised volume on 'Land Problem of India' as soon as it is published by the Indian Society of Agricultural Economics. I should also like you to send me an omnibus volume on business economics (British publication) and also any good on contemporary (or modern) economic theory.

With love,

Sd/- J.P.

[88] J.J. Anjaria; economist; Reader in Economics, University of Bombay in the 1940s; Honorary Secretary and Treasurer, Indian Society of Agricultural Economics, 1944; and member of its Advisory Committee.

c/o The Home Secretary
Govt. of the Punjab
Lahore
20 January 1945

Dear Minoo . . .*

I have already written to you about the five books that I received from you—Burnham's and others. Since then I have received *Your Food* and *Gandhiji*—for which all kinds of thanks. For certain reasons my reading has considerably slowed down and the supply has, for the moment, outstripped the consumption. So, do not send any more books till I ask for them. This does not apply to the books I have already asked for. Burnham's *Managerial Revolution* has affected me rather strongly—in the sense that it has made me realise that the problem is much harder than what I had thought it to be: I mean the problem of democracy and economic planning. I have not, however, been much impressed by his somewhat dogmatic thesis about the three super-state centres of the world. Anyway, Burnham is one of the most clear-headed authors I have read. Are all ex-Trotskyists clear-headed? What has happened to Yusuf? There is no news from him or of him. I hope he has recovered enough to be able to move about. Do let me know about his health. What about yourself—thriving on work as usual? I am very happy to see that the Tatas have not in the least affected your intellectual pursuits or your prolific ideations—not to speak of your equally prolific productions.*

* Blacked out by the censor.

We were nearly frozen here, but the weather is better now.

With love,

Yours,
Sd/-J.P.

Central Jail
Agra, U.P.
8 February 1945

Dear Minoo,
I am very glad to tell you that, after sixteen and a half months, I have at last found deliverence—thanks to my *habeas corpus* petition to the Court—from the Punjab C.I.D. Fort, Lahore. I can't describe to you the great relief I feel—even a prison seems to be a place to be thankful for.

The very day I left Lahore came the last parcel of books that you were good enough to send, containing Romain Rolland,[89] Bernard Shaw,[90] Part II of the *Bombay Plan* and *Twenty Questions about Russia*. I have read through the last and found it rather cheaply done, and the angle of criticism is not acceptable to me.

I think I would have enough quiet here to enable me to put in some work, and I should be glad if you send me some serious (I can't find a better word at the moment) books. You remember I wrote you once that I was anxious to study Indian economic and constitutional problems. I should like to get everything you can find regarding the coal industry (including the miners). You may even send me a book on mining engineering. And what about some magazines? Is the *New Statesman and Nation* available? Can you have me put on their subscribers, list? It is one of the magazines approved by the Government of India. In a previous letter I had asked you to send me an omnibus book on business economics (British publication) and the 2nd volume of Jathar and Bery and any good book on contemporary economic theory. I am reminding you of it.

And what happened to the enquiry I had asked you to make at the Royal Asiatic Society Library? Do let me know.

Here I can write only four letters a month—including two postcards.

[89] Romain Rodland (1866-1944); famous French author and savant; awarded Nobel Prize for Literature, 1915.

[90] George Bernard Shaw (1856-1950); famous British dramatist and critic; awarded Nobel Prize for Literature, 1925.

This means that my letters to you would be less frequent to compensate which you must write oftner.

With love,

Yours,
Jayaprakash Narayan

Mr. M.R. Masani, Bar-at-Law,
Bombay House, Fort,
Bombay.

47. To Mahatma Gandhi, 11 May 1944[1]

C/o The Home Secretary
Govt. of the Punjab
Lahore
11 May 1944

Dear Bapuji,
Loving salutations at your holy feet!
I got the news of your release[2] from newspapers. I am very happy at your release in view of the state of your health. I hope you recover completely very soon. You have the good wishes of millions of people all over the world.

With your grace, I am quite well. I am very anxious to know where Prabhavati was sent after your release. I was expecting that I would get information in this regard from someone by telegram but the fact is that I have neither got any letter from her nor any news about her since the 24th March. I guess, she might have been sent back to Bihar. I may, perhaps, get her letter in a week or two.

Please do not bother to reply. Kindly dictate a few lines to Pyarelalji.[3]

Your affectionately,
Jayaprakash Narayan

[1] *Pyarelal Papers* (NMML).

[2] Gandhi was released from the Aga Khan Palace (Poona) on 6 May 1994.

[3] Pyarelal (1899-1982); Gandhi's Private Secretary for a long time; became editor of *Harijan* after Mahadev Desai's death in 1944; imprisoned several times during the Freedom Movement; publications include: *Epic Fast, Mahatma Gandhi: The Early Phase, Mahatma Gandhi: The Last Phase.*

48. To Kamalashanker Pandya, 18 May 1944[1]

C/o The Home Secretary
Govt. of the Punjab
Lahore
18 May 1944

Dear Kamalashanker,

It was very kind of you to send me the books. Some of them I had read before, but they are nevertheless welcome. I shall return them all as soon as I finish them. Oscar Paul's book is a book in a thousand and I have liked it immensely. Here are the names of the books I have received from you. (i) *Russia Fights On*; (ii) *Education and The Social Order*; (iii) *Tom Paine*; (iv) *Underground Europe Calling*; (v) *The Map of the World*; (vi) *Indian Horizons*; (vii) *Sarat Chandra Chatterji.*

It was good to know that you were out—I thought you were at Nasik. I hope you are keeping good health and are otherwise well and happy. I am keeping fairly well and do a little reading and some fitful writing.

With affectionate greetings,

Yours,
Jayaprakash

[1] *Kamalashanker Pandya Papers* (NMML).

49. To Kamalashanker Pandya, 30 June 1944[1]

C/o The Home Secretary
Govt. of the Punjab
Lahore
30 June 1944

Dear Kamalashanker,

I am sending you by registered parcel (or post) the seven books that you sent me in the first lot. I have finished the other three also that you sent later, but I am keeping them for some time yet. I have liked *All Our Tomorrows* very much, and *Peasant Life in China* is a masterpiece of field study and compact statement. I consider *China Builds for Democracy* to be a very badly written book inspite of Jawaharlal's enthusiasm for it. All its essential matter

[1] *Sampurnanand Collection* (NAI).

could have been brought together, presented better and made more readable in one-tenth of the space.

Since I wrote you last, I also received your letter of April 23, and was concerned to know that you were not keeping well. I hope, however, you have taken care of your health and are much better now. I shall be obliged if you can send me Baden-Powell's[2] *Land Revenue Systems in India* (all the volumes). Please also send me Dantwala's address; has he joined his college again? I am doing fairly well. With best wishes for your health.

Yours affectionately,
Jayaprakash Narayan

[2] Henry Baden-Powell (1841-1901) entered I.C.S., 1861; Small Cause Judge, Lahore, 1866-9; Commissioner of Lahore, 1883-6; Judge, Chief Court of the Punjab, 1886-9; publications include: *A Manual of the Land Revenue Systems and Land Tenures of British India*, *Land-Systems of British India*, *A Short Account of the Land Revenue and its Administration in British India*, and *The Origin and Growth of village Communities in India*.

50. To Sri Prakasa, 16 July 1944[1]

C/o The Home Secretary
Govt. of the Punjab
Lahore
16 July 1944

My dear Sriprakasaji,

I am returning by registered post both the volumes of *The Science of Social Organisation*. I have felt greatly uplifted by a study of this book and I find myself in much greater sympathy with Babuji's views today than in 1935. I also realised with a most pleasant surprise how much in common Babuji has with Gandhiji. That is because both have grasped the basic values of our civilization and the central truth of life. May he live long to carry on and complete the good work which he has undertaken. Please convey to him my most respectful *pranams*.

I trust you are well and are finding life interesting. I am fairly well, and though life is always dull in prison, I am keenly interested in my books. Please remember me to friends there.

With affectionate regards,

Yours,
Jayaprakash

[1] *Sri Prakasa Papers* (NMML).

51. To Kamalashanker Pandya, 29 July 1944[1]

29 July 1944

Dear Kamalashanker,
It was a pleasure to hear from you again. I am writing much earlier than my schedule allowed so that I may prevent you, if it is not already too late, from sending me books that I have read. In your letter of July 13, you mention four books that you intend to send me: *Arrival and Departure*, *Darkness at Noon*, *Out of the Night*, and *Scorched Earth*. I have read these books, so I hope you will not send them. In the future, it may be useful, before you make a selection for me, to consult Minoo. He is fairly in touch with my reading.

No, Kamalashanker, I have no inclination to write anything biographical, and hope will never do so. I did intend to do a little serious writing here, but circumstances have not permitted this. So, I just write to amuse myself or to organise my thoughts when some topical problem agitates me.

Unfortunately, your letter was badly mutilated this time. However, it was good to read the few lines that had been spared. I was glad to know that you will write regularly now. I shall look forward to your letters. Thanking you for your interest in my reading.

Yours affectionately,
Jayaprakash Narayan

[1] *Kamalashanker Pandya Papers* (NMML).

52. To Sampurnanand, 25 August 1944[1]

C/o The Home Secretary
Govt. of the Punjab
Lahore
25 August 1944

Dear Sampurnanandji,
Thanks a lot for *Chidvilas*. I have read only a third of it yet, so I must reserve my comments till I finish it. I shall say only this much today that I find the subjectivism of the title to be strangely at variance with the bold affirmative tone of the 'Upoddhat'. I think you should have been less modest in chosing the title.

[1] *Kamalashanker Pandya Papers* (NMML).

Also, I must compliment you on your style. No nobler prose can be written in any language.

Some time ago I received a parcel of *murabba* from Benares. I could never find out who had sent it. My guess was that you had done so. If I guessed right, will you please accept my belated thanks? If, however, I was wrong and you happen to know the right party, will you kindly take the trouble of conveying my thanks to them?

Trusting you are well, I am.

With affectionate regards,

Yours,
Jayaprakash

53. To Kamalashanker Pandya, 29 September 1944[1]

c/o The Home Secretary
Govt. of the Punjab
Lahore
29 September 1944

Dear Kamalashanker,

It was very kind of you to send me Hemingway's *For Whom The Bell Tolls*. I have liked it immensely. Why have you not written? Didn't you say you would write every fortnight?

I should like to know how your health is now. You said in your last letter that you were going somewhere for a change. I hope the change has done you good.

I am fairly well.

With love,

Yours,
Jayaprakash

[1] *Kamalashanker Pandya Papers* (NMML).

54. To M.R. Masani, 8 April 1945[1]

Agra Central Prison
Agra
8 April 1945

Dear Minoo,

Your letter of March 1 reached me on March 9. I am sorry I could not reply

[1] *M.R. Masani Papers* (NAI).

last month. By the way, it appeared from a letter of Shroff's[2] that my last letter created the impression that we were allowed to write two letters every week. That is not so. We may write only two letters (covered) and two post-cards in a month. In my last letter I had said that as the two covers must be reserved for Prabha,[3] I was left with only two cards a month for friends and relations. That is why I had said I could not write you as often as I did from Lahore, to compensate which I expected to hear oftener from you. Would once a fortnight be too often for you?—remember there were times when I wrote you weekly from Lahore. As for typed letters, I don't mind them at all. In fact I don't care even if you mimeograph your letters—so long as they are from you.

Thanks awfully for copies of the *Life*. We enjoyed them and would rather like to have more. I shall return these copies in a few weeks. Some days ago, I returned three books by registered post: *The Managerial Revolution*, *The Machiavellians* and *Rural Problems*. I liked *The Machivellians* and feel that its wider circulation might offer some wholesome obstruction to that flood of sentimentalism and messianic ardour that envelopes us all in this land of high thinking and starvation.

Please give my affectionate greetings to Shantikumarji and all other friends there. I did not understand how Shantikumarji was sending Prabha all she asked for, because as far as I know, she is not allowed to write except to her nearest relations. My brother Raja (Rajeshwar Prasad) is there these days. If you meet him—he is staying with Mr. Abid Ali[4]—give him my love. Also give my love to my cousin, whom you know and my hearty congratulations on her brilliant success at her exams. I am at a loss to recommend her a career. Everyone likes his own calling, but how can I recommend her life long vagrancy? Let her be guided by her parents, particularly by her grand dad, who is an authority for careers for the young.

It was good to know that Yusuf is so much better now. I hope Shantiniketan[5] would heal him in every way, and he would return whole, not only in the usual sense, but also in a far deeper way—man is only half without a woman, you know. Really I think Yusuf should get married.

[2] N.T. Sharoff—member of Congress Socialist Party.

[3] For biographical sketch on Prabhavati Devi see *JPSW*, Vol. I, p. 41.

[4] Abid Ali (1899-1973); joined Non-Cooperation-Khilafat Movement in 1920-1; General Secretary, Reception Committee, Congress Session, Bombay, 1934; took part in various other Congress movements and was arrested a dozen times; a renowned trade unionist and founder Vice-President, Indian National Trade Union Congress; represented India at I.L.O. in 1953; member, Council of State and Deputy Labour Minister, 1952-62; author of *Mazdoor Se Minister*, an autobiography in Urdu.

[5] Visva Bharati, Santiniketan, Birbhum, West Bengal, Founded in 1921 by Rabindranath Tagore, designated as a Central University in 1951.

I had read in the papers that recently Bombay had the hottest day in many years. How did you face them? Are you also going to Mahabaleshwar[6]? I am afraid Agra[7] is heaps hotter than Bombay can ever be, but it must be our resort for all seasons. I had a legal interview with Mr. Katju[8] yesterday.

With love and best wishes.

Yours
Jayaprakash

P.S. When you send me books again, will you please remember that Marx is no more out of date for me than the Vedas.

[6] Mahabaleshwar—a place near Bombay.

[7] Agra—a district in Uttar Pradesh.

[8] Kailash Nath Katju (1887-1968); Minister of Law & Justice in U.P., 1937-9; Governor of Orissa, August 1947-June 1948; Governor of West Bengal, 1948-51; Union Minister of Home and Law, 1951-2; State Affairs, 1952-5; Defence, 1955-6; Chief Minister of Madhya Pradesh, 1957-61.

55. To M.R. Masani, 6 June 1945[1]

Central Jail
Agra
6 June 1945

Dear Minoo,
I had hoped that before the moon took a full turn and it was my time to write to you, there should be at least one letter, if not two, from you. But—well, let me not trouble you with my importunities.

In your last letter you mentioned getting copies of *Life*; didn't you also get the three books I returned?—*Managerial Revolution*; *Rural Problems*; *Machiavellians*. Please do not omit to acknowledge anything that I return, because it naturally makes me anxious. A few weeks ago I returned a second lot of *Life* numbers and am returning Shaw and Romain Rolland now. You asked me if you could subscribe anything for me: can you arrange to have the *Forum* sent to us?

I was sorry to hear of the relapse of Yusuf's ill-health. I hope he is better now and that everything is being done to prevent a further set-back. It was sad to learn that for another year or so he must be out of things. But, usually his first care, and the care of all of us, must be his health. Other things must wait.

Please tell Yusuf not to worry about the baby you handed over to him,

[1] *M.R. Masani Papers* (NAI).

that is, the job of sending the 'serious books' I wanted. Firstly, I am no longer in the mood for them; secondly, my present environment has made me realise rather sharply my incompetence for any serious work. Some six months ago, or longer, I had asked for something like the *Saint Omnibus*. Saints, I am afraid, are rare birds, but are Agatha Christies too ceased these days? That's the kind of stuff I should like to have to improve my mind—if that is possible.

Looking at the signs of the times, it seems to me Minoo, that I'll be the only benighted Marxist left in this country, as also the only unregenerate materialist. As for the stirrings of your soul, may I present you with this [from] *Zend-Avesta*:[2] Ahmi yad Ahmi. They say if you understand that you understand everything. So help me God! By the way, have you seen Dr. Bhagwan Das' *Science of the Self*? If not, do.

Prabha, as you know, has been released. I am expecting her any day now that she has secured permission to interview me. I'll be seeing her after three years!

Please give my greetings to everybody.

Yours, with love,
Jayaprakash

[2] *Zend-Avesta*—Sacred book of Parsis.

56. To M.R. Masani, 5 July 1945[1]

Central Jail
Agra
5 July 1945

Dear Minoo,

Your letter of June 15. You are a nice one—of course, I got your letter of May 1. How else could I have referred to the stirrings of your soul and the other things? My complaint was irrespective.

Thanks a lot for copies of the *Forum* and thanks particularly to Joachim.[2] Will you give him my congratulations for the fine work he is doing. Such courage is rare, very rare, in the English language journals of this country. I

[1] *M.R. Masani Papers* (NAI).

[2] Joachim Alva (1907-79); one of the pioneers of the youth movement in the old Bombay Presidency; played an active role in the struggle for freedom and was arrested several times; member of the executive of the Bombay Provincial Congress Committee for a number of years; started *Forum*, a popular news magazine, in 1943; member Lok Sabha, 1952-67 and Rajya Sabha, 1968-74.

also feel everlastingly grateful to him for what he did during the difficult Lahore days.

The *Ten Modern Prophets* I read as soon as I got the book, and I confess I was not greatly thrilled by the 'prophets'. I think you had said something about their original thinking. Are they really original? It seemed to me rather that—except for Lawrence and the [leirlogists?]—they were faint echoes of Vedanta and Gandhism. However I hope these prophets succeed in doing something about the black confusion that has overwhelmed this civilisation. They have little to teach others.

We get *The Hindustan Times* here which I think is an excellent paper. By the way, the booby trap[3] seems to be succeeding. A pity.

Prabha was here a few days ago—you must have met her by now. She looked none the good and I am really worried about her health. I don't know where she stayed in Bombay—she said something about intending to put up with our cousin, Mrs. Janardan Prasad.

I had a letter from Narendratara who should be in Bombay now. How I wish to see him! Who can tell when that wish will be fulfilled.

You said in your letter that *Forum* would come to us from 'this week' (June 15). But apart from the back numbers you sent we have received no other issues. Will you please remind Joachim.

How is Yusuf now? Please give him my love and also thanks for the book on The Coal Industry. By the way, you need not register your letters—just parcel.

With love and best wishes.

Yours,
Jayaprakash

[3] Refers to Simla Conference, 29 June-14 July 1945.

57. To M.R. Masani, 19 August 1945[1]

Central Prison
Agra
19 August 1945

Dear Minoo,

Your letter of July 9. I agree you have improved, but don't forget it is August 19 today. However, it is always such a pleasure to read your letters

[1] *M.R. Masani Papers* (NAI).

that I don't think any increase in their number will ever reach the satisfaction point.

Prabha went to Wardha with Gandhiji and came here, via Delhi on the 31st. I had two interviews with her; on the 31st and the 1st. With the usual limitations of a prison interview there was not much she could tell me, but it was good to see her. I am grateful to you for your kindness and help to her. By the way, the Peshawari chappals you sent me were quite half-an-inch too long for me, and I have arranged to have them returned to you. Prabha sent me another pair from Allahabad which are satisfactory.

Some time ago, I returned the copies of *Life* and *Time*, and a little later, the detective novels and *Strangers in India*. There was tremendous activity here as long as the thrillers lasted; no other work or reading was done—even the daily papers suffered. But it was literally a seven days' wonder. By the way, the Agatha Christie was the same that you had sent me at Lahore; but, as Rammanohar[2] had not read it, it was all right. Moon's book[3] I liked, though it is not free from certain presuppositions and attitudes and makes the mistake of generalising for the whole country the experience of a none-too typical province. We are waiting for fresh copies of *Life* and *Time*. And what has happened to the *Forum* again?

Koestler's book,[4] though it came with the thrillers, somehow got detained with the censor for nearly a month, so I was able to finish it only a couple of days ago. This is what I entered in my note-book as I put down the book: A fine book. Shall keep it. The reference at the beginning (I am telescoping the paragraphs) to Gandhiji's [advocacy of] non-resistance to the Japanese made me angry. But it is ignorance rather than malice. The section on Russia is superb. I agree 100%. But [I] don't agree to call it State Capitalism. Needs amending in places along the lines of Lauret and Fromm. The suggestion at the end regarding the way out gives body to my own thoughts. Except for the language, there is page after page in this section of the book which I could have written myself.

The philosophical section at the end is stimulating but leaves a great many questions unanswered. That is natural. But why should Koestler fail for ever to explain the vertical jumps? And, does contemplation give 'knowledge' or 'experience'? At any rate, contemplation does not yield any knowledge of the horizontal levels, for were it so, the *Atma-Vidya* of the East should have laid bare the secrets of matter ages ago. Further, it is also clear that unless contemplation yielded knowledge (or whatever was its product) on a mass scale it could not cure society, and the tragic [spectacle]

[2] For biographical note on Rammanohar Lohia see *JPSW*, Vol. I, p. 91.
[3] Refers to Penderel Moon's *Future of India*, 1945.
[4] Refers to Koestler's *Darkness at Noon*.

of a rare Yajnavalkya or a rare Buddha living side by side with mumbo-jumbo worshipping primitives—which is India past and present—would continue; and, for all its saints and messiahs, the world would remain a savage place. That is if there were no alternative cure to contemplation!

Returning to the Soviet section, it is encouraging to find that Koestler does not think that socialisation of production is inconsistent with democracy. But he does not say how. I wonder if it's possible to get a clarification of this issue from him.

I think I am mainly a commissar type with Yogi leanings.

It was very kind of Yusuf to send me all those lovely books—nine of them (including those for the Doc).[5] It is a wonder how he manages to do all this despite his illness. Prabha told me that he has sent books worth nearly Rs. 10,000 to friends in prison. That is a service unique in its thoughtfulness and resource.

The war has ended. Shall we say the peace too has ended. It strikes me that a most vital provision was left out of the Potsdam decisions[6]: it should also have been provided that all those Germans who showed any signs of genius and threatened to lead the world in the sciences and arts should be decapitated and their brains shared equally (?) between the Academies and Royal Institutes. That should have secured peace for ever, I think. But mistakes will be made, though I see Comrade Wilhelm Pieck[7] does not agree with me. He finds Potsdam generous and humanitarian and unity between the Big Three the only hope for Germany! That shows you. . .

In the meanwhile the Japs have collapsed and Gulmarg is thrilled. But I don't see that the Maulana[8] has shifted the date of the A.I.C.C. from

[5] Doc—Refers to Rammanohar Lohia.

[6] The reference here is to the decisions arrived at after the fall of Germany by the leaders of the victorious powers, popularly known as the Big Three (Truman, Stalin and Churchill) at their Conference at Potsdam (Germany) from 17 July to 2 August 1945. (After July 28 Clement R. Attlee, as Head of the new Labour Government, replaced Churchill at the Conference.) According to them supreme authority in Germany was to be exercised by the Commanders-in-Chief of the armed forces of the United States, U.K., Soviet Union and France, by each in his zone of occupation and also jointly in matters affecting Germany as a whole in their capacity as members of the Control Council. Complete disarmament and demilitarisation of Germany was to be secured. All German land, naval and air forces and all military and semi-military organisations were to be completely abolished. All arms, ammunition and implements of war and facilities for their production were to be held at the disposal of the Allies or destroyed.

[7] Wilhelm Pieck; German Communist leader, worked with Ulbricht; was able to eliminate all opposition and turn his party as the most important Communist Party outside the Soviet Union.

[8] Maulana Abul Kalam Azad (1888-1958); his real name was Muhiuddin, Abul Kalam Azad being his pen name; started an Urdu weekly *Al-Hilal* (1913) and after its suppression by the Government, *Al-Balagh* (1915), for spreading political awakening among Indian

September 20 to August 20. I suppose like all wise men one must wait and see. By the way, that was a great speech[9] that the Sardar delivered the other day, we too had our share of thrill then.

People keep on inquiring if I have written anything. Will you tell them that I have—letters to Minoo Masani and others. Aren't they enough? By the way one of my letters to you has created a rather embarrassing situation. When I wrote from Lahore that I agreed nearly hundred per cent with your *Socialism Reconsidered* I was thinking largely of your treatment of Russia. I do not mean to suggest that I disagreed with the other parts, but my agreement with them was not nearly as complete. Will you please put me right in this matter with those whom it may concern?

It was such a joy to hear of Asoka's release and yesterday The Weekly has brought an article from him. It was good to read it because it enabled me to establish some little contact with his mind and found the experience exhilarating. How is Asoka? Rao says he is not too bad. Well that is something to be thankful for. Will you give him my love and a warm greeting and tell him to treat this letter as meant also for him. I hope to write him next month.

Yes I do remember the walks we had together in Nasik.[10] Here too I have my evening walk, but alone, as Rammanohar is unable to take any exercise due to his oriental sores (they are also called Aleppo and Baghdad, and Peshawar and Lahore and Delhi sores and Deishmaniai Tropica too it seems) which have been troubling for the last five months. In the morning I take some Indian exercises which keep me fairly fit, though as Dr. Erulkar[11] told

---

Muslims; one of the most prominent leaders of the Congress; was in and out of prison several times between 1920 and 1945; elected President of the Congress in 1923 and again in 1940, continuing till 1946; led the negotiations with the Cabinet Mission on behalf of the Congress in 1946; was appointed Union Education Minister in 1947 and continued to hold that portfolio till his death.

[9] This obviously refers to Sardar Patel's speech at Bombay on 9 August 1945 (published in detail in the *Hindustan Times*, dated 15 August 1945). In that speech he was reported to have condemned the hanging of a young political worker, Mahendra Chaudhury, for involvement in violent activities at the time of the Quit India Movement in Bihar. He had also observed that the establishment of a Labour Government in Britain had not brought about any change in British strategy in India.

[10] Refers to Nasik Central Prison where Jayaprakash Narayan was imprisoned during the second civil disobedience campaign (1932-3). Here he felt the need of organizing a Socialist Party. Several of his fellow inmates notably Achyut Patwardhan, M.R. Masani, Asoka Mehta, N.G. Goray and M.L. Dantwala shared his views. This led to the foundation of the Congress Socialist Party in 1934 with Jayaprakash Narayan as its Organizing Secretary.

[11] Abraham Solomon Eurelkar, President Medical Council of India College of Physicians & Surgeons, Bombay.

me in 1934 (was it?) I shall never be rid of my sciatica. I am glad however that it does not give me much trouble apart from affecting generally my nervous energy and capacity for work. Talking of Nasik, Minoo, let me say that the Nasik days were the happiest days I have yet spent in prison, and I cherish dearly the friendship I made there.

I had forgotten to say that I liked Birbal's and Tipu's[12] articles. Tipu's thing I had read already in the Weekly [*Aaj*]. I should like very much to make the authors' acquaintance.

Do remember me to everyone there and give them my greetings. I hope you have work enough not only to keep you busy but also in health. Work is your medicine. My love to Yusuf.

Yours,
Jayaprakash Narayan

[12] Birbal and Tipu—pen names of the authors of the articles.

58. To Khurshed Ben, 17 September 1945[1]

Central Prison
Agra
17 September 1945

Dear Khurshed Ben,[2]
You must excuse me for this delay—with one strictly rationed correspondence these annoying things become unavoidable. I must also beg you not to mind the post-card.

It was good to have your cheering letter, and kind of you to have remembered us.

Many things have happened since you were making your ascent to Simla heights. There are certain things which have to be pushed right before your nose to be believed. For my part, I could never have believed that half of what is happening today was possible. But, as your internationalist friend[3]

[1] *M.R. Masani Papers* (NAI).

[2] Khurshed Ben Naoroji (1894-1966); grand daughter of Dadabhai Naoroji; associated with Gandhian institutions; social reformer and freedom fighter; organized a volunteer organization in 1930, went to N.W.F.P. in 1940 to spread message of non-violence; was arrested in 1941, participated actively in the Quit India Movement in 1942.

[3] Refers to Jawaharlal Nehru.

keeps on reminding us, we are passing through revolutionary times and atomic explosions. If you don't believe it, just see what a revolutionary picture we make!

By the way, I wonder if you could tell me why poor Narendra[4] has been black-balled. Is it his asthma? But isn't there another august member of the club[5] not less addicted to the malady? Perhaps it is the company the wayward professor keeps. Or is it?

I was forgetting to tell you about your 'little Glaxo baby'[6] (now don't quote me—these were your words—I could not use such terms ever). Well he is alive and 'full of beans', as you quote, but rather depressed at the decay of 'internationalism', and troubled somewhat by other oriental sores, which seem to compete with the Almighty in the vanity of their names.

For myself, I have somehow, saved my health (I think I did it by refusing to do any writing in prison!). Anyhow the result is I am physically as fit as I ever was—and as for the mind, well who has a sound mind in these days of atomic demolitions?

If you happen to meet common friends, will you please give them my greetings. Prabha was here yesterday and today and we had two interviews of an hour each. I thought she looked better this time than she did before. She has gone back to her mother's and I expect her again by the middle of October.

I hope you will write again (even though the reply may again be delayed) and tell me about yourself. I hope you are keeping well and enjoyed your recent travels. Are you staying in Bombay for a while or going North again?

Please give my regards to Perin Ben.[7]

With the best thoughts for you,

Yours,
Jayaprakash

[4] Could be Acharya Narendra Deva. For biographical note see *JPSW*, Vol. I, p. 61.

[5] Could be Rajendra Prasad.

[6] Could be Rammanohar Lohia.

[7] Perin Ben (1888-1958); grand daughter of Dadabhai Naoroji; was attracted to the group of distinguished revolutionaries like Madam Bhikaji Cama, Lala Hardayal, Birendranath Chattopadhyaya, etc. She met Gandhi in 1919 and adopted his philosophy of non-violence; founder-member Rashtriya Stree Sabha, 1921; member, Bombay Congress Committee and its first woman president; arrested in 1932 while taking part in Civil Disobedience Movement.

59. To Mahatma Gandhi, 6 October 1945[1]

6 October 1945

Dear Bapuji,
Respectful and loving salutations at your feet!
I received your kind letter[2] sent through Prabha. I am sorry that I was not able to reply to it till now.

I had told Prabha that she should only ask you whether you received the letter I sent you from Lahore or not. I am sorry she made you take the trouble of writing a letter. However, I have felt blessed to receive it.

It is true that in some areas of thought I have been drawn quite close to you. This has given me much happiness. However, I continue to regret that in the area of basic principles I still find myself as far away from you as I ever was. I feel that my field will not only get away from yours, but will also become totally separate. Because of the recent turn of events I find myself moving speedily in this direction. However, as you have written, there is much difference between the emotional experiences of jail life and the world outside. After my release I cannot say in which direction I would be inspired to move.

Although prison is not a place for human beings to live, still I assure you that I am neither counting the days of my release, nor thinking that I am engaged in any penance. In revolutions, it is inevitable that some die, some are ruined and some languish in jails. Where is the question of any kind of deliberation on this. Thousands are still languishing in jails—in future also thousands will continue to languish.

The wilted flowers of the rainy season in our garden have now acquired wrinkles of old age. The seedlings of autumn flowers are peeping up from the veil of the earth to replace them. Now most of my time is being spent in looking after their growth, and in imagining which flowers will brighten which corners of this small world of mine and cover which garden-beds with their smile. The prevailing circumstances convince me that I shall be able to see the fulfilment of my imaginings.

I am afraid I might have only made you angry by wasting your time with this useless talk. In that case I ask for your forgiveness.

I won't like that you should take the trouble of replying. That I always have your blessings is enough to keep me happy and contented at all times.

I was worried to read the news that you got fever in Bombay. I hope you are well now. I shall be grateful if my respectful salutations at the feet of

[1] *Pyarelal Papers* (NMML). Original in Hindi.

[2] Not available.

Sardar Saheb[3] get conveyed to him. It is the great good fortune of the nation that his health is improving as a result of the treatment at Pune.

Prabha came on the 15th and 16th of last month. She is expected to come again by the end of this month.

My health is quite all right. Rammanohar is afflicted with a skin disease called Oriental Sore. However, he is improving with the treatment of a specialist. He is also conveying his respectful regards to you.

Yours humbly,
Jayaprakash

[3] Refers to Sardar Vallabhbhai Patel.

60. To M.R. Masani, 11 December 1945[1]

Central Prison
Agra
11-12-1945

Dear Minoo,
I was very happy to hear from you at long last, and to hear from you at some length. I would have normally replied last month, but for one thing. I was awaiting your promised second letter (lest you should have forgotten I shall quote you: 'I hope to make up for my disgracefully long silence by writing again before the end of this month'—that was on October 12!); and for the other I was somewhat piqued at your 'disgracefully long silence'. Well, but that's neither here nor there.

Let me now congratulate you upon your election to the Central Assembly. I cannot tell you how happy I feel at this. Not because it means honour to you, but for two things; it means a great gain to the Congress Party in the Assembly, and second, which is more important to me personally, it signifies your re-entry into politics. I was never able to reconcile myself to Indian politics without M.R. Masani, and I always considered it to be a major mistake in your life to have left active political work. The fact that even now you intend to keep up your connection with Tatas does not detract from the importance of your new decision. A man must live, and it is far more honourable to live by one's labour than in other ways that many of us are compelled to adopt. I wish you every success in your new work.

I had received all the literature you had sent me, and in a few days I shall be returning all the thrillers and the *Life* and *Time* numbers. How about a further consignment of something interesting? No not thrillers this time.

[1] *M.R. Masani Papers* (NAI).

Some recent publications of the sort you know would interest me.

I am very eager to see the 'Picture of A Plan'—why haven't you sent it yet?

How are all the friends there: Asoka, P.T.[2], Dantwala, Leelubhai, Zuh? Give them all my love. Yusuf I understand is at Igatpuri. Is he better? Do you see him often? Will you please write and send him my love? The same for you.

Yours,
Jayaprakash Narayan

P.S. The 'Plan' has just arrived. What's wrong with *Life*? In the last batch, two copies were of the same issue. This time too, one copy is again of one of the previous issues. That is we have two copies of August 13 and August 20 each.

J.P.

[2] P.T. stands for Purshottam Trikamdas.

61. To M.R. Masani, 8 March 1946[1]

Central Prison,
Agra, U.P.
8-3-1946

Dear Minoo,

It was a pleasure to hear from you twice within such a short period of time. I hope you will keep up the habit; it is such a joy to hear from you.

Sir John Thorne was here again the other day (on March 1 to be exact). Said he thought he would relax by driving down and incidently find out if a further talk could not help to make up his mind. He spoke about you and Sri Prakasa.[2]

By the way, do you think it proper that an individual approach should be made in such cases? I would much rather not. I appreciate greatly your motives and understand them perfectly—but then you have my feelings in the matter.

The Home Member[3] did not say so, but I gathered from his attitude that we were to be held as sort of hostages against the possibility of a fresh outbreak of "disturbances". In other words, if the impending negotiations

[1] *M.R. Masani Papers* (NAI).

[2] For biographical note on Sri Prakasa see *JPSW*, Vol. I, p. 61.

[3] Sir John Anderson Thorne (1886-1964): entered The Indian Civil Service in 1911 and held a number of important positions; Home Member, Viceroy's Executive Council, 1945-6.

were to prove abortive and another storm were to blow over the land, we were not to be left in a position to repeat the Houdini trick. That's national planning for you—rather far-sighted, I admit.

Yes, I read the report of your maiden speech in the "Times" (we get the paper daily and like it immensely—the best English daily in India, I think) as also the reports of your other speeches. Judging from the reports and the press comments on them, I am afraid you were rather mistaken in your estimate of the probable contribution of Mr. M.R. Masani to the Congress Party's work in the Assembly. That shows among other things that, while I am not always wrong, you are not always right.

About that maiden speech, do you think it right to concede that only those who are too gentle to kill flies should be at liberty? Of course, it is well-known that the Empire suddenly went non-violent in 1942, but I don't think it is equally well-known that civilized practice since then has been to allow freedom only to those who believed in non-violence. Is it not still possible, after the unique victory of non-violence in India and elsewhere, to *believe* in violence and be free till one actually committed violence and was brought to book for it? I am afraid a lot of harm has been done to the cause of liberty in this country by overlooking this aspect of the question.

I like your article, *The New Anti-Totalitarianism* (The Home Member also spoke about it), as also the *Picture of a Plan*. But I am waiting for a more elaborate work from you on the subject of democracy and planning.

Will you please give my compliments to Sripukarji and Sethji, and also my grateful thanks to both for the interest they have shown in me.

I hope you are finding your present work interesting. Thanks for the *Life*. I have returned the earlier numbers.

With best wishes,

Yours,
Jayaprakash

P.S. If and when you meet Mrs. Asaf Ali[4] will you enquire from her if she received my letter written more than a month ago. I would be sorry to know that it never reached her. The letter was addressed at your Party Office.

[4] Aruna Asaf Ali (1909-96); freedom fighter; born and educated at Lahore, married Asaf Ali, a prominent Congress leader in Delhi, joined Civil Disobedience Movement, 1930; imprisoned for a year in Lahore; played an important role in the Quit India Movement and remained underground till 1946; joined the Socialist Party; elected President of Delhi Pradesh Congress Committee, 1947; first Mayor of Delhi, 1958. She was recipient of Nehru Award for International Understanding in 1992.

P.P.S. If you wish to have distilled in one sentence the essence of a whole historical period, here it is: *A spectre is haunting Russia—the spectre of Socialism.* Isn't it beautifully said. Some of these American journalists have great penetration. By the way, is it possible for you to get for me some authentic literature on Russia-occupied Europe.

J.P.

APPENDICES

APPENDIX 1

A. Congress Working Committee's Resolution containing the pledge to be taken on Independence Day, 26 January 1930[1]

We believe that it is the inalienable right of the Indian people, as of any other people, to have freedom and to enjoy the fruits of their toil and have the necessities of life, so that they may have full opportunities of growth. We believe also that if any government deprives a people of these rights and oppresses them, the people have a further right to alter it or to abolish it. The British Government in India has not only deprived the Indian people of their freedom but has based itself on the exploitation of the masses, and has ruined India economically, politically, culturally and spiritually. We believe therefore that India must sever the British connection and attain Purna swaraj or complete independence.

India has been ruined economically. The revenue derieved from our people is out of all proportion to our income. Our average income is seven pice (less than two pence) per day, and of the heavy taxes we pay, 20 per cent are raised from the land revenue derieved from the peasantry and 3 per cent from the salt tax, which falls most heavily on the poor.

Village industries, such as hand spinning, have been destroyed, leaving the peasantry idle for at least four months in the year, and dulling their intellect for want of handicrafts, and nothing has been substituted, as in other countries, for the crafts thus destroyed.

Customs and currency have been so manipulated as to heap further burdens on the peasantry. British manufactured goods constitute the bulk of our imports. Customs duties betray clear partiality for British manufactures, and revenue from them is used not to lessen the burden on the masses but for sustaining a highly extravagant administration. Still more arbitrary has been the manipulation of the exchange ratio which has resulted in millions being drained away from the country.

Politically, India's status has never been so reduced as under the British regime. No reforms have given real political power to the people. The tallest of us have to bend before foreign authority. The rights of free expression of

[1] The Indian National Congress, 1930-4. Being the resolutions passed by the Congress, the All India Congress Committee and the Working Committee during the Period between January 1930 to September 1934.

opinion and free association have been denied to us and many of our countrymen are compelled to live in exile abroad and cannot return to their homes. All administrative talent is killed and the masses have to be satisfied with petty village offices and clerkships.

Culturally, the system of education has torn us from our moorings and our training has made us hug the very chains that bind us.

Spiritually, compulsory disarmament has made us unmanly and the presence of an alien army of occupation, employed with deadly effect to crush in us the spirit of resistance, has made us think that we cannot look after ourselves or put up a defence against foreign aggression, or even defend our homes and families from the attacks of thieves, robbers and miscreants.

We hold it to be a crime against man and God to submit any longer to a rule that has caused this fourfold disaster to our country. We recognise, however, that the most effective way of gaining our freedom is not through violence. We will therefore prepare ourselves by withdrawing, so far as we can, all voluntary association from the British Government, and will prepare for civil disobedience, including non-payment of taxes. We are convinced that if we can but withdraw our voluntary help and stop payment of taxes without doing violence, even under provocation, the end of this inhuman rule is assured. We therefore hereby solemnly resolve to carry out the Congress instruction issued from time to time for the purpose of establishing Purna Swaraj.

B. Congress Working Committee's Resolution on New Independence Day Pledge, Wardha, 22 December 1939[2]

The Working Committee draw the attention of all Congress Committees, Congressmen and the country the necessity of observing properly and with due solemnity Independence Day on January 26, 1940. Ever since 1930 this day has been regularly observed all over the country and it has become a landmark in our struggle for independence. Owing to the crisis through which India and the world are now passing and the possibility of our struggle for freedom being continued in an intense form, the next celebration of this Day has a special significance attached to it. This celebration must therefore not only be the declaration of our national will to freedom, but a preparation for that struggle and a pledge to disciplined action.

The Working Committee, therefore, call upon all Congress Committees and individual Congressmen to take the pledge prescribed below in public

[2] Indian National Congress, March 1939 to January 1940. Being the resolutions passed by the Congress, the All India Congress Committee and the Working Committee during the period between March 1939 to January 1940, pp. 60-3.

meetings called for the purpose. Where owing to illness or other physical disability, or to being in an out of way place, individual Congressmen are unable to attend a public meeting, they should take the pledge in their homes, individually or in groups. The Working Committee advise organisations and individuals to notify their Provincial Congress Committees of the meetings held as well as the individual or group pledges taken. The committee hope that none who does not believe in the contents of the pledge will take it merely for the sake of form. Those congressmen who do not believe in the prescribed pledge should notify their disapproval, stating reasons thereof to the Provincial Congress Committee, giving their names and addresses. This information is required not for the purpose of any disciplinary action but for the purpose of ascertaining the strength of disapproval of anything contained in the pledge. The Working Committee have no desire to impose the pledge on unwilling Congressmen. In a non-violent organisation compulsion can have little place. The launching of civil disobedience requires the disciplined fulfilment of the essential conditions thereof.

Pledge

We believe that it is an inalienable right of the Indian people, as of any other people, to have freedom and enjoy the fruits of their toil and have the necessities of life, so that they may have full opportunities of growth. We believe also that if any Government deprives a people of these rights and oppresses them, the people have a further right to alter it or to abolish it. The British Government in India has not only deprieved the Indian people of their freedom but has based itself on the exploitation of the masses, and has ruined India economically, politically, culturally and spiritually. We believe, therefore that India must sever the British connection and attain Purna swaraj or complete Independence.

We recognise that the most effective way of gaining our freedom is not through violence. India has gained strength and self-reliance and marched a long way to Swaraj following peaceful and legitimate methods, and it is by adhering to these methods that our country will attain Independence.

We pledge ourselves anew to the Independence of India and solemnly resolve to carry out non-violently the struggle for freedom till Purna Swaraj is attained.

We believe that non-violent action in general and preparation for non-violent direct action in particular, require successful working of the constructive programme of Khadi, communal harmony and removal of untouchability. We shall seek every opportunity of spreading good-will among fellowmen without distinction of caste or creed. We shall endeavour to raise from ignorance and poverty those who have been neglected and to advance in every way the interests of those who are considered to be backward and suppressed. We know that though we are out to destroy the imperialistic system we have no quarrel with Englishmen, whether officials or non-officials. We know that distinction between the caste Hindus and Harijans must be abolished, and Hindus have to forget these distinctions in their daily conduct. Such distinctions are a bar to non-violent conduct. Though our religious faith may be different, in our mutual relations we will act as children of mother India, bound by common nationality and common political and economic interest.

Charkha and Khadi are an integral part of our constructive programme, for the resuscitation of the seven hundred thousand villages of India and for the removal of the grinding poverty of the masses. We shall, therefore, spin regularly, use for our personal requirements nothing but Khadi, and so far as possible, products of village handicrafts only and endeavour to make others do likewise.

We pledge ourselves to a disciplined observance of Congress principles and policies and to keep in readiness to respond to the call of the Congress, whenever it may come, for carrying on the struggle for the independence of India.

APPENDIX 2

Communist Plot against the C.S.P. by M.R. Masani[1]

Introductory Note

Members of the Congress Socialist Party who are in the know have been aware for a long time past of a deliberate and calculated attempt on the part of the Communist Party to penetrate and capture the Congress Socialist Party. The Central Executive of the C.S.P. has more than once drawn attention to this danger to the Party's very existence and has tried to take certain steps to check this disruptive move.

There are however, many comrades in the Party and others outside who have been sceptical about the existence of this attempt on the part of the Communists. They have wanted concrete proof. The circular issued by the Communist Party to its members which is published here gives them clear documentary proof. The circular is reproduced here verbatim. The titles and emphasis are mine.

This circular has recently come to my hands and I am satisfied that it is an authentitic circular of the Communist Party to its members. I feel it is my duty to share this information with members of our Party as it concerns its very existence. If the Party is to survive this plot, it must be made fully aware of its existence and must take much more drastic steps in its own self-defence than it has hitherto taken.

This document is full of verbiage about "Unity", but I am sure nobody with an open mind will be taken in by this talk. The real intention is perfectly clear. Members will also notice the unashamed directions to Communists inside the Party to resort to "Camouflage", to follow policies to which the Party has refused to be committed but to cloak their actions so that technically they remain within the limits of Party discipline and to smuggle into the Party "unmarked' members of the Communist Party wherever possible. They will also not overlook the insults hurled at certain esteemed members of the Party in this document.

There are many statements in the circular which we may know to be untrue or exaggerated. It may be that the Communists are over-optimistic in thinking that they have already progressed so far in their plot as they imagine. There is no denying, however, the intention and motives of the Communist Party nor the very substantial measure of success they have so far achieved

[1] M.R. Masani, *Communist Plot Against the C.S.P.*, 1938.

through the misplaced generosity and tolerance displayed towards them by the leaders of the Congress Socialist Party.

Much confusion has been caused on this issue by loose talk of "unity" and by the deliberate misuse of that word Unity or unification between two parties or groups can come about only in one legitimate way, and that is by a merger or amalgamation of the two organisations arrived at by mutual agreement and in an open and straight forward manner. That the Congress socialist Party was prepared to consider such a step was stated publicity by Acharya Narendra Deva on the he eve of the Lahore Conference of the Congress Socialist Party. There was no response from the other side to this offer perhaps because the pre-condition of Unity laid down by Acharya Narendra Deva was the liquidation of both the Parties.

What the Communists want to do is to swallow up the Congress Socialist Party and to call it "Unity". They want to keep their own party intact and at the same time to capture the organisation of the C.S.P., to exploit the goodwill it has built up and to make it subservient to the will of the Communist Party. But this is not what the Congress Socialist Party was formed for.

The inevitable consequence of such a policy, if it were to be successful, would be to split the Congress Socialist Party and deprive it, not only of many of those who formed the Party and have built it up in the past four years, but also of its real character and value as an independent Revolutionary Socialist Party of India and to reduce it to a legal platform for the Communist Party.

This circular is a challenge to the Executive of the Congress Socialist Party as well as to every genuine member. If it is not met with adequate and timely action, it may well prove too late to save the Party from disruption. In that event, the responsibility will lie on the shoulders of those who have now no excuse for shutting their eyes to the unpleasant fact of the existence of cold blooded and deliberate conspiracy to swamp the Party with those whose real allegiance is elsewhere.

It is in the hope that this disclosure will lead to timely action which may yet save the C.S.P. that I am making this circular available to comrades in our Party.

M.R. Masani

CIRCULAR OF THE C.P.I.

Plan of Work—C.S.P.—9-5-38

In view of the changed situation inside the C.S.P., the attitude of the C.S.P. leadership and our tasks of working for socialist unity, the following plan of work is adopted:-

1. The composition and character of the All India Contact Committee should be changed. It should consist of five members from each side. This would be a purely political committee and must meet every three months, it would take a review of the political situation and endeavour to evolve through its deliberations a united lead on the major issues facing the movement. These agreed decisions would become the basis not only of joint agitation and work but also be considered the official line of the two organisations unless they are over-ruled by the Executive of either organisation. This committee would endeavour to come to agreement on whatever political issues it is possible to do so. The two organisations would throw in their entire weight, both separately and jointly to implement these agreed decisions. If there are any complaints against the units of either organisation they would be referred to the Sectt. concerned and the results of such investigations and decision will be communicated to the other Sectt. in due course. Complaints against individual or lower units cannot be made a cause, in normal circumstances, for breaking up united front relations nor should these interfere with the work of this committee.

We expect the C.S.P. leadership to circularise to all its units to develop united action with us on as many occasions and as many fronts as possible. We expect that the differences on some issues or even conflicts on some occasions will not be considered as a sufficient cause for stopping joint action on other occasions or other issues etc. The general directive should be to continue U.F. relations on whatever terms possible.

We have already circularised our ranks and are repeating these instructions.

We hope such an All India Committee would become one of the transitional forms for achieving a United Executive and the deliberations of this body would lead in growing measure the ideological political unification of the socialist movement and give concrete guidance to the national movement.

2. In Bombay, Calcutta and Cawnpore, where our differences are the most acute we should take the initiative to form contact committees which should not be of less than three comrades from either side. The functions of this committee would not be only political but it will take initiative to propose and carry out joint actions on whatever terms are possible and over issues the C.S.P. agree and our delegations would be responsible to see that our part of agreement is implemented.

3. We should not suggest any rigid organisational forms for our other provincial and district committees. The existing contacts must be made to function and the necessary changes in composition, etc. introduced to make them to function more regularly, efficiently and smoothly. The main point is to get U.F. work going through whatever mechanism that is possible.

Activists' Groups

4. As the most suitable mechanism to give an organisational form to our U.F. work and to supply it the necessary driving force we should seriously endeavour to form informal Activists' Groups. These should consist of all the active elements from our C.S.P., T.U., and Congress ranks who are easily available at the place of their work of residence. These ad hoc groups through their periodical meetings should take the responsibility for carrying through joint actions, e.g. organising a demonstration, helping or guiding strike, running mass campaign. This would not only be mobilisation of larger number of cadres for day to day work but these Activists' Groups would become through their own experience of working with us the rank and file of united front movement and who would be also a guarantee that united front work instead of being sabotaged is really developed more and more. It is the way we work these Activists' Groups and demonstrate our own worth inside them that we will not only build a U.F. movement but also create socialist cadres who would also struggle along with us, for the achievement of the socialist unity.

5. To inspire confidence in the C.S.P. leadership, to keep the unity of the C.S.P. to be able to enlarge it, we would not, from outside, for the time being press the demand. All the socialists inside the C.S.P. and the leadership who is scared away by this slogan, that since you yet mistrust us and lack confidence in our bonafides and consture our attempts in working for socialist unity to be a partisan move to capture your organisation, we do not advocate a slogan which is being resisted by a section of the C.S.P. and which even threatens to spilt the C.S.P. and with it the unity already achieved if this slogan is accepted. We would endeavour to win your confidence and establish our bonafides and take you seriously at your own word and expect you to implement the slogan of "Joint Action with the C.S.P." and thereby create the preconditions of closer unity.

No Noise

Our comrades within the C.S.P. would continue to popularise the slogan and use every achievement of joint action and every attempt to sabotage it to vigorously pursue the unity policy. In those localities and provinces where it is possible to include all socialists inside the C.S.P., it should be done without fail and without making much noise about it.

It is in this way that the elements working for socialist unity within and without the C.S.P. be strengthened.

6. Our work inside the C.S.P. must be guided by the considerations that we are conscious builders of socialist unity, it is our task to keep up the unity of the C.S.P. and that the anti-unity [*sic*] elements inside the C.S.P. would

seize every opportunity to throw us and our supporters out of the C.S.P. to maintain and guarantee their own organisational domination over the C.S.P. We can achieve the above tasks and defeat the moves of the disrupters only by making a sharp turn in our attitude towards and inside the C.S.P. (on lines indicated in other documents).

The exact nature of our work inside the C.S.P. depends upon our present position inside the C.S.P. units.

Where in Majority

In those provinces and places where we are in a majority: Here we must immediately begin to work in the new way and interpret and act upon the Faizpur thesis, on the lines of Zaheer-Batliwala-Dinkar thesis without giving any chance for technical breaches of discipline. We should defend this as being the logical working out of the Faizpur Thesis. On the basis of our practical work and idelogical campaign we should be able to win over the whole C.S.P. to accept this Draft Thesis and recognise us as the best C.S.P. ers. Systematic efforts must be made to recruit the advanced elements of the C.S.P. who begin to accept our line into our own organisation. We should take particular care not to let other C.S.P. members be banded into a group against us or create the impression that we are rushing the C.S.P. or exploiting our majority in any other cause except strengthening of the C.S.P. itself.

In the majority provinces the Provincial Dist. Executives should discuss both the draft theses which were put forward at the Lahore A.I.C.S.P. conference and should forward their opinion to our C.S.P. committee. In day to day work they should begin to take as their guide the generalisations and directives given in the thesis of Zaheer, etc. With special reference to the proletarianisation of Party [*sic*] and rapidly increasing its membership.

The C.S.P. committee should on the basis of these discussions in the province and districts work out a series of articles for the C.S. work drawing out main conclusions of the thesis on the basis of the experiences of these places and their needs, without referring to the thesis itself, without using its terminology. The main point is to drive home the conclusion that the growth of the mass basis of the C.S.P. arises inevitably out of experience of the growing of the C.S.P. Itself and the tasks it has undertaken.

Unmarked Members

In places where we are in a minority, great vigilance and elasticity in day to day work is needed. We should endeavour to get as many of our new and unmarked comrades or sympathisers as possible inside the C.S.P., promptly undertake to liquidate all sectarian mistakes and silently work towards a majority. It is only through our work that we will earn the right to be inside the C.S.P. In the eyes of all honest C.S.P. ers, not let ourselves be isolated, and make our explusion impossible.

7. The specific tasks in the provinces where we are a majority are the following:-

Andhra: Membership 480. Entirely under our influence no rival group. Provincial C.S.P. headquarters and District Executives function effectively. Our entire might and best of our distt. Cadres should be thrown into the task of organising the local units of the C.S.P. far more effectively and link them up with Provincial headquarters. Along with this organisational consolidation must proceed a serious effort to enlarge the membership still further by admitting into the C.S.P. every honest rank and file who is sympathetic to Socialism and is active on any of the mass fronts-Congress, peasants, T.U. [*sic*], Youth or Students. Andhra can and must become a model C.S.P. Unit.

Tamil Nad: Membership 220. Entirely under our influence. Leadership united. No rival group. Madras city and provincial headquarters function as living units; in the other districts only agitational influence. Ideological level very low; the weekly must not be used only for raising ideological level of the C.S. Pers but by giving them practical guidance re: mass front problems lead to the organisational consolidation of the C.S.P.

Kerala: Membership 200. Entirely our influence and no rival group. Very widespread agitational influence on all fronts. Congress (majority in P.C.C.), peasants and T.U. movements entirely under their influence. The C.S.P. as an organisation is lagging behind its agitational achievements. The comrades have failed to give up Congress methods of organisation and agitation. Individuals function for units.

The foremost task of the leadership is to make the district branches function and during the course of this organisational drive itself double the membership on the basis of a special recruitment campaign from the active workers and peasants. They have recently started a weekly of their own and this should be of inestimable service in fulfilling these tasks.

Orissa: Membership 40. Majority of members with us an assured majority in the provincial executive. Naba Chowdhary who follows J.P.'s lead is the only other element and is considered as a reactionary by our comrades. The membership must be doubled in the course of the next three months by drawing upon students and kisan cadres. Sectarian attitude towards Chowdhary must be immediately liquidated and the danger of his being used as agent by Masani circumvented. Efforts must be made not to let any rival group to be consolidated inside the C.S.P. and draw N. Chowdhary nearer and nearer.

Weaning Away the Centre

Bengal: Membership 250. Though we are a majority inside the Party we are not a majority inside the Executive (8 ours and 9 Centre and Right) owing to our inability to afford to send all our delegates to the Provincial conference. There are Right and centre elements and both have begun to function as a united fraction against us. Through our day to day work and intense ideological campaign we should break up rival fraction and wean away the Centre from the Right on the basis on the unity of the C.S.P. itself.

Our contact is not forthcoming at all satisfatorily, nor is the Provincial leadership boldly carrying out our C.S.P. policy, nor has the sectarian resistance in our district organisations to work inside the C.S.P. been successfully broken. All this must immediately change.

The Labour Party should be made to speed up Unity with the C.S.P. With our strong position inside the Provincial Executive of C.S.P. and with the relative competence of our cadres, unity on terms which may not appear to us as reasonable would be an unqualified advance. It will shift the balance in our favour inside the C.S.P. remove lot of confusion and strengthen the unity elements inside the C.S.P.

If the C.S.P. agrees to have the effective membership 20-40 of the L.P. we should have unity and dissolve the L.P. If the C.S.P. refuses to accept the proposal we should continue to activise [*sic*] the L.P., work cut U.F. with the C.S.P. without any half-heartedness or dilatoriness on our part with a view to bring about unity on the above minimum conditions as soon as possible.

It is not an alternative to C.S.P. nor do we look upon it as a permanent organisation. We retain and activise it only to be able to achieve socialist unity and as transitional measure. The slogan of the L.P. as a necessary political party of the working class and also the slogan of the All India wcrkers' Party separate from the C.S.P. is categorically rejected by us.

The activisation of the L.P. does not mean that it should be extended to the Distt. It should remain confined to Calcutta and be looked upon as our own political platform till unity with the C.S.P. is achieved. Again as many new comrades as can enter the C.S.P. in Calcutta should continue to do so. Inside our own ranks all old prejudice against the L.P. must be cast aside.

The Anushilan is joining the C.S.P. and is likely to join the right and centre fraction in opposition to us and take initiative to start local C.S.P.s. We should not oppose their entry into the C.S.P. but endeavour to work with them to strengthen the C.S.P. itself.

Punjab: Membership 700. Though it would be correct to say that our policy would command an overwhelming majority yet this majority is not stable because of acute faction fights among the socialists as a whole. The biggest [*sic*] problem so far has been the non-understanding and non-acceptance by our own comrades of our policy towards the C.S.P.

This coupled with their own fractional attitude and the fact that the other faction was identified with the C.S.P., has led them to commit a whole series of sectarian and opportunist mistakes. A big forward step has however been taken with the liquidation of the Socialist Party and the unification of all socialists under the C.S.P. The organisational unity of socialists can be immediately made to yield serious political results only if sectarianism and factionalism are rooted out from our ranks in the Punjab. The proletarian movement is rising in the Punjab, headed by the socialists themselves, and the rapid proletarianisation of the Party can alone lead to a permanent solution of the Punjab problems which have so far defied solution.

The two groups within the C.S.P.—Kirti and the Nawajawan Bharat Sabha—are grovelling among themselves. They are likely to seek our support for factional ends. It is our task not to ally with any fraction, keep the unity of the C.S.P. and develop it as a homogenous party.

Within the Congress, the C.S.P. must function as a unit and not ally with either of the Congress factions.

Where in Minority

The Provinces where we are in a minority are the following:-

Bombay: Has problems of its own. Membership 200. Leadership right. We are rigidly excluded. The local units of the C.S.P. do not function. Immediate steps should be for us, to send as many unmarked comrades as possible inside the C.S.P. and they should take the initiative to form local units and press for united action from within. Our joint work and contact is not functioning satisfactorily. Despite difficulties from the other sides the necessary amount of enthusiasm and the needed initiative is not forthcoming on our part. This must immediately change. Joint Work must become a regular feature of our day to day work and begin with a series of campaigns, e.g. Sholapur Prisoners' Release. Recognition of G.K.U., the Bombay Labour Bill etc.

C.P. The C.S.P. was in our hands but was dissolved, the passivity of our responsible comrades and their inability to build up a C.S.P. was used by Masani and others not only to dislodge us by dissolving the party but also to attack our political bonafides.

Later on, our comrades started a Radical Workers League. The C.S.P. is again being reorganised:

A Right!

All comrades who were formerly in the C.S.P. must demand admission into the C.S.P. as a matter of right. We should dissolve the Radical Workers' League and ask its members to join the C.S.P.

Constant contact with the new C.S.P. members must be kept and all steps taken to influence them. The danger of Masani using the C.S.P. in C.P. as his closed preserve must be tactfully circumvented.

We should intensify our Congress work in Nagpur and work to activise the Town Congress Committee along with the C.S.P. comrades and thus win the confidence of the local C.S.P.

Camouflage

Maharashtra: Membership 200. The locals do not function at all nor provincial headquarters. The leadership is definitely hostile.

We must get our comrades to make the locals function, enrol as many members as possible and establish new locals.

These steps must be carefully camouflaged.

Only those of our comrades should remain out of the C.S.P. who are not taken inside it. Leading elements from among them can serve as our contact and take the initiative to launch joint work. It is very necessary in Maharashtra to make a sharp turn in our attitude towards the C.S.P. and implement the above directions immediately.

U.P.: Nominal membership 450. Majority of organised membership with us. All functioning locals ours. The leadership is Centrist and at present suspicious and hostile.

Except at Cawnpore all our comrades are inside the C.S.P.

Our immediate tasks are rapid improvement in our local work, start C.S.P. locals where they do not exist, seriously carrying on joint work at Cawnpore. Our top must keep constant touch with the C.S.P. leaders and endeavour to influence them politically.

Karnatak: Membership 200. Bogus. Our isloated contacts must be asked to join the C.S.P. and form locals. The existing C.S.P. leadership would be unable to prevent this.

As soon as possible a meeting of all our contacts should be called and work for them planned out.

Sindh: The C.S.P. was disbanded. A complete report should be demanded from our comrades and steps taken to find out the exact position of the C.S.P. and investigate about Bechar's corrupt opportunism.

Gujarat: 100. We were in miniority. A part of the leadership had come over to us, but they lost it owing to their own inactivity. The other group has gone over to Masani in Ahmedabad we are a majority. Our group is the very opposite of Andhra comrades, their growing inactivity has completely paralysed and demoralised them.

To-day they have to begin all over again, from the most elementary stage. All the advanced workers of the Mill Kamdar Union must be taken inside the C.S.P. and the Ahmedabad C.S.P. made a functioning body. It is only by improving Ahmedabad work that the situation in Gujarat can be tackled.

Bihar Needs Organiser

Bihar: 200. Solidly with J.P. Provincial headquarters function, but not district units. They supply cadres and political leadership to the kisan Sabhas but function as loose group of individual agitators. The party is not built through Kisan work, not attempted to draw in new cadres. If we could send a good orgniser a first rate C.S.P. could be organised but we cannot afford to send any. We have contacts with some recently released Andman prisoners and they are working inside the C.S.P.

Delhi: Membership 70. Torn with factionalism. The Left section is with us but they are really nothing more than left C.S.P. ers. Some advanced workers who had previously been in contact with us in other towns and are very good elements have joined the C.S.P. and the Congress but are dissatisfied with both sections of the C.S.P. leadership. Since we cannot afford to send a whole time organiser there, comrades on their way to and from Punjab should drop down at Delhi.

N.W. Frontier. Punjab C.S.P. ers have contacts with them and they go along with them. They are generally Left. Our C.S.P. comrades should get in direct touch with them through the Punjab comrades.

Ajmer. There are ex-terrorists, Left Congressmen working among the States peoples and some advanced workers and with them all a good local C.S.P. can be formed. The B.B.C.I. Union comrades should get in touch with all these contacts in Ajmer and help to organise a C.S.P.

APPENDIX 3

A.I.C.C. Resolution on War Crisis, Wardha, 9-10 October 1939[1]

The declaration of war in Europe has created in international situation of the gravest import to the world and to India, and the All India Congress Committee charged with the heavy responsibility of guiding the people of India in this moment of world crisis, has sought guidance from the principles and declarations of the Congress in considering this grave situation. The Congress has been guided throughout by its objective of achieving the independence of the Indian people and the establishment of a free democratic state in India wherein the rights and interests of all minorities are preserved and safe-guarded. The means it has adopted in its struggles and activities have been peaceful and legitimare, and it has looked upon war and violence with horror and as opposed to progress and civilisation. In particular, the Congress declared itself opposed to all imperialist wars and to the domination of one country over another.

In spite of the repeated declarations of the Congress in regard to war, the British Government have declared India a belligerent country without the consent of the Indian people, and various far-reaching measures have been hurried through the legislatures and promulgated in the form of ordinances vitally affecting them and circumscribing and limiting the powers of the Provincial Governments.

The All India Congress Committee, however, does not wish to take any final decision precipitately and without giving every opportunity for the war and peace aims of the British Government to be clarified, with particular reference to India. The Committee approves of and endorses the statement issued by the Working Committee on September 14, 1939 on the war crisis, and repeats the invitation contained therein to the British Government to state their war aims and peace aims.

While the Committee condemns fascism and Nazi aggression, it is convinced that peace and freedom can only be established and preserved by an extension of democracy to all colonial countries and by the application of the principle of self-determination to them so as to eliminate imperialist control. In particular, India must be declared an independent nation and present application should be given to this status to the largest possible extent. The A.I.C.C. earnestly trusts that this declaration will be made by

[1] Indian National Congress, March 1939 to January 1940. Being the resolutions passed by the Congress, the All-India Congress Committee and the Working Committee during the period between March 1939 to January 1940, pp. 16-17.

the British Government in any statement that it may make in regard to its war and peace aims.

The Committee desire to declare afresh that Indian freedom must be based on democracy and unity and the full recognition and protection of the rights of all minorities to which the Congress has always pledged itself.

The Committee approves of the formation by the Working Committee of the War Emergency Sub-Committee and authorises the Working Committee to take such steps as may be necessary to give effect to this resolution and to their statement on the war crisis.

APPENDIX 4

Joint Statement by Jayaprakash Narayan, Narendra Deva, Asoka Mehta and Rammanohar Lohia on Viceroy's speech, 12 January 1940[1]

The Viceroy is only exacerbating nationalist India which is the only living India, by continuing to harp on the tune of dominion status and on the role of the imperialist Government as protector of the minorities and the princes. He is doing no credit to his intelligence by demonstrating that he has failed to appreciate that the old tune has been played out.

The goal of nationalist India has been irrevocably determined by its sole representative organ, the National Congress. That goal is full and unfettered freedom. The British power must go together with every vestige, and in its place must arise the power of the sovereign people of India, through an assembly elected on adult suffrage and deriving its sanction from their revolutionary will. Millions of Indians are preparing under the command of the Congress and their generalissimo, Mahatma Gandhi, for their last battle for independence. As a first step towards that battle, millions will take a new the Pledge of Independence on January 26, which declares, in the clearest possible terms, India's intention of severing the British connection.

At such a time as this, the Viceroy is only making himself and the British Government ridiculous by running around the country displaying the rusty and broken toy of dominion status. The Liberal stalwarts of the south who have wired to Mahatma Gandhi to accept the so-called offer of the British Government, might fall for such a tinsel but not the freedom-loving people of India, not the downtrodden millions, who under the rigorous schooling of the Congress and their economic struggles, have grown to a sturdy manhood.

The days of empire are gone, and those who do not appreciate it are destined to wake up one fine morning to a most unpleasant truth. It is time the British people realised that unless they parted with empire they too shall perish along with it.

It is also necessary to remind the Viceroy of another unpleasant fact. This war is not India's war, and even when it has been adequately demonstrated that the allies are fighting for freedom and democracy as they are most definitely not doing today, a free India, as Mahatma Gandhi has pointed out, will give no more than its moral support to the British Govern-

[1] *National Herald*, 13 January 1940. The Statement was issued at Lucknow on Viceroy Lord Linlithgow's speech delivered at the Orient Club, Bombay, 10 January 1940 in which he had exhorted the Indian leaders to end the constitutional deadlock.

ment in this war. Its efforts will all be directed to establishment of peace and goodwill among the nations.

As for the repeated emphasis of the Viceroy on the differences between sections of the Indian people, it is, to all self-respecting Indians, more disgusting than anything else. The Viceroy poses as the protector of minorities and the princes. India never invited the British to come and protect its minorities. They came to rule. While they have pampered rajas and nawabs, the ravages of their rule have visited every home in India, whether Hindu, Muslim, Sikh or Christian. Those who seek the protection of the British power are traitors to their country and should remember that they too will be swept aside along with imperialism in the onward march of freedom.

Freedom is one and indivisible. It knows no communal compartments. Those who wish to restrict its forward motion by communal barriers are not the true servants of their community.

The Indian people are indeed divided into religions and creeds, but these are not economic and political divisions. Economically and politically India is one and one also in economic and political freedom.

As for religious freedom, India has always enjoyed it and the Congress has always uncompromisingly stood for it.

In any case, difference among sections of the Indian people are matters for adjustment among the people themselves. An outside power has nothing to say in the matter and it is the height of unpatriotism to allow them any say in it. The only question about which it has any say is when and how it will take its leave of the country. And on this question there are not many Indias and one Britain, but one India—Nationalist India—and one Britain—Imperialist Britain. These two will decide the issue.

APPENDIX 5

Mahatma Gandhi to Jayaprakash Narayan
[before 19 January 1940][1]

Your opposition is proper and you have expressed it in a language of restraint. You could not have done anything else.

[1] *National Herald*, 19 January 1940. Also published in *The Collected Works of Mahatma Gandhi*, Vol. LXXI.

APPENDIX 6

"The Dissentients": Article by Mahatma Gandhi in the *Harijan*, 20 January 1940

Shri Jayaprakash Narayan and Shri Sampurnanand have spoken in no uncertain terms against the addendum to the pledge to be taken on the 26th inst. I have great regard for them. They are able and brave and have suffered for the country. I should count it a privilege to have them as companions in arms. I should love to win them over to my viewpoint. If the battle is to come and I am to lead it, I should not be able to do so with half-convinced or doubting lieutenants.

I am not spoiling for a fight. I am trying to avoid it. Whatever may be true of the members of the Working Committee, I wholly endorse Subhas Babu's charge that I am eager to have a compromise with Britain if it can be had with honour. Indeed satyagraha demands it. Therefore I am in no hurry. And yet if the time came and if I had no follower, I should be able to put up a single-handed fight. But I have not lost faith in Britain. I like the latest pronouncemnt of Lord Linlithgow. I believe in his sincerity. There are undoubted snags in that speech. Many *is* have to be dotted, many *is* have to be crossed. But it seems to contain germs of a settlement honourable to both nations. Those, therefore, who work with me have to appreciate this side of me. Perhaps from the standpoint of the dissentients this compromising nature of mine is a disqualification. If it is, the country should know it.

Shri Jayaprakash Narayan has done well to clear his and the Socialist Party's position. He says of the constructive programme:

> We have never accepted it as the only or even as an adequately effective weapon in our struggle. . . . Our views regarding these matters have remained unchanged. Rather they have been strengthened by the helplessness of the national leadership in the present crisis. . . . Let students come out of their schools and colleges on that day and let workers lay down their tools.

If the majority of Congressmen entertain the views that Shri Jayaprakash propounds on behalf of the Socialist Party, I can never hope to lead such an army to success. He has no faith either in the programme or in the present leadership. I suggest to him that he has quite unconsciously discredited the programme he would carry out merely "because the nation's High Command desire it". Imagine an army marching to battle without faith in the weapons to be used and in the leaders who have prescribed them. Such an army can only bring disaster to itself, its leaders and the cause. If I were in Shri Jayaprakash's place and if I felt able to tender discipline, I would advise my party to remain indoors and silent. If I could not, I would preach open revolt and frustrate the designs of an ineffective leadership. Again, he would have the students come out of their colleges and schools and workmen lay down their tools. Now this is a lesson in indiscipline. If I had my way, I would invite every student to remain in his school or college unless he got leave or the Principal decided to close the college or school in order to take part in the celebration. I should give similar advice to the workmen. Shri Jayaprakash complains that the Working Committee has given no details about the work to be done on the Independence Day. I thought that with the programme of fraternizing and Khadi there was no need for detailed instructions. I should expect Congress committees everywhere to arrange spinning demonstrations, khadi-hawking, and the like. I observe that some committees are doing so. I had expected Congress committees to make preparations from the day the Working Committee resolution was published. I shall measure the strength of the nation's response not merely by the quantity of yarn spun but mainly by the khadi sales throughout the country.

Finally Shri Jayaprakash says: "We advanced for our part a new programme, that of labour and peasant organization, as the foundation of a revolutionary mass movement." I dread the language used. I have organized both but not perhaps in the way Shri Jayaprakash has in mind. The sentence demands further elucidation. If they are not organized on a strictly peaceful footing, they may damage non-violent action as they did during the Rowlatt Act Satyagraha and later during the hartal in Bombay over the Prince of Wales's visit.

Shri Sampurnanand has raised a spiritual issue. He thinks that the original pledge should not have been tampered with though as he says, and rightly, it was discursive. I was its author. I wanted the people not merely to repeat the *mantra* of independence but to educate the people as to its why and wherefore. It was later amended when certain portions of the original had become meaningless. I admit the sacredness of the mantra of independence. That was given to us when the Lokamanya first uttered: "Swaraj is my birthright." It was caught by thousands and is gaining strength from day to day. It is now enshrined in the hearts of millions. I hold that the addendum this year was necessary. It adds to the sacredness of the original and tells the people how everyone can contribute to the realization of national freedom.

I feel, therefore, that Shri Sampurnanand's objection really arises from his disbelief in the constructive programme. Thus he says:

> If making it an integral part of the pledge means that we are definitely committing ourselves to a policy of village industries as opposed to mass production, then I, as a socialist, cannot accept it.

Of course I cannot give the legal interpretation of the pledge. It can only be given by the Working Committee. But as the General responsible for declaring and conducting a non-violent war I am bound to say that this mentality must interfere with mass propaganda. A leader like

Sampurnanandji can either throw himself whole-heartidly in the struggle or not at all. He will create confusion in the mass mind by being half-hearted in his exposition of the addendum. If khadi has not an abiding place in the national programme, it should have no place in the addendum. If there is anything more effective, it should be put before the nation. There need be no hush-hush policy because a big fight is said to be impending. It is not necessary for all to be of one mind. But it is absolutely necessary that those who have to be in charge, as he would have to be, have a living faith in the programme they have to work out. No make-believe will answer the present requirements.

It has been suggested to me by a Congressman wielding great influence that as soon as I declare civil resistance I would find a staggering response this time. The whole labour world and the kisans in many parts of India will, he assures me, declare a simultaneous strike. I told him that, if that happened, I should be most embarrassed and all my plan would be upset. I must confess that I have no positive plan in front of me. Let me say that God will send me the plan when He gives the word as He has done before now. He has been my unfailing Guide and has sustained me throughout my stormy life. This, however, I know that no plan that I may put before the country will admit of unregulated and sporadic strikes, because that must lead to violence and therefore automatic suspension of the non-violent struggle. It would amount to my dismissal. I am sure that socialist leads and other dissentients do not expect me to embark on a struggle which I know beforehand is likely to end in disaster. I ask for lieutenants and men who will act as one mind.

Even if somehow or other we achieve nominal independence, we cannot conduct national affairs with any degree of success unless we have won the struggle in the manner prescribed by me. Without real non-violence there would be perfect anarchy. I hope I am not expected knowingly to undertake a fight that must end in anarchy and red ruin.

Segaon, January 16, 1940
Harijan, 20-1-1940

APPENDIX 7

Joint Statement by Narendra Deva and Jayaprakash Narayan on the Working Committee's Draft Resolution for the Ramgarh Congress, 4 March 1940[1]

The draft resolution prepared by the Working Committee for the Ramgarh session of the Congress must mark a turning point in current Indian history. A distinct break with the policy of statement has been made. Dominion Status has been definitely rejected; complete independence and Constitutent Assembly based on adult suffrage have been reiterated; complete non-cooperation with the Imperialist War has been enjoined upon all who would answer to the call of the congress; the inevitability of civil disobedience has been unequivocally proclaimed. No other obstacle to resumption to civil disobedience remains, except indiscipline within the Congress. The British attempt to use communal differences and the Princes as obstacles has been finally put out of the way by pointing out that both these problems are British creations and, therefore, could be solved only when the British power has been overthrown.

We hope that in view of these fateful decisions, those who in the name of leftism have of late been trying to disrupt the congress and lower its prestige will realise now that the time has come when we must put our house in order and repair the breaches that have been made in the national front. Their sole justification for all their actions has been that the Congress would not fight any more and that the Working Committee was soon to enter into a pact with Imperialism. These deductions as we often endeavoured to show, at some risk of misunderstanding, were based on a false reading of Congress policy and perhaps a certain amount of wishful thinking. The anti-Right vendetta must be based on some thing and what better basis could be found than the scare of a dishonourable deal with Imperialism. However, the draft resolution leaves no doubt about a national struggle. Its perspective is no longer dim or distant. Our duty, therefore, is also clear. Let not false notions of prestige stand in the way of duty. Differences may remain, as they must, but internal chaos and indiscipline must cease. The greatest responsibility in this connection lies on Shri Subhas Chandra Bose who, we hope, will rise to the occasion. The unseemly quarrel within the Congress in Bengal must cease. Let all our efforts be directed not to the sole end of preparing for the national struggle about which no uncertainty remains any longer.

[1] *Searchlight*, 5 March 1940. Statement issued at Patna, 4 March 1940.

APPENDIX 8

Mahatma Gandhi's Comments on Draft Resolution of Jayaprakash Narayan for the Ramgarh Congress, 20 April 1940[1]

I liked it and read his letter and the draft to the Working Committee. The Committee, however, thought that the idea of having only one resolution for the Ramgarh Congress should be strictly adhered to, and that the original, as framed at Patna, should not be tampered with. The reasoning of the Committee was unexceptionable, and the draft resolution was dropped without any discussion on merits. I informed Shri Jayaprakash of the result of my effort. He wrote back suggesting that he would be satisfied if I could do the next best thing, namely, publish it with full concurrence of such as I could give it.

I have no difficulty in complying with Shri Jayaprakash's wishes. As an ideal to be reduced to practice as soon as possible after India comes into her own, I endorse in general all except one of the propositions enunciated by Shri Jayaprakash.

I have claimed that I was a socialist long before those I know in India has avowed their creed. But my socialism was natural to me and not adopted from any books. It came out of my unshakable belief in non-violence. No man could be actively non-violent and not rise against social injustice no matter where it occured. Unfortunately Western socialists have, so far as I know, believed in the necessity of violence for enforcing socialistic doctrines.

I have always held that social justice, even unto the least and the lowliest, is impossible of attainment by force. I have further believed that it is possible by proper training of the lowliest by non-violent means to secure redress of the wrongs suffered by them. That means is non-violent non-co-operation. At times non-co-operation becomes as much a duty as co-operation. No one is bound to co-operate in one's own undoing or slavery. Freedom received through the effort of others, however benevolent, cannot be retained when such effort is withdrawn. In other words, such freedom is not real freedom. But the lowliest can feel its glow as soon as they learn the art of attaining it through non-violent non-co-operation.

It therefore gladdens me to find Shri Jayapraksh accepting, as I read his draft, non-violence for the purpose of establishing the order envisaged by him. I am quite sure that non-violent non-co-operation can secure what violence never can, and this by ultimate conversion of the wrong-doers. We in India have never given non-violence the trial it has deserved. The marvel

[1] *The Collected Works of Mahatma Gandhi*, Vol. LXXI.

is that we have attained so much even with our mixed non-violence.

Shri Jayaprakash's propositions about land may appear frightful. In reality they are not. No man should have more land than he needs for dignified sustenance. Who can dispute the fact that the grinding poverty of the masses is due to their having no land that they can call their own?

But it must be realised that the reform cannot be rushed. If it is to be brought about by non-violent means, it can only be done by education both of the haves and the have-nots. The former should be assured that there never will be force used against them. The have-nots must be educated to know that no one can really compel them to do anything against their will, and that they can secure their freedom by learning the art of non-violence, i.e., self-suffering. If the end in view is to be achieved, the education I have adumbrated has to be commenced now. An atmosphere of mutual respect and trust has to be established as the preliminary step. There can then be no violent conflict between the classes and the masses.

Whilst, therefore, I have no difficulty in generally endorsing Shri Jayaprakash's proposition in terms of non-violence, I cannot endorse his proposition about the Princes. In law they are independent. It is true that their independence is not worth much, for it is guaranteed by a stronger party. But as against us they are able to assert their independence. If we come into our own through non-violent means, as is implied in Shri Jayaprakash's draft proposals, I do not imagine a settlement in which the Princes will have effaced themselves whatever settlement is arrived at the nation will have to carry out in full. I can therefore only conceive a settlement in which the big States will retain their status. In one way this will be far superior to what it is today; but in another it will be limited so as to give the people of the States the same right of self-government within their States as the people of the other parts of India will enjoy. They will have freedom of speech, a free Press and pure justice guaranteed to them. Perhaps Shri Jayaprakash has no faith in the Princes automatically surrendering their autocracy. I have. First because they are just as good human beings as we are, and secondly because of my belief in the potency of genuine non-violence. Let me conclude, therefore, by saying that the Princes and all others will be true and amenable when we have become true to ourselves, to our faith, if we have it, and to the nation. At present we are half-hearted. The way to freedom will never be found through half-heartedness. Non-violence begins and ends by turning the searchlight inward.

APPENDIX 9

C. Rajagopalachari's Draft Resolution for Congress Working Committee Meeting, Delhi, 3 July 1940[1]

The Working Committee is of opinion that the proposals communicated by His Excellency the Viceroy in his conversation with Mahatma Gandhi do not meet the requirements of the present situation in any satisfactory manner.

According to these proposals the claim of the Congress that the status of India should be declared by Britain to be one of complete independence remains unsatisfied. Any declaration that India shall be in the same position as the self-governing countries in the British Commonwealth does not meet the case of India. Nor has it any real meaning in the present state of world affairs.

Apart from this and what is even more important in relation to the immediate activities in regard to Defence efforts, the working committee is emphatically of the opinion that the congress cannot withdraw its non-cooperation unless the entire field of central government including defence is immediately placed incharge of a national government, which, though formed ad hoc and as a transitory measure, should be so constituted as to command the confidence of all the elected elements of the Central Legislature and of the Responsible Governments in the provinces. Unless such a central national government is immediately formed, any efforts in the direction of the defence of India will not only be contrary to the fundamental principles of justice and democratic government, but will also prove utterly futile.

[1] *Collected Works of Mahatma Gandhi*, Vol. LXXII, p. 466.

APPENDIX 10

Resolution adopted by Congress Working Committee, Delhi, 7 July 1940[1]

The Working Committee have noted the serious happenings which have called forth fresh appeals to bring about a solution of the deadlock in the Indian Political situation; and in view of the desirability of clarifying the Congress position, they have earnestly examined the whole situation once again in the light of the latest developments in world affairs.

The Working Committee are more than ever convinced that the acknowledgment by Great Britain of the complete Independence of India, is the only solution of the problems facing both India and Britain and are, therefore, of opinion that such an unequivocal declaration should be immediately made and that as an immediate step in giving effect to it, a provisional National Government should be constituted at the centre, which, though formed as a transitory measure, should be such as to command the confidence of all the elected elements in the Central Legislature, and secure the closest co-operation of the responsible government in the provinces.

The Working Committee are of opinion that unless the aforesaid declaration is made, and a National Government accordingly formed at the Centre, without delay, all efforts at organizing the material and moral resources of the country for Defence cannot in any sense be voluntary or as from a free country, and will therefore be ineffective. The Working Committee declare that if these measure are adopted, it will enable the Congress to throw in its full weight in the efforts for the effective organisation of the Defence of the country.

[1] Indian National Congress, March 1940 to September 1946. Being the resolutions passed by the Congress, the All-India Congress Committee and the Working Committee, Allahabad, pp. 74-5.

APPENDIX 11

J.P. and others to Superintendent, Deoli Detention Camp, 29 May 1941[1]

To
The Superintendent,
Deoli Detention Camp.

Sir,

You are aware that there has been among us for a long time past, very strong feelings concerning the Camp hospital and the Medical Officer. The Camp Committee have had several occasions to bring complaints to you notice concerning both. The demand for the removal of the present M.O. has also been a long standing one. Quite recently, that is on 27-5-41, when matters had become grave, the Camp Committee sent you an urgent note, setting forth certain immediate demands. Among these were (1) the transfer of the serious cases to the Ajmer Civil hospitals or to any other suitable civil hospital, (2) the immediate removal of the present M.O., (3) weekly visits to the Camp hospital of the Civil Surgeon, Ajmer, till a new M.O. arrives. Before any reply was received from you concerning these demands, a very grave situation was created in the hospital, when an attempt was sought to be made to remove by force Mr. Beni Madhav Rai, who was seriously ill, to another place outside the enclosure meant for us. For this purpose a posse of armed guard had been called. This was an act not only of extreme provocation but also of the atmost callousness. After that incident, when the Camp Committee met you, they reiterated their demands, previously communicated, that is on 27-5-41. They also made the further demand that Mr. Satrughan Koomar, who has been most vindictively punished, and against which punishment the Committee at the same time strongly protested to you, should be immediately removed from the cell and sent to nurse Mr. B.M. Rai. This request was made entirely on medical grounds, for it was known that the sudden removal of Mr. S. Koomar from the hospital, had caused a great shock to Mr. B.M. Rai in his extremely weakened state of health and mind, due to which, his mind seemed to have been deranged, and he was constantly demanding that Mr. Koomar should be brought back to him. The Committee was led to believe that in consultation with the M.O., this could possibly be done. But this was not done and Mr. Rai was transferred to Ajmer this morning. Not only was not Mr. Koomar sent with him, as he should have been , considering the patient's mental condition, but no one else from amongst us either was allowed to go with him. It should be pointed

[1] Home Political Department, F. No. 43/96/41, NAI.

out here that the arrangements made for his removal to Ajmer were also extremely unsatisfactory.

Further, the Civil Surgeon came here yesterday and though the Committee had desired to be allowed to see him, this was not done. Neither did the Civil Surgeon recommend the other serious cases, to be transferred from here.

In these circumstances, we the undersigned have been forced to the conclusion that since all manners of protest and action have failed, we must take recourse now to the final weapon in our power and invite upon us the utmost suffering by resorting to hunger strike in order to correct this deplorable state of things. We demand again that (1) the other serious cases should be immediately transferred to Ajmer or any other civil hospital, (2) Mr. Satrughan Koomar should be immediately sent to Ajmer to attend Mr. B.M. Rai, (3) the Civil Surgeon Ajmer, should visit the Camp hospital twice a week till a new Medical Officer arrives, (4) the present M.O. should be immediately removed. Unless satisfaction is given to us on these points till 10 a.m. tomorrow morning, we shall refuse to take any food thereafter.

We remain
Yours truly,

(Signed)	(1)	Mohanlal Gautam, M.L.A.	U.P.
	(2)	Dayaram Beri	U.P.
	(3)	Virendra Nath Pandey	U.P.
	(4)	Bal Gangadhar Tripathi	U.P.
	(5)	Roop Narain Pande	U.P.
	(6)	Keshav Prasad Sharma	U.P. (detenue of last Camp)
	(7)	Jogeshwar Prasad Trivedi	U.P.
	(8)	Krishna Shanker Srivastav	U.P.
	(9)	B.N. Roy	U.P.
	(10)	Amrik Singh Bendra	U.P.
	(11)	Ram Dulatey Upadhyaya	U.P.
	(12)	Surendranath Pande	U.P.
	(13)	Gokuldas Shastri	U.P.
	(14)	Kamta Prasad	U.P.
	(15)	Harbans Singh	U.P.
	(16)	S. Usmani	U.P. (connected with Beawar and Ajmer)
	(17)	Manmohan Gupta	U.P.
	(18)	S.N. Pathak	U.P
	(19)	S.N. Sanyal	U.P.
	(20)	A.K. Chakravarty	U.P.
	(21)	Jayaprakash Narayan	Bombay
	(22)	Jogesh Chandra Chatterji	U.P.
	(23)	G.K. Jetley	U.P.

APPENDIX 12

Mohanlal Gautam and Jayaprakash Narayan to Civil Surgeon, Ajmer, 30 May 1941[1]

Copy

To
The Civil Surgeon,
Ajmer.
(Through the Superintendent, Deoli Detention Camp.)

Sir,
As you will learn from the bearer some of us have gone on hunger-strike since 10 A.M. this morning. This step has been forced upon us entirely by the deplorable conditions obtaining in the camp Hospital and our grievances pertaining there to. In our talks with the Camp authorities this morning. It was pointed out to us that many of the points raised by us fall into your jurisdiction. We have been therefore advised by the authorities to address this letter to you.

Firstly, our demand is that the serious cases that are in the camp Hospital should be immediately transferred to the Ajmer or any other suitable Hospital. You will appreciate the justice and urgency of this demand if you realised, as you probably do, that we have lost all confidence in the capacity and humanity of the camp Medical Officer. Some of the cases have been in the hospital for months, now and there has been no improvement. The conduct of the M.O. and his unsympathetic, even hostile, treatment are producing a very bad reaction in the minds of the patients.

Secondly, in the case of Mr. Beni Madhav Rai, whom you were good enough to recommend to be transferred to Ajmer, his mind has been greatly affected by the sudden removal of Mr. Shatrughan Koomar who was his particular friend and was nursing him in the hospital. Evidence of the effect of Mr. Koomar's removal on Mr. Rai's mind is found in the fact that his mind seems to have been deranged and he kept on demanding constantly that Mr. Koomar be brought back to him. He also failed to recognise people and thought everyone who went near him to be Mr. Shatrughan Koomar.

In view of these facts, the Camp Committee demanded entirely on medical grounds, that Mr. Koomar should immediately be sent to the hospital to attend Mr. Rai. This was not done, with obvious results to the patient. When it was learnt that Mr. Rai was to be transferred to Ajmer, it was demanded

[1] Home Political Department, F. No. 43/96/41, NAI.

that Mr. Koomar should be sent along with him. This too was not done. Our present demand is that considering the mental condition of Mr. Rai, Mr. Koomar be immediately transferred to Ajmer to attend Mr. Rai. We believe that not to do so would be cruel, and that if it were done his mental condition would immediately improve.

Thirdly, we have demanded that in view of our lack of faith in the Camp Medical Officer, you should visit the Camp Hospital at least twice a week. We believe that in the circumstances this is the best that can be done in the interests of our health. When we have been confined in such an out of the way place, proper arrangements should be made at least for our medical treatment.

Fourthly, we have demanded that the Medical Officer should be immediately removed from here.

This in brief is our case. It is not possible to explain it at greater length. We had expected that when you came here last you would see our representatives who would have put the whole case before you. But for some reason or the other you did not see us. It would help, if you could come here immediately and discussed the matter with us. In the meanwhile our hunger strike naturally continues.

We are, Yours Truly,

Sd/- Mohanlal Gautam
Sd/- Jayaprakash Narayan
{On behalf of the hunger-strikers
Camp No. 1}

Deoli,
30.5.41.

APPENDIX 13

Draft Press Note by J.P. and others [before 31 July 1941][1]

Copy of a press note that we had prepared, but could not send out. It may be used.

Nearly fifty security prisoners in the Deoli detention Camp including S. Mota Singh, Messrs. Jayaprakash Narayan, Mohanlal Gautam, Jogesh Chatterji, Dr. G.K. Jetely and Jogendra Shukla, had been on hunger-strike from May 30 to June 4. For a long time past the prisoners in this Camp have been agitating for the redress of their grievances and for certain demands. In this connection they have sent repeated memoranda to the Government of India. While it is true that some minor demands have been fulfilled, the important ones, such as the demand for repatriation, family allowance, for the abolition of classification, the demand that no book that is not proscribed should be disallowed, and several others remain still unfulfilled. In connection with the last demand it may mentioned that even such books as Pandit Jawaharlal's autobiography, Dr. Seetaramayya's History of the congress, novels of Dostoievsky, Capital of Karl Marx have been disallowed. While these questions were deeply agitating the minds of the prisoners here, matters were brought to a head by the conduct of the authorities and their callous attitude towards patients seriously ill in the Camp Hospital. The Medical Officer of the Camp is not only an incompetent doctor but also extremely unsympathetic and hostile to the prisoners. The demand for his removal has also been a long standing one. Deoli climate is very unsuitable and fever and stomach troubles are common. The diseases too are not uncommon. There were at least five very serious cases in the Hospital of prisoners who had been very ill for weeks, and some of them for months. Repeated requests to send them to the Ajmer Civil Hospital for treatment had been rejected. Recently one of them suddenly developed symptons of delirium due to extreme pain in abdomen. The Medical Officer on the pretext that the patient was insane, advised the camp authorisies to have him removed from the Hospital and threatened even to have him chained to his cot. On the patient's refusal to leave the Hospital a posse of armed guards was brought in to have him removed by force. This was resisted by all the patients in the hospital. When the news of all this reached the Camp, the Hospital being some furlongs away, there was great indignation. Nearly fifty prisoners, as mentioned above, soon thereafter gave notice to the authorities that unless steps were urgently taken to remove the serious cases to Ajmer or any other suitable Civil hospital, to transfer the Medical Officer, to improve conditions in the Camp Hospital,

[1] Home Political Department, F. No. 43/96/41, NAI.

to arrange for the Civil Surgeon, Ajmer, to visit the Camp Hospital at least once every week till a new Medical Officer arrives, they would refuse to take any food. The lives of their sick fellow prisoners were sufficiently precious to compel them to stake their own lives for their sake. On the fifth day of the hunger strike the authorities agreed to all the demands and the hunger strikes was broken.

From this the public should not be led to believe that all is now well in Deoli. All the important demands for which the prisoners had been agitating for months and in connection with which they had made representations to Government remain still unfulfilled. There is no doubt that unless something is done about them in the near future a very serious situation, much more serious than the one recently created, would develop in the Deoli Camp. Even with regard to the last hunger strike, though the authorities definitely promised that the Medical Officer would be immediately transferred, this has not yet been done. Nor the medical department is working satisfactorily enough. One of the patients who had been transferred to Ajmer has returned, and he reports that he was very badly treated by the Civil Surgeon, Ajmer, and was kept in a locked room. It is necessary that the public should demand a non-official enquiry to be made into the affairs of the Deoli Detention Camp. Unless this is done and the grievances and demands are looked into the satisfactorily settled, a grim fight will soon have to be launched, the consequences of which will all be the responsibility of the Government.

APPENDIX 14

J.P. and others to N.M. Joshi [before 31 July 1941][1]

Copy of letter given to Mr. N.M. Joshi

Dear Sir,

We take this opportunity of informing you of a serious situation that had developed in this Camp some time ago. We do not know if any news of it appeared in the press, or if it did how for did it represent things correctly.

Some time ago, to be exact from May 30 to June 41 over forty of us security prisoners in both the camps here (over thirty in Camp I and about 12 in Camp II) were on hunger strike. We state briefly the circumstances that led to the strike and the sequence of it.

As you will come to know from the Camp representatives who will acquaint you with the general position, we have been agitating here for certain demands and for the removal of certain grievances. In the midst of this agitation matters were brought to a head by the conduct of the camp authorities and particularly by their callous attitude towards patients seriously ill in the Camp Hospital. As you will have come to know one of our most serious grievances has been in connection with the medical department of the camp. The Medical officer who has now been removed, was not only an incompetent doctor but also extremely unsympathetic and hostile to us.

For some time prior to our hunger strike there were a number of serious cases in the Camp Hospital. Repeated requests to send them to the Ajmer Civil Hospital for better treatment were rejected on various grounds. Suddenly one of the serious patients developed symptons of delirium due to extreme pain in the abdomen. The Medical Officer, on the pretext that the patient had gone insane, advised the Camp authorities to have him removed from the Hospital, and threatened to even have him chained to his cot. On the patient's refusal to leave the Hospital a posse of armed guards was brought in to remove him by force! This was naturally opposed by all the patients in the Hospital.

When the news of all this reached the Camp, there was great indignation. Over forty of us, as mentioned above, soon thereafter gave notice to the authorities that unless steps were urgently taken (1) to remove the serious cases to Ajmer or to any other suitable Civil Hospital, (2) to transfer the Medical Officer, (3) to arrange for the civil surgeon, Ajmer, to visit the Camp at least once every week till a new M.O. arrives, we would refuse to

[1] Government of India, Home-Political, F. No. 43/96/41, NAI.

take any food. There was also a fourth demand which would require a little explanation. Our friend, Mr. Beni Madho Rai, who has been mentioned as having developed delirium was being attended upon by a friend of his. This latter Comrade one day slapped a ward-boy in the hospital for his refusal to do something which it was his duty to do. For this the Camp authotities gave our Comrade solitary cell punishment and convict diet for a week. Since this happened Mr. Rai, though he was not informed of the punishment, kept demanding for his friend to be brought back. Considering the mental condition of this patient we had demanded simply on medical grounds, that the punished Comrade should be sent back to the hospital or to Ajmer if Mr. Rai is sent there. We were forced to take recourse to this grave step on account both of the provocation caused by the calling of military guards to use force on a patient and of the realisation of our helplessness to effect any improvement in the Hospital through any other means we felt that the lives of our sick friends were sufficiently precious to justify our staking our own for their sake.

Our strike ended on June 4, all our demands having been conceded. But prior to this, an ugly incident occurred which we wish to bring to your notice so that you may realise better the attitude of the Camp authorities towards us. A day prior to our ending the strike the Superintendent who had been on leave took over charge and he called our representatives to discuss the issues of the strike. There was some difficulty in reaching an agreement on which the Superintendent ordered our representatives to be segregated from us and to be confined in Camp III, which was unoccupied. To call representatives of hunger-strikers for negotiation and then to punish them in this manner is a species of conduct which we better leave it to yourself to describe.

In this connection there are two other incidents which need to be mentioned. Mr. Rai whose case has been mentioned was finally sent to Ajmer as a result of our pressure. There he was treated very badly by the Civil Surgeon who personally participated in having him dragged from the Hospital verandah to his room in which he was kept locked up day and night. Being treated in this manner, the patient asked to be sent back to Deoli and said that unless he was sent, then he would not take any food or medicine. There upon he was brought back, but the Civil Surgeon, Ajmer, sent along a report that he was malingering and was not ill at all! We demanded that a Medical enquiry be made into his case and the truth or otherwise of the report be established. But nothing has been done so far about this. On the report of the C.S. the Supdit. Immediately put Mr. Rai in solitary confinement for the offence of malingering! Fortunately at this very time the Chief Medical Officer, Ajmer-Merwara, a European gentleman visited the Camp. At our request he examined Mr. Rai and on his recommendation he was taken out of the cell and his punishment was remitted.

Such is the manner in which the Medical Officer, the Supdt, and the C.S. have been behaving and such is the extraordinary manner in which this Camp is being run.

Among the hunger-strikers were the following:

Professor Mota Singh
Mohanlal Gautam
Jogesh Chatterji
Dr. G.K. Jetley
Jogendra Shukul
Dhanraj Sharma
Keshav Prasad Sharma
Jayaprakash Narayan

APPENDIX 15

R.F. Craster to V.T. Bayley, 31 July 1941[1]

SECRET

D.O. No. X-1407

Deoli, Rajputana
31 July 1941

My Dear Bayley,

Prabhavati Devi, wife of Security Prisoner, Class I, Jayaprakash Narayan, arrived here on the 28th July for an interview with her husband.

She was allowed one on the evening of the 28th. It passed off normally only domestic matters being discussed. She was therefore given a second interview on the morning of 29th.

During the second interview Jayaprakash Narayan attempted to pass certain letters to his wife (copies enclosed).

2. There was a short struggle for the possession of the papers. Sub-Inspector Bhola Nath Banerjee, with the help of a guard did very well in getting the papers without much damage being done to them. Security Prisoner Jayaprakash Narayan tried hard to destroy them.

I saw Prabhavati Devi immediately after the scuffle and informed her that the rest of her interview was cancelled. She informed me, in tears, that she belonged to Mr. Gandhi's Ashram and had no intention of taking anything out of the Camp as she believed in non-violence. However, from the letters from Jayaprakash Narayan to his wife it will be seen that she is a messenger for the "cause".

I afterwards saw Security Prisoner Jayaprakash Narayan and punished him under the Deoli Detention Camp Order, 1940.

He beseeched me to burn the papers in his presence and he would accept any punishment I liked to award him.

He said he was a revolutionary and that he was only working for his party and not for himself. This was refused.

He then asked what I proposed doing with the papers. I informed him that I regretted that I could not discuss the question further with him.

He again appealed to my justice and left my office under protest.

3. I think you will find most of the papers worth reading and I do not propose contradicting any of the statements as it would take too long. However, if there are any questions you would like to ask I will be only too pleased to answer them.

[1] Home Political Department, F. No. 43/96/41, NAI.

4. I am taking disciplinary action against Security Prisoners
(1) Mota Singh
and (2) Munshi Ahmed Din
and I presume you will take action against Prabhavati Devi and others mentioned in the correspondence if you think fit.

5. I enclose 2 spare copies of the correspondence in case you wish to send them on to the Punjab and Bihar Governments. I have sent a copy of their letter together with copies of enclosures to Simms for information of the Home department.

Copies of this correspondence have been forwarded to the Inspector-General of Police, Ajmer-Merwara, with an extract, regarding contacts in Ajmer and Deoli to the Superintendent of District Police, Ajmer-Merwara, for the information of Jumna Pershad, Liaison Officer.

V.T. Bayley, Esqr., I.P.,
Assistant Director, Intelligence Bureau,
Government of India, Home Department,
Simla.

Enclosures:
(1) A Hindi letter from Jayaprakash Narayan to Prabhavati Devi (together with English translation);
(2) A letter in English from Jayaprakash Narayan to P.T. (probably Purshottam Trikamdas) regarding political and other affairs. This is in two parts i.e. Old Report and New Report. There is a Hindi letter for Ganga Babu on the last page of the Old Report (together with its English translation).
(3) A document in English for the press containing the following papers:-
(a) statement regarding recent hunger strike at Deoli;
(b) copy of a letter meant for N.M. Joshi when he came to visit this camp;
(c) a copy of a memorandum said to have been sent to the Government of India in connection with their grievances. (This has not been received in my office to date);
(4) Document containing the policy regarding war in two parts i.e. old report and new report;
(5) An Urdu letter from Mota Singh to Sardul Singh Caveeshar regarding the policy of Forward Bloc and Congress Socialist Party etc.
(6) Three Urdu letters (together with English translation) from Munshi Ahmad Din, Security Prisoner, to the following political workers:-
(1) Nisar Ahmad, Lahore
(2) Ram Kumar, Lahore
(3) Pt. Mangal Dass, Lakshmi Insurance Co. Ltd., Lahore

The original of (5) and (6) above will be forwarded to you in the near future.

APPENDIX 16

Mota Singh to Sardul Singh Caveeshar[1]
[before 31 July 1941]

I was thinking of knowing your activities since long but could not get any source through which I could send my message. The important issue is political struggle. The proceedings of the Forward Bloc meeting in Delhi have not appeared in the press. Any how your attitude is apparent from the report of a press correspondent regarding the prospective conduct of the actual meeting. Our views on national an international affairs are nearly the same as expressed and almost similar views have been published by the General secretary of the Congress Socialist Party. In the last meeting which Sri Jayaprakash Narayan held with Sri Subhas Chandra Bose, it was considered possible that on the basis of co-operation of joint programme or ideological affinities both the parties (Forward Bloc and Congress Socialist Party) may weld together to take one shape for the solution of political issues etc.

2. Afterwards the demonstration staged in Calcutta by the communists' Party under the presidency of Mrs. Ranga and with the consultation of Swami Sehjananda is not only conducive to the widening of gulf but is detrimental to the interests of Kisan Movement and general political life of the country. It is hoped that you will try to persuade Swamiji and Mrs. Ranga.

In the light of the present circumstances any co-operation with the Communist Party is not only difficult but has reached the borders of impossibility. If possible the answer to this letter should be sent through the communicating agency verbally. It is necessary to send a written reply.

3. You may be knowing Babu Nanak Singh. The more about him you can know from Sardar Kirpal Singh. I don't want to say anything more except that you will oblige me by taking any national services from him under your guidance.

Anandpuri

P.S. Note: For sometime I have not received any letter from Babuji nor has Kirpal Singh written anything in this connection. Has he been arrested? If he is leading a free life I hope you will try to make him useful for the country by entrusting him some service. He has much influence in his illaqah and is sufficiently intelligent and clever. But the lines on the which work should be done at present necessarily requires your instructions.

4. Baba Party is hand in gloves with the Communist Party but the Akali elements can come nearer. In the economical and political domain most of them have imbibed socialist ideas. It is hoped that by approaching their

[1] Home Political Department, F. No. 43/96/41, NAI, Original in Urdu.

chosen leaders you would evolve a way by which they may prove more useful for the struggle for emancipation. Sri Jayaprakash Narayan and other Socialists have asked me to convey their regards and good wishes to you and so I do it. The word "Pardhan" used in the letters to Kirpal Singh means your goodself.

Anandpuri

Under emergent circumstances, if you try, contacts for communication can be made with some local reliable person through the Congress Committee, Ajmer. Insinuation can be made about him in the course of interview.

APPENDIX 17

A. Munshi Ahmed Din to Nisar Ahmed [before 31 July 1941][1]

I am at a loss to understand as to what I should write. Suffice it to stress upon you that whatever the circumstances may be you should come in the field and run the party work. You would be helped by Pt. Mangal Dass and Ram Kumar. I do not think it proper to dilate any more but this request should not be committed to the waste paper basket. I will have consolation in the Jail.

Munshi Ahmed Din

Today I am going to Deoli.

[1] Home Political Department, F. No. 43/96/41, NAI, Original in Urdu.

B. Munshi Ahmed Din to Ram Kumar[1]

Dear Comrade Ram Kumar,
I am writing this letter before my departure from Motgomery. My advice is in the shape of request. It is most necessary to bring Comrade Mangal Dass and Nisar Ahmed into the party by all possible efforts. Both of them are already in the party and now they are to be compelled to do only party work. Mangal Dass should not go in for Satyagraha and should do party work only. Comrade Nisar is silent which should be broken. It is most necessary. It is not necessary to write more. It is hoped that reply would be given on success. It will be beneficial to the interests of the party.

Yours,
Munshi Ahmed Din

[1] Home/Pol/43/96/41-Poll (I), NAI, Original in Urdu.

C. Munshi Ahmed Din to Mangal Dass[1]

Dear Comrade Panditji,
I request you that you should do party work in conjunction with Ram Kumar. If you are released it is not necessary that you should do Satyagraha. It is

[1] Home/Pol/43/96/41-Poll (I), NAI, Original in Urdu.

most necessary. Nisar should be approached and compelled that he should come into the field. It is not proper to sit inside in these days. I do not want to write any more as you might have comprehended I mean. Tonight is our departure to Deoli camp. I am writing to Nisar Sahib separately.

Ahmed Din

APPENDIX 18

J.P. and others to Chief Secretary, Government of India, New Delhi, 12 October 1941[1]

To
The Chief Secretary,
Govt. of India,
New Delhi

Sir,
We, the undersigned, find ourselves constrained to intimate Govt. that in view of their attitude of continued indifference to our very fair and reasonable demands communicated to them nearly seven months ago, we are compelled to take recourse to the last weapon that is at the disposal of prisoners anywhere in the world namely that of hunger-strike.

We shall briefly refer to the circumstances that have led to this decision. On and about March 31, 1941, a memorandum was sent to Govt. incorporating a number of our demands, the chief among which were: (i) granting to us the status of State prisoner, (ii) abolition of classification of detenus, (iii) payment of an adequate family allowance to all those who have got dependents or such liabilities to meet as insurance premimus, (iv) a daily diet allowance of Rs. 16/- and a pocket allowance of Rs. 32/- per month, (v) repatriation to our respective provinces, and (vi) payment of traveling expenses to those who come to interview us.

A few months later we wrote to Govt. Again for permission to correspond with friends and relations who may be in other camps or prisons.

We had several occasions to remind Govt. of these demands through official visitors who happened to visit the camp.

After considerable delay Govt. granted a few of our minor demands. But all the major demands remain unfulfilled to this day. Besides, such ever-present grievances as lack of proper medical treatment, particularly of such serious cases as are beyond the competence of the local medical officers, the case of Sardar Kulbir Singh is an instance in point—the irksome treatment of the Camp authorities, censoring of letters, newspapers, books etc. continue to remain unredressed. Lately the system of cell punishment has become intolerably common and the authorities seem to think that they are free to do with us as they please. Furthermore, even in the gravest circumstances such as the death of a near relation, parole, for which provision is made in the rules has been persistently denied to us. There has been only one such [*sic*] instance in all these many months which goes rather to support than deny our case.

[1] Home/Pol/43/96/41-Poll (I), NAI, Original in Urdu.

Taking all these facts and circumstances into consideration, we have come to the conclusion that there is no other self respecting course open to us but to stake our lives for what we consider our just rights & privileges.

Accordingly we hereby intimate Govt. that unless we are satisfied before Oct. 22, 1941 regarding the questions stated above and in our memoranda of previous dates as also those that were mentioned by us from time to time, we shall resort to hunger-strike beginning from Oct. 22, 1941.
We remain

Yours faithfully,

1. Jayaprakash Narayan, General Secretary, A.I. Congress Socialist Party, Ex-member Congress Working Committee.
2. Damodar Swarup Seth, formerly General Secretary U.P. Congress Committee.
3. Mohanlal Gautam, M.L.A., President All India Kisan Sabha.
4. Dr. G.K. Jetley, M.B.B.S., Kisan leader of U.P.
5. Benimadho Roy, Revolutionary leader of U.P.
6. Kabul Singh, M.L.A. (Punjab).
7. Harjap Singh, M.L.A. (Punjab).
8. Munshi Ahmed Din, Leader, Punjab Congress Socialist Party.
9. Kulbir Singh and Kultar Singh, Brothers of Sardar Bhagat Singh.
10. Professor Tilak Raj Chaddha, Rawalpindi College.
11. Balwant Singh Dukhia, President District Congress Committee Hoshiapur.
12. Jogendra Shukla, Andaman-returned Revolutionary leader of Bihar.
13. Shyama Charan Bhartwar - do -.
14. Shaukat Usmani, Member Communist International.
15. Jogesh Chatterji, Ex-Kakori prisoner.
16. Mota Singh Anandpuri, Sikh leader of Punjab.
17. Ramchandra, President, District Urban Congress Committee Lahore, and 191 others in all 208 Security prisoners in Deoli Detention Camp.

APPENDIX 19

Mahatma Gandhi's Statement on the Government's publication of J.P.'s Deoli letters, 21 October 1941[1]

Statement to the Press

Wardhaganj
21 October 1941

The publication of the statement attributed to Shri Jayaprakash Narayan, which he is stated to have attempted to smuggle from his place of detention, does not, so far as I can see, lead us anywhere.[2] If the motive was to discredit the organization of which Jayaprakash Narayan is a distinguished member, it must fail.

Assuming the correctness of the charge against Jayaprakash Narayan, the method advocated by him is against the policy of truth and non-violence adopted by the Congress, and he deserves the severest condemnation. But it becomes ill for the Government to condemn or discredit it. Frankly, all nationalist forces, no matter by what name they are described, are at war with the Government. And, according to the accepted canons of war, the method adopted by Jayaprakash Narayan is perfectly legitimate. He has had his training in America for seven long years and is a student of the methods adopted by Western nations in their fight for freedom. To practice deception, to resort to secret methods and even to plot murder, are all honourable and turn the prepetrators into national heroes. Are not to Clive and Warren Hastings British heroes? If Jayaprakash Narayan was in the British Diplomatic Service and by secret diplomacy achieved something of importance, he would be covered with distinction.

The sensation with which the event has been disclosed to the Indian world is ill-conceived. The annotations in the communique are probably wholly unwarranted. When it is borne in mind that Jayaprakash Narayan is an untried detenu, the annotations look very like hitting below the belt. The Government should have shown Jayaprakash the document or documents seized, and published his answer if he had any to give.

[1] *Collected Works of Mahatma Gandhi*, Vol. LXXV (1941-2), p. 34.

[2] A communique issued by the Government on October 16 said: "Plans to consolidate the position of the Congress Socialist Party by winning over important members of the terrorist organizations, known as the Revolutionary Socialist Party and the Hindustan Republican Socialist Association and by isolating the Communist Party, were seized from Mr. Jayaprakash Narayan, security prisoner, Deoli Camp, when he attempted to pass them to his wife, Prabhavati Devi, at an interview."

The way in which his poor wife has been dragged in is unfortunate. She knew nothing of the attempt, for it was frustrated before anything could reach her. I may inform the public that Prabhavati does not share Jayaprakash Narayan's view. She was put under my charge by her parents when she was not yet fifteen and while her husband Jayaprakash was still in America. She has wholly accepted my view of Indian politics and is one of my most faithful co-workers. As husband and wife, Jayaprakash Narayan and Prabhavati Devi are an ideal couple. Jayaprakash has never sought to impose his views on Prabhavati. He has never prevented her from freely coming to me. Indeed, he has encouraged her to come to me whenever she has been ill. She has never been taken into the secrets of the Socialist Party. The alleged communication has completely upset her, for she never thought that her husband would advocate the method attributed to him.

The suggestion made in some newspapers that the restriction on prisoners should be tightened is wholly irrelvant to Jayaprakash Narayan's attempt. That it was frustrated is enough proof of the efficiency of the C.I.D. Even if there is laxity, it can be no warrant for giving them bad or insufficient food, or keeping them in places far away from their homes, making it difficult or expensive for relatives to visit detenus. I have read Shri N.M. Joshi's very careful and over-moderate recommendations[3] about the Deoli camp. I have learnt enough about it to enable me to say, in the name of humanity, that the camp should be disbanded and the prisoners should be sent nearer their homes. It is wrong, from every point of view, to bring prisoners from their provinces and concentrate them in a place where there is no facility either of provisions or medical assistance or other amenities of life. Prisoners of war are treated like princes compared to political prisoners, whose status would be any day superior to that of prisoners of war.

One word to Congressmen. While Jayaprakash Narayan remains the patriot we have known him, they must realize that his method is harmful in the extreme while a non-violent struggle is going on. I have said, repeatedly, that secrecy has no place in a non-violent organization. No underhand or underground movement can ever become a mass movement or stir millions to mass action. I am glad, therefore, that Shri Purshottam Trikamdas, Secretary of the Socialist Party, has repudiated the method said to be advocated by Jayaprakash Narayan. Indeed, I would appeal to Jayaprakash Narayan to reconsider his philosophy and, if his reason can approve, to repudiate the method as lapse from sound reason and the loyalty he owes to the congress. What he has stigmatized as a farce of satyagraha is not a farce. It is the fine fruit of mature experience of thirty-three years'

[3] N.M. Joshi had, with the Government's permission, visited Deoli in July and published his impressions and suggestions.

experimenting in truth and non-violence; and, if God wills it, I hope to demonstrate that from this farce will rise a reality which will compel admission even by Jayaprakash Narayan and those who think with him. Jayaprakash did not indeed go to prison as a satyagrahi, but he has not ceased to be a member of the Congress, and so it is not proper for him and others who think with him to retard the movement by their action, which is admittedly disloyal to the Congress.

The Hindu, 23-10-1941.

APPENDIX 20

J.P. and others to Superintendent, Deoli Detention Camp, 4 November 1941[1]

To
The Superintendent,
Deoli Detention Camp.

Sir,
We have been greatly disturbed by the news of the condition of Syt. Jogesh Chatterji. We understand that he has been passing acetone in his urine for the last several days. The Medical Officer will tell you how serious this is. It is particularly serious and means certain death in the case of Syt. Chatterji, because it is not possible to feed him forcibly.

The other day Syt. A.K. Ghosh and Jayaprakash Narayan wrote to you on our behalf that no further attempt should be made to feed Syt. Chatterji as, in his peculiar condition, that would merely bring his death sooner, beside causing him intense pain and suffering. They had also informed you that recently when Syt. Chatterji was on hunger-strike, the Superintendent of the Lucknow Central and District Jails, Lieut.-Col. Jaffri, had also failed to feed him.

We understand now that fresh attempts have been made to feed him by force. Jayaprakash Narayan informs us that when he visited the 'B' hospital and discussed the case of Syt. Chatterji with the M.O., the latter told him that after having personally tried it, he could say conscientiously that it was impossible to feed Syt. Chatterji. We fail to understand, therefore, why the doctors are tormenting Syt. Chatterji again. We wish to make it clear that every attempt to feed him drags him nearer to his death. If that be your intention and that of the doctors, you may do as you please. We shall also do what we consider necessary then. You will have the satisfaction of taking not only one life but perhaps several.

If, however, you are prepared to be fair and listen to reason we wish to request to you to inform government telegraphically of Syt. Chatterji's condition and recommend his immediate release. The Government are of course free to arrest him again if they wish to after he is well. We strongly urge upon you this suggestion, and we hope that when a precious life is involved, no further time will be lost. If Government are not prepared to release him, they have only two alternatives: either to let him die in peace or to concede to his demands immediately.

[3] Government of India, Home-Political, F. No. 43/96/41, NAI.

In this connection we are sending herewith three telegrams, which we request you to pass and to have despatched immediately. We also request you to telegraphically inform Mrs. Chatterji of her husband's condition and allow her interview him.

Yours Faithfully,

Sd/- A. Mota Singh Anandpuri.
Jayaprakash Narayan.
A.K. Ghosh.
Z.A. Ahmed.
Bishwa Nath Roy.
Keshav Prasad Sharma.

APPENDIX 21

Mahatma Gandhi to Jayaprakash Narayan, Telegram 12 November 1941[1]

Strongly advise discontinuation of the hunger-strike by you and others. Public opinion being created for securing relief. Dr. Rajendra Prasad and Mian Iftikharuddin join me in the appeal. Prabhavati anxious to meet you. Restraining her pending developments.

[1] *The Hindu*, 16 November 1941.

APPENDIX 22

Mahatma Gandhi to Jayaprakash Narayan, Telegram 17 November 1941[1]

Kamaladevi here. She and I consider your demand for same treatment as Deoli incapable literal execution. Puts you wrong box. You should be satisfied with repatriation and end strike and again [*sic*] you will estrange public feelings by persisting if repatriation assured. Sardar Rajenbabu Kripalani join.

Gandhi

[1] *Collected Works of Mahatma Gandhi*, Vol. LXXV (1941-2), p. 102.

APPENDIX 23

Congress Working Committee's Resolution, 11 April 1942[1]

The Working Committee have given their full and earnest consideration to the proposals made by the British War Cabinet in regard to India and the elucidation thereof by Sir Stafford Cripps. These proposals, which have been made at the very last hour because of the compulsion of events, have to be considered not only in relation to India's demand for independence, but more especially in the present grave war crisis, with a view to meeting effectively the perils and dangers that confront India and envelop the world.

The Congress has repeatedly stated, ever since the commencement of the War in September 1939, that the people of India would line themselves with the progressive forces of the world and assume full responsibility to face the new problems and shoulder the new burdens that had arisen, and it asked for the necessary conditions to enable them to do so to be created. An essential condition was the freedom of India, for only the realisation of present freedom could light the flame which would illumine millions of hearts and move them to action. At the last meeting of the All India Congress Committee, after the commencement of the War in the Pacific, it was stated that: 'Only a free and independent India can be in a position to undertake the defence of the country on a national basis and be of help in the furtherance of the larger causes that are emerging from the storm of war.'

The British War Cabinet's new proposals relate principally to the future upon the cessation of hostilities. The Committee while recognising that self-determination for the people of India is accepted in principle in that uncertain future, regret that this is fettered and circumscribed and certain provisions have been introduced which gravely imperil the development of a free and united nation and the establishment of a democratic State. Even the constitution-making body is so constituted that the people's right to self-determination is vitiated by the introduction of non-representative elements. The people of India have as a whole clearly demanded full independence and the Congress has repeatedly declared that no other status except that of independence for the whole of India could be agreed to or could meet the essential requirements of the present situation. The Committee recognise that future independence may be implict in the proposals but the accompanying provisions and restrictions are such that real freedom may well become an illusion. The complete ignoring of the ninety millions of the people of the Indian states and their treatment as commodities at the disposal

[3] Indian National Congress, March 1940 to September 1946.

of their rulers is a negaion of both democracy and self-determination. While the representation of an Indian State in the constitution-making body is fixed on a population basis, the people of the State have no voice in choosing those representatives, nor are they to be consulted at any stage, while decisions vitally affecting them are being taken. Such States may in many ways become barriers to the growth of Indian freedom, enclaves where foreign authority still prevails and where the possibility of maintaining foreign armed forces has been stated to be a likely contingency, and a perpetual menace to the freedom of the people of the States as well as of the rest of India.

The acceptance before hand of the novel principle of non-accession for a province is also a sever blow to the conception of India unity and an apple of discord likely to generate growing trouble in the provinces, and which may well lead to further difficulties in the way of the Indian States merging themselves in the Indian Union. The Congress has been wedded to Indian freedom and unity and any break in that unity, especially in the modern world when people's minds inevitably think in terms of ever larger federations, would be injurious to all concerned and exceedingly painful to contemplate. Nevertheless the committee cannot think in terms of compelling the people in any territorial unit to remain in and Indian Union against their declared and established will. While recognising this principle, the Committee feel that every effort should be made to create conditions which would help the different units in developing a common and co-operative national life. The acceptance of the principle inevitably involves that no changes should be made which result in fresh problems being created and compulsion being exercised on other substantial groups within that area. Each territorial unit should have the fullest possible autonomy within the Union, consistently with a strong national State. The proposal now made on the part of the British War Cabinet encourages and will lead to attempts at separation at the very inception of a union and thus create friction just when the utmost co-operation and gooodwill are most needed. This proposal has been presumably made to meet a communal demand, but it will have other consequences also and lead politically reactionary and obscurantist groups among different communitites to create trouble and divert public attention from the vital issues before the country.

Any proposals concerning the future of India must demand attention and scrutiny, but in today's grave crisis, it is the present that counts, and even proposals for the future are important in so far as they affect the present. The Committee have necessarily attached the greatest importance to this aspect of the question, and on this ultimately depends what advice they should give to those who look to them for guidance. For the present the British War Cabinet's proposals are vague and altogether incomplete, and it would appear that no vital changes in the present structure are contemplated. It has been made clear that the Defence of India will in any event remain under British control. At any time defence is a vital subject; during war time it is all important and covers almost every sphere of life and administration. To take away defence from the sphere of responsibility at this stage is to reduce that responsibility to a farce and a nullity, and to make it perfectly clear that India is not going to be free in any way and her Government is not going to function as a free and independent government during the pendency of the War. The Committee would repeat that an essential and fundamental pre-requisite for the assumption of responsibility by the Indian people in the present, is their realisation as a fact that they are free and are in charge of maintaining and defending their freedom. What is most wanted is the enthusiastic response of the people which cannot be evoked without the fullest trust in them and the devolution of responsibility on them in the matter of defence. It is only thus that even at this grave eleventh hour it may be possible to galvanise the people of India to rise to the height of the occasion. It is manifest that the present Government of India, as well as its provincial agencies, are lacking in competence, and are incapable of shouldering the burden of India's defence. It is only the people of India through their popular representatives, who may shoulder this burden worthily. But that can only be done by present freedom, and full responsibility being cast upon them. The Committee, therefore, are unable to accept the proposals put forward on behalf of the British War Cabinet.

APPENDIX 24

Mahatma Gandhi's Draft Resolution for Congress Working Committee [before 24 April 1942][1]

Whereas the British War Cabinet's proposals sponsored by Sir Stafford Cripps have shown up British imperialism in its nakedness as never before, the A.I.C.C. has come to the following conclusions:

The A.I.C.C. is of opinion that Britain is incapable of defending India. It is natural that whatever she does is for her own defence. There is an eternal conflict between Indian and British interests. It follows that their notions of defence would also differ. The British Government has no trust in India's political parties. The Indian army has been maintained up till now mainly to hold India in subjugation. It has been completely segregated from the general population who can in no sense regard it as their own. This policy of mistrust still continues and is the reason why national defence is not entrusted to India's elected representatives.

Japan's quarrel is not with India. She is warring against the British Empire. India's participation in the war has not been with the consent of the representatives of the Indian people. It was purely a British act. If India were freed her first step would probably be to negotiate with Japan. The Congress is of opinion that if the British withdrew from India, India would be able to defend herself in the event of Japanese or any aggressor attacking India.

The A.I.C.C. is, therefore, of opinion that the British should withdraw from India. The plea that they should remain in India for protecting the Indian Princes is wholly untenable. It is additional proof of their determination to maintain their hold over India. The Princes need have no fear from unarmed India.

The question of majority and minority is a creation of the British government and would disappear on their withdrawal.

For all these reasons the Committee appeals to Britain, for the sake of her own safety, for the sake of India's safety and for the cause of world peace to let go her hold on India even if she does not give up all Asiatic and African possessions.

This Committee desires to assure the Japanese Government and people that India bears no enmity either towards Japan or towards any other nation. India only desires freedom from all alien domination. But in this fight for freedom the Committee is of opinion that India while welcoming universal

[1] *Collected Works of Mahatma Gandhi*, Vol. LXXVI, pp. 63-5.

sympathy does not stand in need of foreign military aid. India will attain her freedom through her non-violent strength and will retain it likewise. Therefore, the committee hopes that Japan will not have any designs on India. But if Japan attacks India and Britain makes no response to its appeal the Committee would expect all those who look to Congress for guidance to offer complete non-violent non-co-operation to the Japanese forces and not render any assistance to them. It is no part of the duty of those who are attacked to render any assistance to the attacker. It is their duty to offer complete non-co-operation.

It is not difficult to understand the simple principle of non-violent non-co-operation:

1. We may not bend the knee to the aggressor nor obey any of his orders.

2. We may not look to him for any favours nor falls to his bribes. But we may not bear him any malice nor wish him ill.

3. If he wishes to take possession of our fields we will refuse to give them up even if we have to die in the effort to resist him.

4. If he is attacked by disease or is dying of thirst and seeks our aid we may not refuse it.

5. In such places where the British and Japanese forces are fighting our non-co-operation will be fruitless and unnecessary. At present our non-co-operation with the British government is limited. Were we offer them complete non-co-operation when they are actually fighting, it would be tantamount to placing our country deliberately in Japanese hands. Therefore not to put any obstacle in the way of the British forces will often be the only way of demonstrating our non-co-operation with the Japanese. Neither may we assist the British in any active manner. If we can judge from their recent attitude, the British Government do not need any help from us beyond our non-interference. They desire our help only as slaves-a position we can never accept.

It is necessary for the Committee to make a clear declaration in regard to the scorched-earth policy. If, inspite of our non-violent resistance, any part of the country falls into Japanese hands we may not destroy our crops, water-supply, etc., if only because it will be our endeavour to regain them. The destruction of war material is another matter and may under certain circumstances be a military necessity. But it can never be the Congress policy to destroy what belongs to or is of use to the masses.

Whilst non-co-operation against the Japanese forces will necessarily be limited to a comparatively small number and must succeed if it is complete and genuine, the true building up of swaraj consists in the millions of India whole-heartedly working the constructive programme. Without it the whole nation cannot rise from its age-long torpor. Whether the British remain or not it is our duty always to wipe out unemployment, to bridge the gulf between rich and poor, to banish communal strife, to exorcise the demon of untouchability, to reform dacoits and save the people from them. If crores of people do not take a living interest in this nation-building work, freedom must remain a dream and unattainable by either non-violence or violence.

Foreign Soldiers

The A.I.C.C. is of opinion that it is harmful to India's interests and dangerous to the cause of India's freedom to introduce foreign soldiers in India. It therefore appeals to the British Government to remove these foreign legions and henceforth stop further introduction. It is a crying shame to bring foreign troops inspite of India's inexhaustible manpower and is a proof of the immorality that British Imperialism is.

APPENDIX 25

Resolution adopted by A.I.C.C., Allahabad, 2 May 1942[1]

In view of the imminent peril of invasion that confronts India, and the attitude of the British Government, as show again in the recent proposals sponsored by Sir Stafford Cripps, the All India congress Committee has to declare afresh India's policy and to advise the people in regard to the action to be undertaken in the emergencies that may arise in the immediate future.

The proposals of the British Government and their subsequent elucidation by Sir Stafford Cripps have led to greater bitterness and distrust of that Government and the spirit of non-co-operation with Britain has grown. They have demonstrated that even in this hour of danger, not only to India but to the cause of the United Nations, the British Government functions as an imperialist government and refuses to recognise the independence of India or to part with any real power.

India's participation in the War was a purely British act imposed upon the India people without the consent of their representatives. While India has no quarrel with the people of any country, she has repeatedly declared her antipathy to nazism and fascism as to imperialism. If India were free she would have determined her own policy and might have kept out of the war, though her sympathies would, in any event, have been with the victims of aggression. If, however, circumstances had led her to join the war, she would have done so as a free country fighting for freedom, and her defence would have been organised on a popular basis with a national army under national control and leadership, and with intimate contacts with the people. A free India would know how to defend herself in the event of any aggressor attacking her. The present Indian army is in fact an offshoot of the British army and has been maintained till now mainly to hold India in subjection. It has been completely segregated from the general population, who can in no sense regard it as their own.

The essential difference between the imperialist and the popular conceptions of defence is demonstrated by the fact while foreign armies are invited to India for that defence, the vast man-power of India herself is not utilised for the purpose. India's past experience teaches her that it is harmful to her interests and dangerous to the cause of her freedom to introduce foreign armies in India. It is significant and extraordinary that India's inexhaustible man-power should remain untapped, while India develops into a battleground between foreign armies fighting on her soil or on her frontiers, and her defence

[1] Indian National Congress, March 1940 to September 1946.

is not supposed to be a subject fit for popular control. India resents this treatment of her people as chattels to be disposed of by foreign authority.

The A.I.C.C. is convinced that India will attain her freedom through her own strength and will retain it likewise. The present crisis, as well as the experience of the negotiations with Sir Stafford Cripps, make it impossible for the Congress to consider any schemes or proposals which retain, even in a partial measure, British control and authority in India. Not only the interest of India but also Britain's safety, and world peace and freedom demand that Britain must abandon her hold on India. It is on the basis of independence alone that India can deal with Britain or other nations.

The Committee repudiates the idea that freedom can come to India through interference or invasion by any foreign nation, whatever the professions or that nation may be. In case an invasion takes place, it must be resisted. Such resistance can only take the form of non-violent non-co-operation as the British Government has prevented the organisation of national defence by the people in any other way. The Committee would , therefore, expect the people of India to offer complete non-violent non-co-operation to the invading forces and not to render any assistance to them. We may not bend the knee to the aggressor nor obey any of his orders. We may not look to him for favours nor fall to his bribes. If he wishes to take possession of our homes and our fields we will refuse to give them up even if we have to die in the effort to resist them. In places wherein the British and the invading forces are fighting our non-co-operation will be fruitless and unnecessary. Not to put any obstacle in the way of British forces will often be the only way of demonstrating our non-co-operation with the invader. Judging from their attitude the British Government do not need any help from us beyond our non-interference. *They desire our help only as slaves, a position which we can never accept.*

The success of such a policy of non-co-operation and non-violent resistance to the invader will largely depend on the intensive working out of the Congress constructive programme, and more especially the programme of self-sufficiency and self-protection in all parts of the country.

APPENDIX 26

Rajagopalachari's Formula, May 1944[1]

(i) The Muslim League endorses the Indian demand for Independence and will co-operate with the Congress in the formation of a Provisional Interim Government for the transitional period. (ii) After the termination of the War, a Commission shall; be appointed for demarcating contiguous districts in the North-West and East of India, where the Muslim population is in an absolute majority. In the areas thus demarcated, a plebiscite of all the inhabitants, held on the basis of adult suffrage or any other practical franchise, shall ultimately decide the issue of separation from Hindustan. If the majority decide in favour of forming a Sovereign State separate from Hindustan. Such a decision shall be given effect to, without prejudice to the rights of districts on the border to choose to join either State. (iii) It will be open to all Parties to advocate their points of view before the plebiscite is held, (iv) In the event of separation, mutual agreement shall be entered into for jointly safeguarding Defence, Commerce, communications and for other essential purposes. (v) Any transfer of population shall only be on an absolutely voluntary basis. (vi) These terms shall be binding only in case of transfer by Britain of full power and responsibility of the government of India. (vii) Gandhiji and Mr. Jinnah agree to these terms of settlement and will endeavour respectively to get the approval of the congress and Muslim League for these terms.

[1] *Gandhi-Jinnah Talks*, text of correspondence and other relevant matter. Preface by C. Rajagopalachari, New Delhi, 1944.

APPENDIX 27

Mahatma Gandhi's Statement on Underground Activities, 28 July 1944[1]

The question most discussed with me by visitors is whether I approve of underground activities. These include sabotage, the publication of unauthorized sheets, etc. It has been suggested to me that without some workers going underground they could have done nothing. Some have contended that destruction of property, including dislocation of communication, provided that safety of human life could be ensured, should surely be counted as non-violence. Examples of other nations as having not hesitated to do all these things and much worse have been cited. My reply is that no nation has, so far as I know, deliberately used truth and non-violence as exclusive means for the attainment of freedom. Judged by that standard, I say unhesitatingly, that underground activities, even though utterly innocent in themselves, should have no place in the technique of non-violence. Sabotage and all it means, including destruction of property, is in itself violence. Though these activities may be shown to have touched the imagination and enthusiam, I have no doubt that they have harmed the movement as a whole.

I swear by the Constructive Programme. Let me recount the items of that programme:

1. Communal unity
2. Removal of untouchability
3. Prohibition
4. Khadi
5. Other village industries
6. Village sanitation
7. New or basic education
8. Adult education
9. Uplift of women
10. Service of the so-called aboriginals
11. Education in health and hygiene
12. Propaganda of *rashtra bhasha*
13. Love of one's own language
14. Working for economic equality

Unfortunately the workers have not developed in that programme the

[1] *The Bombay Chronicle*, 29.7.1944; *Collected Works of Mahatma Gandhi*, Vol. LXXVII, pp. 429-30.

living faith which I have. I can put re-emphasize the importance of that programme. And, if the whole of India could be converted to take to that programme, we should reach our goal in the quickest manner possible.

To the workers who are still underground, I advise:

If you share my conviction that underground activity is not conducive to the growth of the spirit of active non-violence, you will discover yourselves and take the risk of being imprisoned, believing that imprisonment, thus undergone, itself helps the freedom Movement.

INDEX